American Empire and the Political Economy
of Global Finance

International Political Economy Series

General Editors: **Timothy M. Shaw**, Professor and Director, Institute of International Relations, The University of the West Indies, Trinidad & Tobago

Titles include:

Leslie Elliott Armijo (*editor*)
FINANCIAL GLOBALIZATION AND DEMOCRACY IN EMERGING MARKETS

Eudine Barriteau
THE POLITICAL ECONOMY OF GENDER IN THE TWENTIETH-CENTURY CARIBBEAN

Gabriel G. Casaburi
DYNAMIC AGROINDUSTRIAL CLUSTERS
The Political Economy of Competitive Sectors in Argentina and Chile

Peter Clegg
THE CARIBBEAN BANANA TRADE
From Colonialism to Globalization

Matt Davies
INTERNATIONAL POLITICAL ECONOMY AND MASS COMMUNICATION IN CHILE
National Intellectuals and Transnational Hegemony

Yvon Grenier
THE EMERGENCE OF INSURGENCY IN EL SALVADOR
Ideology and Political Will

Ivelaw L. Griffith (*editor*)
THE POLITICAL ECONOMY OF DRUGS IN THE CARIBBEAN

Jerry Haar and Anthony T. Bryan (*editors*)
CANADIAN–CARIBBEAN RELATIONS IN TRANSITION
Trade, Sustainable Development and Security

Tricia Juhn
NEGOTIATING PEACE IN EL SALVADOR
Civil–Military Relations and the Conspiracy to End the War

R. Lipsey and P. Meller (*editors*)
WESTERN HEMISPHERE TRADE INTEGRATION
A Canadian–Latin American Dialogue

Don Marshall
CARIBBEAN POLITICAL ECONOMY AT THE CROSSROADS
NAFTA and Regional Developmentalism

Juan Antonio Morales and Gary McMahon (*editors*)
ECONOMIC POLICY AND THE TRANSITION TO DEMOCRACY
The Latin American Experience

Leo Panitch and Martijn Konings (*editors*)
AMERICAN EMPIRE AND THE POLITICAL ECONOMY OF GLOBAL FINANCE

Eul-Soo Pang
THE INTERNATIONAL POLITICAL ECONOMY OF TRANSFORMATION IN ARGENTINA, BRAZIL, AND CHILE SINCE 1960

Henry Veltmeyer and James Petras and Steve Vieux
NEOLIBERALISM AND CLASS CONFLICT IN LATIN AMERICA
A Comparative Perspective on the Political Economy of Structural Adjustment

Henry Veltmeyer and James Petras
THE DYNAMICS OF SOCIAL CHANGE IN LATIN AMERICA

International Political Economy Series

Series Standing Order ISBN 0–333–71708–2 hardcover
Series Standing Order ISBN 0–333–71110–6 paperback
(*outside North America only*)

You can receive future titles in this series as they are published by placing a standing order. Please contact your bookseller or, in case of difficulty, write to us at the address below with your name and address, the title of the series and the ISBN quoted above.

Customer Services Department, Macmillan Distribution Ltd, Houndmills, Basingstoke, Hampshire RG21 6XS, England

American Empire and the Political Economy of Global Finance

Edited by

Leo Panitch
York University, Canada

Martijn Konings
University of Amsterdam, The Netherlands

palgrave
macmillan

First published 2008 by
PALGRAVE MACMILLAN
Houndmills, Basingstoke, Hampshire RG21 6XS and
175 Fifth Avenue, New York, N.Y. 10010
Companies and representatives throughout the world

PALGRAVE MACMILLAN is the global academic imprint of the Palgrave Macmillan
division of St. Martin's Press, LLC and of Palgrave Macmillan Ltd. Macmillan® is a
registered trademark in the United States, United Kingdom and other countries.
Palgrave is a registered trademark in the European Union and other countries.

ISBN-13: 978–0–230–55126–8   hardback
ISBN-10: 0–230–55126–2   hardback

This book is printed on paper suitable for recycling and made from fully managed
and sustained forest sources. Logging, pulping and manufacturing processes are
expected to conform to the environmental regulations of the country of origin.

A catalogue record for this book is available from the British Library.

Library of Congress Cataloging-in-Publication Data

The American Empire and the political economy of global finance /
    edited by Leo Panitch, Martijn Konings.
        p. cm. — (International political economy series)
    Includes bibliographical references and index.
    ISBN 0–230–55126–2 (alk. paper)
    1.   United States—Foreign economic relations. 2.   International
    finance. I. Panitch, Leo. II. Konings, Martijn, 1975-
    HF1455.A676 2008
    332'.042—dc22

                                                                2008015888

10 9   8   7   6   5   4   3   2   1
17 16 15 14 13 12 11 10 09 08

Printed and bound in Great Britain by
CPI Antony Rowe, Chippenham and Eastbourne

Contents

List of Figures and Tables

Figures

Tables

Notes on the Contributors

Scott Aquanno previously worked in the financial services industry as an investment broker and securities consultant with a multinational brokerage firm. He is currently completing a PhD in Political Science at York University in Toronto.

Ruth Felder is completing a PhD in Political Science and is a Research Associate at the Center for Research on Latin America and the Caribbean, at York University in Toronto.

Sam Gindin was for many years Research Director of the Canadian Auto Workers Union and currently holds the Packer Chair in Social Justice at York University in Toronto.

Martijn Konings recently completed a PhD at York University in Toronto on the rise of American finance and is currently a Researcher in the Amsterdam Institute for Metropolitan and International Development Studies at the University of Amsterdam.

Eric Newstadt formerly worked in the Canadian banking sector and is now completing a PhD in Political Science at York University in Toronto.

Leo Panitch is the Canada Research Chair in Comparative Political Economy and Distinguished Research Professor of Political Science at York University in Toronto and the co-editor of the *Socialist Register*.

Christopher Rude has a PhD from the New York School of Social Research and was a Postdoctoral Fellow at York University in Toronto during 2004–5.

Thomas Sablowski is a Researcher at the Social Science Research Centre in Berlin and was a Postdoctoral Fellow at York University in Toronto during 2005–6.

David Sarai was a Fulbright Fellow at American University, Washington, D.C. and is completing a PhD in Political Science at York University in Toronto.

Preface

The relationship between states and globalization is one of the burning questions of our time. The processes of capitalist globalization, initially widely perceived as bypassing and marginalizing the state, have not only transformed the world's states; at least some capitalist states have been key authors of those processes. Among these, the American State has been most central to launching a globalized capitalism *and* the transformation of other states, thereby extending the unique place it came to occupy as an imperial power in the twentieth century. Just seven years into the twenty-first century, this active role of states, and above all of the American state, was evident amidst the turmoil in international markets that began in the summer of 2007, starting with when the world's central banks acted in unison on 10 August to provide liquidity to the tune of hundreds of billions of dollars. While every movement in a vast array of financial markets was being closely scrutinized by US Treasury staff massed in front of their flat-screen monitors in the 'markets room', *The New York Times* reported that Secretary Henry M. Paulson Jr., 'spent the day in hourly contact with the Fed, other officials in the administration, finance ministries and regulators overseas and people on Wall Street – where until last year he had worked as an executive at Goldman Sachs'. Meanwhile, the staff at the Federal Reserve, where the newly appointed Chairman Ben S. Bernanke could draw on his academic work as an economist at Princeton University in the 1980s on how the 1929 crash could have been prevented, were in contact with the European Central Bank, the Bank of England and the Bank of Japan as to the role they would play as 'lenders of last resort'.

Over the ensuing months, the US Treasury would organize, first, a consortium of international banks and investment funds, and then an overlapping consortium of mortgage companies, financial securitizers and investment funds, to try to get them to take concrete measures to calm the markets; and officials in the Federal Reserve would stay in close touch with their counterparts in the other central banks in deciding what they would each do about interest rates in face of the ongoing credit crisis. Both the Treasury and Federal Reserve staff also worked closely with the Securities Exchange Commission and Commodity Futures Trading Commission under the rubric of the Working Group on Financial Markets, which for twenty years had overseen such crisis interventions inside the American state. At the same time, they burnished their close contacts, developed over some three decades of coordinated promotion of both financial globalization and crisis management, with the finance ministries and central bankers of the G7, and with those of the twenty-six states organized under the Financial Stability Forum since 1999, in order (as the latter put it in October 2007) 'to enhance market discipline and institutional resilience'. As the crisis wore on to the end of the year, the central banks of the advanced capitalist states undertook a further highly coordinated provision of liquidity to sustain the interbank market, while the sovereign wealth funds of other states were encouraged to invest directly in Wall Street banks to beef up their capital.

As 2008 began with stock markets in Asia and Europe shaken at the prospect of an American recession, the US Federal Reserve undertook a large emergency cut in interest rates before the New York stock exchange could follow suit. Insofar as this might have caused a vicious downward spiral in world stock markets, the Fed was acting as much as the world's central bank as the American. By March the Fed had undertaken another coordinated move with the other central banks, supplying them with dollars to provide liquidity to their banks, while simultaneously making no less than $200 billion available to Wall Street's investment banks. Yet even this could not save one of these – Bear Stearns, ironically the lone major investment bank which had refused to cooperate with the Fed-engineered bail-out of Long Term Capital Management a decade before. When Wall Street woke up on St Patrick's Day greeted by headlines like 'Wall Street quakes as the parade passes by', it was revealed – not dissimilar to when in 1998 the Fed had locked the principals of New York investment houses in a hotel room until they jointly agreed to bail out LTCM – that after all-day and night weekend sessions, the Fed had directed, overseen and guaranteed to the tune of $30 billion J.P. Morgan's takeover of Bear Stearns. It was hardly surprising that, by the end of the month, when the Treasury issued its long-awaited 'Blueprint for a Modernized Financial Regulatory Structure' (in preparation since March 2007, before the onset of the crisis), it was primarily designed to 'enhance' the Fed's regulatory authority over the whole financial system, not least over the investment banks for whom it now was so openly the lender of last resort. Nor was it surprising that it was also revealed that the US and British Treasuries would start to formalize with a new working group of their respective officials their decades-long close coordination of interventions to stabilize London and New York's intertwined financial markets. The US President's Working Group on Financial Markets, for some twenty years euphemistically dubbed the 'Plunge Protection Team' by market insiders, was going international.

All too often, and with especially good reason at the beginning of the twenty-first century, it is US military interventions that draw attention to the imperial nature of the American state. Yet the proper measure of American empire today needs to include the quotidian ways US power is embedded in and operates through the structures of global finance, and the central role it has played in the expansion of international financial markets and in managing the economic crises that emanate from them. While the US position in the international financial system has become a key pillar of modern-day American empire, the institutional connections between the American state and finance have not received as much attention as they deserve, and as a result the concrete mechanisms through which US power operates in this arena still stand in need of considerable clarification. It is precisely such clarification that this book seeks to provide; although the chapters were all drafted before the onset of this financial crisis (with the final drafts in December 2007 only able to comment on a crisis still very much in train) every chapter is highly germane to understanding the American state's behaviour in relation to it.

The Department of Political Science at York University, building on Canada's rich political economy tradition, has long been recognized as one of the foremost academic sites for the critical study of both International Political Economy and Comparative Political Economy, gathering together a remarkable community of scholars and graduate students from around the world. This book is a product of an ongoing major research project on 'Production, Finance, Empire', funded by the Social Sciences and Humanities Research Council and conducted at York's political science department under the auspices of my Canada Research Chair in Comparative Political Economy. The chapters here all began as research papers for this project and most were presented to the Seminar Series in Comparative Political Economy (affectionately dubbed 'the empire seminar') which has over the past five years also attracted many international scholars as speakers, and faculty and graduate students from various departments at York and other universities.

Among the contributors to the book, my co-editor and co-author Martijn Konings took up a postdoctoral fellowship under my Canada Research Chair after completing his PhD at York, before moving on to his current position at the Amsterdam Institute for Metropolitan and International Development Studies at the University of Amsterdam. Sam Gindin, who holds the Packer Chair in Social Justice at York University, has been my co-investigator in the 'Production, Finance, Empire' project. Chris Rude and Thomas Sablowski came from the New School University and Frankfurt University respectively to take up positions as Postdoctoral Fellows under the project and as visiting professors in the Department of Political Science. David Sarai, Eric Newstadt, Scott Aquanno and Ruth Felder were actively engaged members of the research team while working on their PhD dissertations at York. It is indicative of the practical as well as scholarly expertise that this volume draws on that Rude worked at the Federal Reserve and Aquanno and Newstadt in the private financial sector before taking up their academic work; that Sarai was a Fulbright Fellow at American University in Washington, D.C., while conducting research at the US Treasury; that Felder worked in Argentina's public sector when it was undergoing restructuring under Word Bank auspices; that Sablowski worked as a consultant and researcher with the IG Metal Union and ATTAC in Germany; and that Gindin was for many years the Chief Economist and Research Director of the Canadian Auto Workers Union.

The broader research team of which the contributors have been part has included Patrick Bond and Ellen Russell as Postdoctoral Fellows; Travis

Fast, Khashayar Hooshiyar, Frederick Peters, Alan Zuege, Aidan Conway, Jeno Krouzil, Peter Brogan, Dan Crow, Marcel Nelson, Tori Ingham, Honor Brabazon and Michael Skinner have been among the graduate students at York who at various times and in various ways have contributed to it. This book would probably never have come to fruition without their inspiration and feedback, as well as that from the students in my Globalization and the State graduate seminar over the years. I am grateful for the support of colleagues like Greg Albo, John Saul and Ted Winslow who have been so active in the Seminar Series in Comparative Political Economy at York; of the Chairs of the Department of Political Science, Steve Newman, Isa Bakker and David McNally as well as the Dean of Arts, Bob Drummond; and of such dedicated members of the political science staff as Angie Swartz, Marlene Quesenberry and Carolyn Cross. Finally, this research project has coincided with the annual preparation and production of the *Socialist Register* (where in the 2005 volume earlier versions of the chapters here by myself and Sam Gindin and by Rude first saw the light of day), and I want to express my gratitude to my co-editor of the *Register*, Colin Leys, and our publisher at Merlin Press, Tony Zurbrugg, for their encouragement and cooperation.

Leo Panitch

Toronto, April 2008

1
Demystifying Imperial Finance

Leo Panitch and Martijn Konings

To a large extent, the discipline of international political economy (IPE) emerged in response to the perceived tendency of economic and financial globalization to undermine the power of nation-states, including that of the US state. The Bretton Woods system of fixed exchange rates was seen as the high point of American power in international finance. The decade of the 1970s saw international and domestic confusion, with several countries pursuing policies that were little to the liking of the US, while at home stagflation produced great regulatory perplexity. Not surprisingly, then, IPE scholars saw the end of Bretton Woods and the subsequent globalization of financial markets as signifying the decline of America's power in international finance. In this perspective, America's neoliberal policy turn during the late 1970s and early 1980s was seen as giving it some short-term advantages, but doing little to halt the decline: the huge inflows of capital that followed the artificially high interest rates were seen as serving to finance American indulgence (the hallmark of an imperial power in decline) as the American people and government borrowed more than ever before. While American banks continued their slide in the international rankings, and as the US's financial woes were complemented by troubles in other areas, theories of hegemonic decline flourished.

In fact, however, the American financial system continued to grow, American intermediaries innovated like never before, the US continued to attract large flows of capital, and American banks quickly returned to the top of the international league tables. By the last decade of the twentieth century it appeared that the crises of the 1970s and 1980s had done little lasting damage to the American financial system as a whole; the liquidity that the US state had pumped into the financial system after the 1987 stock market crash proved fairly effective, as did many of the (highly market-friendly) reforms. It was the US that was most active in opening up the economic and financial systems of other countries, and it was the US that benefited the most.

Under these circumstances, critical strands in IPE began to concentrate more on the sources of the asymmetrical effects of financial globalization. The globalization of financial markets, it was argued, had not only undermined

1

the US-dominated institutions of Bretton Woods, but had also been the driving force behind the creation of more indirect, structural relations of power in which the US was much more favourably positioned than other countries. However, what has never really been sufficiently worked out in this literature are the precise ways in which US power relations, practices and institutions are embedded in expanding financial markets, i.e. the organic institutional linkages between the operation of global finance and the US state that are at the root of America's privileged position. Accordingly, the literature developed in critical IPE soon began to develop its own decline thesis: financial globalization has created extraordinary opportunities for the US, but those opportunities are no longer properly embedded in and supported by hegemonic institutional structures.

This volume is premised on the idea that attempts to analyse US power in terms of America's ability or inability to defy the laws of capitalist finance represent a dead-end. The chapters in this volume try to uncover the concrete institutional mechanisms and historical sources of what often appears to be a mysterious, ungrounded ability of the US state to manipulate and benefit from the operation of global financial markets. To that end, it recasts the problematic as one of American empire – a concept that serves to emphasize that the relations between financial globalization and the US state are internal and mutually constitutive. The power of global financial markets and the power of the American state are not separate entities, to be articulated only after their respective constitution. Rather, they are connected through a dense web of organic institutional linkages.

Of course, American empire is qualitatively different from previous forms of imperialism, which were based on colonial rule and the geographical transplantation of the authority of the formal state. In such eras imperialism was obvious and visible in a way it is not when it assumes the form of a more subtle process of socio-economic interpenetration and informal political domination. But that makes it more rather than less important to adopt a perspective that emphasizes the imperial dimension of globalization: precisely because it appears as driven by neutral economic mechanisms, the expansion of practices and institutions acquires a tacit, indirect quality that often enhances its legitimacy and hides its imperial nature. For critics of neoliberal globalization and imperialism, the point is precisely to look behind the neutrality of appearances, i.e. to decode institutions and to conceptualize the patterns of economic power and imperial domination shaped through them.

The difficulty of grasping this elusive, tacit quality of American power[1] is borne out by the fact that it is rarely explicated in concrete historical terms; analyses are either theoretical and abstract or, when addressing historical questions, tend to focus once again on the more immediately visible aspects of American power. What tends to get lost is the distinctive nature of American international economic power. For it is precisely its hard-to-pin-down, indirect quality that allows American economic power to straddle the globe, and endows American policies with the leverage they possess – even when their military reach confronts hard limits (as in the Middle East today) and even when the roots of global financial crises (as with the credit crisis that hit in the summer of 2007) are directly traceable to US domestic financial markets.

Finance epitomizes the unique quality of American power. Pieces of paper bearing the imprint of the US state are accepted as valuable even in the world's most underdeveloped areas with only the most tenuous connections to the formal structures of the world economy. America's financial strength allows the US state to attract capital and run massive budget and payment deficits and as such constitutes a crucial element in the power of the American state at large. However, scholars have experienced considerable difficulty conceptualizing the sources of these phenomena and the mechanisms through which they are produced. They certainly are invisible to mainstream economics, premised as it is on the assumption of markets as neutral structures. But it seems that the foundations of America's financial power have been so thoroughly buried in the depoliticized realm of economic mechanisms that they tend to elude even those who study finance in its political aspects.

From the perspective offered here, the demise of Bretton Woods appears in a new light. The crisis of Bretton Woods coincided with the rapid expansion of American finance, both domestically and internationally. When the dam finally broke, US economic and political institutions proved eminently capable of exploiting the opportunities. The problems and regulatory contradictions of the 1960s and 1970s can be seen in this light as representing not the decline and malfunctioning of American finance but rather the difficulty of controlling and steering a financial system that was bursting at the seams. And the embrace of neoliberalism and monetarism in response to this is less fruitfully seen as a perverse reversion to misguided ideologies[2] than as a political turning point that reconfigured America's relation to the world and gave American capitalism a new lease of life.

It is not just that America's financial power seems to have outlived the Fordist age of undisputed industrial pre-eminence and current account surpluses. After all, Britain too reached its height of financial power after its decline as 'workshop of the world'. What is more extraordinary is the fact that the US benefited rather than suffered from its transformation from an international creditor to an international debtor. In contrast to what happened with Britain, America's ability to accumulate gigantic amounts of debt was not compromised by the fact that its debts to the world came to far exceed its assets. This was precisely because America's debts became a central element of the infrastructure of the international financial system. Thus, since the early 1980s, as ever more states became subject to the disciplinary pressures of global finance, the leverage of the US state seemed to grow and grow. While not ignoring the many challenges to American financial power, nor the contradictions that have attended its elaboration over time, the perspective presented in this volume seeks to offer a more comprehensive understanding of the various aspects of American financial power, and shows how it has been facilitated through the imperial penetration of global financial structures, including those of other states.

Markets and states in international and comparative political economy

The existing IPE literature has remained too wedded to the discourse of states and markets to arrive at a satisfactory account of the growth of American financial power. More specifically, its continued reliance on an external conception of market power and state power has prevented it from fully conceptualizing the institutional linkages between global finance, American finance and the US state. Indeed, the very fact that the discipline of IPE has come to rely so heavily on the notion of 'globalization' in its analysis of international finance is testimony to the ideological strength of American empire and the failure of mainstream and even critical scholarship to penetrate fully beneath its appearances. And because the constitutive dimensions of US power in the operation of global financial markets are not fully theorized, the IPE literature remains prone to revised notions of hegemonic decline, according to which the globalization of financial markets must at some point inevitably overwhelm the capacities of the US state. A century ago, however, it would have been unthinkable for contemporaneous observers of international finance to write about financial markets as though their constitution was external to the power relations among states: there was little question that the mechanisms governing financial internationalization reflected the imperial interests of Britain as well as the specific institutional characteristics of British finance.

For a long time the most prominent account of the rise of US financial power was that presented by the neorealist theory of hegemonic stability (e.g. Kindleberger 1973; Gilpin 1987). Premised on the notion that a liberal international economic order requires political leadership for its stable reproduction, hegemonic stability theory understood the history of the international system in terms of the rise and fall of hegemonic nations, each overseeing the expansion of the world market. The absence of hegemonic leadership (i.e. the breakdown of British imperialism and American unwillingness to assume the mantle of hegemony) was seen as responsible for the instability and ultimate collapse of the international economy during the interwar period. After the Second World War, the US did assume the role of hegemon, ensuring the stable reproduction of the capitalist economy by embedding it in regulatory institutions. As the institutional expression of the ideology of 'embedded liberalism', the Bretton Woods system represented the high point of American financial leadership in this mode of thought.

Financial globalization, understood as a process without an author, was seen to upset this highly specific model of international power and thus came to be seen as the cause of American decline. It was the re-emergence of global finance from the late 1960s, now apparently untied from its state moorings, that was seen as marking the beginning of the loss of US hegemony, ultimately leading to the collapse of the Bretton Woods system. The American state's role in bringing this collapse about, reinforced by neoliberal and monetarist policies during the early 1980s, only further undermined America's long-term economic position and prospects and so its capacity to perform the role of hegemon.

Relying on the notion that there is a structural isomorphism in the way that hegemonic nations relate to the world economy, hegemonic stability theory conceptualized American leadership in international finance as a variation on the theme of a hegemonic nation taking responsibility for the reproduction of a liberal world order. This stark, abstract distinction between international economic structures and the national state and the disregard for the specific institutional linkages between them has drawn considerable criticism from mainstream and more critical IPE approaches alike. But especially within mainstream IPE, assertions concerning the relatedness of politics and economics have always been somewhat perfunctory and gratuitous. While Ruggie's analysis of how post-Second World War liberalism was embedded in multilateral institutions led him to the idea that perhaps the post-war global political economy should be understood not as a function of 'American *hegemony*' but rather as constituted by '*American* hegemony' (1992: 568), this notion has been studiously ignored by himself and others. Ultimately, any theory not actually focused on the institutional (re)construction of the global economic system by the US state and financial system will be incapable of grasping their transformative impact on the rules of the world economy and the qualitatively unique nature and distinctive dynamics of American power.

To be sure, within mainstream IPE the reaction to the problems of hegemonic stability theory has revolved around an engagement with the theme of institutions and regimes. While scattered evidence of some sort of resurgent protectionism during the 1970s might have seemed to confirm the predictions of neorealism, as the world emerged from the confusion of that decade it became clear that the end of American hegemony had not meant the return to economic nationalism or the breakdown of the world economy. The institutional regime on the basis of which the world economy functioned turned out to possess more internal coherence and it was thus concluded to be less singularly dependent on US hegemony than had been assumed. Neoliberal institutionalism (Keohane 1984) in particular proposed supplementing the neorealist focus on state power and national interest with attention to the network of international institutions that functioned to support international order and stability. Moreover, the broader theoretical strand with which neoliberal institutionalism can be said to be associated, i.e. regime theory, pays a great deal of attention to the 'softer' and more informal institutions that are necessary for the regulation and reproduction of economic structures (see Krasner 1982).

Yet these approaches understood institutions primarily in terms of the rather technical cooperation among non-market actors faced with processes of growing economic interdependence that in principle elude their grasp. In this sense, they never really challenged the external conception of states and markets. The greater concern with institutions never translated into a precise understanding of the historical, institutional and social dimensions of state power, and it especially continued to give short shrift to the concrete, organic institutional linkages between the American state and the operation of global financial markets (either at the formal-organization level or at a more informal social level). Accordingly, these approaches did nothing to challenge the thesis of American decline: globalization was still understood as undermining the power of the US state – and globalization was now treated as being capable of flourishing as it did so. In some ways the emphasis on the inherently stable nature of globalization processes made the analysis of neoliberal institutionalism and regime theory even more peculiarly depoliticized than hegemonic stability theory, with its visions of global economic breakdown, had ever been.

Thus, mainstream IPE has largely failed to get to the actual nature and quality of the 'political' that lies at the heart of the institutional constitution of the world economy. It was more critical approaches in IPE that sought to theorize this with the notion of 'structural power'. This shifted the focus from the behavioural aspects of state power (e.g. resources and direct control) towards its indirect, not immediately observable aspects. It proposed thinking about state power with reference to its broader socioeconomic, class and institutional dimensions and sources (e.g. Strange 1988; Gill and Law 1989; Helleiner 1994; Arrighi 1994; Germain 1997). The resurgence of global finance outside the 'embedded liberal' structures of Bretton Woods was recognized not to have in any straightforward way undermined US power in international finance: while it was responsible for the demise of the US-dominated Bretton Woods institutions, it also laid the basis for a more market-based and structural form of power.

Critical IPE scholars thus tend to understand US structural power in terms of the ability of the US state to harness global markets to its international ambitions, but it remains unclear what institutions, techniques and relations are embedded in the very constitution of the international economy that reflect US power and bias its operation in favour of the US. Structural power, it seems, is primarily conceived as the power of capital or the market, and what remains underdeveloped are its organic linkages to the American state, i.e. the historical sources and institutional basis of the US's privileged relationship to processes of financial globalization. Consequently, there remains an element of uncertainty as to what determines whether the structural power of global finance will work for or against the purposes of the American state.

It is in this light that we can understand why the critical IPE literature has been prone to adopting some variation of the mainstream thesis of hegemonic decline. Even though it generally recognizes that for the time being the US retains a huge degree of financial power, this is not seen as having any inherent, organically privileged relationship to processes of globalization. While it acknowledges that financial globalization has created extraordinary opportunities for the US, it fails to register sufficiently that the reasons for this are embedded in the basic structures of global finance. Eventually, it is argued, the American state will have to bow before the power of globalizing financial markets. America's ability to exploit the rest of the world through the dynamics of international finance is seen as marked by a somewhat ephemeral quality: the US is dominant yet its power is no longer firmly supported by hegemonic institutional structures.

Critical IPE's historical interpretation can perhaps be said to be rooted in conceptual tensions that are similar to those of mainstream IPE, i.e. the problem of articulating the economic and the political. It does not entirely succeed in overcoming the idea of markets and institutions as separate entities, leaving them to be articulated only after their respective constitution. In this sense, we can say that critical IPE authors often still adhere to an 'outside-in' approach (Panitch 1996, 2000) to the study of the relation between states and the global political economy: structural power tends to be conceived as market power and its connections to state power tend to be articulated in largely external terms. The historical sources and institutional bases of state power remain underdeveloped. It thus becomes difficult to theorize the internal connections and organic institutional linkages between the global economy and nation-states and the transformative effect of hegemonic power on the nature of global economic processes.

The approach adopted in this volume also takes its distance from the analysis of national political institutions offered by the new institutionalism and the associated 'varieties of capitalism' literature in comparative political economy (CPE). Its theoretical programme is quite different from that of IPE: instead of viewing states primarily as either the victims or authors of processes of financial globalization, it aims to show that states are entirely capable of maintaining their own institutional integrity and that the era of global capital has seen the persistence – indeed, flourishing – of a variety of national models (Zysman 1983; Hall and Soskice 2001). Yet in making this argument it shares with IPE a tendency to ontologize the distinction between markets and institutions as well as a focus on formal state institutions and organizations that is oblivious to the social sources of state capacity. Like IPE, this literature remains caught in a methodological perspective that separates and juxtaposes institutions and economic structures. The 'varieties of capitalism' literature in particular examines the institutionally generated ability of states to react and respond to the pressures of economic globalization, but does not consider how institutions shape these pressures in the first place. It does not understand the very formation of international economic imperatives as a process of institutionalization of power relations. As a consequence, the CPE literature is not very helpful in construing the organic institutional linkages between national states and globalizing financial markets (Coates 2005).

Overcoming the dichotomies and reifications of both IPE and CPE discourse requires more than mere theoretical assertion: it requires a research focus that guides our efforts to construing the constitutive impact of political power on the nature and dynamics of economic structures and the resulting linkages between economic dynamics and political power – connections that are often difficult to see as they have been covered under layers and layers of ideological representations. If we are to break with an outside-in mode of analysis, our historical analysis of the state should commence not after the political and economic have already been legally, ideologically and discursively constituted as separate entities but it should precisely trace and understand this process as itself a source of power. This is what this volume tries to do in its analysis of the American state. The key is to conceptualize and research how the institutional framework of American finance shaped the system of global finance in the first place as well as how the institutional linkages between the American state and the structural power embedded in the system of global finance have functioned to enhance the power of the US state.

But it is important to be clear on what such a perspective entails; opening up states and deconstructing the appearances of institutional authority is not something that one can do a little bit, just to add it on to an otherwise 'outside-in' or state-centric analysis. Thus, by examining the constitution of what Gramsci calls the 'integral state' rather than merely the state's formal institutions and official representations, the perspective adopted in this book differs from other approaches that also try to open up the state and pay more explicit attention to the role of particular institutions.[3] Once one looks beneath the state's official presentation of itself and questions its professed purposes and nature, a virtually endless network of connections becomes visible that organically ties formal institutions and organizational actors to lower-level institutions and practices, travelling all the way down to social relations as people experience them in their daily lives. This volume not only opens up the American state by examining actors and institutions such as the Treasury and the Federal Reserve, but also examines the way in which these institutions are connected to the constitution of social process and class relations both in the US and internationally. In other words, while this volume certainly engages with current debates about the role of the US state in the world at large, it does so not merely by looking for the ways those institutions are furthering the objectives of a narrowly conceived American 'national interest' but by paying ample attention to the social construction of the American state capacities that have become so actively engaged in the construction and management of a global capitalism.

The meaning of crisis

As this book goes to press, the financial world is still in the throes of the liquidity crunch brought on by the crisis in the 'subprime' sector of the US mortgage market. The exact scale and significance of such events can only be determined with the benefit of hindsight. Yet it is clear that this is more than a minor upheaval. Comparisons have already been made with the 1987 stock market crash and the bursting of the dot-com bubble at the turn of the century. Lending by commercial banks and mortgage providers has taken a serious hit, money market interest rates have jumped, and even the operations of hedge funds and private equity funds – until recently seen to be operating in a rarefied world of high finance largely unaffected by events in the real world – have been brought up short. Moreover, while the US and European monetary authorities have been prepared to pump liquidity into the markets, this has had less immediate effect than they hoped.

Almost as soon as the US subprime crisis struck in the summer of 2007, the crisis of the British mortgage bank Northern Rock made clear how quickly and effectively the tensions in a relatively small corner of the US financial markets were transmitted across the world. While very much a product of integrated global financial markets, the Northern Rock crisis produced images that negated pretty much everything that modern people have come to believe about the credibility of money and the seemingly autonomous operations of the financial system. The pictures of long lines of people waiting to empty their bank accounts seemed reminiscent of the bank failures of the Great Depression and peculiarly disconnected from the modern twenty-first-century financial system with its highly sophisticated techniques for risk and liquidity management.

In other words, the current crisis is a serious one that has laid bare some key networks of the central nervous system of global finance. Moreover, it is one that emanated from the heart of empire – unlike the crises during the previous decade (such as the Mexican, Asian, Russian and Argentinian ones), which seemed bound up primarily with the inability of developing countries or emerging markets to accept the discipline needed to participate in a fully liberalized world order. Other crises – such as the LTCM crisis – played themselves out entirely at the level of high finance. The end of the dot-com boom and the stock market run-up it sustained already had a serious impact on the value of Americans' investment portfolios. But it is the subprime crisis that has really exposed the connections between such a key component of the American dream as home ownership and the mechanisms of financial expansion and innovation. To many, the situation is yet another illustration of the fundamentally unsustainable nature of the neoliberal system of Americanized global finance, reliant as it is on massive mountains of virtual money and paper-debt created through financial engineering and speculative practices that appear so disproportionate in relation to the wealth-generating capacity and manufacturing competitiveness of the US economy.

However, it is precisely the understanding advanced in this volume of the historical evolution and present state of the American financial system and its global role that leads us to view with some scepticism strong claims concerning the disastrous outcome of the current liquidity crunch for the structural dynamism of the global system of finance and America's position in it. If there is one thing that we especially hope the essays in this volume demonstrate, it is that the present system of global finance has been shaped so profoundly by specifically American institutions and practices that it will not do to evaluate the changes and transformations of this system on the basis of either an abstract, generic model of capitalism or mere extrapolations from conjunctural crises. American financial power did not latch on to an existing system of international finance but shaped this system to its core through a long history of imperial expansion. The decades-long build up of American power has been punctuated by multiple crises and instabilities, but this has primarily been a reflection of the depth of the transformation effected and the dynamism generated by American-style financial globalization. Crisis and instability are part and parcel of the dynamics of imperial finance and so are the difficulties experienced by the US state in managing them. Neither the crisis nor the managerial difficulties are likely to prove fatal unless they generate the kinds of social and political conflicts that shake the system to its core.

The plan of the book

The chapters in Part I of this volume set the table by laying out the basic contours and sources of American financial power, and identifying the key aspects and moments of its growth and expansion. Chapter 2, by Panitch and Gindin, presents an interpretation of America's role in shaping the dynamics and institutions of post-Second World War global finance that differs in important respects from the analysis offered not only by mainstream but also by more critical approaches. The story told is one of Americanization, the processes of institutional penetration whereby distinctly American forms and practices have spread and often been willingly embraced in other countries. It discusses the various ways in which the American state and its financial system have shaped the political economies of other states as well as the rules that regulate the financial relations among them – and in the process the global financial system at large. Konings' essay (Chapter 3) goes back further into history to examine the social and historical roots of the US financial system and traces the way in which the institutions and practices of American finance have evolved and expanded to assume a central role in the making of the modern global financial system. He shows how the integrative capacity of the American financial system has been at the core of the mutually reinforcing dynamics between empire at home and empire abroad.

Part II moves on to a more concrete account of the modalities of American financial power through examinations of several of its institutional pillars and the processes through which these were constructed. The order of the chapters, in keeping with the inside-out approach outlined above, is configured so as to trace the process of Americanization: starting on the domestic side of things, they work their way back to the international realm and finally address traditional IPE themes informed by a much fuller understanding of the social and historical sources of American state power.

Thus Chapters 4 and 5 by Newstadt and Sarai, respectively, begin where Part I left off, presenting detailed accounts of the role of the two key state institutions in the construction of American financial power. In most IPE work the Treasury features as a crucial but largely unexamined actor. This leads, among other things, to a lack of awareness of the relation between its international and domestic roles. Sarai's account of the Treasury in the making of American finance explicitly situates its international role in this context. Newstadt's chapter provides a detailed examination of the Federal Reserve's evolving management of the expansionary dynamics of the American financial system in a relationship of functional interdependence with the re-emergence of global finance. He shows that the Fed's turn to monetarism was a crucial moment both in domestic financial management and in the reconfiguration of global financial power, and goes on to trace the Federal Reserve's emergence as the 'world central bank' in the very process of playing a more and more crucial role in domestic policy-making and global financial management.

The following three chapters trace the trajectory of Americanization processes into the global arena, beginning with Aquanno's examination (Chapter 6) of the fundamental role that US Treasury bills play in valuing risk in global financial markets and the historical role of American bond markets in the construction of imperial financial power. While the Eurodollar markets have always received considerable attention in the literature, these are not normally situated within the broader complex of bond markets – which is crucial to a full understanding of the institutional linkages between global financial markets and the American state. Sablowski's chapter on the Americanization of European finance (Chapter 7) tries to understand this process through a case study of the transition to a finance-led regime of accumulation in Germany. He shows that the transition towards a market-oriented financial system should not be seen as an effect of a generic process of globalization but is more usefully understood as involving the internalization by the German state and financial system of American regulations and practices. Chapter 8, also by Sablowski, addresses the international politics of accounting standards, and shows how, especially during the neoliberal era, an international accounting standard regime has been put into place that reflects the nature of American financial practices and tends to work to the advantage of the US state and American intermediaries.

The last two chapters in Part II focus on the more traditional IPE territory of international financial institutions (IFIs), and in doing so reveal how much the analysis of international regulation can be enriched by this volume's focus on the historical roots, social sources and institutional pillars of US imperial power. Felder's essay (Chapter 9) on the International Monetary Fund and the World Bank demonstrates how these institutions have from their very inception been shaped by American power, and traces their successive transformations in relation to the policies and strategies of the US state, revealing how, when it comes to the current era, IFIs do not just feature as agents of neoliberalism, but as agents of empire. At the same time she poses the challenging question of whether strategies of disengagement from the IFIs, as advanced by certain Latin American governments today, are likely to succeed. In Chapter 10 Rude brings Part II to a dramatically insightful close with an analysis of the development of capital adequacy rules for banks via the Basel I and II regimes for international bank regulation. He reveals how even the most technical and seemingly apolitical questions should in fact be seen as involving a crucial element of class and imperial power in the international arena. The structural effects of this in the sphere of international banking regulation result in asymmetrical financial discipline being placed on banks in the global South compared to those in the core capitalist states, very much to the advantage of the latter, and this has become an important element in the reproduction of imperial relations.

The editors' concluding chapter in this volume draws together some of the lines of argument presented in the various essays and addresses their broader implications in terms of political contestation, crisis and democracy not only historically but right up to the present. It theorizes the relationship between American empire and global finance by emphasizing the distinctive interaction between class and finance in the US, the mutually constitutive relationship between the state and financial markets, and the fact that processes of financial internationalization have entailed not only the *externalization* of American financial forms and practices but also the *internalization* of a variety of heterogeneous and geographically dispersed practices and relations into spaces structured by American rules and institutions. The critical assessment it offers in the final section of the political orientations and implications of IPE and CPE theorizations will hopefully help reveal how the kind of alternative analysis undertaken in this volume can usefully inform progressive and transformative political forces and strategies.

Notes

1. Hardt and Negri (2000) appropriately call this 'network power' and trace its roots to the American constitution, but they mistakenly see this quality of power in global capitalism as having been disconnected from the US via the process of globalization (Panitch and Gindin 2002a).
2. The tendency to give unwarranted causative force to the ideas of Hayek or Friedman in the emergence of neoliberalism can be seen in such diverse and sophisticated accounts as Helleiner (1994), Harvey (2005) and Klein (2007).
3. Broz (2005) and Broz and Hawes (2006), for instance, have tried to understand the US strategy in international finance by focusing on the role of the US Congress and its relations with international financial institutions, but the analysis is marked by its formalistic character and the lack of attention to the social sources of power and policy. For his part, Seabrooke (2001), engaging directly with debates on US structural power, has tried to develop a richer understanding of the domestic institutional sources of American financial power in terms of the 'interactive embeddedness' of Washington and Wall Street. Yet it is important that this notion not be treated too abstractly and employed too generally, and thus come to function as a substitute for, rather than as an invitation for an analysis of, the relations among private and public American financial institutions.

Part I

Contours and Sources of Imperial Finance

2
Finance and American Empire

Leo Panitch and Sam Gindin

'Today, there are no more worlds to find. Upon us is the responsibility never laid before on a people – building the world's capital for all time to come.'

(Wall Street lawyer and Congressman
John DeWitt Warner, 1898)[1]

'Remember the song, "We Are the World?" In matters of finance and politics, if not culture, we are becoming the world and much of the world wants to become us.'

(Chairman of the New York Stock Exchange
Richard Grasso, 1997)[2]

'I do believe New York is the financial capital of the world, that the strongest capital markets in the world are in New York, and they benefit our whole country. But I also believe that having strong capital markets in London benefits us all.'

(Secretary of the Treasury Henry M. Paulson, 2007)[3]

Despite the hubris that has attended the global ambitions of American financiers for over a century, the actual rise to world dominance of American finance was far from smooth or inevitable. The goal of 'building the world's capital for all time to come' in New York, already articulated in the late nineteenth century, looked set to be realized by the end of the First World War. Yet it was only a decade later that the Wall Street crash triggered the Great Depression and the breakdown of the international financial order. And while New York took its place as the world's principal financial centre at the end of the Second World War, this seemed much less important when the new Bretton Woods order had supposedly marginalized finance relative to production and trade. As the story of twentieth-century capitalism is usually told today, only the neoliberal 'revolution' of the 1980s and 1990s finally unleashed the forces that made Wall Street the central location of the world economy. But far from this marking the end of history, the scandal that enveloped Richard Grasso in 2003 over his $150 million salary not only epitomized the venality of New York as the capital of global finance, but it also appeared to symbolize its fragility. And Hank Paulson's recent bold statement of confidence in New York as the financial capital of the world – expressed in the midst of the global credit crisis that had its roots in the collapse of the US domestic subprime mortgage market (with Paulson's own Wall Street firm Goldman Sachs having played a large role in making that market) – could be taken as yet another example of whistling in the dark (Stein 2007).

From this perspective, it is perhaps not surprising that puncturing the hubris of New York's financial elite and its political representatives has become a favourite game of critical political economists. Playing this game may be dangerous, however, insofar as it underestimates the material significance as well as the obvious salience of global finance in the American empire. With this in mind, this chapter tries to come to a deeper understanding, first, of the actual historical process that led to the realization by the end of the twentieth century of a global financial order with New York as its operational centre, and with the American imperial state as its political carapace; and, second, of the way in which finance and empire reinforce each other today.

We begin in section 1 with the unique position of the American state at the time of the reconstruction of capitalism after the Second World War. We argue that this did not allow for the repression of finance, as many believe the Bretton Woods arrangements accomplished, but rather that the seeds planted at that time for a new liberal trading order both reflected and contributed to the influence and power of financial capital. Section 2 examines the two-decade-long period of confusion and hesitation about whether, and if so how, the American state could manage the emerging global capitalist economy in the context of the inflationary pressures and class conflicts of the 1960s and 1970s. Section 3 addresses the central moment in the neoliberal reconstitution of the global capitalist order: the domestic economic discipline introduced by the US Federal Reserve under Paul Volcker (the 'Volcker shock') at the beginning of the 1980s – which built upon the privatization and internationalization of financial markets that had already occurred, and carried them further still. We show that at each of the turning points in the evolution of the international capitalist economy, the American state both registered and extended the power and depth of financial capital at home as well as abroad.

Section 4 examines not only the crises and contradictions but also the synergies involved in the relationship between finance, production and American empire today. It makes three central points. First, the expansion of finance has not been something apart from, but rather integral to the deepening of accumulation, as seen in both the continued internationalization of production networks and – as part and parcel of this – the continuing strength of the American economy. Second, liberalized finance needs to be seen less as a new constraint on the US state and more as a developing mechanism through which the state addresses its goals – including its capacity to contain the depth, breadth and duration of the crises that are inherent in the volatility of liberalized finance. Third, it is wrong to see the financialization of the American empire as a symptom of its decline: the globalization of finance has included the *Americanization* of finance, and the deepening and extension of financial markets has become more than ever fundamental to the reproduction and universalization of American power. It is an American empire strengthened rather than weakened by its financialization that we need to confront.

1. The post-war era as the cradle of global finance

Most liberal and even critical political economists have emphasized the 'embedded liberalism' of the post-war era, stressing in particular what often has been called the 'repression' of finance (Helleiner 1994: 3). In turn, the growth of untrammelled global financial markets over the past quarter century has usually been seen in terms of the 'liberation' of finance from its post-war constraints. But the 1980s did not suddenly launch the liberalization and Americanization of international finance. No less a practitioner of financial capital and American power than Paul Volcker has stressed the continuity: 'I take it almost as an article of faith (a faith that in this case can be backed by facts) that the United States, as the dominant power after World War II and for decades afterwards, was the driving force toward a liberal trading order and the freedom of international investment' (Volcker and Gyohten 1992: 288). Concentrating on what distinguishes the two eras leads to the neglect of the processes at work that led from the first era to the second, and the extent to which neoliberalism's spread in the 1980s and 1990s depended on the structures previously established. As a recent study of international banking put it, '[T]he Bretton Woods years should be regarded in a number of respects as the cradle of the global financial order that eventually emerged in the two final decades of the last century' (Battilossi 2002a: 27).

This itself cannot be properly understood except in terms of the new type of imperial order that emerged in the decades after the Second World War.[4] It was defined above all by the American state successfully overcoming the earlier fragmentation of capitalism into rival empires. The unique informal empire it now fashioned was characterized, most notably, by the US state's economic penetration of, and close institutional linkages with, the other advanced capitalist states. This was an imperial order very different from the one that had been characterized by the ties between the imperial states and their colonies in the pre-First World War era.

In rethinking today how capitalist globalization was relaunched in the post-Second World War era, the American interest in such a project seems obvious enough: the exhaustion of the old empires during the war provided new opportunities too tempting to ignore. But more generally, the thirty-year crisis of capitalism, and its declining legitimacy in the face of both Soviet communism and the strength of the left in the West European labour movements, meant that more than just an American-led post-war economic reconstruction of Europe was at stake: the tendency towards the establishment of a liberal global capitalist order, so severely interrupted since the First World War, now depended for its realization on the unique capacity of the American state for its revival and extension.

But why did Europe accept the American project? After all, hadn't liberalism proved to be a failure? And how could Europe possibly compete with the US economically – or, even if it accepted the need for American capital and technology for post-war reconstruction, how could it possibly pay for this? Wasn't inward, self-reliant development the only real option? Insofar as these questions have been neglected, it is in large part because of the assumption that the post-war order was in fact *not*, even tendentially, a liberal-capitalist one, but one that 'embedded' capitalist relations within a political and social regulatory framework designed to limit and control its logic and dynamics. In this narrative the 'suppression' of finance in favour of production, and the adoption of Keynesian fiscal policies and the Bretton Woods rules and institutions for managing global adjustments, created the foundations for the establishment of distinctive national, welfare-state capitalisms, especially in Western Europe.

But the reality was very different. At the time of the entry of the US into the Second World War there was a broad consensus in American capitalist and state circles that a top priority for the post-war world would be the reconstruction of a global free trade system. 'We have profited by our past mistakes,' Roosevelt said as early as September 1942. 'This time we shall know how to make full use of victory.' What he meant by this was that, unlike at the end of the First World War, the US government would now 'conquer its allies in a more enlightened manner, by demanding economic concessions of a legal and political nature instead of futilely seeking repayment of its wartime loans' (Hudson 2003).[5] The editors of *Fortune,Time* and *Life* magazines, in a joint statement in 1942, called for a 'new American imperialism' whose goal would be 'to promote and foster private enterprise, by removing the barriers to its natural expansion', through the creation of 'an expansionist context in which tariffs, subsidies, monopolies, restrictive labour rule ... and all other barriers to further expansion can be removed'. This vision was strikingly similar to what would later be called neoliberalism, in which 'universal free trade' was seen as 'the *ultimate* goal of a rational world' (*Fortune Magazine* 1942: 59–63).

This imperial vision was articulated just as the US Treasury was taking the initiative, in conjunction with the British Treasury, to develop the plans that eventually led to Bretton Woods. Roosevelt's Secretary of the Treasury, Henry

Morgenthau, promised a 'New Deal in international economics'. Important to the final outcome were Keynes' influential attacks on financial orthodoxy in the context of the new 'facts on the ground' – the comprehensive wartime controls over currency and capital flows. But this should not obscure the compromises that were made with the bankers, reflecting the continuing importance of financial capital both inside and outside the state.

The key issue was what role capital controls would be allowed to play after the war. As far as the US itself was concerned, the outcome had already been prefigured before the war. The New Deal at home had meant corporatist regulation and suppression of competition between financial institutions, but not the suppression of financial capital as a powerful force in American society (Ferguson 1984; Helleiner 1994: 31). The fact that the New Deal at home never extended to controls over the international movement of capital meant that rhetorical bravado of the kind occasionally heard from politicians like Morgenthau, about 'driving the usurious money lenders out of the temple of international finance', should never have been taken too seriously.

By the time many of America's leading capitalists entered the government during the war, the bankers' adamant opposition to an international treaty re-establishing controls over capital movements was well understood. Henry Dexter-White wrote a position paper for the US Treasury in 1941 which correctly recognized that any really effective international system of capital controls would require recipient states to cooperate in policing incoming flows of capital that had escaped the controls of other countries. This proposal, however, ultimately got nowhere, as did Keynes' attempt to secure at least voluntary multinational cooperation against currency speculation. To be sure, even the New York bankers were pragmatic enough to see that most countries – with the key exception of the US – would continue to require capital controls after the war. But they never relinquished their view that such controls should be only temporary. They were motivated by their concern to protect investors' rights and for investors to exert discipline on the fiscal policies of governments – and this would 'continue to be part of Wall's Street rhetoric for the remainder of the century' (Seabrooke 2001: 53).[6] So while the Bretton Woods Agreement recognized that states could operate capital controls, what was more significant was the US state's own refusal to use such controls, and the expectation in both Washington and New York that other states would use them only for a transitional period of reconstruction.

How short the transitional period was initially expected to be was evident from the great pressure the US put upon the British to quickly make sterling convertible, and the open arms with which Wall Street received a wave of capital flight from Europe immediately after the war. Even when it was recognized that if this continued it would spell the end of European capitalist reconstruction (and thus that even currency convertibility, let alone the removal of capital controls, would have to be postponed), the American state was not prepared to make European controls more effective by controlling capital inflows to the US. Rather, the funds pumped into Europe under the Marshall Plan were provided on terms that were meant to reinforce what European finance was demanding of European governments, i.e. 'to balance their budgets, restore financial stability, stabilize the exchange rate at realistic levels and enhance mutual cooperation'.[7] The use of 'offsetting financing' – which would become the primary means of coping with capital flight in the neoliberal era – had been discussed at Bretton Woods but was formally rejected there in favour of capital controls. Yet this is what the Marshall Plan in a certain sense amounted to, at a time when the new International Monetary Fund had insufficient resources to play much of a role.[8]

The Bretton Woods rules and international institutions like the IMF did allow more flexibility in national adjustments to international imbalances. But what was really crucial was the way the American state's acceptance of what it always saw as temporary and transitional barriers to selected US exports and investments abroad, helped to incorporate the Western European (and Japanese) states into the new imperial order. It tolerated their under-valued exchange rates, and used its financial and military aid to facilitate their access to American equipment and technology, while at the same time encouraging European economic integration. An important study under-taken in the early 1950s by leading American bureaucrats and academics concluded that 'the inability to realize the goals of Bretton Woods policy except marginally inevitably shifted the center of gravity and the orienta-tion of American foreign policy away from attempts to apply universal trade and monetary prescriptions'. By 1948 it was already clear that 'internation-alist trade and monetary policies and universal inter-governmental agencies play a peripheral or waiting part', while American programmes and gov-ernment agencies 'occupy the center of the stage' (Study Group sponsored by the Woodrow Wilson Foundation and the National Planning Association 1955: 213).

The American state did not so much dictate to the European states as struc-ture their options in the post-war period so that the reproduction of European capitalism depended on its international integration. It thereby 'internation-alized' these states in terms of their goals and consequent responsibilities. Given the challenge (and potential contradictions) facing Europe in rebuild-ing its infrastructure while also rebuilding its social relations, relying on Bretton Woods alone was doomed to fail. The overwhelming economic dom-inance of the US would have led to balance of payments crises that the newly formed IMF clearly could not handle; 'fixed' exchange rates would have had to be repeatedly adjusted; beggar-my-neighbour trade policies would have been revived. It was the intervention of the American state in shaping the pattern of European reconstruction which – far more than the 'suppres-sion' of finance via Bretton Woods, or the deployment of Keynesianism as a policy technique – made the post-war golden age of capitalist growth possible.

Marshall aid itself had obvious strategic, trade and ideological purposes apart from financial stabilization and economic growth, all linked to strengthening Europe's capitalist classes. The post-war balance of class forces meant that labour could not be repressed as it had been before, which made it all the more important that financial capital should be reinforced. How far this could be accomplished varied from country to country. But it was certainly expressed in the determination with which the Bundesbank and the Finance Ministry in Germany espoused neoliberal monetarist policies throughout the post-war period. And, in the UK, the Bank of England – even after its nationalization by the post-war Labour government – continued to represent the interests of the City of London, often in alliance with a UK Treasury increasingly obsessed with restraining union wage power under conditions of high employment. Meanwhile, the Bank for International Settlements (BIS) was preserved as a bastion of financial orthodoxy. With the help of Keynes' intervention at Bretton Woods, it had survived the US Treasury's attempt to extinguish it in the face of strong opposition from both European and American private and central bankers (Skidelsky 2000: 354; Ozgercin 2005: 242–56). The BIS was turned to practical as well as ideological use when it became, now with strong backing from the US Treasury, the vehicle for running the European Payments Union mechanism in the late 1940s.

But all this paled beside the special place that American financial capital itself occupied in the world capitalist order. The outcome of the war had effectively put the world on the dollar standard, and the Bretton Woods agreement had effectively ratified this. Although the dollar was nominally backed by gold, the day could already be foreseen when gold would be demonetized 'along with copper, nickel, silver, not to mention wampum and clam shells' (Kindleberger 1981: 103). The dollar already had a unique status: as reserve currency; as vehicle currency through which firms were generally invoiced and other currencies were exchanged in international commerce; and as store of value for financial assets (including for the issuance of public and private long-term bonds). And this status was based, above all, on the immense size, depth, liquidity and openness of the US domestic financial markets.

The New York bankers had considerable influence in the Treasury under the Truman administration, even though 'lingering New Deal suspicion of Wall Street [had] culminated in one last cannonade' in the form of an antitrust suit launched in 1947 by the Justice Department against the investment houses that handled 70 per cent of Wall Street underwriting. But when this suit failed in the courts a few years later, it was a 'watershed in the history of Wall Street' that 'finally freed the Street of its image as the home of monopoly capitalists...the investment bankers finally proved they were vital to the economy' (Chernow 1990: 402; Geisst 1997: 272).

The post-war economic boom and the financial bull market through the 1950s provided the space for American finance, even while still operating within the framework of the New Deal regulations, to further deepen its markets at home and expand abroad. Financial institutions of various types across the country not only participated in the rapid growth of industry but also found ways to encourage and take advantage of rising consumerism to draw in the working classes, especially through state-backed mortgage securities and consumer loans. International portfolio investment recovered slowly in the 1950s, but New York's investment banks, far from suffering from their exclusion from commercial banking under the New Deal financial legislation, became unrivalled in terms of the role they played (and the fees they earned) in capital-intensive infrastructural 'project financing' and in the placement of corporate, state and World Bank bond issues.[9] Although interest rates were low during this period, rising volumes and stable spreads between interest charged and interest paid supported profitability. The profits of financial firms grew faster than non-financial profits through the 1950s and 1960s: between 1945 and 1952 the average annual growth in profits in finance was 18 per cent compared to 11 per cent in the non-financial sector; from 1953 to 1969 the comparison was 7.5 per cent vs. 4.5 per cent.[10] Robert Rubin, the future Secretary of the US Treasury who joined Goldman Sachs in 1965, recalls one of the old guard telling him in the early 1970s 'that we junior partners would be unlikely to ever do as well financially as the older partners had because there would never be another period as good as the one that had just passed' (Rubin 2003: 81).

In the new dollar-centred international financial system the relationship of the rest of the world, and especially of Europe, to American finance could not be limited for very long to borrowing through financial services located in New York. Before the war, the branches of American investment banks had acted mainly as diplomatic outposts for their home offices, but by the late 1950s and early 1960s they had become dynamic financial actors *inside* Europe. This involved the export of American banking techniques and expertise, and facilitated an explosion of foreign direct investment by American multinational corporations. And US commercial banks, barred since the New Deal from investment banking activity at home, also jumped at the chance to set up foreign branches in Europe so that they could conduct the full range of activities requested by their American clients – and soon were also wooing European companies. This penetration of Europe by American corporations and banks meant the implantation of American capital as a class force inside European social formations, whereby 'economic expertise, social norms, and cultural habits are transmitted by the investing firm. This ties the recipient economies into the broader social totality out of which the investment has come, thereby broadening the basis of social relations upon which it rests' (Germain 1997: 82).

The emergence of the Eurodollar market advanced this process considerably. Initially using loopholes in exchange control regulations to set up external dollar accounts for Soviet-bloc and Arab states that were wary of banking in New York, British merchant banks switched their international operations from sterling to the dollar to take advantage of currency convertibility and the loosening of capital controls in Japan and Europe at the end of the 1950s. This provided a completely unregulated international repository for the dollar at a time when rates of interest in New York were still limited by New Deal regulations. Encouraged by the British authorities as a way of maintaining the City of London as an international financial centre, the effect of the Eurodollar market's emergence was to move the City – and through it, European finance in general – more closely into the American imperial embrace. In this type of new imperial order, moreover, capital controls based on the distinction hesitatingly drawn at Bretton Woods between 'productive' and 'speculative' financial flows increasingly broke down. Not only the unregulated Eurodollar market but also the intra-firm transfers that characterize so much foreign direct investment lay at the root of the eventual abandonment of capital controls in the 1970s.

Perhaps most important, the form that capitalist integration had by now taken affected the social formations of all advanced capitalist states, so that, even while economic competition among the advanced capitalist states returned, any revival of inter-imperial rivalry was foreclosed. Taking Germany as an example, the trade patterns in place by the late 1950s were themselves a factor in limiting protectionism, but even more important the penetration of American direct investment affected (amongst other things) the nature of German capital – not just directly (GM, Ford, IBM) but also via suppliers, banks and customers. This was reinforced by German firms' consequent need to establish a countervailing presence in the US, all of which tended to create cross-border networks of finance and integrated production.

The point is not that a transnational capitalist class had emerged, operating in a transnational ether beyond states, but something more complex. The capitalist class of each country retained its distinctiveness, but both the capital historically rooted there and the foreign capital that established itself alongside it now depended on each other's states, and especially on the American state, to expand and manage the capitalist order.

2.   From Bretton Woods to neoliberalism: 'hesitations and false starts'

Once we recognize the post-war period as the cradle of a new, globalizing and liberalizing American imperium, its implications for future developments become clearer. At the end of the 1950s the American state was not merely at the apex of a hierarchy of states, but was by now a qualitatively different kind of state from the rest, and was internationalized in a distinct way. To be sure, the US had not simply imposed itself on Europe; it required the *active* participation of European states in the transformation of capitalist order in the post-war period.[11] But while all the advanced capitalist states increasingly recognized (to varying degrees) the responsibility they had to participate in the management of international capitalism, they also recognized – and increasingly insisted on – the central role the American state had to play in this. Only the American state bore the burden – and had the accompanying capacity and autonomy – to take on the task of managing the system as a whole.

Yet how exactly the American state was to do this became the burning question of the 1960s and 1970s. It might have been thought that the provisions of Bretton Woods would really come into their own once the period of reconstruction was completed towards the end of the 1950s. As European economic competitiveness was restored and currencies were made convertible, the post-war dollar shortage turned into a dollar glut thanks to European and Japanese exports to the USA as well as American military expenditures and foreign investments. In this new context, the contradictions of the Bretton Woods framework, above all those involved in its treatment of the US state as equivalent to any other state, increasingly began to reveal themselves. The fact that the deep penetration of Europe by US capital at this time coincided with an emerging crisis of the dollar meant that the deepening of the new structure of imperial power was sometimes obscured. It was a situation that proved confusing to all the main actors – including the Americans. The *sang froid* with which the *Fortune* editors had proclaimed in 1942 that the new American empire would not be 'afraid to help build up industrial rivals to its own power...because we know industrialization stimulates rather than limits international trade' was no longer in evidence in 1960, as both the outgoing Eisenhower administration and the incoming Kennedy administration panicked over the new American balance of payments deficit.

The introduction in the early 1960s of American controls on the export of capital for the first time since the war was certainly not welcomed by the New York bankers, who instead demanded – as did central bankers in Europe – higher American interest rates to cope with the problem. But the fact that these controls were seen as temporary and were accompanied by further US encouragement of other states to remove their capital controls, showed how limited an about-face it really was; it actually had the effect of further encouraging American banks to set up as direct participants in the Eurodollar market. This was an effect that the American state was well aware of and even encouraged, as it served to sustain the value of the dollar and provide access to European funds, as well as to reinforce the international predominance of US banks. In any case, given the option for the holders of dollars of converting them into gold, the controls would have had to have been much more stringent to stem the falling confidence in the dollar.

Yet balance of payments deficits did not have the same meaning for the United States as they did for any other state. This was not widely recognized at the time, but as an obscure paper prepared for the Federal Reserve of Boston in 1971 pointed out: '[t]his asymmetry appears to be appropriate, for it corresponds to an asymmetry in the real world' (quoted in Hudson 2003: 327, italics added).[12] Before this perspective could be universally accepted (especially amongst bankers), however, the fiction of a gold standard behind the dollar standard would have to be abandoned and replaced not only by flexible exchange rates but types of global financial markets that could sustain them. And it would have to come to be seen that, far from necessarily representing a diminution of American power, the outflow of capital and the balance of payments deficits were actually laying the basis for a dollar-based credit expansion and financial innovation, both domestically and internationally – what Seabrooke appropriately calls the 'diffusion of power through the dollar' (2001: 68). Above all, it would be necessary for the American state, as the imperial state, to retain the confidence of the ever more dynamic and powerful financial capitalists in the face of the pressures on the dollar. All this implied addressing the deeper contradictions of the Bretton Woods arrangements for fixed exchange rates and tying the dollar to gold, which by then had become a barrier to the American state's capacity to navigate between its domestic and imperial responsibilities.

Especially important in this regard was the way class relations had developed in the advanced capitalist states during the Keynesian era. Under the near full employment conditions that had arrived by the early 1960s, the militancy of a new generation of workers drove up money wages and challenged managerial prerogatives, with negative implications for both productivity and profits. At the same time, new social justice political movements drove up the social wage, and the 'new left' that emerged from the rapid expansion of post-secondary education had radicalizing effects in the political arena. But this did not amount to the kind of fundamental class realignment that could have sustained policies to move beyond Bretton Woods-style controls on external capital flows, to democratic controls over investment itself. Without this, inflation was the inevitable result of the 1960s militancy – and it was exacerbated by a growing revolt in the 'third world', leading to increased military costs as well as rising commodity prices.

Because capital – and not least financial capital with its natural aversion to inflation – was also strong, the contradictions became intense. Finance felt doubly pressured in the 1970s. Not only was it affected by the general crisis in profitability, but the form this crisis took particularly affected financial assets. As industrial capital – supported by the state's accommodative fiscal and monetary policies – raised prices to protect its profits, the resultant inflation devalued financial holdings. Yet financial capital was not passive in this period. Matching the rise of the new left was a new generation of MBAs, 'bright and ambitious students ... paying more attention to business strategy, product development, marketing, and costs, the stuff of business-school curricula' (Sylla 2002: 62). Amidst a wave of takeovers and mergers, banks competed to recruit this ambitious new generation who developed key innovations in financial services, building on the development of certificates of deposit that initiated the 'securitization' of commercial banking (i.e. the shift from depositing money in a bank to buying a tradable financial asset from the bank). This transformed the role of banking from direct credit intermediation (taking deposits from and loaning money to particular customers) to mediating the interactions of lenders and borrowers in depersonalized securities markets. The vast expansion of risk arbitrage and 'block trading' for institutional investors soon followed, and it was out of this that, in turn, the revolution in derivatives and hedge funds so crucial to the globalization of finance eventually emerged.

The privatization and liberalization of finance, which is usually dated from the 1980s, actually began much earlier, with the state playing a direct and active role. In the 1960s, the decline of American foreign aid created pressures on foreign governments to find ways to get access to private credit; and this occurred alongside the advent of the deregulated Eurodollar market and the expansion of private foreign direct investment as the major form of capital flows. Later, in the 1970s, after the Americans ended the convertibility of the dollar into gold, leading to the end of fixed exchange rates, there was an explosion of new market-based securities designed to meet the need of traders to hedge against the risk associated with floating exchange rates. Meanwhile, as economic growth slowed down, not only was the increasing public debt of the advanced capitalist states financed through private channels, the American state also insisted on recycling petrodollars to the third world through the private banking system. The increased opportunities, greater risks, and especially intensified competition that flowed from this privatization of credit led to further dramatic innovations in finance, especially the magnification of the range of securities.

The impact on American financial institutions of inflation, low real interest rates and stagnant profits in the 1970s accelerated the qualitative transformations of these years, which increasingly ran up against the old New Deal banking regulations. This was what prompted the global 'financial services revolution' that Moran (1991) dates as beginning in the mid-1970s with the abolition of fixed rates on brokerage commissions on Wall Street. Monetary instruments that had previously seemed exotic now became basic parts of the financial landscape: money market mutual funds, for example, emerged to account for $25 billion in assets by 1979 – and by 1981, they had further quadrupled. The assets of foreign banking offices in the US increased eightfold in the 1970s (matching the growth of the Eurodollar market), while the assets of American banks abroad increased almost seven-fold, and portfolio flows amongst the G7 increased eleven-fold. By the end of the 1970s, the foreign earnings of the five largest American banks accounted for over half of their total earnings. Nor should it be thought that these developments took place within a self-contained financial sphere divorced from production and trade. US trade actually doubled as a share of GDP in the 1970s, and foreign direct investment amongst the G7 increased almost six-fold.[13]

As financial capital outgrew the cradle of Bretton Woods, however, it ran up against the militant labour and other popular forces of the period. Every advanced capitalist state had to deal with this underlying problem of class relations. Since none of them was about to repress financial capital, they had to curtail the power of labour. Social democratic governments in Europe tried to cope by wooing trade unions into corporatist arrangements for wage controls, a strategy that increasingly proved unstable as workers revolted against their own unions (Panitch 1986: chs. 4–6). In France, where low union density and communist strength in the labour movement ruled this out, de Gaulle tried to return to the gold standard as a way of imposing austerity at home. Going back to the gold standard had the added attraction of undermining the dollar internationally. In the end this led nowhere. In May 1968, after de Gaulle granted a huge wage-hike to derail a general strike and induce labour away from the revolutionary ambitions of the students, he acknowledged that the gold standard would have denied him this flexibility and 'stopped daydreaming about a return to gold' (Arrighi 2003: 35–6).

As for the US itself, the Nixon administration elected in 1968 was caught between the call for higher interest rates to reduce capital outflows and the political costs associated with the increased unemployment this would cause. As Gowa's study shows, when it finally terminated the dollar's link with gold in 1971 after two years of trying to 'muddle through', this was more an act of expedience than one conceived as a dramatic break with Bretton Woods (Gowa 1983: 147, 166). Far from providing any long-term solution, it was a way to avoid addressing the underlying contradiction of class relations that lay at the root of the inflation and dollar crisis of the period, which nothing less than breaking both the New Deal framework and the domestic power of American labour would accomplish. Such a neoliberal solution was presaged by the measures the US Treasury and New York Federal Reserve Bank required of the British Labour government during the 1976 IMF crisis, leading to the explicit abandonment of Keynesianism even before the election of Margaret Thatcher (Panitch and Leys 2001: chs. 5–6). But the asymmetry amongst the capitalist states in the new imperial order was such that until the American state dealt with the problem at home, no such solution abroad could be stable.

In spite of the problems faced by the American state through the 1970s, no serious challenge surfaced to its international dominance. This was partly because, despite the incontrovertible *force majeur* the US displayed in ending the dollar's convertibility to gold, the American state still remained concerned not to play up its dominant position too much. As an interdepartmental group chaired by Paul Volcker (then under-secretary for monetary affairs in the Nixon Treasury) said in a 1969 report, even while seeking 'a substantial degree of U.S. control [of the international monetary system] ... in the interests of facilitating international harmony the appearance of US hegemony should not be sought' (quoted in Gowa 1983: 129). But at a deeper level it was the American penetration of the other developed capitalist countries, and the dense institutional linkages that had evolved between them

and the US, which determined that inter-state tensions were limited to rene-
gotiating the terms of the imperial relationship, not questioning its essence.
Within the third world, instances of attempted withdrawal from American-
led global capitalism were contained (the American defeat in Vietnam had
not led to any domino effect) or turned around (the overthrow of Allende
being followed by the introduction of neoliberalism under Pinochet), while
the recycling of petrodollars further integrated the third world into global
financial circuits.

Yet the management of global capitalism remained problematic. What had
not emerged were the disciplinary mechanisms needed to adjust national
economies to the rhythms of international accumulation. An immediate barrier to such a development was that the American state itself had not imposed
the necessary domestic discipline that would allow it to maintain the value
of the dollar as the international currency, a failure that was manifested in
inflation in the US, and turmoil in international financial markets. While the
end to dollar–gold convertibility in 1971 allowed for greater American foreign policy autonomy and the avoidance of drastic domestic austerity, it did
not overcome the contradiction between the American state's imperial and
domestic roles. It did not yet mark, as is sometimes suggested, 'the dawning
of a new international regime for money and international relations' (Gowan
1999: 33).

In the context of the floating exchange rates, petrodollar recycling, expanding financial markets, continued labour militancy and 'soft' monetary policy
that characterized the 1970s, by the end of the decade the American state was
scrambling to deal with double-digit inflation, a declining dollar and, above
all, large outflows of capital. Even the sober Bank for International Settlements went so far as to speak of 'a genuine Dollar crisis' (BIS 1979: 3); and
there was a degree of discontent on Wall Street 'not seen since the last days of
the Hoover presidency' (Geisst 1997: 320). Looking back to his appointment
as Chairman of the Federal Reserve at the end of the 1970s, Paul Volcker
recalled 'all the hesitations and false starts, the uncertainty and questions'
after a decade in which 'theorizing and empirical analysis about stable and
predictable relationship[s] ... seemed to break down in the United States and
other countries' (Volcker 1990: 5).

3.   The Volcker shock: finance and the reconstitution of empire

It was in this context that the 'Volcker shock' of 1979–82 brought to a definitive end two decades of policy confusion amidst severe tension between the
state's imperial and domestic roles, through what Volcker himself called a
'triumph of central banking'.[14] This triumph was political, not technical.
Like the first panic over the value of the dollar that marked the transition
between the Eisenhower and Kennedy administrations in 1960, the Volcker

shock also spanned the transition between Carter and Reagan, two presidents of otherwise very different temperaments. Volcker was himself no more than a 'pragmatic monetarist' (having first worked in the New York Fed and the US Treasury under Kennedy and Nixon trying to patch up the holes in the Bretton Woods system). What the Volcker shock entailed in policy terms, as he admitted, was not 'very fancy or very precise' (1990: 5). For all the pseudo-scientific econometrics that provided ideological cover for the operation, it simply involved limiting the growth in the money supply and allowing interest rates to rise to whatever level – and at whatever short-term economic cost – was necessary to break the back of inflation and the strength of labour. The Federal base rate rose from an average of 8 per cent in 1978 to over 19 per cent at the beginning of 1981 and did not consistently return to less than double digits until after 1984.

The Fed's brief embrace at this time of the Friedmanite goal of controlling the money supply was contradicted by the diversity of financial instruments that had already developed – and that would soon spread much further under the impetus of extremely high interest rates. As Greenspan (1997) later explained: 'Increasingly since 1982 we have been setting the funds rate directly...in the current state of our knowledge, money demand has become too difficult to predict...As the historic relationship between measured money supply and spending deteriorated, policymaking, seeing no alternative, turned more eclectic and discretionary.' The Federal Reserve now explicitly took responsibility for directly declaring an interest rate that would project an unwavering anti-inflationary commitment so as to become the global anchor of a dollar-based world economy. This gave it, as Volcker put it, a central 'role in stabilizing expectations [that] was once a function of the gold standard, the doctrine of the annual balanced budget, and fixed exchange rates' (quoted in Johnson 1998: 178).

The only possible alternative to this would have involved extensive American capital controls over Wall Street, with cooperation from the European states. The outflows of capital from the US that so worried American leaders by the late 1970s came from American investors as much as disenchanted foreigners. Because the flow went to the unregulated Eurodollar and Eurobond markets, the Fed had at one point proposed that reserve requirements be put on Eurodollar deposits, which in order to be effective would have required other central banks to do the same (Hawley 1984). Yet this was nothing like the early wartime proposals for cooperative capital controls. With Nixon's rescinding of the temporary capital controls that had been introduced in the 1960s, the American state was now more adamantly opposed than ever to the use of capital controls (Helleiner 1994: 101–21). But the rejection by the European central banks of an American proposal to set reserve requirements on Eurodollar deposits also indicated the lack of genuine interest on the part of European states for cooperative capital controls. Even on the few occasions when they themselves raised controls as a possibility during the turmoil of the 1970s, it was notable that the European (and Japanese) governments did not push the idea very hard. What they did push hard was that the Americans should apply discipline to themselves.

Indeed, given the degree to which capital markets were already internationalized, effective controls now implied not only a much more far-reaching intervention in financial markets than ever before, but intervention in trade and investment as well. Just as the internationalization of finance had earlier accompanied the internationalization of production, so any attempt to control finance by the 1970s would not be able to leave industrial capital untouched. Not even social democratic governments in Europe were inclined to seriously contemplate such a radical intervention, as was shown by the hostile treatment of Tony Benn's Alternative Economic Strategy in Britain in 1975–6, and the rejection at the same time of the German unions' much milder proposals for investment planning (Panitch and Leys 2001). And however committed (or not) the Mitterrand government in France was to the radical programme on which it was elected in 1981, by then extensive controls on capital and investment had already been ruled out in Europe no less than in the United States.

Thus when the Federal Reserve acted as it did in 1979–82 to show the imperium's own determination to win the confidence of the financial markets through the radical use of monetary policy, it was endorsing the inclination of European governments. They had been trying to cope with inflation in their own economies by shifting away from Keynesianism and the commitment to full employment, since holding on to these seemed bound to take them in a much more socialist direction than they wanted to go. With global capitalism structured around the dollar as the international currency, and instability of the dollar creating instability everywhere else, the focus was on whether the American state could in fact maintain the value of the dollar in the face of domestic pressures, and thus meet its imperial responsibilities. Having dispensed with a gold-related standard (because the discipline involved had proven too rigid), and in the absence of a solution based on cooperative capital controls (because its de facto implications were too radical even for European social democracy), the issue became the capacity of the American state to act unilaterally to preserve its access to global resources while re-establishing confidence in the dollar.

With the Volcker shock, the US effectively secured acceptance by other states and financial capital of the asymmetric treatment of its external deficit because, indeed, *'it correspond[ed] to an asymmetry in the real world'*, which, as we saw above, the Fed itself had slowly begun to realize as early as 1971. The way American banks had spread their financial innovations internationally in the 1960s and 1970s, especially through the development of secondary markets in dollar-denominated securities, allowed the American state – unlike other states – to substitute the sale of Treasury bills for a domestic pool of foreign exchange reserves and run its economy without large reserves.

The only proviso, as Seabrooke notes, was that it had a liquid financial system and could attract buyers for its securities in the international markets. Rather than evidence of the origins of a collapse of American hegemony, as many commentators have supposed, 'the US's ability to constantly re-finance its debt obligations is not a sign of weakness but evidence of its great structural power in financial relations' (Seabrooke 2001: 105).

The Fed's policy thus placed the need to 'discipline ourselves' (in Volcker's own words) at the centre of both America's economic revival and its international role (Volcker and Gyohten 1992: 167). The reconstitution of empire, in other words, began at home. And crucial to this, for all the tensions between regions and fractions of capital that attended this restructuring, was that it produced no split in either the American ruling class or between the American and other ruling classes. By the end of the 1970s, the non-financial sectors of capital had themselves generally come to acknowledge the need to give priority to fighting inflation and thereby to accept that strengthening financial capital was in their own interests. Far from fighting the emerging leading role of financial capital, industry leaders accepted the costs implied by a finance-led revival of domestic and international accumulation.[15]

Of course, the US-led attack on inflation was only effective in combination with the strong underlying capacities of the American economy: its technological base, depth of financial institutions, and the resources that came with its imperial role. In breaking the inflationary spiral in the US through breaking the economic power of labour, the American state not only won back the confidence of financial markets, but also put itself in the position to be able to tell other states – all too ready to blame the US for their own inflation – to likewise address their own balance of class forces. And by further liberalizing its own financial markets, it not only deepened the domestic strength and liquidity of these markets but supported their further internationalization. It was this that now crucially sustained the dollar as an international currency and made US government securities seem as good as (indeed, because they paid interest, better than) gold. The resolution of the crisis of the 1970s through the strengthening of the structural power of finance thus reinforced the capacity of the American state to revive global capitalism.

The means by which American inflation and the wage militancy of US labour were broken – high interest rates and an induced recession – also led to an inflow of capital, a stronger dollar, and greater public debt (the Reagan defence expenditures adding to the costs of the recession). The consequent increase in international holdings of highly liquid US Treasury bills not only had a major impact on furthering the development of massive secondary markets in bonds, but lay at the core of the reconstituted form of American imperial rule. It allowed the American state to consistently rely on global financial reserves to expand its – and capitalism's – global reach. As this direction was consolidated and international confidence in the US was firmed up, access to foreign capital became less dependent on offering a higher rate of interest. Foreign capital came to the US again because it was a safe haven in a world that had not yet generally followed the American example, and because of the prospect of profitable investment there, given the definitive defeat of the unions in the US. Over the four years from 1975–8, foreign direct investment in the US had totalled $18.5 billion; in the period 1981–7, it averaged $22.9 billion *per year* (Guttman 1994: 334).

The Federal Reserve's success in initiating this turn rested on how convincing it was in its determination that not just short-term, but long-term inflation would be controlled. This introduced a new parameter in state policy that implicitly accepted lower rates of growth as a corollary to the priority of low inflation, so as to stabilize the dollar and assure its international role. But the Volcker shock's contribution to the new priority of 'breaking inflationary expectations' in the early 1980s depended on something more fundamental still. However it was articulated, the real issue was not so much finding the right monetary policy, as restructuring class relations. Breaking inflationary expectations could not be achieved without defeating the working class's aspirations and its collective capacity to act to fulfil them. Notably, once the government entered directly into the Chrysler bankruptcy proceedings in 1980, Congress insisted that Paul Volcker sit on the public board responsible for the negotiations with the company, its creditors and suppliers, and the union; and Volcker was indeed finally responsible for securing from the UAW, the highest-profile union in the US, the conditionality (wage cuts and outsourcing) attached to the loan that Chrysler was granted. Meanwhile, outside the purview of the Fed but by no means unrelated to its objective, was President Reagan's smashing of the air traffic controllers' strike in 1981. Indeed, Volcker would later say that 'the most important single action of the administration in helping the anti-inflation fight was defeating the air traffic controllers strike' (quoted in Taylor 1995: 778).

It was on this basis that the American state regained the confidence of Wall Street and financial markets more generally. This proved pivotal to the reconstitution of the American empire by unleashing the new form of social rule subsequently labelled 'neoliberalism' – promoting the expansion of markets and using their discipline to remove the barriers to accumulation that earlier democratic gains had achieved. As vehicles for the most mobile form of capital, the new financial markets contributed strongly to the universalization of neoliberalism in the 1980s and 1990s. The deepening and extension of financial markets that had already occurred by this time – their domestic and international growth, their increasingly multidimensional and innovative ties to business, and their penetration of consumer savings – were central to this new form of social rule. The new global market in foreign exchange that had emerged when the gold standard was terminated in 1971 did not itself immediately lead to 'the active international market in financial claims as a whole' that best defines the term 'global finance' (Grahl 2002: 1).[16] This awaited the development of financial capital's new capacities in creating, assessing and selling new kinds of securities that would spread throughout the monetary system after the Volcker shock.

Crucial here was the increased international liquidity of credit and its contribution to the management of risk. This allowed for what Dick Bryan has called the international 'commensurability of value' (Bryan et al. 2000). Financial markets, especially through the invention of a large number of financial instruments called derivatives (swaps, options, futures not based on the trade in physical products), put a price on the various dimensions of risk associated with exchange rates, trade, long- vs. short-term investments, political developments, etc., vastly extending the basis for comparing the performance of assets not only across space and time but also across the various dimensions of risk themselves (see Tickell 1999: 249–51). All this has become central to the dynamics of competition and accumulation in global capitalism.

No less important was the imperial basis of this financialization, above all the full international acceptance, a decade after the dollar was freed from gold, of the dollar's continuing role as the fulcrum of the international financial system. Ultimately, the risks involved in international accumulation are contingent on confidence in the dollar. This is founded on its material foundations in the strength of the American economy and on the capacity of the American state to manage the inevitable volatility of financial markets. The post-war boom had reflected this kind of confidence in American power; the reconstitution of empire that began in the early 1980s was about restoring it after the uncertainties of the 1960s and 1970s.

The turning point marked by the Volcker shock thus represented a convergence of imperial and domestic responsibilities. Bound up with renewed capitalist confidence in the US was the free-market, anti-statist rhetoric of Reaganism and Thatcherism. This did not mean the end of regulation, of course – any more than Keynesianism had, conversely, meant the suppression of markets. When the Depository Institutions Deregulation and Monetary Control Act was passed in 1980 right in the midst of the Volcker shock, it revealed by its very title the futility of any discourse cast in terms of a dichotomy between 'regulation' vs. 'deregulation', or state vs. market.

Encouraging finance to spread its wings demanded new forms of state intervention to manage the uncertain implications of that freedom. A textbook on American finance published at the turn of the century casually noted, for example, that, 'the financial system is amongst the most heavily regulated sectors of the American economy' (Mishkin 2000: 41). What was at issue was not deregulation but the form that regulation would take. Regulation was reconceived to emphasize managing, as opposed to preventing, the volatility implied by more open financial markets: improving supervision, requiring self-regulation and, of course, setting interest rates and acting as lender of last resort. This was especially necessary since, alongside the enormous shake-out that interest rates approaching 20 per cent brought about in

American industry in the early 1980s, an enormous shake-out in the financial sector also began at this time. Over 4500 banks – 36 per cent of the total – shut their doors between the end of the 1970s and the early 1990s, not including the savings and loans industry collapse, making the period what one Congressional study subsequently called 'undoubtedly the most turbulent years in US banking history since the Great Depression' (Berger et al. 1995: 57). The concentration and centralization of banking was offset by the emergence of new financial institutions offering new instruments and services. The financial sector as a whole expanded explosively, both in the US and globally.

This was facilitated by legislation through the 1980s and 1990s that provided more and more space for banks to operate in securities markets, and non-bank institutions to engage in commercial property-lending (and thus gradually reversing the provisions of the New Deal's Glass-Steagall Act long before it was formally repealed at the turn of the century). The legislation facilitating competition in the financial services sector was also designed to expand consumer credit markets. The American working and middle classes maintained their standards of living by working longer hours and going into debt. They often remortgaged their homes to do so, and commercial banks sold off the resulting debt in packages to investment banks which in turn repackaged them for sale in the derivatives market. On the other side of the ledger, commercial banks relied less and less on deposits for their funding and more and more on selling and trading securities. Meanwhile the New York investment banks famously made out like bandits. As Michael Lewis said in his Wall Street memoir, *Liar's Poker*: 'Had Volcker never pushed through his radical change in policy, the world would be many bond traders and one memoir the poorer . . . A Salomon salesman who had in the past moved five million dollars' worth of merchandise through the traders' books each week was now moving three hundred million dollars through each *day*' (Lewis 1989: 35–6).

This trading in securities was so profitable that it not only swept across all the different sectors of finance but soon encompassed industrial corporations themselves. The New York investment banks, moreover, not only increasingly asserted their dominance in the City of London, but became significant actors in all other financial centres. Apart from the competitive advantages they enjoyed from having pioneered the innovations in securitized finance, they were also aided by the other financial centres' emulation of New York's 'big bang', and by the American state's own concerted actions aimed at the diffusion of its neoliberal regime. The fact that the major New York investment banks took the lead in providing financial services and advice for mergers and acquisitions in all the regional financial centres from Europe to East Asia meant that they came to play a significant role in transforming not only financial markets, but business practices generally, on US lines. Under these conditions, the widely held belief of the 1980s that Japanese

banks were poised to displace American financial dominance was soon shat-
tered. Even the close industry–bank networks for which Japan and Germany
were famous could not remain immune for long from the transformations
this entailed. A truly global financial system 'based on the deregulation and
internationalization of the US financial system', as John Grahl has put it, 'is
neither a myth nor even an alarming tendency, but a reality' (2001: 43–4).[17]

4.   Finance and empire in global capitalism

The historical account we have offered above challenges the conventional
bifurcation of the second half of the twentieth century into one era based on
the suppression of finance (associated with the golden age of capitalism and
a beneficent American hegemony) followed by another based on finance's
liberation (associated with a decline of both the dynamism of capitalism and
the hegemony of the American state). For all the attention that has been
paid to the Volcker shock as a momentous turning point in contemporary
capitalism, too little attention has been paid to the extent to which its great
impact was conditional on the earlier strengthening of financial capital by
virtue of its markets having become notably liberalized, with domestic and
international developments reinforcing each other.

Many critics at the time insisted that the Volcker shock could not work.
High interest rates would induce austerity in the short term, and not only
block growth but also fail to reverse the competitive threat from Europe and
Japan. Above all, it was argued, shifting power and resources to finance, a
section of capital that was unproductive of surplus, would not only increase
inequality but also limit long-term accumulation. How far can we say the
dire predictions have proved correct? It is certainly the case that the defeat of
labour and the reinforcement of financial capital's power since the early 1980s
have led to stark and increasing inequality within the US and internationally.
But this by no means entailed a decline in capitalism's dynamism. As we have
argued at length elsewhere (Panitch and Gindin 2002b, 2005c), while it is true
that giving priority to the defeat of inflationary expectations implied slower
growth, that in itself hardly qualified as a crisis for capitalism. As Maddison
(2001: 265) has shown, average annual growth rates in the quarter century
after 1973, while below those of the golden age, were still above every earlier
period in world capitalism from 1820 to 1945.

As for the implications of the relative increase in the role and power of
financial institutions, there was an underestimation of how the deepening of
capital markets, and the competitive pressures and mobility they generate,
could lead to increased capital productivity and profit rates. They did this
not just through their disciplinary impact on firms and governments, but
also by reallocating capital and supporting the dissemination of technology
across firms and sectors (more rapid exit of relatively inefficient firms, support
for risky but innovative start-ups, dissemination of new technologies into

old sectors). Both the decline in the rate of profit that signalled the end of the golden age and its subsequent recovery after the early 1980s have been convincingly linked, empirically, to corresponding decreases and then improvements in the 'productivity' of capital (i.e. the output per unit of capital stock) (Duménil and Lévy 2002, 2003; Webber and Rigby 1996).

To be sure, this doesn't answer some larger questions about the contributions of finance to restructuring – questions made more controversial because of disputes about how to conceptualize 'finance'. Of course, credit creation in itself does not necessarily imply an increase in productive activity. But the historical development of financial institutions, accelerating from 1960 onwards, has included the expansion of services beyond the acquisition of savings and the provision of credit. A major change occurred in the very nature of what financial institutions do. As investment houses challenged the former dominance of banks, and as banks remade themselves to counter this threat, 'finance' evolved far beyond its classical role in credit provision and was placed directly at the heart of the accumulation process, essentially introducing a new sector that straddled credit and production. Forms of money themselves became commodities that could be packaged and sold to an unprecedented degree. Furthermore, these financial packages frequently came with new business services, including many previously performed by other sectors (accounting, payroll, information systems, consulting). And they included consumer services that, like Fed-Ex, completed the delivery of a product or saved time in acquiring a product or service (ATM machines, credit cards). Financial institutions have, at the same time, been early and crucial players in the information revolution, providing the major market for computers and software, and developing key information technologies and systems for themselves and others (Klein et al. 2003; Berger et al. 1995).

Moreover, the global spread of capitalism could not be sustained without overcoming barriers to managing risk. The development of markets that commodify risk was a response to this. It is clear enough that such markets include morally repulsive speculation, appalling waste and conspicuous inequalities. They have also added new risks (see Tickell 1999: 251–7). Indeed, their very necessity within a globalizing capitalism is another reason to question the acceptability and indeed rationality of this social system. But all of this does not erase their importance to *capitalist* development. The deepening of financial markets and the strengthening of financial institutions did increase volatility, but they were also crucial to limiting the negative effects of the very volatility that they engendered. This contributes to capitalism's overall dynamism – which of course often works through crises – as well as supports the durability of the system. Like transportation, risk management adds a cost to the final product, yet it is a cost that non-financial capitalists have had to accept as part of what makes the expansion of global accumulation possible. The larger share of overall profits that has recently gone to finance certainly includes speculative and rentier gains, but it also needs to be seen as representing in part a return for finance's contribution to keeping general profits higher than they would otherwise have been.

Finally, the deepening of financial markets played a directly imperial role. It made it possible for the American economy to attract global savings that otherwise would not have been available to it. Those capital inflows were often identified by critics as an imperial tithe the US imposes on other countries, but this ignored how much of this capital came to the US for reasons of prudent investment and profitability. In any case, they sustained the dollar at exchange rates that otherwise would have been lower, making imports cheaper for American consumers and reducing the reproduction costs of labour for American industry, while keeping the cost of capital low in the US. And it was not only the relative strength of the US economy that these financial markets maintained. They also contributed to making the empire easier to manage: the inflows of capital and imports of commodities to the US allowed global savings to be channelled and global exports to be expanded, while mobile financial markets promoted the neoliberal restructuring and integration of other economies.

While liberalized finance proved to be 'functional' for both global accumulation and the American empire, it not only brought with it grotesque inequalities and injustices but also threw up its own contradictions. This was seen in a series of severe disruptions in the accumulation process, above all in the third world, ranging from repeated crises in Latin America to the massive East Asian crisis of 1997–8, while Africa experienced a more or less perpetual crisis. Much of this had its roots in the way the crisis of the developed capitalist states in the 1970s was resolved. Neoliberalism was born out of a response to that crisis, and focused mainly on stabilizing the relationship between the American economy and the rest of the advanced capitalist world, even though it was third world countries which eventually suffered the worst long-term effects.[18] The reconstitution of the American empire in the early 1980s through higher interest rates launched the third world debt crisis, and the subsequent promotion of neoliberal globalization left a debt overhang that has made it hardly surprising that every application of 'structural adjustment' has itself proved crisis-prone. Moreover, the shift to a greater reliance on markets, and especially volatile financial markets, has meant that the advanced capitalist countries themselves have not been immune from crises. These were registered in the savings and loans collapse and the stock market crash in the US in the latter 1980s, the exchange-rate crisis in Europe in the early 1990s, Japan's decade-long deflation through the 1990s (with its stock and property asset crashes being followed by bank insolvencies), the bursting of the American 'dotcom' bubble in 2000, and most recently the 'subprime'-induced credit crisis of 2007.

Yet the relative containment of these crises in terms of their depth, duration and tendency to spread has been remarkable. In other words, the fact that financial crises are now such a common event is only half the story. Though financial crises may be inevitable, in certain circumstances they may also, as Peter Gowan (1999: 35, 105) has emphasized, be functional to neoliberalism's reproduction and extension. Analogous to the impact of business cycles, but in a more extreme form and involving more direct imperial intervention, financial crises may be exploited to reduce or remove barriers to capitalist interests that 'ordinary' market or diplomatic pressures could not dislodge. The other half of the story, then, is that over this same period, the capacity to cope with these crises has also grown. The development of this capacity involves an acceptance of the fact that crises cannot, in the present stage of capitalism, be prevented. '[P]eriodic financial crises of one sort or another are virtually inevitable,' Robert Rubin concluded from his period as US Secretary of the Treasury in the 1990s; equally inevitable, in his view, was that the US state would act as 'chief of the fire department' (2003: 213, 276).

The ability of the American state to manage domestic and international economic crises is based not just on the institutional learning and development that has occurred over time within the Federal Reserve and the Treasury (supplemented by cooperation with their counterparts across the G7) and in international institutions such as the BIS, the IMF and the World Bank, but also on the strength of economic structures outside the state. This is what Greenspan (1999) meant when he said that the existence of a complex of financial institutions and markets can act as 'a backup' to one another 'to mitigate financial crises', citing how capital markets 'were able to substitute for the loss of bank financial intermediation' in the 1990 recession, and how, conversely, during the 1998 crisis 'banking replaced the capital markets'. To this one might add the way Wall Street was mobilized by the Federal Reserve in bailing out the Long Term Capital Management Fund in the shadow of the Asian and Russian crises.

The durability of the American banking system (and the importance of the spreading of risk through securitization) was seen when the bursting of the stock market bubble of the late 1990s, to the surprise of many, did not register a crisis of any significance amongst major banks. This was largely accomplished through the lowering of interest rates by the Federal Reserve followed by the liquidity pumped into the global economy with the cooperation of the Bank of Japan.[19] Meanwhile the banks themselves profited by creating off-balance sheet Security Investment Vehicles that repackaged and sold subprime mortgages as asset-backed securities. This created a new bubble which, when it inevitably burst in 2007, led central banks to once again pump liquidity into the banking system as the Fed lowered interest rates while the US Treasury coordinated the creation of a 'superfund' by private American banks to refinance the security investment vehicles.[20]

The widespread predictions that the ballooning US trade deficit portended a much more serious crisis waiting to happen were based on the expectation that this deficit was likely to prove unmanageable because it was bound to undermine the dollar as the imperial currency. But it is also necessary to put this in historical perspective. When the balance of payments deficit first emerged in the early 1960s, it led to what now is generally seen as an excessive panic. Robert Roosa, speaking from his experience of trying to address the problem within the Treasury, concluded prophetically in 1970: 'Perhaps, by conventional standards, the United States would have to become a habitual renegade ... barely able to keep its trade accounts in balance, with a modest surplus on the current account, with an entrepot role for vast flows of capital both in and out, with a more or less regular increase in short-term dollar liabilities used for transaction purposes around the world' (quoted in Hudson 2003: 319).

In the 1970s it was widely assumed that the American trade deficit would necessarily lead to American protectionism. There has certainly been plenty of nationalist sentiment in the US, but rather than withdrawing from world markets the American state has consistently used the threat of protectionism to beat down foreign opposition to the global neoliberal project, thereby transforming 'nationalist impulses into strategies for opening up other nations' markets' (Scherrer 2001: 591). The continuous deficit since the 1980s did not alarm investors. Even while that deficit increased dramatically in the early years of the new century and peaked at almost 6 per cent of GDP by 2006, this did not scare off foreign creditors. To understand this properly it is necessary to reconsider what is often seen as a structural decline in American manufacturing competitiveness. While American foreign direct investment continued to expand through the 1990s, manufacturing at home in that decade actually grew faster – much faster – than in any of the other developed countries.[21] Furthermore, the US led the rest of the G7 in the growth of exports right through the 1980s and 1990s.[22] The US trade deficit was thus not caused by a loss of manufacturing and export capacity but by the enormous importing propensity of a US economy which experienced much greater population growth, and had a much greater proportion of its population working – and working for longer hours – than any other developed capitalist economy. Imports contributed to lowering the cost of reproducing labour and obtaining both low- and high-tech inputs for business, each of which facilitated low inflation at home as well as increased exports. There were, of course, particular sectors that were hit hard by the restructuring of American industry, but the overall picture was one of a *relatively* strong capitalist economy which, while increasingly unequal and exploitative, in overall terms held its own in exports, while being able to import ever more by virtue of its relative financial strength.

In considering whether the inflow of capital implies that the US economy is vulnerable to capital flight, it is once again important to note that the inflows did not come in just as compensation to 'cover' the deficit, as imagined by those focusing exclusively on international trade statistics. The inflow of capital was mainly the product of investors being attracted by the comparative safety, liquidity and high returns that come with participating in American financial markets and the American economy. The dollar stayed at relatively high levels until recently because of that inflow of capital, and it was the high dollar that allowed American consumers and businesses to import foreign goods cheaply. In recent years the inflow mainly came from central bankers abroad motivated by the goals of padding their foreign exchange reserves and limiting the decline in the value of the dollar relative to their own currencies.

All this precisely reflected how the new imperialism had come to differ from the old one. While financial markets in the old pre-First World War imperialism were quite developed in terms of the size of capital flows, they generally took the form of long-term portfolio investment, much of it moving only one way, from the imperial centres to the periphery. In contrast, international markets in short-term securities today are massive and, in the absence of the gold standard, it is American Treasury bills that stand as the world's monetary reserves. In addition, the old imperialism limited the extent of manufacturing in the third world, while the division of labour in the new imperialism has, by way of foreign investment and outsourcing, included the expansion of manufacturing in the third world. This not only contributed to the American trade deficit but as the trade surpluses, especially in South-East Asia, were recycled into capital flows to the US, it also contributed to making the imperial power itself, remarkably, a debtor in relation to some third world countries. Yet at the same time these very developments sustained the American economy's ability to have privileged access both to the world's savings and to cheaper goods.

Even though the recent downward adjustment of the dollar relative to other currencies has reduced the size of the trade deficit, a major speculative run on the dollar is of course not impossible. But the form that the globalization of capitalism now takes makes this less rather than more likely. The largest holders of the dollar in Asia and Europe (the respective central banks) want to block the dollar's collapse because that would threaten their exports to the US, and because it would devalue the dollar assets they hold. The global economy has developed with and through the dollar as the dominant currency, and there is no evidence to date that the only other remotely serious candidate, the Euro, is about to replace the dollar in this respect. This is primarily not an economic issue but an imperial one – and neither Europe nor Japan has shown either the will or the capacity to displace the US from its leading role in the capitalist world. In contrast to the old paradigm of inter-imperial rivalry, the nature of the current integration into the American empire means that a crisis of the dollar is not an 'American' crisis that might be 'good' for Europe or Asia, but a crisis of the system as a whole, involving severe dangers for all. To suggest that because the holders of American Treasury bills are now primarily in Asia we are therefore witnessing a shift in the regional balance of power, is to confuse the distribution of assets with the distribution of power (Arrighi 2001).

5. Crises, contradictions and class in global capitalism

Although traditional Marxist theories of structural crises provide valid insights into the nature of these discontinuities, they sometimes tend to fetishize crises in the sense of abstracting them from history. As Arrighi once argued, the economic crisis of the late nineteenth century was rooted in a capitalism very different from that of the 1930s or the 1970s in terms of class formation, industrial and financial structures, and state capacities (Arrighi 1978). Clinging to the notion that the crisis of the 1970s remains with us today flies in the face of the changes that have occurred since the early 1980s; over the following quarter century the capitalist system was spreading and deepening, including through sponsoring another technological revolution, while the opposition to it was unable to mount any effective challenge. If crisis becomes 'the norm', this trivializes the concept and diverts us from coming to grips with apprehending the new contradictions of the current conjuncture.[23]

We therefore need to be careful not to try to counter the conservative conceit of the 'end of history' by renewing predictions of the implosion of global capitalism. A future beyond capitalism is possible, and increasingly necessary from the perspective of social justice and ecological sanity, but capitalism is still in the process of being made. The American state has a privileged position in today's 'making' of capitalism, albeit not an omnipotent one insofar as its rule must operate through other states. The nature of this empire – its complexity, its incompleteness especially with regards to the third world, the fact that it depends on other states and hence the social formations and class struggles within them, and the weight given in its functioning to inherently volatile financial markets – all these factors combine to create a context in which crises repeatedly occur. Yet alongside the developments that make such crises virtually inevitable has come a capacity – based on structures inside as well as outside the American state – to limit their extent, a capacity that is considerably reinforced by the relative weakness of working classes everywhere. That is, while capitalism is unable to avoid crises, it has so far proved able to manage them. This does not mean that it is no longer useful to speak of contradictions inherent in capitalism, but we must be careful not to make too much of their consequences unless they take the form of class contradictions that raise challenges to both capital (in terms of whether it can adapt and respond) and labour (in terms of whether it can develop the political capacity to build on the openings provided). It is time to dispense with a notion of 'crisis' as something that leads capitalism to unravel on its own; our theories of crisis must be politicized to integrate the responses of both states and class actors.

The openings for radical change in the present era of capitalism will generally revolve around problems of political legitimacy rather than any sudden economic collapse. In the third world, the neoliberal restructuring of states to support global accumulation, accompanied by foreign takeovers of third world banking sectors, has not led to coherent patterns of internal development. The pressure to open up their economies leaves these countries extremely vulnerable to financial crises, given the lack of depth of their financial institutions. The 'new financial architecture' promoted by the American Treasury after the 1997–8 financial crises to require transparency and accountability in the new market economies came to look increasingly hypocritical and implausible as a spate of scandals hit Wall Street. This has tended to delegitimize both the empire itself and the governments of those third world states that embraced neoliberalism. The restructuring of other states through direct military intervention, as in the case of Afghanistan and Iraq, not to mention the unlimited 'war on terrorism', makes imperial rule more visible, and less legitimate.

In the developed world, neoliberalism has also weakened the legitimation functions of the state; and as pressures mount in Europe for further structural 'reforms', especially to 'flexibilize' labour markets, the fact that this must be done without the US economy's privileged access to global savings only intensifies the degree of exploitation that must be achieved in those countries. The American state depends on other states to develop popular backing for its imperial role, and this is becoming increasingly difficult for those states to secure. The economic costs of empire at home are correspondingly higher as popular forces abroad limit the ability of other states to share the military, economic and rhetorical burdens of empire. Meanwhile, measures taken inside the US to secure support for this burden by creating paranoia and suppressing dissent (as in the Patriot Acts) are subverting the very freedoms the US is supposed to be fighting for. Resentment against this at home as well as abroad could coalesce with the instabilities and tribulations that volatile financial markets bring to people's daily lives.

The creation of new political possibilities out of such contradictions will not be enhanced by waxing nostalgic about a previous golden age of capitalism, when empire was apparently beneficent and finance allegedly repressed. This illusion is one of the unfortunate legacies of the post-war era. That is why in trying to analyse the nature of global finance and American empire today, this chapter began by tracing the actual historical process that brought us here since 1945 – and indeed it is necessary to go back further than this, as the next chapter demonstrates. The way out of global capitalism and American empire will not be found in a return to a reformism modelled on the post-war order. The fact that the globalization of capitalism has left virtually no national bourgeoisies for labour to ally with, and few divisions to exploit between finance and industry, helps make the case for struggles at the level of the national state that are anti-capitalist as well as anti-imperial. While renewed inter-imperial rivalries or financial crises spiralling out of control are unlikely to clear the way to social transformation, the openings provided by the problems of neoliberal and imperial legitimacy provide ample global terrain for the development of new political strategies that do fundamentally challenge capitalist social relations.

Notes

1. Quoted in Drainville (2004: 65).
2. Quoted in Seabrooke (2001: 151).
3. Quoted in the *Financial Times*, 27/28 October, 2007; see also Stein (2007).
4. For our understanding of the specific nature of the American empire today and a more detailed account of its historical evolution, see Panitch and Gindin (2004).
5. The policies the American state had adopted at the end of the First World War, insisting on the repayment by its allies of its war loans, made the latter dependent on the German state meeting the heavy reparations payments imposed upon it – and at the same time made all the European states dependent on the loans of New York bankers to meet these obligations.
6. Seabrooke (2001: 53) goes on to say: 'The rejection of capital controls on the dollar provides an obvious example of how Washington's and Wall Street's *interactive embeddedness* impacted upon the framework of international finance'. But 'embeddedness' in this sense, meant the very opposite of the repression of finance, let alone the decommodification of social relations that Polanyi meant by the term. On this, see Lacher (1999).
7. These are the words of W. F. Duisenberg, the first head of the European Central Bank, looking back on the occasion of the 50th anniversary of the Marshall Plan, in the context of recalling that 'before receiving that aid each recipient country had to sign a bilateral pact with the US...Along with the carrot thus came the stick. In many ways this is similar to the approach followed in later years by the International Monetary Fund in its macroeconomic adjustment programs' (speech at dinner held by the President of the Netherlands Bank and the Bank for International Settlements, Washington, D.C., 15 May 1997).
8. In any case, the IMF was staffed with officials who shared the views of the US Treasury and thus employed the 'conditionality' of macroeconomic austerity from the beginning. See the opening chapters of Harmon (1997). On 'offsetting financing' see Helleiner (1994: 61).
9. 'In reality, the Banking Act of 1933...did the embryo US investment banks, operating (until then) mostly as subsidiaries of commercial banks, a big favour. As independent entities they were able to create and mould the business free from the restraints of the traditional slow-moving commercial banking culture. Put simply the US investment banks wrote the rules while everyone else...was busy trying to work out what investment banking was all about! With such a head start, it is hardly surprising that they remain so dominant' (Golding 2001: 25–6). On the expertise of US banks in 'project financing' (going back to the role they began to play for oil companies in the 1930s), see Smith and Walter (1997).
10. US Bureau of Economic Analysis, National Income and Product Accounts, Table 6.16D (available at http://www.bea.doc.gov).
11. Most theorists of 'hegemony', with their focus on consent and coercion among states, never quite capture the American penetration that structured this active participation. Poulantzas' notion of American 'penetration' is much richer, yet to the extent that American direct investment is crucial to his analysis, it does not explain the fact that Europe was already well integrated into the American project before the wave of American investment that began in the mid-1950s and did not really become significant until the 1960s.

12. Kindleberger (1981: 43) was one of the few economists in the 1960s who questioned the significance of the balance of payments crisis in the US, arguing that the deficit largely reflected the American supply of financial intermediary services through borrowing short-term capital and lending long in terms of foreign direct investment – a 'trade in liquidity profitable to both sides' – rather than a trade deficit or over-investment abroad as was commonly understood.

13. The calculations in this paragraph are derived from 'Flow of Fund Accounts 1975–84', Federal Reserve Board, September, 2003; 'International Operations of US Banks', *Federal Reserve Board Bulletin*, 84/6, June, 1998; and 'International Capital Markets September 1998 – Annex V', International Monetary Fund, October, 1998. See also Cohen (1986: 21–31).

14. As a Federal Reserve paper later exulted: 'In the early 60s, the Federal Reserve was little known outside of the financial services industry and university economics departments. Twenty years later Fed Chairman Paul Volcker was one of the most recognized names in American public life' (Goodfriend 1997: 1). What follows is partly based on our personal interview with Volcker in March 2003, and draws as well on Woolley (1984: 102–5), Johnson (1998) and Rude (2004).

15. This interpretation has been confirmed by our personal interviews with senior executives of the American auto corporations as well as with Paul Volcker. For the UK case, see Leys (1985) (also based on interviews with industry leaders).

16. By the end of the 1970s, foreign exchange transactions were already ten times higher than those of trade, although this represented only a taste of the explosive growth to come.

17. On the growth of American investment banks abroad, see Smith (1990: 45–6); Thomson Financial (http://www.thomson.com) offers the best data on these banks in mergers and acquisitions.

18. This was an outcome overdetermined by the fact that the American state in the post-war era had allowed European and Japanese reconstruction to take place via the kind of export-led development that built on and sustained the internal coherence of their domestic economies, while the developing world (which was only, at best, a secondary concern among the architects of Bretton Woods and later received no comparable assistance from Marshall aid) had much more limited space and fewer possibilities to establish their own internal coherence. Sticking to policies that could create such internal coherence was beyond the capacities of most developing countries, pressured and tempted as they were by the promise of access to already developed technologies, rich markets and ready finance. If this was so even under the import substitution industrialization strategies permitted in the Bretton Woods era, it proved to be all the more the case under neoliberalism.

19. See Duncan (2005).

20. See Mollenkamp et al. (*Wall Street Journal*, 15 October 2007); and Guha (*Financial Times*, 16 October 2007).

21. Manufacturing did of course grow faster in Asia, but the US maintained an impressive record vis-à-vis Europe and Japan. According to a US Department of Labor report, the average annual rate of growth in manufacturing between 1990 and 2001 was 3 per cent in the US but only 2.2 per cent in France, 1.3 per cent in Italy, 0.4 per cent in the UK, 0.3 per cent in Germany and 0.2 per cent in Japan. (Chao 2003: 21).

22. See World Trade Organization, *Trade Statistics, Historical Series*, August, 2003, available at www.wto.org. Note, however, that after 1998 there was a lag in US exports in good part due to the relatively slower economic growth in Europe.

23. Our analysis clearly differs in fundamental ways from Robert Brenner's *The Boom and the Bubble* (2002). Apropos the argument being made here, three such differences are especially important. First, while Brenner does give some historical specificity to the source of the crises of the early 1970s – the limits to exit that followed the concentration of capital and the subsequent tendency to over-accumulation – we argue that those limits were in fact not of a technical nature but of a political nature, as the escalation of factory as well as bank closures in the early 1980s following the Volcker shock clearly shows. That is, even in analysing 'market competition', the state must be brought into the analysis (and not only in regard to exchange rates). Second, and related to this, Brenner underestimates the capacity of the American state to restructure its domestic base, in part because he reduces the role of finance to an external, ad hoc, instrument that can only postpone 'real change'. Third, while Brenner rightly argues that an economically strong but politically weak working class could not sustain a profit squeeze in the face of capitalist restructuring, had he acknowledged that capital *did* in fact restructure and that the breaking of the working class was fundamental to that project, he might have provided a more credible interpretation of both the earlier crisis and capital's current success. But by insisting that the crisis never ended, he shifts attention away from working-class resistance as both a pivotal factor in causing the crisis and a target of its resolution at the end of the 1970s and beginning of the 1980s.

3
American Finance and Empire in Historical Perspective

Martijn Konings

If there is no lack of marvel at the historically unprecedented reach of American imperial power, we often find little indication as to the concrete institutional roots and sources of this distinctive capacity. This chapter tries to conceptualize the institutional foundations of American power in the sphere of international finance, which epitomizes both the global reach and the indirect nature of American empire. It argues that the distinctiveness of American financial power derives from specific institutions that are the product of its own domestic development. Of course, the idea that the make-up of the international order varies with the institutions and interests that characterize the hegemonic country's domestic order is not new. Yet it is not clear that its implications are always fully pursued and appreciated. The notion that transhistorical principles apply to the relation between a hegemonic power and a liberal international financial order continues to have considerable force, and it continues to direct more research efforts than the idea that the web of institutional linkages that connects a dominant state to the world economy needs to be studied in all its historical and institutional contingency.

Even critical strands in the international relations literature have remained wedded to an external conception of the relationship between financial globalization and American state power: what has never really been sufficiently worked out are the precise ways in which US power relations, practices and institutions are embedded in global financial markets, i.e. the organic institutional linkages between the operation of global finance and the US state that are at the root of America's privileged position. The insufficient attention to the qualitative ways in which domestic institutions shape an imperial order is evident in the tendency to trace the origins of American hegemony back to the interwar period, when, according to the orthodox interpretation, Britain's imperial power passed to the US – even if the latter's capabilities were not accompanied by a willingness to shoulder its hegemonic responsibilities for the reproduction of a liberal world economy (Kindleberger 1973; Costigliola 1984; Gilpin 1987; Nye 1990; Burk 1992; Hybel 2001).

By treating the interwar US state as a reluctant imperial heir, this interpretation implicitly relies on British financial imperialism as a template for the rise of American power (Ingham 1994). As we will see, that is a very problematic assumption: the institutional foundations of American finance are qualitatively different from those of British finance.

The (often implicit) assumption of a certain structural isomorphism in the relation between hegemons and international orders has also found its way into accounts of post-Second World War global finance, which tend to give insufficient attention to the ways in which specifically American institutions have shaped the world of global finance. The reliance on a conception of imperial financial order primarily modelled on the institutions of nineteenth-century liberalism is evident in neorealist and liberal-institutionalist interpretations, which view the post-Second World War period in terms of the US deploying its capabilities for the stable reproduction of the financial order by embedding it in stabilizing regulatory institutions, and the subsequent erosion of this capability as from the 1960s financial globalization began to undermine the institutional parameters of embedded liberalism (Ruggie 1982; Keohane 1984; Gilpin 1987). More critical authors focused on the pro-American bias that marked post-Bretton Woods financial globalization (Strange 1988; Arrighi 1994; Helleiner 1994; Germain 1997). Yet what endured even in this literature was the notion that these dynamics, while greatly benefiting the US in the short term, tended to upset the American state's hegemonic relationship to world finance, i.e. they undermined its structural ability to ensure the reproduction of a liberal world order.

This chapter tries to conceptualize the linkages between the system of global finance and the US state by showing how the US first developed domestically a set of highly distinctive financial practices and institutions and how those later shaped the global financial system. As we shall see, the institutional specificities of American finance are intricately bound up with the fact that, for most of its history, American finance was a purely domestic and highly politicized affair. The prevalence of republican and populist sentiments among the American lower classes prevented the formation of a coherent, integrated system of financial markets and intermediaries. This sparked the development of strategies and techniques for the creation of credit and debt relations that were much more flexible and expansionary in nature than those that had prevailed under British financial hegemony. Until well into the twentieth century, American finance was characterized by an inwardly oriented dynamic of expansion that resulted in the rapid growth of domestic government, corporate, personal and mortgage debt. It was only after the Second World War that this system began to assume substantial international dimensions, resulting in the growth of US global financial power. Financial globalization, which began under the Bretton Woods system, gathered pace after its demise and was shaped by practices and institutions of American provenance, served as the vehicle for American imperial power. The traditionally fragmented and highly regulated nature of American finance had sparked a revolution in instruments and techniques that now proved themselves to be highly functional to the growth of American financial power globally.

But the internationalization of American finance has not only been shaped by the nature of its domestic institutions; it also exists in a perennial relationship of functional interdependence with the dynamism of American finance at home. The idea that the nature of the international order is affected by domestic political institutions and social relations is of particular importance for understanding US power, as it holds in a very specific sense: in stark contrast with the case of British hegemony, the international expansion of American finance always has been and continues to be inextricably connected with its domestic expansion. In an important sense, the growth of US international power is best grasped not in terms of externalization but rather as the internalization of foreign financial practices and credit relations into the dynamics of American finance. American financial imperialism functions by sucking in a variety of heterogeneous and geographically dispersed practices and relations and concentrating them into a space structured by American rules and institutions. This vortex-like quality is what underlies the non-territorial, network-like power of American financial imperialism – and its continuing strength at the beginning of the twenty-first century.

Lineages of American finance

Long before the US was an imperial power in the world, it was an imperial power at home. Its nineteenth-century continental expansion was marked by a speed and rapaciousness that has few precedents in world history and contrasts starkly with America's relative lack of interest in overseas territorial expansion. This 'internal' expansion was a profoundly bloody affair that obliterated entire civilizations and was, from the very beginning, at the heart of the political projects of the American ruling classes (Egnal 1988). At the same time, however, America's imperialist impulse was driven by and justified in terms of unusually progressive objectives and modern ideas, i.e. the maintenance of popular independence and republican self-government rather than the greater glory of the crown. The ideal of a new kind of society that would not fall prey to the decadence and corruption rampant in the Old World was a central ingredient of the institutional make-up of the new republic and its expansionist impulse (McCoy 1980). Personal autonomy and civic virtue could only be preserved in a republic based on independent yeoman production, and such guaranteed access to the agrarian way of life was crucially dependent on the ample availability of land – as most famously expressed in Turner's frontier thesis.

In the case of European countries, the link between the rise of the working class and pressures for democratization on the one hand, and the material and ideological benefits of colonization during the late nineteenth and early twentieth centuries on the other, has often been observed (e.g. Hobsbawm 1994). But in many ways internal social relations and the dynamic of outward expansion were much more intimately linked in the US. Continental expansion was central to the hegemonic integration of the masses into the American polity and in this sense, America's imperialism has been more 'social' in nature than European colonialism ever was. In few places has the connection been made more explicit than in Thomas Jefferson's celebration of 'extensive empire and self-government' (Jefferson quoted in Panitch and Gindin 2004: 10).

Thus, manifest destiny was less a consensual cultural trait of the new country than the ideological underpinning of a protracted and contradiction-ridden process of hegemonic socialization. Extensive empire and continental expansion was a precondition for republican self-government, but the unprecedented degree of opportunity for democratic influence and popular independence that marked the social and political structures of the new republic in turn profoundly shaped the process of expansion. American elites' attachment to democracy and republicanism was instrumental, but for the vast majority of American settlers, a central objective was to secure yeoman independence and to avoid dependency on either feudal relations of authority or the imperatives of trade and commerce.

The dialectic of continental empire and republican self-government was evident in the development of American finance during the nineteenth century. American farmers were much more connected to markets than pre-modern farmers in feudal Europe had ever been (Kulikoff 1989; Clark 1990), and financial relations and institutions emerged wherever people settled. Because exchange relations were relevant to farmers' everyday lives, their precise organizational make-up remained at the centre of social struggle and political regulation. The weight of agrarian interests limited the expansion of commercial networks and the short-term mercantile obligations used in them. To be sure, farmers did need credit, but precisely long-term mortgage credit for farms and land. Moreover, farmers' populist sentiments led them to resist any policies and institutions oriented towards the creation of a more coherent and centralized financial system (Goebel 1997).

The fact that the American economy generated primarily non-mercantile types of debt, in combination with the existence of a regime of tight, decentralized regulation, had important implications for both the domestic constitution of American finance and its international role. The discount market for short-term, well-secured, trade-related sterling credits was a key institutional foundation for Britain's domestic financial system and its international financial power (Scammell 1968). Its absence in the US and repeated failures to create one meant that the international role of US markets and intermediaries remained very limited. The promissory notes generated by the American economy were long-term, unsecured and often unendorsed, and therefore unsuitable for the financing of international transactions (Myers 1931; Goodhart 1969). Domestically, the absence of a sizeable, nationwide discount market meant that there was very little liquidity in the domestic financial system – a huge problem for already heavily regulated banks (Hammond 1934). Politically imposed fragmentation meant that, as the nineteenth century progressed, the expansion of American finance resulted in the creation of an incoherent patchwork of unstable and incommensurate financial practices and institutions. The American banking system was consistently illiquid and forever prone to crises.

A federal banking system was only established during the Civil War. National banks were required to hold Treasury securities as backing for outstanding bank notes, which served to guarantee a steady demand for government debt. This 'effectively brought the Treasury into a central position within the New York money market' (Sarai, this volume, p. 74) and allowed it to use the credit-creating capacities of the commercial banking system to ensure a steady demand for government debt. The expansion of the market for government debt was also facilitated by the methods of the investment firm of Jay Cooke, who, instead of restricting the sale of bonds to known and trusted individuals from elite circles, actively tried to market government bonds to ordinary Americans all around the country (Hidy 1951; Gaines 1962). This meant that it could tap into a huge pool of domestic capital and that it became much less dependent on large Anglo-Saxon private fortunes for the placement of public debt.

The legislation also established a system of reserve funds, which had the effect of concentrating massive amounts of funds in the hands of New York banks (Hedges 1938). This greatly increased New York banks' need for liquid assets, and did so at a time when the birth of the commercial paper market (made up of unendorsed promissory notes) allowed borrowers to bypass ('disintermediate') banks and so contributed to a further contraction of the opportunities for making loans (James 1995). Banks responded by turning away from classical commercial banking (based on the extension of well-secured, trade-related, short-term and non-speculative credit) and towards 'financial banking' (Youngman 1906). That is, they began to 'securitize' their asset portfolios: they invested funds in the growing market for call loans (made on the basis of stock collateral, typically by banks to brokers), and set up securities affiliates in order to be able to purchase stock directly (Myers 1931). The flipside of banks' ample access to liquidity was that they were in a position to extend credit across the board, including unsecured and illiquid personal debt. This was a much more expansive basis for credit extension than traditional practices developed in Britain, which largely limited the extension of credit to short-term, well-secured mercantile transactions. It enabled American financial intermediaries to engage the economic basis of the American dream: the populist sentiments that during the nineteenth century had prevented the emergence of a coherent financial system and so forced financial elites to adopt new financial techniques were very similar to the ones that during the twentieth century would drive the growing density and network power of American finance.

The new system of financial intermediation was highly dynamic, speculative and therefore volatile, and it is against this background that the foundation of the Federal Reserve System in 1913 should be understood (Livingston 1986). But even before the Federal Reserve System was in working order, the First World War broke out and it immediately became enlisted in the Treasury's efforts to place massive amounts of debt. By rediscounting government debt at a preferential rate, the Fed promoted banks' own purchases as well as their extension of credit to the public to enable it to buy Treasury securities (Anderson 1965). Banks' easy access to liquidity dramatically loosened the limits on their credit-creating capacities, and after the war they deployed these to extend credit for a variety of purposes in addition to government debt.

Banks increasingly became 'financial department stores' offering a wide range of services to an ever larger public and holding a wide range of financial assets and liabilities (De Cecco 1984; Cleveland and Huertas 1985). They began to promote the widespread holding of securities by the public (Geisst 1990) – ushering in a process which Seabrooke (2001) has aptly termed the 'socialization of high finance'. But the public's participation in the financial system grew not only in its role as investor, but also in its capacity as borrower. After the consolidation of corporate capitalism and the defeat of populism's programme for a producers' republic at the end of the nineteenth century, popular concerns had shifted towards issues of consumption and distribution. This represented a transformation rather than an abandonment of the ideology of republican independence: it was thought that consumer credit would allow farmers and workers to create a certain distance from the pernicious imperatives of the market and the discipline of wage labour. But these ambitions soon became subject to a process of depoliticization – not least due to the efforts of civic-minded progressive reformers, who sought to integrate the American public into the financial system as responsible citizen-consumers (Cohen 2003: 21). Moreover, the real world of consumer credit turned out to impose rather more obligations on debtors than populist notions of 'social credit' suggested. The period following the end of the First World War saw the rapid growth of consumer and mortgage lending (Olney 1991; Calder 1999: 19). Consumption and consumer credit were thus transformed from a potential arena of political contestation into a world of potentially endless economic opportunities.

These dynamics served to embed financial relations ever more deeply into American life. The financial integration of the American population provided what already was a highly dynamic and expansionary financial system with great density and momentum. The same republican and populist sentiments that during the nineteenth century had been responsible for the fragmentation of American finance now drove the continuous expansion of this system. The American dream was now not merely allied to extensive empire, but rather to intensive empire – not to the geographical expansion of American institutions, but rather the inwardly directed intensification and growing connectivity of social life. Finance no longer appeared to be an obstacle to self-government and economic independence, but an excellent means of realizing it. This made it a potent instrument of hegemonic socialization.

However, this process of financial expansion generated ever greater volatility. The foundation of the Federal Reserve System had done nothing to undermine the network of structural relations and institutional connections between banks and financial markets that was responsible for America's unique pattern of financial growth (Myers 1951a: 582). Indeed, the presence of such an ever-available source of liquidity meant that banks could intensify the pursuit of their old strategies and so really served to *harness* the ability of banks to engage in what would later be considered unsound and risky banking practices (Phillips 1921). To be sure, over the course of the 1920s, the expansion of speculative and consumptive credit became increasingly cause for concern. But the Fed was not a modern central bank with capacities for macroeconomic management (Chandler 1971). Its main task was to keep the banking system liquid by functioning as a lender of last resort and accommodating banks' demand for credit in the money market (Hardy 1932), and this passive approach limited its ability to regulate the dynamics of an expanding financial system. The dangers of financial expansion were only acknowledged when it was too late.

The US certainly bore its share of responsibility for the economic depression that engulfed the world in the 1930s. However, it is not clear that this is best understood as a 'huge blunder' (Hybel 2001: 45), i.e. as a failure to live up to its imperial status. For the early twentieth-century expansion of American finance was predominantly internal and only had a very limited international dimension. To be sure, the period around the First World War saw some changes in the organization of American finance: the constraints on banks were loosened and the Federal Reserve System was charged with the task of creating an American discount market (Broz 1997). But these changes could hardly be said to represent a turning-point (Phelps 1927): relatively few banks went abroad and the discount market remained artificial and was limited in size and duration. That is not, of course, to deny that the inter-war period saw a significant challenge to Britain's position in international finance: the intergovernmental capital flows spawned by the First World War signified a major reconfiguration of global financial power (Hudson 2003). Yet the new structure of public credit relations was not part of the formation of an organic set of connections between American finance and the world economy; they did not replace but were rather superimposed on the existing, organically grown system of sterling-centred private credit relations (Langley

2002). The American challenge was not based on the competitive emulation of English financial practices. Thus, the idea that the US was capable but unwilling to assume hegemonic responsibility seems a poor way of capturing the constellation of forces during the interwar period. In one sense, due to the absence of an infrastructure of dollar-centred private credit relations, the US was not only unwilling but also incapable of providing organic hegemonic leadership (Ingham 1994: 32). In another sense, the US was all too willing and capable of pursuing its own imperial interests; it was just that those interests were not really bound up with the stable reproduction of an international financial order along the lines of British nineteenth-century liberalism.

The New Deal order and financial expansion

The New Deal response to the Depression was a critical episode in the reconstitution of the American state and the making of US financial imperialism. It was marked not by an ambition to restore the relatively restrictive financial conditions of nineteenth-century liberalism, but rather by the idea that the expansionary dynamics of American capitalism needed to be actively managed. Thus, while the New Deal was very much a response to widespread discontent (Vittoz 1987) and sought to restore popular faith in the financial system, it should not be understood primarily in terms of the re-embedding or social-democratization of American capitalism. The New Deal reflected an acute awareness of both the potential benefits of the hegemonic integration of the American population into the financial system and the fact that the volatility of financial expansion needed to be managed through modern policies of macroeconomic stabilization.

Thus, the extent of statist redistribution was very limited and furthermore came under attack during the second half of the 1930s (Brinkley 1995) and during the Second World War (Waddell 2001). For all the opposition that New Deal labour legislation elicited from capitalists, in the financial sphere the New Deal institutions were all along oriented more towards promoting than reducing the working classes' integration into and dependence on the financial system. In particular, they sought to restore popular faith in the financial system by compartmentalizing it, fortifying sectors with populist appeal (such as the market for mortgages, which had strong links to the American dream), and through policies favourable to insurance companies and pension funds. In this sense, the New Deal involved a conception of enhanced state capacity that enjoyed considerable support among financial and corporate elites. Indeed, the expansion of the state's capacities in the run-up to and during the war occurred in a process of continuous interaction with the growing capacities of private financial actors. This new conception of state capacity rested in part on a modern, 'macro' conception of the economy as sufficiently system-like that it could be regulated by manipulating key institutional parameters. Thus, the Fed became responsible for the monetary stabilization of the macroeconomic system as a whole and received a range of new powers (Greider 1987: 313); the Treasury became increasingly aware of the macroeconomic impact of its budget and debt-funding operations and it was put in charge of foreign financial policy with a view to insulating the American recovery from destabilizing external influences; and the securities industry came to be overseen by its own regulator, the Securities and Exchange Commission.

Even what appeared to be the New Deal's most punitive measure – the Glass-Steagall separation of the financial system into heavily regulated commercial and investment banking sectors – became a key institutional foundation for further financial expansion. This was apparent in the securities sector during the 1930s and 1940s: in response to the decline in corporate issues in the post-crash climate (Myers 1951b) and the fact that the bulk of the federal wartime debt was placed through the commercial banking system (Carosso 1970: 458), investment bankers began to reorganize their industry on a more cooperative basis. Of key importance in this regard was the facilitating role of the Securities and Exchange Commission (SEC), which declined to pursue a very activist role and saw cooperation with Wall Street as 'a means to enhance the agency's regulatory reach' (Khademian 1992: 40). The securities sector thus became organized on the basis of the principle of self-regulation by industry organizations, overseen by the SEC. This highly oligopolistic and concentrated industry structure gave investment firms ample opportunity to maintain close ties with specific firms and allowed them to engage in syndicated project financing. It thus formed an excellent basis for the re-emergence and further development of the financial techniques and capacities responsible for the dynamism of American capital markets. While investment bankers were now less central figures than they had been in the late nineteenth and early twentieth centuries, they did well for themselves in a growing sector. The decade of the 1950s was marked by steady growth not only of corporate issues but especially of municipal and state bonds, and the rise of institutional investors also gave a boost to the securities sector (Schmidt and Stockwell 1952).

But financial expansion and its interaction with the new framework of regulatory institutions was even more pronounced in the commercial banking sector. Due to the interest rate ceilings which placed strict limits on price competition, banks enjoyed a steady supply of cheap funds. And they had ample opportunities for investing these funds: banks bought large amounts of Treasury securities and also extended credit to individuals using the proceeds of these loans to purchase government debt (Degen 1987: 103). The banks' buying and lending activities were greatly facilitated by the fact that from the second half the 1930s until the early 1950s the Fed was in a subordinate position vis-à-vis the Treasury and applied itself to supporting its debt funding policies by standing by to purchase any amount of Treasury securities at a fixed price. In this way the Fed provided the banking system with ample liquidity and consequently it lost even more control over the creation of money and credit than during the First World War. Banks' credit-creating capacities were responsible for a massive expansion of the market for government debt, and after the war the banks again applied them to other ends.

Commercial banks, for the time being without access to speculative financial markets, expanded their industrial lending and, in many ways, this period witnessed the birth of modern corporate finance: the 'term loan' could be fully customized according to a corporation's specific needs and came with extensive bank involvement in the long-term financial health of a corporation (Sylla 2002). Consumer lending, too, grew (Grant 1992). Somewhat paradoxically, the Depression years had in fact further strengthened the reputation of consumer finance as repaying instalment debt had risen to the top of many people's list of priorities (Calder 1999). Consumer credit now increasingly appeared as an excellent disciplinarian of the working classes, giving them a stake in the system and locking them into a life devoted to repaying the debt they had incurred in acquiring that stake. The extension of mortgage credit by commercial banks and thrifts was greatly facilitated by the activities of the Federal National Mortgage Association (Fannie Mae), which guaranteed the liquidity of mortgages by buying them from banks and thrifts and selling them on in securitized form, i.e. as so-called mortgage-backed securities (Vidger 1961). After the Second World War, the American working classes would become ever more fully integrated into the financial system, as lenders and savers but above all as borrowers and consumers. The ideological resiliency of popular aspirations for republican independence, having taken on more consumerist qualities after the defeat of populist hopes for a producers' republic, was thus responsible for the ever fuller integration of the lower classes into a world of privatized consumption and the financial system that regulates it.

Financial globalization and imperial power

After the Second World War, the vigorous expansion of American finance contrasted starkly with the weak state of European economies. Unlike during the interwar period, US policies were mindful of Europe's predicament. The Bretton Woods Agreement of 1944 envisaged a multilateral system of trade and payments organized around the dollar as key currency. But since American policy-makers realized that there existed a potential conflict between stable international trade and the ability of European countries to reconstruct their economies on the one hand and fully liberalized finance on the other, the agreement also provided for control of speculative capital movements and allowed for a transitional period of exchange and import controls. However, the weakness and dependence of European economies was still greater than American planners had anticipated. After the failed attempt to make sterling convertible in 1947 had made this abundantly clear, a rapid return to currency convertibility was ruled out and the aim of putting in place the conditions for Europe's recovery and enabling it to pay for US exports – first through the Marshall Plan and later through the European Payments Union – became paramount (Battilossi 2002a). This greatly limited the extent of financial liberalization during the late 1940s and 1950s. Capital and exchange controls were used widely, bilateral trade and currency arrangements proliferated (Kaplan and Schleiminger 1989: 7; Walter 1993: 161) and international financial relations remained of a predominantly intergovernmental nature (Battilossi 2002a: 8).

Thus, with weak European economies and a non-liberal system of private international finance, American finance *was* global finance. While European economies were weak and only beginning to recover, the domestic expansion of American finance proceeded at a rapid pace. Moreover, New York became the main international financial centre almost by default (Battilossi 2002a: 10): it was the only open financial centre and became the place where foreigners – especially European governments – could issue long-term bonds. Having been established as numeraire currency at Bretton Woods, over the 1950s it grew into the main official reserve currency (Mikesell and Furth 1974). The system of fixed exchange rates made it more necessary than ever for European central banks to hold reserves because they needed to be able to intervene in foreign exchange markets to maintain the par value of their currency. Of course gold had traditionally been the most obvious reserve currency, but European central banks chose not to convert their dollars into gold, preferring instead to hold dollar assets. That was not only because of American suasion but also because, due to the Federal Reserve's long-standing support of the Treasury's debt management, US Treasury bills had become highly liquid assets, virtually as liquid as gold yet earning interest. Thus, what was crucial to the rise of the dollar as a reserve currency was the existence of an open market in US government debt deep enough to absorb the demand from a number of foreign central banks (Scott 1965).

The US fully exploited the dollar's special status and spent freely on national security and foreign aid. However, over time the US's exploitation of the dollar's privileged position came to undermine the dollar's ability to function as the source of international liquidity (Odell 1982). From the late 1950s capital flows began to outstrip the trade surplus and by the early 1960s the dollar shortage had been transformed into a dollar glut, fuelling the growth of an offshore pool of American dollars (the Eurodollar market). European economies and balance of payments had improved dramatically, and the return to convertibility in 1958 had sparked the re-emergence of a system of private global finance in which they participated on more equal terms than before. Concern regarding the stability of the dollar was widespread by the early 1960s, but the Treasury opposed any proposals for fundamental reforms to the financial system and instead adopted capital controls (Hawley 1987). The latter, however, did little to reduce the outflows of capital associated with foreign direct investment by American companies. Of crucial importance in this regard was precisely the Euromarket (Levich 1988), which constituted a huge incentive for American banks and corporations to establish overseas affiliates.

Yet it was the very same processes of internationalization that were laying the basis for a loosening of the external constraints on the American state. Throughout the decade but especially during the second half of the 1960s, US banks put a distinctly American stamp on the resurgent system of private global finance (Konings 2008). Banks' reasons to go abroad had everything to do with their domestic operations. By the late 1950s, after years of steady expansion of their lending business, banks' opportunities for making loans had become constrained by the limits of their supply of funds. As market interest rates began to rise, with the rates that banks could pay on deposits subject to interest rate ceilings, depositors began to shift their funds into financial markets. Banks became strapped for funds and found themselves unable to respond to the continued high demand for credit generated by Fordist patterns of production and consumption; consequently corporations and consumers now turned to financial markets for their borrowing requirements as well. The funding squeeze, in other words, had set in train a cycle of disintermediation. Accessing new funds to finance their lending activities was therefore of vital importance to the banks (White 1992a: 8–9). Circumventing the New Deal restrictions and giving a boost to the securitization of financial relations, banks turned to financial markets in order to raise funds through 'liability management' techniques. The most important of these was the negotiable certificate of deposit (CD), which was a time deposit (on which banks could offer higher rates than on demand deposits) for which banks created a secondary market (Degen 1987: 131).

These developments created significant problems. The banks' new ways of accessing reserves greatly loosened the constraints on their capacity to create money and credit. Inflation was a problem from a domestic point of view, but, given the growing balance of payments deficits, no less from a foreign policy perspective. Moreover, the continuous raising of the rate on time deposits allowed banks to lure funds away from the savings banks and so precipitated a major crisis in the thrift sector. Thus, during the second half of the 1960s the Fed began to clamp down on the new bank strategies. Banks responded by inventing new financial techniques and instruments, and the Fed and the banks became involved in what seemed like an endless tug of war (Mayer 1974).

It was the international arena that offered American banks an additional escape from Federal Reserve control. Already from the early 1960s American banks had been going abroad in steadily growing numbers, as banks followed corporations into the Euromarket. But the internationalization of American finance gathered real pace only towards the end of the 1960s, when, following the domestic credit crunches of 1966 and 1969, banks went abroad in ever larger numbers and began to systematically exploit the ability of their overseas branches to raise funds in the Eurodollar market (Degen 1987; Battilossi 2002a). Bank branches operating in the Euromarket would use Eurodollar CDs to attract dollar funds and then send these home to the parent bank in the US. The role that the Euromarket played in banks' liability management strategies grew exponentially (De Cecco 1987; Dickens 1990, 1995). Thus, a major reason for US banks to go abroad during the 1960s was to import funds and secure funding for *domestic* operations (Huertas 1990: 254). In other words, the very same practices, strategies and techniques that drove the international expansion of American finance also laid the foundation for its continued domestic expansion.

The internationalization of American finance had the effect of creating a highly integrated and liquid financial structure that bore the stamp of specifically American practices and institutions and was shaped by American techniques to sell dollar debt. In this way, it did much to loosen external constraints and to reduce the threat posed by the dollar overhang. As the decade of the 1960s drew to a close, the Treasury and policy-makers in the Nixon administration adopted a much more laid-back attitude to the growing dollar overhang. The awareness that America's debts to the world were not just America's own problem motivated a number of policy shifts that opened the floodgates of domestic and international finance. The Nixon administration adopted a strategy of benign neglect, allowing the balance of payments deficit to grow unchecked in an effort to shift the burden of adjustment on to Europe. This move had the effect of making clear to Europeans that dollars had *already* ceased to be backed by gold in any meaningful way and that an attempt by Europeans to cash in their vast amounts of dollars would be self-defeating (Mikesell and Furth 1974; Hudson 1977). The convertibility of the dollar into gold was suspended, the dollar was devalued and capital controls lost much of their relevance.

After the end of Bretton Woods, financial markets expanded at an unprecedented rate. Once outside American borders, US banks were no longer subject to any of the New Deal regulations (Frieden 1987) and the separately developed capacities of commercial and investment banks began to merge. Floating exchange rates greatly expanded the opportunities for the application of the new financial techniques through financial speculation and hedging activities (Berger et al. 1995). Also, increased competition in international banking motivated American banks to pioneer sophisticated techniques for liquidity and risk management (Forsyth 1987; Harrington 1987; Battilossi 2002b: 127), which gave a tremendous boost to the market in speculative derivatives (such as futures and options) (Tickell 2000; Dodd 2005). Moreover, all this financial expansion occurred on the basis of the new dollar standard: US liabilities had become the basis of the international monetary system, and balance of payment deficits became ever less of a concern (Parboni 1981). As it grew aware of the fact that the demise of Bretton

Woods and the expansion of global financial markets allowed it to exercise extraordinary seigniorage privileges, the US resisted attempts to construct a new formal international financial regime. Such continued unilateralism lay at the root of the lack of international regulation of the massive flows of capital into the Euromarkets during the 1970s (most prominent among which were the so-called petrodollars, Middle Eastern oil earnings channelled into the Euromarket).

However, the ability of the US state to loosen its external constraints was by no means without contradictions or challenges. The growth of global financial markets caused a degree of instability that received its most visible expression in the failure of two large banks (the American Franklin National Bank and the German I.D. Herstatt) due to currency speculation in the Euromarket. The hegemony of the dollar was not entirely uncontested and at various times private investors and central banks sought to diversify their portfolios. What prevented this from constituting a fundamental redirection of capital movements was the fact that the financial markets of countries such as Britain, Germany and Japan lacked the depth and liquidity that characterized dollar markets. But the most fundamental challenge to America's position in international finance was the flipside of the very processes of internationalization that had loosened its external constraints: the very same strategies of liability management and financial innovation that were responsible for the loosening of external constraints were also at the root of the loss of control by American monetary authorities over the domestic financial system. That is, the most fundamental constraint on America's ability to rewrite the rules and fully exploit the dynamics of the international financial system was the continued lack of control over money and credit creation at home and the inflation that resulted from this.

The banks' ability to access reserve funds supported a dynamic of rapid financial expansion at home. Corporate, governmental, consumer and mortgage debt all grew rapidly. And the incentives for banks to pursue financial innovation only grew, as during the 1970s the disintermediation threat was reinforced by the rapid financialization of economic life (which refers not to shifts of funds within the financial system but the entry of new funds into the financial sphere that had previously remained outside it). With opportunities for productive investment under pressure and financial instruments offering high rates and capital gains, corporations began channelling large amounts of funds into the financial markets (Arrighi 2003; Krippner 2003). A similar blend of financialization and disintermediation was represented by the dramatic growth of mutual funds: investment funds that applied themselves to attracting not the fortunes of wealthy private investors but the kind of funds that would normally be held as small bank deposits (Edwards 1996: 16). Over the period 1975–9 the assets of mutual funds grew more than ten-fold (Cargill and Garcia 1985: 49). Other institutional investors, such as pension funds, grew rapidly too, although generally less spectacularly.

As the growth of institutional investors fuelled the expansion of financial markets, they did much to facilitate the raising of funds by banks and other intermediaries and so the further growth of credit extension (Kahn 1993; James 1995). In this way they helped to lay the basis for the further expansion of corporate and consumer credit facilities. Institutional investors also bought mortgage-backed securities, thereby allowing for the growth of mortgage financing (Fink 1996). The post-Second World War baby-boomer generation had grown up and were ready to follow in their parents' footsteps of suburban home ownership. To secure the baby-boomers' access to this key ingredient of the American dream, in 1970 Freddie Mac was founded to compete with Fannie May (Brendsel 1996). This gave a huge boost to the amount of mortgage debt enjoying direct or indirect support from the federal government (Grant 1992: 352). The expansion of American finance was now driven on by a mutually reinforcing interaction of the public's role as borrowers and their role as investors.

Institutional investors also played a central role in the liberalization of the securities industry, whose self-regulatory structures privileged a cartel-like structure of insiders (Khademian 1992). The liberalization lobby emphasized the interests of ordinary investors and such arguments found wide appeal (Moran 1991). The SEC responded with a shift away from its support for self-regulation and took aim at insider trading practices, promoting market transparency and enforcing more competitive market structures. The restructuring of the securities industry sparked a revolution in financial services (Moran 1991). The abolition of the fixed brokerage rate 'unleash[ed] a free-for-all among investment houses for the consumer dollar' (Zweig 1995: 540). Commercial banks, under ever greater competitive pressures but still faced with interest rate ceilings and restrictions on branch banking, now embarked on their own campaign for the deregulation of the banking sector (Sobel 1994) – also in the name of the small saver. But it would take time for these efforts to bear fruit.

Thus, throughout the 1970s, banks had few options other than to continue devising new financial techniques (Berger et al. 1995). They relied on CDs and repurchase agreements and they invented new kinds of deposit accounts. Banks also stepped up their off-balance sheet activities: through securitization, they transformed illiquid traditional bank loans into tradable asset-backed securities which could then be sold to a third party or transferred to so-called 'special purpose entities' (Berger and Udell 1993: 229). They took on ever more investment banking functions and gave a huge boost to derivatives and foreign exchange markets (Sylla 2002: 67; Ennis 2004). Moreover, they lent large amounts to less developed countries that had poor credit ratings and did not enjoy ready access to international bond markets.

As the 1970s progressed, the situation became increasingly untenable for the Federal Reserve. Pursuing restrictive policies within the New Deal framework merely fuelled disintermediation tendencies and financial innovation, while credit creation and inflation continued. A further constraint on the Fed's ability to combat inflation was the effects of restrictive policies on the politically sensitive housing sector. Higher market interest rates resulted in a flow of funds from thrifts to the money market, forcing thrifts to cut down on their lending (Johnson 1998). Ever larger swathes of financial activity were outside the Fed's jurisdiction and this greatly complicated its capacities for macroeconomic stabilization (Degen 1987). A high rate of inflation was not only a problem for purely domestic reasons, but it also began to affect foreigners' willingness to hold dollar debt, putting considerable pressure on the dollar. This contradiction received its most vivid illustration in the 1978 dollar crisis, when speculation against the dollar came close to sparking a redirection of capital flows away from the US.

The vortex of neoliberalism

Thus, as the 1970s progressed, it became clear that financial regulation and monetary policy needed to be adapted in essential respects. This awareness underlay the shift towards monetarism and neoliberalism during the late 1970s and early 1980s (Panitch and Gindin, this volume). The idea behind the Fed's introduction of monetarist operating procedures in 1979 under chairman Volcker was that instead of regulating banks' demand for credit in the money market, it would control the total amount of reserves in the banking system and so directly control the total amount of credit and money created (Meulendyke 1988; Volcker and Gyohten 1992). However, the creation of credit and money failed to slow down. In a definitional sense it was of course true that there was a direct correspondence between total reserves and the creation of money and credit, but there was little in the Fed's approach that undermined banks' ability to employ the new financial techniques allowing them easy access to reserve funds (Greider 1987). Indeed, the 'Volcker shock' was followed by a programme of deregulation – implemented by the Reagan administration in the name of the American worker and the American dream – that gave financial innovation free rein (Cargill and Garcia 1985; Khoury 1997).

However, after some time it became clear that the ongoing expansion of money and credit no longer resulted in high rates of inflation. Banks' access to Euromarket funds no longer had the same effects as in the 1970s. Something had changed in the institutional parameters within which the expansion of American finance occurred. The Fed's new operating procedures were still not effective in restricting credit creation; the difference with the previous decade was that now little of that credit created found its way into the real economy. Instead, skyrocketing interest rates – in large part precisely the result of banks stepping up their liability management strategies (Greider

1987) – served to suck funds into the financial sphere, thus simultaneously containing inflation and promoting financial expansion. The Fed's policies accelerated processes of financialization and drew in large capital flows (Wigmore 1997; Krippner 2003; Duménil and Lévy 2004). The capital inflows also pushed up the exchange rate of the dollar, thereby reinforcing the economic recession and fuelling financialization.

The redirection of financial flows from productive investment into financial channels, the savings that fuelled the growth of institutional investors and the massive inflows of foreign capital served to finance growing public and private indebtedness (Guttmann 1994; Duménil and Lévy 2004: 78–85). America was borrowing like never before: total American debt in 1984 was twice as high as in 1977 (Greider 1987: 658). The extraordinarily high demand for credit may seem incongruous in view of the high interest rates. However, a great deal of credit was extended precisely for the purpose of financial speculation. Moreover, the Reagan administration suffered huge budget deficits and if there is a relation between government deficits and interest rates, it is probably a positive one: the government borrows to finance its interest payments, and high rates therefore result in a rapid growth of the debt and higher financing requirements. The growth of mortgage and consumer debt was characterized by a similar cumulative logic: insofar as people are already locked into certain commitments, rising rates will lead to higher rather than lower financing requirements. In addition, for the middle classes the 'wealth effect' of rising asset prices did much to take the edge off the reality of higher interest payments. Moreover, the culture of debt deepened further, extending from responsible middle-class borrowing for durable consumer items to desperation-driven lower-class borrowing for necessary everyday items. The Reagan administration's dismantling of social services and its assault on labour unions had a devastating impact on the income of the lower strata of the American population, leaving them with little choice other than to borrow against unfavourable rates, and often to borrow more in order to be able to repay their loans and interest charges when they came due. Many became caught in a cycle of consumer debt.

Capital inflows and America's growing debt to the world did not undermine, but rather served to further lubricate the mechanisms of imperial finance: they fuelled the depth and liquidity of financial markets, and this dynamic of expansion served to promote the kind of strategies that had driven the formation of the new framework of US-centred financial relations. And these strategies no longer generated the same contradictions as before the Volcker shock: financial innovation and credit creation had been embedded in a new institutional regime that directed credit flows in a way that increased rather than jeopardized US financial power (Arrighi 2003). The US dealt with its increasing indebtedness during this period – marked by its transformation from a net creditor into a net debtor in 1985 – not by developing strategies to settle these debts or to cut down on the amount of new debt it was taking on (e.g. by taking measures to improve the trade balance), but precisely by developing strategies to enhance its ability to sell its debt (Seabrooke 2001).

Thus, the period following the Volcker shock is a particularly strong reminder that American financial imperialism is as much a process of internalization as of externalization. In many respects, the financial dynamics of the early 1980s are better understood as exemplary of the vortex-like process whereby foreign systems and credit relations are sucked into the American financial system than as the outward expansion of American finance. This is best illustrated by the liberalization of international banking: American banks' ability to run overseas branches through International Banking Facilities effectively served 'to internalize aspects of [the Euromarkets] within the US domestic financial system' (Seabrooke 2001: 111) – or, as Kapstein (1994: 52) puts it, it had the effect of at least partly bringing the Euromarket back home. Deregulation pulled in new foreign financial capital and entailed a diminished centrality of offshore financial centres (Sassen 1991). The neoliberal turn and the subsequent accumulation of American debt in foreign hands gave a dramatic boost to the size and status of New York as an international financial centre (Silver and Arrighi 2003: 346). Financial globalization during the early 1980s was based on a massive increase in foreign purchases of American securities (Frankel 1988).

Of course, the vortex metaphor should not be extended too far; it is certainly not meant to deny that the US became much more active in the world of international finance than it had been during the 1970s. In particular, the US Treasury abandoned its benign neglect approach and has been, in close cooperation with the US-dominated yet formally neutral and multilateral IMF and World Bank, active in opening up the financial system of other countries. Moreover, imperial power operates not only through exerting pressure from the outside, but also tends to affect states' internal configuration of power and, through the promotion of transnational linkages among financial interests, creates political bases for liberalization within other countries (Sobel 1994).

But as much as the US benefited from its ability to promote the securitization of credit relations both at home and abroad, this was not a smooth or straightforward process. For the explosion of American finance resulted in considerable instability: the debt crisis and the savings and loan crisis made apparent the often reckless behaviour of American intermediaries and so highlighted the downside of deregulation, and the 1987 stock market crash threw into question the solidity of the new international financial regime and America's place in it. But these crises were effectively managed in ways that did nothing to jeopardize further financial expansion. The Treasury repeatedly acted to bail out intermediaries in trouble. The government's interventions during the debt crisis, the Continental Illinois failure and the S&L crisis all created expectations for the way in which monetary authorities would deal with the imminent failure of financial intermediaries in the future. It amounted to an acknowledgement of the state's responsibility for the soundness of the financial system – which also introduced a major element of moral hazard into the financial system. Moreover, subsequent years saw a dramatic increase in the resources made available for state interventions to provide liquidity to the market during a crisis. In addition, in 1988 the Basel Capital Accord was signed. It established an international framework to measure the risk associated with different types of bank assets and imposed capital requirements on banks (Rude, this volume). The Accord also promoted the sale of American government debt, as Treasury obligations were rated as low-risk assets.

Thus, by the early 1990s, the US had put in place a regulatory regime that was highly market-friendly yet did much to stabilize the vast and highly securitized American financial system. Together with the dismantling of the last remnants of the New Deal system of financial regulation – the separation of commercial and investment banking and the restrictions on branch banking – this laid the foundations for the continued expansion of American financial markets. Corporate, consumer and mortgage debt grew dramatically (Brenner 2002). The massive growth of household debt was especially crucial during the second half of the 1990s, when it served to compensate for the temporary decline in the supply of government debt – a consequence of the Clinton administration's policy to reduce the budget deficit and the national debt (Dupont and Sack 1999). Banks engaged en masse in the creation of asset-backed securities. And due to the role of agencies such as Fannie Mae and Freddie Mac, the amount of securitized debt enjoying direct or indirect government support continued to grow exponentially. The banks achieved large profits through other derivative operations as well, such as interest rate and currency swaps. At the same time, institutional investors continued to grow in size.

The IMF and WB applied themselves to opening up and liberalizing the financial systems of other countries, thus ensuring that American financial innovations and policies had maximum leverage and reinforcing the mutual interaction of the domestic and international expansion of American finance (Grahl 2001). Speculative capital flows put a great deal of pressure on countries that were seen not to have their financial affairs in order. American hedge funds, speculating with fantastic amounts, played a crucial role here. But at the same time it was precisely American finance that was the main beneficiary of these crises. For it was the extraordinary deep and liquid American financial markets that provided investors with a safe haven for their funds. Of course, America's ability to benefit from the misery of other countries was contingent on the crisis not spreading – something that the Asian crisis of 1997 threatened to do – and it was precisely for this reason that the active management and intervention by the Treasury in conjunction with the IMF and WB was so important. Precisely because financial markets had become much more globally interconnected and instabilities were transmitted much more rapidly across the globe (Solomon 1999), the American state began to assume an ever greater responsibility for the management of the global financial system.

The regulatory capacities of the 'Washington consensus' were complemented by the growth of the Fed's governing capacities at home (Krippner 2007). Over the course of the 1990s it found that the same phenomenon that had created so many regulatory difficulties in the past – i.e. the undiminished growth of credit and financial innovation – also allowed it to develop an extraordinary degree of control over the direction of financial flows. The growth of market size and liquidity improved market arbitrage and this meant that Federal Reserve changes in the rate for bank funds were almost instantly transmitted to other financial markets (Phillips 1996). By the beginning of the twenty-first century, the Fed had acquired an uncanny ability to steer financial markets in particular directions with minimum effort, i.e. it had learned to 'talk' markets up or down.

Thus, the period since the early 1990s can be seen as the decade during which the mechanisms of US financial imperialism were consolidated. It could perhaps be argued that the relative stability of the 1990s was primarily a consequence of the prudent fiscal policies of the Clinton administration which did a great deal to bring ingoing and outgoing capital flows into balance, and that such prudence has been jettisoned by the imperial hubris of the Bush II administration (Seabrooke 2004). What the policies of the Bush administration will turn out to have done to America's financial imperialism several years from now is an open question of course. Clearly, there are more and less effective ways of governing empire. Yet to study the state of American imperialism by contrasting prudent, multilateral modes of governing with aggressively unilateral, reckless cowboy-style ones seems somewhat myopic. Each of these approaches is part and parcel of a long history of imperialist expansion, and what stands out from this history is the strength of the interaction between internal expansion and external expansion. This dialectic may weaken or change at any point in time, but when it comes to questions of social transformation we are probably better advised to look to the forces that might have reason to break out of the dynamic of internal and external imperial expansion than to the failures and misconceptions of American policy-makers.

Conclusion

Scholars of history and international relations have tended to conceptualize American hegemony primarily with reference to other modern forms of imperialism. However, in America's popular imperial imagination, it is antiquity and not modernity that has always occupied a special place. As illustrated by a range of Hollywood movies, Americans seem to find it much easier to relate to the imperial grandeur of Ancient Rome than that of Britain. This is especially puzzling because some of the most central characteristics of American imperialism – its capitalist character, the sheer geographical scale of imperial control and its genocidal nature – would much more readily seem to invite comparisons with more modern varieties of imperialism. What explains Americans' intuitive affinity with the Roman Empire is of course its republican nature: Roman conquests were not legitimated in terms of the greater glory of the crown but rather as furthering the *res publica*, the interests of 'the Senate and People of Rome' as the ultimate source of public authority. Similarly, America's role in the world is invariably justified in terms of the interests of the American people, the imperative of maintaining the American way of life. This was as true of the nineteenth century, when continental expansion secured access to land and agrarian independence, as it is of the current era, when America's international entanglements are presented as essential to the continued viability of a transformed notion of personal independence and security based on privatized consumption and suburban home ownership. American public discourse is forever absorbed by the theme of the barbarians at the gate, seeking to bring down the essence of modern civilization, and the need to strengthen the distinction between citizens and non-citizens. Thus, at least at the ideological level a certain kind of unilateralism is a permanent feature of American foreign policy. In few areas of life is America's claim to its non-imperial nature more plausible than in international finance, seemingly governed by the neutral rules of markets and the technocratic expertise of policy-makers. Yet, as this chapter hopes to have shown, the rules, practices and governance of contemporary global finance have been profoundly shaped by the particular imperial nature of America's financial relations, and continue to evolve in a dynamic of permanent interaction and functional interdependence with these.

Part II

Constructing the Pillars of Imperial Finance

4
US Structural Power and the Internationalization of the US Treasury

David Sarai

All too often the US Treasury has been portrayed as an instrument of the Wall Street financial community in international affairs. Yet the important connection that does exist between financial capital and the US Treasury needs to be seen in structural more than instrumental terms. The Treasury's central responsibility is financing the American state through taxation and borrowing. Its exclusive role in debt management brings it into close contact with financial markets (where government securities are floated) and in effect means that the Treasury, while a part of the state, is also a very important part of the market. In the international sphere, where the Treasury's main role is maintaining and managing the international standing of the US dollar, the connection with Wall Street is no less intimate. Indeed, it is the Treasury's management of the national debt in globalizing American financial markets that shapes the Treasury's role in managing the dollar globally.

This chapter will argue that the Americanization of global finance has involved an internationalization of the Department of the Treasury alongside the internationalization of US financial markets. This process has tended to generate structural power for the US state while at the same time strengthening the structural power of capital on a global scale. This dual form of structural power can be traced back historically to the dynamic relationship that developed between the Treasury as the financial heart of the US state and the domestic US financial system.

The structural power of finance and the internationalization of the state

The concept of structural power points to a diffuse and indirect form of social power that is mediated through social institutions and practices (Gill and Law 1993; Strange 1996). It can be understood as the 'non-intentional' power that specific actors have within a prevailing framework or set of institutions (Guzzini 1993). Yet, it can also be understood in terms of the ability to shape and define the rules, frameworks or institutions in which other social actors participate. This especially applies to the financial market – which is not a fixed institution or an automatic mechanism of economic coordination but rather a dynamic set of practices that are continually being constructed. The state plays a key role in defining the basic rules and parameters of this market, yet its ability to do so depends on actors' willingness to recognize and participate in these frameworks – what Seabrooke (2001) calls 'interactive embeddedness'.

Conceptualizing structural power in this manner is particularly useful for understanding the Treasury's interaction with the financial sphere. The US Treasury market is the largest, deepest and most liquid financial market in the world with $4.84 trillion of securities and on average $531 billion transactions carried out by primary dealers daily.[1] Furthermore, it is a truly global financial market with 24-hour trading centres in New York, London and Tokyo (Fleming 1997). Crucially, US government debt forms the most secure and liquid asset available in financial markets and is not simply a liability for the US government: it has much wider significance within the global financial structure. From this broader function of debt, the US state derives a great deal of structural power. Treasury securities provide basic building blocks for the increasingly complex and sophisticated financial instruments which are key to the operation of global financial markets.[2]

Researchers attached to the IMF capital markets section have identified five important roles that Treasury securities play within global financial markets (Schinasi et al. 2001). First, they provide a benchmark for interest rates, allowing investors to distinguish changes in credit risk, on a particular security or class of securities, from the general level of interest rates and thereby assume an important role in pricing private securities. Second, given the benchmark role they play, Treasury yields correspond closely with private yields and therefore provide an important means for hedging against interest rate risk. Third, the active cash and repo markets in Treasury securities make them an important tool for short-term cash management and even a functional substitute for bank deposits. Fourth, the liquidity of Treasury securities makes them ideal instruments for market actors from institutional investors to small speculators who can easily shift in and out of position within the highly fluid Treasury market. Fifth, Treasury securities act as risk-free international near-money which provides an ideal safe haven for investors during any period of instability in the financial markets.

All these roles are particularly important in the context of the tremendously fast-paced, high-risk and high-reward capitalism that financial globalization has wrought. This market extends far beyond government debt into all other financial markets, providing a common point of reference for the entire global financial system as well as for all business enterprises operating on a transnational scale, thereby facilitating the overall circulation and mobility of capital. Indeed, the tremendous liquidity of the Treasury market has created a new form of global financial intermediation. The US's ability to finance massive budget and current account deficits has not simply been a matter of 'exorbitant privilege' but rather needs to be understood as deriving from this intermediary function which has been so integral to capitalist globalization.[3] At the same time, insofar as this intermediation has enhanced the mobility of capital, it has underpinned the increasing power of capital on the global level. This structural power of capital is not something external but rather integral to the power of the US state.

The Treasury market has come to play such an important role not simply because of its unrivalled size and the low credit risk of the US state, but also because of its institutional structure. Even the large Japanese and German government bond markets cannot match the highly internationalized and sophisticated market infrastructure that has developed around the US Treasury (Schinasi and Smith 1998). Rather than attempting to simply restrict or limit this market, the Treasury has developed debt management techniques that are adjusted to the dynamics of US financial markets. The Treasury works to maintain an orderly and predictable market, not simply to boost US financial markets but also to provide the best terms for financing the US state, thereby concurrently cooperating with the market and competing within the market. The internationalized character of this market has also given US financial firms distinct advantages globally: their own institutional structure and expertise have been shaped by this interactive dynamic with the US Treasury. At the same time, the Treasury market has allowed internationally mobile capital to exploit the asymmetry of national financial systems, thus drawing capital from all over the globe into its interactive dynamic with the US state.[4] In this manner, although US capital has a clear advantage within the institutional framework of the state, the US state has come to represent global capital in general.

The concept of 'the internationalization of the state', as advanced by Cox (1987), sought to capture how the forces of globalization external to any given state lead those domestic state institutions, such as finance departments and central banks, that are most closely related to these forces, to take on added international roles and increased prominence within the structure of the state. Panitch (1994) has correctly argued that this internationalization is not simply driven by political and economic relations at the global level but emerges from within states themselves as they become increasingly penetrated by foreign capital. As such, states begin to adjust their institutional and policy structures towards the global economy from the 'inside-out' as opposed to simply in response to external 'outside-in' pressures. Yet insofar as the US Treasury has come to play a unique role in this process on behalf of the pre-eminent capitalist state, oriented to supporting the expansion of US capital abroad and responsible for the management and reproduction of the global capitalist order (Panitch and Gindin 2005a), it was in fact not penetration by foreign capital that determined this trajectory, but rather the interactive relationship between the US Treasury and US financial actors as it developed domestically. As we shall see, the highly internationalized market in Treasury securities developed out of the historical interplay between the US state and its domestic financial sector. The Treasury's political authority combined with its position within the financial market to allow it to shape the framework in which this market was developed and internationalized. Indeed, the process surrounding the internationalization of US finance tended to be driven as much, and at times more, by the state than by private financial institutions during much of the twentieth century.

The Treasury and the development of US finance

The Treasury has always played an important role within the US economy, although its primary functions of keeping government accounts and financing government operations combined with the Independent Treasury legislation of the early nineteenth century to segregate government finances from the US financial system at large. The heavy financing requirements of the Civil War led the Treasury to greatly overstep the bounds of these restrictions via innovations such as an income tax, temporary fiat currency ('greenbacks'), and a national banking system. The new national banks, by being given the right to issue bank notes that would be backed by holdings of certain Treasury securities, at once provided both a stable national currency and a ready market for federal government debt (Gaines 1962). The national banking system effectively brought the Treasury into a central position within the New York money market (Myers 1931: 243–4). By 1875, 63 per cent of the investment portfolios of the New York national banks were made up of Treasury securities, and the Treasury played an increasingly central role in the provision of liquidity to the market.[5] However, the Treasury did not formally acknowledge this role and it proved quite ineffective during financial crises (Kinley 1893). Moreover, the Treasury's debt repayments tended to drive bond prices up, making it difficult for national banks to support their note issues and resulting in a contraction of the money supply. This problem led to the development of a specialized market as dealers would provide independent financing for the carrying trade in Treasury securities, thereby allowing national banks to obtain backing for their note issue without disturbing their required reserves (Gaines 1962: 199–200). This network would become central to the Treasury's method of marketing debt as these dealers would provide a second layer of support and liquidity for Treasury issues by purchasing Treasury debt in volume, maintaining large inventories of these securities, and developing retail networks for them.

   Although the Treasury paid much more attention to the impact of its operations on the money market by the turn of the century, there was growing pressure for financial reform. The New York financial sector was not enthusiastic about the Treasury extending its powers over financial markets because of concerns about undue political influence as well as the Treasury's prior mis-management of the market (Livingston 1986). Instead, the Federal Reserve System was founded to supervise the creation of money, liquidity and credit. While the Treasury was keen to subordinate the Federal Reserve to its own authority (Broesamle 1973; Shook 1987), the Federal Reserve's independent status proved useful in effectively freeing the Treasury from its rather pre-carious position in managing domestic financial crises. By serving as the Treasury's fiscal agent, it also did away with the need for the problematic Independent Treasury system – which was formally abolished in 1920. Most significantly, the Federal Reserve's support for Treasury debt issues would become central to the development of the state's key tool for monetary management – the Fed's 'open market' operations.

This intertwining of the Fed's monetary management with the Treasury market only developed gradually during and especially after the First World War.[6] But with this basic structure already taking shape, the enormous increase in US government debt during the Depression and the Second World War provided an animating force which firmly entrenched the US Treasury market's position at the heart of the US financial system. As investors had few profitable outlets for their funds, a massive flood of capital, drawn from every part of the economy as well as abroad, poured into Treasury securities. This flight to quality then concentrated the nation's finances in the Treasury market. Further, the 1933 Banking Legislation Act which shifted the US off the gold standard effectively tied the US currency to the Treasury market though with a residual link to gold reserves. The increasing demands of government financing also reaffirmed the Federal Reserve's subordinate posi-tion vis-à-vis the Treasury, which effectively set interest rates through its strict control of the price of Treasury securities. This lasted until the Treasury–Fed Accord of 1951, which left interest rates to be determined through the market, and gave the Federal Reserve independence in the area of monetary policy through the influence it could bring to bear on the market by 'leaning against the wind' through its buying and selling of Treasury bills. This represented a significant constraint on the Treasury's ability to pursue Keynesian policies since the price for the Treasury securities needed to cover the US govern-ment's massive public debt was allowed to reflect financial markets' inherent anti-inflationary biases (Epstein and Schor 1995).

This ensured that the Treasury's debt management techniques were developed in close alignment with the orientations and practices current among bond dealers and other private financial actors, and led to a grow-ing tendency for US Treasury securities to play a liquidity role in portfolios as opposed to an investment function (Gaines 1962: 247). Along with the development of the repo market in the 1950s, this added to the liquidity of the Treasury market and extended the geographical and institutional reach of the money market. This furthered the integral relationship between the Treasury and the wider US financial system. The Treasury–money market nexus would become increasingly central to the operation of global finance as US financial markets became internationalized throughout the 1970s and 1980s.

The internationalization of the US Treasury

The Treasury Department did not have a very prominent role in international affairs before the First World War, when Treasury Secretary McAdoo's ambitions and efforts to promote US banking abroad were massively enhanced by the place that both New York and Washington (with its massive lending to allied governments after 1917) immediately came to occupy as the world's creditors (Broesamle 1973; Shook 1987). Even so, the Treasury, under the highly conservative Mellon, remained clearly subordinate to the State Department right through the 1920s. Until the Great Depression, even the most sensitive financial negotiations after the war were organized through networks of private financiers such as J. P. Morgan & Company (Parrini 1969; Hudson 2003). Secretary of State Hull was still the lead representative at the London Economic Conference in 1933. But the New Deal's prioritization of domestic reflation over international financial stability, beginning with taking the US off the gold standard, devaluing the dollar and vesting the newly created Exchange Stabilization Fund with the Treasury, gave it the main role in buffering the US economy from the effects of the international economy. This elevated the Treasury to a leading role within the US state apparatus in international financial affairs (Myers 1970; Henning 1999). This role was further reinforced by the creation of the Treasury's Division of Monetary Research (headed by Henry Dexter-White) which provided an alternative for international economic policy to that of the State Department.

This set the stage for the central role the Treasury played in planning for and orchestrating the 1944 Bretton Woods Agreement conference, the highpoint in the Treasury's new-found influence over international affairs. The institutional framework that White and Keynes negotiated and brought to the conference reflected as much the Treasury's interest in the unblocking of the sterling balances and the breaking of the British imperial preference trade system as it was designed to insulate macroeconomic and trade policy from speculative international financial markets (Helleiner 1994; Hudson 2003). But in establishing the dollar as the centre of the fixed exchange-rate system and the influence it effectively gave the American Treasury in the constitution of the IMF and the World Bank, it appeared to signal a major internationalization of the Treasury's role in the post-war era. In the event, the Treasury's international role would soon decline significantly as Morgenthau and White were quickly ousted under Truman, and, with the onset of the Cold War, the main responsibility for international economic affairs shifted back to the State Department under the rubric of the Marshall Plan (Block 1977). Partly due to Wall Street's and Congress's suspicions, the Bretton Woods institutions would be rendered marginal in this process; and in light of the dismal failure of both the Treasury's and State Department's attempts to force premature convertibility on sterling as the condition of the post-war loan to Britain, the current account liberalization envisioned by Bretton Woods was postponed until 1958. As the Bretton Woods framework was rendered inoperative, the Treasury's agenda largely concentrated on domestic issues until the late 1950s.

Nevertheless, the Bretton Woods framework – reanimated as it became with the substantive issues arising from the restoration of current account convertibility in Europe and the emergence of US balance of payments deficits in the late 1950s and the desire to preserve the dollar's international role – did provide the formal structure for the renewed internationalization of the Treasury's role in the 1960s (Cohen 2000). Since the dollar's status gave the US considerable financial advantages and seigniorage privileges, but at the same time produced pressures on the dollar's position that could not be addressed through devaluation (Seabrooke 2001), the Treasury implemented a series of measures to defend the dollar. This included setting up a network of credit swaps among central banks, the General Arrangement to Borrow (GAB) and the gold pool as well as issuing foreign currency denominated US Treasury securities that became known as the Roosa Bonds (Roosa 1967; Coombs 1976; Solomon 1977). These were strictly defensive (and ultimately unsuccessful) measures which were seen as unfortunate temporary measures to be removed as soon as conceivably possible (Conybeare 1988). However, they had some important lasting implications. While European states largely rejected the Treasury's rationale for the payments imbalance, these states were nevertheless drawn into the multilateral process of managing the contradictions and tensions in the Bretton Woods institutions. Through these measures the Treasury developed substantive links with other states' financial ministries, and further drew European monetary authorities into the Treasury securities market. This went well beyond simply coordinating exchange rate policy or later discussions of international monetary reform: it increasingly led the Treasury – beginning with the austerity it pressured the British Labour governments to implement after 1964 – to infringe on other states' domestic economic policies (Roy 2004).

The deterioration of the US balance of payments deficit in the late 1950s and early 1960s was largely due to increased US foreign investment (reflecting both European firms and governments drawing on US capital markets and the overseas expansion of US multinationals). The US was playing the role of a financial intermediary in the international economy – borrowing short-term funds on favourable terms while providing long-term financing (Kindleberger 1965; Kindleberger et al. 1966; Odell 1982). The New York financial markets tended to serve this function not only because of their relative openness to the international economy, but also due to their high degree of sensitivity to short-term interest rate changes in the money market. However, inflows of short-term capital tended to be invisible in terms of the balance of payment statistics, leaving only the outflows of long-term capital apparent. Under the constraints of the Bretton Woods framework, the openness and strength of US capital markets perversely left the Treasury rather weak in multilateral negotiations, resulting in growing antipathy towards supporting the dollar.

As this situation was increasingly registered in the Treasury by the late 1960s (Roosa 1967: 223), it responded by attempting to broaden the base of the international monetary and financial order while maintaining US primacy via the creation of an international reserve unit (the so-called Special Drawing Rights) to supplement (rather than replace) the US dollar (Cohen 1970). It also attempted to broaden the base of other states' financial markets in order to take some of the pressure off the New York markets. A detailed comparative study of European capital markets undertaken by the Treasury had determined that such pressures were exacerbated significantly by government controls within European capital markets (US Treasury 1964). The Treasury viewed its own programme of capital controls as necessary to offset these problems with European markets. In the first major move to push financial liberalization, the US Treasury tried to encourage European countries to liberalize their domestic financial systems. The Treasury believed that this would lead to a decline in European use of US financial markets and, at the same time, provide US multinational corporations (MNCs) abroad with domestic sources of capital. The Treasury also believed that such domestic reforms would allow European capital to flow into US markets and possibly provide an important domestic source of support for international financial liberalization within Europe.

While the initial efforts of the Treasury to push for financial liberalization were unsuccessful, international financial markets were in fact being broadened in a different, and largely unforeseen, way: namely, through the development of the Euromarket. Its growth was a central part of the internationalization of the US banking sector which was increasingly seeking out this offshore market in order to escape the constraints imposed by the new capital controls programme as well as by the New Deal's US domestic banking regulations (Seabrooke 2001; Konings 2008). Although Treasury officials were at first somewhat hesitant about the Euromarket's effects, they came to recognize that London's re-emergence as a financial entrepôt would defray some of the pressure from the US financial system. This offshore market, not covered by US capital controls, or for that matter, restrictive US banking regulations, was also seen as providing a way for US banks to compete internationally and to provide a source of capital for US MNCs abroad.[7] The growth of the Euromarkets thus functioned to take pressure off the dollar and US financial markets, at the same time as it exacerbated the US balance of payments problem and contributed to destabilizing the Bretton Woods system. The Treasury now began to contemplate ever more seriously the possibility that maintaining the privileged status of the dollar was not synonymous with maintaining the Bretton Woods system.

The Treasury in the global economy

The 1970s would see the Treasury lead the US state into bringing about a radical shift away from the restrictive Bretton Woods system, drawing together the structural power of the state and the structural power of capital into what Gowan has termed the 'Dollar-Wall Street regime' (Gowan 1999). By 1970, the Treasury regarded the Bretton Woods system as no longer tenable for the US; that is, none of the efforts at monetary reform within this fixed exchange rate system were likely to alleviate the situation. The Treasury pushed to unilaterally close the gold window, ending convertibility of the dollar (Odell 1982; Gowa 1983) and thereby removing the immediate constraints on the US balance of payments position. The desired devaluation of the dollar was achieved through the seemingly automatic mechanism of the market, and the burden of adjustment was thus shifted to other countries (Helleiner 1994). The very same internationalizing trends in US capital markets, as well as in the Euromarket, which had presented such a problem under the Bretton Woods framework, now became a great advantage to the US.

The end of Bretton Woods had the effect of enhancing the autonomy and structural power of the US state. The US was suddenly in a far stronger bargaining position, and Treasury Secretary Shultz, an ardent advocate of free markets, took a hard line in international negotiations concerning the development of a new monetary framework (Williamson 1977). The result was a permanent shift to floating exchange rates: private markets now determined currency values. In subsequent negotiations, the Treasury resisted attempts to set formal guidelines for official exchange rate intervention, preferring instead to justify intervention only in reaction to 'disorderly markets', and it ardently defended the Euromarket against charges that this market was highly inflationary. In addition, during the oil crisis the Treasury insisted on the primacy of private financial markets in recycling petrodollars while resisting proposals for a multilateral recycling mechanism. Nevertheless, the Treasury pushed US banks to keep up their level of foreign lending and to further internationalize their operations. This resulted in a massive build up of loans to developing countries, tying these countries into the emerging global financial system and making them extremely vulnerable to changes in global interest rates.

As the Treasury moved towards lifting the capital controls of the 1960s, it also initiated a major study of foreign investment in the US (US Treasury 1976), followed by an increasing push for the removal of other states' impediments to foreign investment and the extension of tax treaties to developing countries in order to open transparent channels for investment. Treasury officials now fully embraced the position that the expansion of both American and global financial markets reinforced the position of the dollar as the key international currency: the US dollar was secure as the global reserve currency because of the unmatched role of open US capital markets within the international economy (Ludlow 1982: 121). At the same time, Treasury officials further concentrated on strengthening the US position within emerging global financial markets by drawing foreign investment flows into US financial markets. However, by far the most important source of foreign investment in the US Treasury market continued to be other governments. Indeed, there was a significant increase in foreign official holdings, the result of countries attempting to moderate the rise in their exchange rates vis-à-vis the dollar.[8] The Treasury also directly recruited Saudi Arabian petrodollars through a series of highly secretive negotiations with the Saudi government (Spiro 1999). In doing so, the Treasury was particularly concerned with off-setting the highly volatile financial flows moving continually in and out of the US financial system and Euromarkets which threatened to disrupt the money market. Channelling these funds and ensuring liquidity within the Treasury market tended to then stabilize and underpin the money market with which the Treasury market was enmeshed.

The liquidity within the Treasury–money market nexus would spark considerable financial innovation throughout the 1970s and 1980s. There was an increased need for banks and financial institutions to develop adequate liquidity and risk-management techniques due to the pronounced volatility of flexible exchange rates and competitive pressure. The wave of financial innovation in new and complex derivatives allowed firms flexibility in hedging their positions within the flux of the markets. With their high degree of liquidity and the expansion of repo markets, Treasury securities provided the ideal assets. They allowed firms to hedge and restructure the value of cash flows in order to balance their portfolios within the context of a particular risk-management strategy (Fabozzi 1990). The Treasury market, then, was at the very centre of the process of financialization and tended to give a unique advantage to US financial firms that developed linkages to this market.

However, by the late 1970s, ever higher rates of inflation – itself related to financial expansion and the ample availability of credit – and the increasing weakness of the US dollar were threatening to undermine US financial markets. The high interest rate regime put in motion by the Volcker shock would begin the process of arresting inflation and strengthening the dollar that set the stage for the Reagan revolution. The Treasury was a firm proponent of the magic of the marketplace, which it saw as serving to extend the Dollar-Wall Street regime and US structural power. Although this neoliberal approach did not suggest much interest in reviving multilateral economic management, the Treasury did have a clear international economic policy. Indeed, as suggested by Under-Secretary Beryl Sprinkel, the Treasury's international policy was now seen as an extension of domestic American economic policy (Sprinkel 1981). In particular, despite mounting international protest and the unfolding third world debt crisis, the Treasury was initially very supportive of the high interest rates resulting from the Federal Reserve's monetarist policy.

The Treasury's push for greater market discipline in IMF and World Bank lending and the broader development of the Washington Consensus would bring enormous pressure to bear on developing countries to liberalize their economies and financial systems in the wake of the debt crisis. However, high interest rates also caused problems for the Treasury as the rapidly rising budget deficits of the Reagan administration threatened to collide with the Fed's hard-line policy against monetary growth (Greider 1987; Krippner 2003). There were worries that this disjuncture between monetary and fiscal policy would lead government borrowing to crowd out private investment, potentially crippling capital markets. Yet, this crowding out scenario never materialized as massive inflows of foreign capital, much of it from Japan, poured into the US financial markets and Treasury securities, thereby offsetting the budget deficit and pushing up the value of the dollar. The Treasury quickly recognized the benefits that such inflows provided. First, these inflows would provide the Treasury with necessary financing to cover growing budget deficits in spite of the Fed's tight money policy. Second, they provided US financial markets with abundant capital, touching off a wave of financial expansion. This fitted closely with Secretary Regan's calls to further deregulate banking and financial services in order to modernize and firmly entrench the US financial sector's leading international status (Reinicke 1995).

The expansion of the Treasury securities market itself was a crucial element in this. The Treasury saw the inflows of capital and the strong dollar as an affirmation by financial markets of the US's role as the leading capitalist state. In fact, beginning with the high capital inflows that followed the French Socialists' 1981 election, the Treasury openly defined US capital markets as a 'safe haven', affirming that it was not simply higher returns alone that were drawing capital into the US, but that the security offered by the US financial system was a key driving factor (Sprinkel 1983). The Treasury was thus also affirming its role in protecting capitalist class interests in other countries from political turmoil, government policies or social forces that would damage profitability, and inviting these capitalists to identify with the neoliberal vision of the global economy promoted by the US.

During the 1980s, the Treasury implemented several measures to further promote inflows of foreign capital. For example, the Treasury finally managed to persuade Congress to eliminate the withholding tax on foreign investment. In addition, the Treasury established a programme to issue securities specifically targeted towards foreign investors (Destler and Henning 1989). While this programme only resulted in two major issues, it showed that the

Treasury recognized the important shift to increasing private foreign invest-ment in Treasury securities – which would, by 1989, represent 46 per cent of total foreign holdings of US Treasury securities. Finally, and most import-antly, the Treasury initiated a series of negotiations with Japan directed at securing the liberalization of its financial system (Brown 1994). Though these negotiations were publicly framed as an attempt to open up Japan to foreign investment and US banks, the Treasury also recognized that Japanese finan-cial liberalization would lead to further Japanese capital flowing into the US financial system and the Treasury market (Krippner 2003). And this was fol-lowed by the Treasury's insistence that financial liberalization be included in the negotiations of the GATT's Uruguay round, marking the beginning of the broad global push for financial liberalization.

While the appreciation of the dollar after the Volcker shock strengthened the US financial sector and was a source of structural power for the US state, there were significant domestic costs as the US manufacturing sector grew more and more vocal about declining competitiveness. This resonated with an increasingly protectionist Congress. Treasury Secretary Baker, eager to dampen this protectionist mood, initiated an intensive period of foreign exchange rate intervention. This was coordinated multilaterally with Japan and Germany under the Plaza and Louvre Accords to first adjust downward and then stabilize the dollar (Funabashi 1988; Henning 1994). Although the US experienced the acute savings and loans crisis and the brief 1987 stock market collapse which punctuated a period of intense restructuring in the banking industry, the continued dynamism and innovation in American financial markets suggested a significant underlying strength. By the late 1980s the dollar seemed to have achieved some balance with the yen and Deutschmark and the debt crisis in the developing world moved towards a resolution with the Brady plan. This served to strengthen the Dollar-Wall Street regime which, in turn, further entrenched the structural power of the US state.

In the 1990s, the Treasury worked to extend and deepen the integration of the global financial order while managing recurrent financial crises to pre-serve this order. Again, domestic policy would play a key role in the way foreign economic policy was conceived. The Treasury was a leading voice for deficit reduction from the outset of the Clinton administration, overrul-ing many policies on which Clinton had campaigned (Woodward 1994). It anticipated that reducing the need for government financing would reduce long-term interest rates and so free up capital within the financial market for private investment. But this strategy would require continued high levels of private foreign investment. The Treasury got off to a rather shaky start with foreign exchange markets: Secretary Bentsen's comments concerning the benefits of a weaker dollar led to a decline in the dollar vis-à-vis the yen and this tended to destabilize the bond market. The Treasury quickly reversed track with Robert Rubin's succession of Bentsen. This continued throughout the rest of the Clinton administration. The result was a continual inflow of foreign capital into US financial markets, which was a key driving force behind the historic run-up of the stock market through the late 1990s. This boom in US financial markets tended to strengthen US structural power due to increasingly high rates of return and the prevailing sentiment among market participants that the US Treasury was now following financially 'sound policies'.

The Treasury would also continue to push for financial liberalization domestically and globally. Within the US, the Treasury would continue the long drawn-out battle begun in the mid-1970s and heightened during the Reagan administration to sweep away the last vestiges of the Glass-Steagall restrictions on banking, thereby allowing banks to operate fully in all branches of financial services following the Financial Services Modernization Act. The Treasury, as well as the Federal Reserve, increasingly presented this as a regulatory shift away from futile efforts to eliminate crises by containing the dynamism of financial services towards a framework that is designed to manage crises and prevent systemic breakdown and so allows for ongoing financial expansion (Litan and Rauch 1998). This approach carried over to the global level where the Treasury consistently pushed for financial liberalization in international forums such as the G7, OECD, APEC and WTO, as well as through individual trade/investment treaties modelled after the 1994 NAFTA agreement. The Treasury was also broadly supportive of the push for capital account liberalization and increased global financial integration. A broad consensus had already formed within the G7 concerning the desirability of capital account liberalization, including those states which had heretofore remained sceptical of capital account liberalization such as France and even Japan (Baker 2006). In large part, this reflects the structural power of the US embodied in the Dollar-Wall Street regime as countries came under increasing pressure (not least by those elements of domestic capital within these countries which operated at the global level) to partake in competitive deregulation.

The Treasury as global crisis manager

The Treasury's most significant role internationally during the 1990s was that of a global financial crisis manager. In sharp contrast to the 1980s, when the debt crisis in the developing world had been allowed to drag on for almost a decade, under the Clinton administration the Treasury assumed a much more activist role. In this respect, Secretary Rubin established his credentials shortly after assuming office by organizing a daring bail-out for Mexico during the 'peso' crisis of 1995 (Rubin and Weisberg 2003). Recognizing that US banks were heavily exposed due to holdings of short-term Mexican government dollar-denominated securities (tesobonos) and that the newly signed NAFTA agreement was in jeopardy, Rubin skirted Congressional approval and used the Treasury's Exchange Stabilization Fund (supplemented by contributions from the IMF and the BIS) to provide the greater portion of the rescue package (Henning 1999). Subsequently, the Treasury would experiment with a variety of techniques to handle crises, e.g. 'bailing in' investors by requiring exposed firms to provide emergency financing during a crisis.

Several principles underlay all of these efforts. First, as with domestic financial regulation, the priority of the Treasury was less to prevent crises through restrictive regulatory measures than to prevent systemic breakdown of the international financial order when crises occurred. Such a focus on systemic crisis management tends to accept that financial crises, along with the tremendous social costs such crises unleash, are inevitable, especially in developing countries whose financial systems are less integrally related to the global financial order. Second, the Treasury has attempted to defuse any attempts for reform that would threaten to change the basic structure of the open global financial order. During the fall-out from the Asian financial crisis, a variety of potential proposals – from capital controls to reforming the IMF – for changing the international financial system emerged with considerable international support (Soederberg 2004). The Treasury attempted to defuse this movement for reform by acknowledging the problem of financial instability and developing the more inclusive G20 forum which would include many of the leading developing countries. But, within this forum, the Treasury promoted a series of market-based reforms. The proposal for a 'New Financial Architecture' was oriented to preventing market 'breakdowns' presumed to flow from flaws such as inadequate information or undeveloped market institutions. The emphasis of the reform agenda therefore still focused on measures such as improving market transparency, disseminating codes of conduct and best practices, and extending the existing framework for international banking regulation/supervision (Rude, this volume).

By 2000, it appeared that the financial order on which US structural power was based was rather firmly entrenched globally, and that the Treasury was also increasingly the leading state apparatus engaged globally in coordinating and managing the Dollar-Wall Street regime, both through the markets and multilateral frameworks. However, there was also opposition and resistance developing to the trajectory of globalization. While a good deal of this opposition tended to overlook the Treasury's specific role, the Treasury's international operations were coming under fire within Congress. This criticism tended to be bipartisan – liberal Members of Congress were concerned about the humanitarian and social costs of IMF/World Bank programmes with which the Treasury was linked, while conservatives saw the Treasury's international operations as an irresponsible use of taxpayers' dollars. At the very moment when US structural power seemed to be greatest, the Treasury faced the prospects that its international role might be constrained or reduced.

The Treasury and the 'war on terrorism'

In fact, under the Bush administrations after 2000, the Treasury's international operations were not so much reduced as their focus was shifted, placing far greater emphasis on supporting the American state's 'war on terrorism'. Of course, the Office of Foreign Assets Control (OFAC) had long played a role in enforcing sanctions and in blocking financing on national security grounds. There also existed a variety of branches devoted to combating money laundering and illegal financial transactions. However, these operations were not well integrated into the broader national security/intelligence apparatus or the Treasury's wider international operations.[9] In addition, the Treasury had generally resisted expansion of this international enforcement role by regularly opposing measures such as financial sanctions. The rationale was that sanctions or other types of economic controls would be ineffective and would impair the United States' standing as an open economy.

Almost immediately after the 11 September 2001 attacks, there was a reorientation in the Treasury to playing the role of 'global financial warrior' (Taylor 2007). The Treasury also received increased powers in the area of financial crimes in order to crack down on 'terrorist financing' (E.O. 13224 and E.O. 12947). This authority was later extended to include measures to combat proliferation of weapons of mass destruction (WMD) (E.O. 13382). The initial efforts in these areas were conducted on something of an ad hoc basis as it took time to refashion the institution to accommodate this new mandate, but the creation of the Office of Terrorism and Financial Intelligence (OTFI) in 2004 concentrated the focus on matters related to terrorist financing and national security concerns and allowed for coordination between offices and operations within the Treasury.[10] Further, the creation of an Office of Intelligence and Analysis within the OTFI gave the Treasury a dedicated intelligence office which was tied into the wider national security intelligence structure including the CIA and National Security Council (NSC). The Treasury was now able to access a broader range of intelligence and to offer its own financial perspective on terrorist activities and national security issues. This in turn facilitated the integration of existing operations such as OFAC and the Financial Crimes Enforcement Network (FinCEN) into the larger US strategic/national security framework. As such, efforts were not confined simply to criminal investigations or to rooting out terrorist financing networks, but increasingly expanded to target 'rogue states' such as North Korea and Iran.[11] OTFI took a lead role multilaterally in emphasizing the need to crack down on terrorist financing and 'rogue states'. Efforts to network with financial intelligence units within other countries, which often lie outside the purview of finance ministries, to collect information and to provide technical assistance, served to integrate these units with the US security apparatus.

While these initiatives marked an important shift, the Treasury continued to draw on US structural power in its new emphasis on financial intelligence and enforcement. In fact, Treasury officials emphasized that the global role of the dollar and the dominant position of US financial markets internationally were critically important to their operations (Glaser and Szubin 2007). The fact that most international commerce involves transactions in US dollars means that these funds routinely pass through US banks at some point, thereby giving the Treasury the opportunity to seize targeted assets. In addition, the success the Treasury had in getting foreign banks to cooperate with its initiatives had much to do with the latter's own concern to ensure continued unimpeded access to US financial markets.

Conclusion

The Dollar-Wall Street regime continues to underpin US financial strength but aspects of this highly interdependent system are nonetheless fragile. Certainly, this regime was not strengthened by the significant shift in the role of the Treasury just discussed and the corresponding neglect of multilateral economic management. Furthermore, the run-up of the budget deficits along with the current account deficit again under the Bush administrations increasingly called attention to the unequal power dynamics of this financial order and led to growing disquiet about the imbalances within the global economy. Insofar as it is true that structural power functions best when the relationships that created this power are embedded in the unremarked, 'common-sense', day-to-day operation of the economy, all this risked testing the limits of the structural power inherent in the global financial order.

To what extent does the recent decline of the US dollar bespeak this? The fall of the dollar against other major currencies is indeed often taken as a sign of the US state's growing financial, productive and political weakness. However, its effects have been able to increase competitiveness, reduce the external value of the debt burden and, at the same time, increase the value of US assets abroad through what amounts to a relatively orderly devaluation of the dollar. This orderly decline has been in part underpinned by the shift from private foreign investment in Treasury securities to foreign official holdings: since 2002 Japan, China and major oil producers have poured investment into the Treasury market.[12] While this has often been interpreted as increasing the vulnerability of the US, the shift has tied China's economy into the Dollar-Wall Street regime. It is notable in this respect that the Treasury, whose focus after 9/11 reflected the ability of the Pentagon and the Department of Homeland Security to set the agenda, seems to be regaining influence since Secretary Paulson's appointment in 2006. Paulson has made the newly created 'US–China Strategic Dialogue' the centrepiece of international economic policy. This fits quite closely with the pattern the Treasury has tended to follow, engaging surplus countries bilaterally and directly recruiting capital such as in the case of Saudi Arabia in the 1970s and Japan in the 1980s. The nature of the relationship with China will likely determine the future development of the Dollar-Wall Street regime.

Certainly the global credit crisis which exploded in the summer of 2007 directly out of the mounting problems in the US subprime market is indicative of the enormous managerial challenges the Treasury faces. The Treasury under Paulson had been more focused on concerns about the competitive position of New York due to the falling dollar as well as the deleterious effects of the Sarbanes–Oxley legislation, and on taking initiatives to improve the competitiveness of US capital markets and review the broader regulatory structure. Treasury officials believed the problems in the subprime market, which were thought to be somewhat contained, could be addressed mainly by improving transparency and extending regulatory oversight to new investment vehicles. Even in August 2007, when wider money markets began to experience pronounced liquidity problems, Secretary Paulson, though clearly concerned, continued with this rather passive response and deferred to the actions of the Federal Reserve (Weisman 2007). However, as the ramifications of this credit crunch reverberated through banking sectors globally, the Treasury organized a series of meetings with major US financial services firms (Mollenkamp et al. 2007b), out of which came the ultimately aborted attempt by major banks to set up a private fund to buy up distressed asset-backed securities. This was followed by the Treasury's more successful organization of mortgage providers to provide a collective respite to their clients.

At first glance, this seems to be a return to the Treasury's role as a crisis manager. The Treasury acted as a seemingly neutral party to help market participants coordinate an intervention to stabilize financial markets. The reluctance of the Paulson Treasury to provide direct public financial support to the banks and mortgage companies – which might be seen as a government bail-out – was marked, yet as the problems in global credit markets dragged on, and threatened to generate broader economic and financial instability, the Treasury's position softened at least as regards indirect support via aid to those threatened by foreclosures, and via the $170 billion fiscal stimulus that it shepherded through Congress at the beginning of 2008 (almost doubling the size of the annual budgetary deficit). It remains to be seen what kind of international leadership the Treasury under a new administration will be prepared to provide in the reviews that the G7 and other multilateral forums will now inevitably undertake of the regulatory structure of global financial markets in light of this latest market failure.

But this only reinforces the central point that the internationalization of the US Treasury is tightly intertwined with the expansion of the US financial system. This expansion has been shaped by the US Treasury and the latter occupies a privileged position as well as a burdensome set of responsibilities within it. The structural power that is generated by this relationship helps to explain the seemingly paradoxical position of the US state which, as Seabrooke (2001) points out, has been empowered through indebtedness. Furthermore, the mutually reinforcing dynamic between the structural power of the US state and the structural power of capital has underpinned the social/political restructuring associated with what Gill (1998, 2003) calls 'disciplinary neoliberalism', whereby market reforms have been increasingly 'locked in' by the world's states through a hardening of the outward distinction between the economic and political spheres designed to insulate them from popular democratic challenges. But this distinction may be increasingly hard to sustain, and democratic challenges even harder to resist, not only in the face of American military interventions and occupations abroad, but also in light of the explicit role the US Treasury plays as both the maker and the manager of global financial markets.

Acknowledgements

I would like to thank Stephen Gill, Leo Panitch, Martijn Konings, Leonard Seabrooke, Samuel Knafo, Randolf Persaud and Randall Hennings for various comments which contributed to this chapter. I would also like to thank the librarians at the United States Department of the Treasury who assisted me with my research and the US–Canada Fulbright Foundation for their generous financial support.

Notes

1. These are 2006 figures taken from Federal Reserve Bank of New York's primary dealer statistics and the *Treasury Bulletin*. See also Dupont and Sack (1999).
2. This explains the concern among financial analysts and economists when it appeared in 2000 that the Treasury market was shrinking due to the success of the Clinton administration in reducing the outstanding debt (Kosterlitz 1999; Fleming 2000; Wojnilower 2000; McCauley 2002). Such concerns were quickly put to rest by the marked expansion of budget deficits under the Bush administration.
3. Focusing on the current account deficit, Hausmann and Sturzenegger (2005) have developed the concept of 'dark matter' to explain the discrepancy between the consistently positive returns on the US net financial position despite mounting current account deficits. This 'dark matter' includes the unaccounted value of liquidity services provided by the US financial system as well as an 'insurance premium' due to the security of US assets, in particular Treasury securities.
4. Dooley et al. (2004) have argued that the US current account deficit supplies a form of collateral to developing countries by supporting a two-way trade in financial assets that frees capital from 'inefficient' financial markets, pointing to the way the accumulation of financial assets through direct investment has been offset by developing states' accumulation of Treasury securities.
5. The continuing restrictions of the Independent Treasury legislation still meant that the Treasury was unable to deposit government funds directly into banks and had to continually sell gold and greenbacks while buying back government

bonds in order to provide domestic funds and foreign exchange to the money market (Bensel 1990: 261).

6. With the US entry into the war, the Fed's priority became to support increased wartime borrowing and there was pressure from the Treasury to keep interest rates low. This provided banks with easy credit and encouraged a 'borrow and buy' campaign to sell Liberty Bonds which greatly broadened the ownership of Treasury securities among the US public (Myers 1970: 276). Following the war, the Treasury became somewhat concerned about the large holdings of government debt that Federal Reserve banks had accumulated. The Treasury pressured the banks to sell off some of these securities, and when they began doing so, they found that such sales had an effect on the level of bank reserves and the money market, thus leading to the development of the Fed's open-market operations in which government debt plays such a key role (Brawley 1999). The other important post-war innovation was the extension of repurchase agreements by the Federal Reserve to Treasury dealers, providing the dealer market with additional liquidity (Gaines 1962: 201). This then linked all three levels of support (the banks and the money market, the security dealers, and the Fed) for the Treasury securities market together.

7. Some have seen this as finally consolidating a transnational historic bloc, in formation since the 1920s, which aligned the financial sector with increasingly internationalized US multinational corporations. See van der Pijl (1984).

8. In 1974 foreign official holdings amounted to 96 per cent of marketable US Treasury securities held by foreigners. While foreign official holdings had averaged approximately $14 billion throughout the 1960s, this figure shot up to $32.7 billion in 1971 and reached $125.2 billion by 1979 (note that these figures include non-marketable securities). Figures taken from the Treasury's *Report on Foreign Portfolio Holdings of US Securities* 2003 and *Annual Reports of the Secretary of the Treasury*, various years.

9. Former Under-Secretary Taylor (2007) has described OFAC as being a rather obscure institution within the Treasury that operated largely independently prior to the 11 September attacks.

10. Interview with former Treasury official, 18 May 2007.

11. Indeed, the Treasury seems to have been one of the most hawkish elements in cracking down on North Korea in 2006 even when this ran foul of the State Department's efforts to reach an agreement on disarmament.

12. Foreign official holdings shifted upward in 2002 and represented 66 per cent of foreign holdings of US Treasury securities in 2005. Figures taken from the Treasury's *Report on Foreign Portfolio Holdings of US Securities* 2005.

5
Neoliberalism and the Federal Reserve

Eric Newstadt

The debate that has emerged over the last decade about the nature of the present world order – the degree to which an era of American empire or hegemony is being consolidated (Gill 2003; Panitch and Gindin 2004, 2005a), or whether we have entered a period of monumental transformation and relocation of supremacy (Wallerstein 2006; Arrighi 2007) – touches on a huge series of significant theoretical and empirical issues, one of the most central being how to read the tendency of capitalism to produce crises and capitalist states' ability to manage, redirect and elide them, generally to their own advantage. This chapter addresses some of the issues that stem from this debate, above all whether the centrality of the American state and political economy in the post-Bretton Woods era has been consolidated in an institutional form within which actors are sufficiently aware so as to manage with relative efficiency the process of capitalist accumulation. Focusing on the US Federal Reserve system since 1970, we shall argue that the American state has in fact developed significant managerial capacities, particularly relative to other institutional bodies and state agencies. This took place only very unevenly, in fits and starts, and has only recently been consolidated. Moreover, the Fed did not always develop such managerial capacities with either the strategic intent of doing so, or the immediate understanding that they had done so; as often as not key capacities developed and emerged almost by accident, in the context of panicked attempts to manage crises. Nevertheless, in the process of 'globalization' the Fed certainly became, both structurally and politically, one of the primary state agencies involved in the global extension and management of the American empire.[1]

The development of such capacities has today reached a turning point. In a context where the power and dominance of the American state remains unmatched, the Fed has been able to position itself as the world's central bank, thereby sustaining the centrality of the American political economy with greater ease than at any point in the post-war era. There are, however, countervailing tendencies and trends, as the edifice of American power has begun to show significant signs of wear, not least in respect of the US's ability to corral and condition the behaviour of other states. Nor has it evolved sufficient new practices to cope with the changes and problems appearing in the global economy. This has become especially clear in terms of the tightrope that the Fed now appears to be walking in seeking to cope with the 2007 credit crisis that has emerged out of the bursting of the housing bubble. This crisis reveals serious contradictions in the capital adequacy regime for global banking that the Fed has sponsored and is especially problematic as it has hit in the context of a falling dollar which, while welcome in terms of improving massive trade imbalances, restricts Fed options in terms of preventing either an inflationary or, more disturbingly, a deflationary spiral.

This issue of the development of states' managerial capacities indicates something very important about the nature of contemporary neoliberalism: neoliberalism has always crucially depended on the state, but only in the 1990s did neoliberals openly admit and endorse this. We shall see, in this light, that the monetarist policies of the Fed which are associated most closely with the Volcker shock need to be understood as particularly crude and early instances of a policy programme that today finds its articulation in various forms of government subsidy and intervention. Much more was involved here than the neoclassical definition of monetarism allowed for, premised as it was on the idea that inflation is a strictly monetary phenomenon and/or a result of inflationary expectations. Indeed, in neoclassical terms, monetarist policy was concerned to effect price stability through a tight (albeit presented as neutral) monetary policy – i.e. through the control of credit generation affected through the manipulation of interest rates and/or reserve requirements. Yet while the Volcker shock did reflect an intention to bring the money supply under the control of the Fed, it largely failed in this particular respect, as we shall see. Moreover, the continued fiscal injections by the US government acted to buoy the American economy in a manner quite antithetical to monetarist doctrine. In other words, monetarism, neoclassically defined, never came to pass; monetarism, historically defined, involved a broader range of practices directed at establishing fiscal discipline and social regulation. The actual neoliberal form of monetarism that was developed by the Fed evolved not via effective controls over the quantity of credit but via the way monetary policy came to be related and made ancillary to the establishment of qualitative social control of capitalist class relations through a type of fiscal discipline functional to capitalist accumulation.

In making these arguments, I maintain that since the 1970s we have moved through five phases in the transition to, and the evolution of, contemporary neoliberalism. The identification of these phases is primarily based on my reading of the New York Federal Reserve's annual reports between 1970 and 2003.[2] The first phase occupies the years between 1970 and 1979 when the Fed struggled, along with its G5 partners, to deal with a rapidly changing environment marked by the failure of Bretton Woods arrangements. What the reports from this period denote is some significant understanding of how states in the South could be incorporated once Bretton Woods had failed – namely through IMF conditionality. The same reports, however, indicate significant confusion with respect to the reconstitution of American centrality and dominance in the advanced capitalist world. The second phase is that of the Volcker shock, beginning in 1979 and lasting until 1984, the first year of consistent low inflation growth following the Fed's intentionally induced recession while expounding the classical monetarist doctrine. Here the reports indicate that the Fed's centrality and power were becoming increasingly clear, that the Volcker shock had in fact worked to the advantage of the American empire. However, the mechanisms that the Fed would use as tools of imperial dominance did not take their initial juridical form until 1985, the start of the third phase, when the US began to construct a supervisory and regulatory regime – both internationally and at home – that provided advantage to American banks and supervisors, as well as to the US Treasury Department.

By 1992, Fed reports indicate that a turn to a fourth phase was in train, this time in the direction of a reworked neoliberalism based in part upon a series of theoretical revisions packaged as New Growth and portfolio management theory. The finance-related agencies of the state solidified their positions both at home and abroad through the development of a series of institutional strategies that proved highly adaptive and fluid, premised on the recognition that state intervention and management can re-enforce, not limit, market-based exchange. During this fourth phase, the Fed also took on a cultural significance previously unseen – the Fed began writing grade- and high-school curricula, worked with the BIS to develop a new school for the training of central bankers from around the world (primarily from the underdeveloped world), hosted more conferences, published more papers and journals, and even started the 'Fed Challenge', an annual national elementary school competition aimed at creating and testing financial literacy. Most importantly, during this era, the tendency of capitalism to over-accumulate was intentionally situated within an institutional complex that facilitated concurrently: (1) the extension of capitalist social relations on neoliberal lines (fiscal austerity, price stability and labour market flexibility); and (2) the centralization of the managerial apparatus and capacity necessary to deal with whatever crisis the extension of capitalist social relations created.

The fifth phase, taking shape after the bursting of the dot-com bubble and reinforced by 9/11, has not only been one in which the American state has reapproached the process of globalization through a neoconservative and militarist lens, but also one in which neoliberal economic policy seems to have become entrenched. Since 2001, the Federal Reserve appears to have been far less focused on developing new and different programmes and policies adequate to maintain US supremacy over the medium to long term in light of the structural transformations taking place within the global economy. This helps explain why even in the face of the credit crisis of 2007, the

Fed appeared to remain wedded to the risk management and reserve setting assessment procedures it previously established and which helped spawn the crisis.

The evolution of the Federal Reserve

Concentration on the Federal Reserve over any of the other key agencies within the American state can be justified on a number of grounds. A central bank is a kind of lynch-pin that ties together the advanced capitalist economy. The role of banks as clearing houses between debtors and creditors requires a central bank to solve the problem of interbank settlement. As Harvey (1999: 247) has explained, the central bank in a capitalist state

> provides the means for banks to balance accounts with each other without shipping gold around. To do this the central bank must possess high quality money, which can guarantee the safety of the transactions between banks. The money of individual banks is freely convertible into central bank money only when the central bank is satisfied as to the quality or soundness of the individual bank money. The central bank forms the next tier in the hierarchy of monetary institutions. From these commanding heights the central bank seeks to guarantee the creditworthiness and quality of private bank moneys.

In economies operating with a currency that has no underlying store of value (a fiat currency) and which have increasingly complex systems of credit, decisive and constant action on the part of a centralized state authority becomes decidedly more necessary and important; because the connection between money and an underlying money commodity is cut off, the political and legal backing of the state is fundamental to the continued use of money as a medium of exchange. As Harvey (1999: 244) put it:

> Pure paper money – 'inconvertible paper money issued by the State and having compulsory circulation' – completely severs the connection between money and the process of production of any money commodity. The money supply is thereby liberated from any physical production constraints and the advantages of flexibility of supply and economy of circulation can be achieved. But the power of the state then becomes much more relevant, because political and legal backing must replace the backing provided by the money commodity if users of pure paper moneys are to have confidence in their stability and worth.

Apart from the importance of lender-of-last-resort liquidity functions which a central bank also vitally performs, there is also the international dimension of which we need be cognizant: central banks must themselves be able to operate cooperatively in settling international trade and exchange transactions; the complexities central banks need to attend to in relation to their domestic economies are simply replicated at a higher level insofar as economies become ever more densely internationally integrated in the context of the unleashing of capitalism's tendencies to globalization. This was in large part the reason, during the Second World War, for the construction of the International Monetary Fund (IMF): if international trade was to blossom again it was seen as necessary to coordinate international settlement between central banks. Of course, the IMF was destined never to become a world central bank, nor was the World Bank. No international institution was built under Bretton Woods with lender-of-last-resort capabilities, and its dollar-based gold standard clearly implied that state backing was to come from the US. In fact, the dollar-based gold standard did not operate on the basis of rapid convertibility into the underlying store of value, at least not until its very end, and then mainly at the apex of international finance, through interbank flows. In fact, it could be argued that a world central bank was not required until the 1970s and 1980s when trade *and* production had become more truly international amidst the rapid processes of capitalist globalization already set in motion.

The evolution of the Fed's mandate, first nationally and then internationally, has always been historically contingent – and an intensely political matter. As Henwood (1997: 92) has succinctly put it, the history of the Federal Reserve System, which is perhaps the most decentralized central bank in the industrialized world, is 'a study in how money and the moneyed constitute themselves politically'. James Livingston's (1986) excellent account of the Fed's creation traces its roots to the 1890s when an emergent corporate capitalist class 'learned a good deal ... both about itself and about the larger society', through its campaign to secure public support for 'sound money' in the wake of the extensive class conflicts that opened that decade. Attaching the dollar to the gold standard system was explicitly intended to provide a mechanism for structurally disciplining farmers and workers in the context of the emergence of large-scale corporate capitalism. 'Ultimately, the education the corporate business community received by making its own sound money propaganda effective enabled it to conceptualize and erect a new, corporate industrial society' (Livingston 1986: 124–5). When the Fed was created by an act of Congress in 1913, it was structured as a system of twelve regional banks (on each of whose governing boards big business was heavily represented), anchored by a Washington-based board, which included government-appointed representatives, namely the Secretary of the Treasury and the Comptroller of the Currency. This structure was a clear reflection both of a liberal ethos in an emerging corporate America and of the battles between populist/democratic forces and the new corporate ruling class: the Fed was built as both an arm of government that could perform public functions, and as an institution that channelled and was answerable to the 'expertise' of corporate America.

Over time, power within the Fed system was gradually centralized in the Washington-based Board of Governors, a change that reflected the concerted efforts of America's corporate community relative to those of small business owners and the working class and the unintended consequences of policy designed to increase Fed accountability. First, in the wake of the Great Depression and amidst massive New Deal restructuring, the Glass-Steagall Act of 1933 separated commercial from investment banking functions, effectively giving the Fed control over the bulk of deposits in the US, even though the Act was more directed at preventing wild speculation with private deposits. Subsequently, the Banking Act of 1935 institutionalized the role of the Federal Open Market Committee (FOMC), empowered a renamed Board of Governors to manipulate member banks' reserves, eliminated the ex officio seats that had been held until then by the Secretary of the Treasury and the Comptroller of the Currency, and gave the Fed exclusive domain over the sale of government issues, all so as to limit the influence of democratic pressures on monetary policy (Gayer 1935). Then with the Treasury–Fed Accord in 1951, in what the Fed now celebrates as a victory for sound and intelligent policy design when its 'overriding goals became price stability and macroeconomic stability', power was further centralized in the Washington-based Board and autonomy was secured from the Treasury as it was accepted that the interest rate on Treasury bills should be constrained by Wall Street's perceptions and expectations of government policy (Hetzel and Leach 2001). How the Fed actually practised monetary policy in light of the position it now occupied as the central mediator between financial markets and the American state has remained an intensely political affair (see especially Dickens, 1996, 1997, 1998). For most of the post-war period, however, it was mainly a domestic affair; it was only with the 'financialization' of the 1960s, both in the US itself and with the growth of the Euromarkets, that the affair really became international and tied up with the politics of capitalist globalization.

Muddling through the crisis of the 1970s

To be sure, by establishing the centrality of the dollar so as to facilitate the growth of international trade, Bretton Woods had in a certain sense already set the stage for the emergent centrality of the Fed in the global economy. This should not be taken to mean that the stage was set consciously, or with any intention at all. The IMF was designed to provide short-term bridge financing, not to act as the world's central bank, and US policy all along was to dismantle currency and capital controls once adjustment and catch-up had occurred. But it was not envisioned that this would necessarily undermine the dollar–gold standard or create massive transnational speculative flows. On the contrary, as the New York Fed's annual reports of the early 1970s make clear, while capital controls were arguably never intended as a long-term component of the Bretton Woods order, their dismantling was likewise never intended to produce what it did – the urgent need for state-backed management of the explosion of private speculative financial flows at the international level (Federal Reserve Bank of New York Annual Report 1974: 15–19). Still, the Fed was well positioned, largely because of the nature of Bretton Woods and the Treasury–Fed Accord, to work with financial capital to develop a new regulatory regime and supervisory footing that would in effect increase the importance of its role as the central bank. This was true internationally as well as nationally, as in the process of globalization the Fed became, both structurally and politically, one of the primary state agencies involved in the global extension of the American empire.

However intense the 1970s were as a decade of change and transformation in the international political economy, it must nonetheless be acknowledged that the US remained central if not entirely hegemonic in the capitalist bloc, if only because of its relative size and importance rather than because of its strategic imperial capacity. Indeed, we find that at the very moment Bretton Woods was being torn apart, the American state was scrambling to find a more consistent and stable footing upon which it could in turn exercise its imperial might. Certainly between 1970 and 1979 the Fed itself stumbled about in terms of policy, and if it ended the decade having laid much of the groundwork for the much more coherent set of policies and practices in the 1980s and 1990s, it could not be said to have prepared for this with much consistency or foresight.

The New York Federal Reserve's Annual Reports between 1971 and 1974 all indicate a desire to re-establish fixed exchange rates and the opposition to such from both the British and the Germans, and later the French as well. While the American state was never sold on the idea of capital controls, even under Bretton Woods, there was nonetheless strong support within the state, and the financial sector generally, for fixed exchange rates well after the de-linking from gold in 1971. In fact, even as the American state moved towards abandoning the capital controls it had introduced in the 1970s, it was not until around 1974/5 (after the failure of both the Smithsonian and Ramboillet Agreements) that the Fed finally abandoned the idea of re-establishing a system of fixed exchange rates.[3] While the Fed did develop a firm understanding that exchange rates needed to be maintained within certain parameters through frequent and often massive coordinated interventions in the market, what is also clear from the same reports is that such interventions were coordinated on the fly, since the standing arrangements that existed were hardly effective in allowing the Fed, or any other central bank, to defend a national currency.[4]

The US's balance of payment deficits – and Germany's and Japan's surpluses – alongside the re-emergence of international money markets triggered a significant downward 'correction' of the dollar in 1973. US markets became 'disorderly', particularly in the absence of 'central bank guidance'. Coordinative mechanisms were difficult to organize in the immediate post-Bretton Woods moment when each of the advanced industrial countries dealt with the de-linking of the dollar from gold in markedly different ways (some by floating, some by pegging, etc.). In this context, increased US-led coordination became

> inherently a matter of international concern, since any exchange rate change entails reciprocal variations in the exchange rates of other countries and may introduce new problems in the management of other economies. It follows, therefore, from the very nature of exchange rate relationships that the determination of exchange rates under virtually any regime, is a matter of international negotiation and reconciliation. The Bretton Woods System, as implemented in practice, provided an effective solution to this problem for many years but one that placed the US in a passive role. That role is no longer feasible for the United States. (FRBNY 1973: 18)

The Fed also became increasingly aware that interventions were needed to underscore efforts at domestic readjustment, even though there was not any clear consensus on what this would entail. The 1974 report, for instance, notes the dissent of the Federal Open Market Committee (FOMC) Chairman, Arthur Burns, who had wanted to impose a 'tighter' monetary policy than the FOMC in fact stipulated. And at least until the latter part of the decade the Fed seemed intent on trying to manipulate the quantity of credit being generated in the economy. The Fed sought to formalize the communication of quantity controls, presumably with an eye towards securing the tacit cooperation of private finance, via the Fed's target ranges for the monetary aggregates, a programme with which the Fed began experimenting in 1971 and which was formalized by an act of Congress in 1975.

Yet there was increasing clarity and consensus in terms of the Fed's understanding that what they were facing was both remarkably complex and potentially disciplining. For example, the 1975 report reads:

> It was understood of course that while cooperative efforts could do much to improve the functioning of the exchange markets, no amount of official intervention would be useful if it ran against fundamental market forces or if intervention were viewed as a substitute for fundamental policy actions. Stability in exchange markets cannot be sought independently of stability in domestic economies. Of course, there are great difficulties in coordinating policies internationally. Dilemmas and conflicts in domestic and external policies are unavoidable. And because the exchange

market is multi-sided, the difficulties increase when numerous countries are involved. (FRBNY 1975: 21)

The 1977 report went somewhat further in outlining what 'fundamental policy actions' might actually mean: 'In the end, exchange rate stability must rest on effective economic policies to attain the more basic objectives of steady growth, reduced inflation, and appropriate international adjustment' (FRBNY 1977: 18). Significantly, the report suggested that exchange rate stability was dependent upon jettisoning a full employment platform; fiscal and monetary conservatism, not employment, became, in the Fed's own words, 'the *sine qua non* of price stability' (FRBNY 1977: 10). As early as 1976, moreover, the Fed appeared to have understood that it could work through the IMF and WB – and in conjunction with private finance – to facilitate the structural adjustment of economies in the South.[5] But even though in terms of content, the policy conditionalities that this would entail were more or less identical to what would be contained under that heading by the mid-1980s, the IMF and the Fed were simply not aware in the 1970s of how to package and sell the apparent efficacy of structural adjustment – such capacities would only develop in the 1980s.

Finally, it is important to note that the Fed never really anticipated in the 1970s the new imperial architecture in terms of its main economic partners. In fact, in respect of Germany and Japan, the Fed seemed very concerned in both its 1977 and 1978 reports about how it would maintain structural centrality in the post-Bretton Woods order, panicking momentarily about emergent payments imbalances, increasing rates of Japanese investment, and the fact of catch-up in general. And there is no obvious sense, as there is in later reports, that institutions like the BIS could be used to design a regulatory and/or supervisory programme, which would be structurally advantageous to American banks relative to their European and Japanese counterparts.[6] In fact, quite the opposite – the Fed, without a full understanding of its imperial capacity, simply warned Germany and Japan about lowering currency values to gain competitive advantage.[7] In the end, the Volcker shock was a kind of last-ditch effort to re-establish a renewed basis for American growth and power, even though the anticipated results, outside of a recession, were not really understood.

The monetarist moment

The notion that monetary policy aimed at producing price stability through control of the monetary aggregates should be used as the principal economic instrument of the state became ascendant between 1979 and 1984 simply because it appeared as the only available option to deal with the economic crisis that was by then well underway. Simply put, the Volcker shock was, for the Fed, about providing a basis upon which the Bank could re-establish, if only temporarily, sufficient control over credit generation so as to effectively kill off inflation. Of course, what had puzzled the Fed through the 1970s was high inflation despite persistent unemployment. Stagflation was admitted as a possibility only once it occurred.[8] By the middle of the 1970s a series of theoretical contortions had delivered an explanation of stagflation that ultimately rested on the idea that inflationary expectations were being priced into wage demands, and that these were in turn being fuelled by the failure of government policy to recognize and respect a 'natural level of unemployment'. By the late 1970s, after multiple failed attempts to quell inflation by slowly reducing its accommodative money supply, the Fed issued its call to arms 'to break the growing momentum of inflationary expectations that threatened to undermine the struggle against inflation' (FRBNY 1979: 5).

The Fed was prepared by 1979 to let interest rates rise so as to quash demand for credit (and therein the growth rates of the monetary aggregates) and thus stifle inflationary expectations. It expected that it would in this way regain the ability to control credit generation. If this was a reasonable extension of both the neoclassical and Keynesian logics to which it was then married, the Fed also understood quite well that high interest rates would break the back of labour, which in the manufacturing sector especially was seen to threaten both accumulated stores of wealth and corporate profits.

Panitch and Gindin (this volume) read the Volcker shock as involving the 'reconstitution' of the American empire by creating a regulatory structure for global finance in the wake of the demise of Bretton Woods that would maintain the US's centrality. In fact, what is interesting about the New York Fed's reports between 1979 and 1984 is that there was no indication that it then understood how its actions would function to reinforce its central position within the global economy. The global structural and disciplinary capacities that the shock created for the Fed were not realized immediately, not until 1985 when the Fed formally surrendered any pretence of targeting growth trends for the monetary aggregates, and began to exercise more consciously its new structural power. The Fed did not appear to comprehend until 1985 either that it had the power to revise and set the rules of international finance and banking, or that the best set of rules should build upon the experience of American banks and financial services firms in the American market. Put still another way, only once targeting was dispensed with did the Fed come to understand that it could coordinate and empower American banks and financial services firms to exercise their expertise in relatively deep and broad American financial markets so as to maintain an advantage in the US and develop leads in foreign markets.

That said, even if it was not until 1985 that the Fed came wholeheartedly to divorce itself from notions of quantity controls, at least the Fed rather rapidly came to understand that quantity controls were no longer within its grasp and that this in fact placed the Fed in a special position within the American and global political economy. Thus, while in 1979 the Fed outlined a new procedure aimed at controlling the growth rates of the monetary aggregates, by 1981, the New York Fed Chairman, Anthony Solomon, admitted that 'we may already be nearing the point where the Federal Reserve can influence the growth of the broad measures [M1, M2, & M3] only indirectly by first influencing the behaviour of the economy itself' (FRBNY 1981: 12). By the time of its 1983 Annual Report, there is a distinct sense that targeting is rapidly becoming a meaningless exercise:

> When financial innovation and deregulation impinge on the economic meaning of the monetary measures, however, some of their value as a means of focusing on the longer run is lost – perhaps permanently, certainly temporarily. When the monetary targets must be subject to frequent review, adjustment, and reevaluation, some of the pristine simplicity of the approach is bound to be lost ... This is undoubtedly unfortunate. But the alternative is to ignore the problems of the monetary measures, to treat as sacrosanct numerical values whose meaning is necessarily surrounded by uncertainty. Such an approach would not make sense. And it is likely that this kind of ambiguous situation with regard to the aggregates will remain with us for some time to come. (FRBNY 1983: 11–12)

The same reports, and even reports from earlier in the 1970s, did pay lip service to the idea that monetary policy could only be effective if sufficiently coordinated throughout the G10 economies. However, it does not appear that the Fed really believed that its efforts to slow the growth rates of the monetary aggregates would require concerted action. First, the flow of investment dollars (most in the form of petro-profits) was seen as unsustainable in the long run. Second, there was not, at that point, any indication that the American consumer market was understood to be fundamental to Japanese and German growth. Third, the balance of payments problems that had begun to develop in the late 1970s were, like the flow of petrodollars, not understood to be emergent structural trends. Finally, there is no indication that the Volcker shock was understood as a new means of driving innovation and competition, propelling the American services sector to the heights it would shortly thereafter obtain. Again, imperial ambition and hubris should not be mistaken for either a definitive plan or even any significant understanding of the effects that the Volcker shock would have, even given some tacit recognition of the US's centrality.

In fact, the Fed hardly quashed demand for credit throughout the economy. In that sense, monetarism failed. Indeed, the Volcker shock arguably increased the demand for credit within the financial sector, where financial institutions of all kinds, though particularly banks, suddenly needed to rapidly revolve instruments based on short-term liabilities, in order not to have to call in long-term loans. The resultant 'innovation', all of which was and remains ultimately dollar-based, was phenomenal. However, the Fed did in fact crush the demand for credit within the manufacturing sector, and not just in the US, but the world over. As Konings (2006: 138) has it:

> the Volcker shock did not eradicate inflation but, by transforming con-sumer price inflation into asset inflation, made it more functional to US financial power. The creation of credit and debt was not brought to a halt but rather embedded in a new institutional regime that served to redirect financial flows in a way that increased rather than jeopardized US power in international finance.[9]

While true, the implication here is that the Volcker shock signalled the ascen-dance of American finance, and a renewed American empire. But capacity and structural centrality must not be mistaken for intent and design.

The 'moment of monetarism' marked the Fed's ascension within the finan-cial sector and arguably within the US state more generally. This was when the Fed began transmitting monetary policy through what has since been jokingly referred to as the 'Federal Open *Mouth* Committee'. In the 1980s the reports of the New York Fed indicate that it had begun to notice a relationship between public speeches by the Fed chairman and movements in the market (of the Federal Funds Rate). The sarcastic renaming of the FOMC did not appear within popular discourse, however, until 1994, when the Fed began, and subsequently formalized the practice of, announcing policy inten-tions immediately following meetings of the FOMC. However, the Fed very clearly understood quite early on that policy announcements had immediate consequences in the markets (even the famously obscure ones associated with the Volcker years): the 'open mouth' relationship actually pre-dates the emergence of both the practice and the term.

This can also be read as a change in the relative proximity of the Fed and financial markets, and therein the Fed's power to effect economic outcomes, generally to the benefit of financial capital. Simply, beyond a clear social proximity, the Fed was in the process of developing a functional proximity to increasingly decentralized markets. Moreover, the Fed developed during the Volcker shock an effective mechanism through which to affect monetary policy both nationally and internationally, given that American dollar values were to remain central to the valuation of other currencies. Though his term was intended to apply to the plethora of media surrounding market activ-ity, Doug Henwood's (1999: 99) notion of markets operating in a 'reflexively fellative' manner is quite instructive here; the fact that the Fed was and is able to communicate both through its 'open mouth' (i.e. through the announce-ment of interest rate policy) as well as through occasionally massive moves in the market, indicates just such a 'reflexively fellative' relationship between the Fed and financial capital, one that has only strengthened over time.

Monetarism transformed: neoliberal regulation and supervisory design

Between 1985 and 1991 the Fed was coming to understand more clearly how national and international supervisory frameworks could be built and leveraged to the advantage of both the American state and American banks. The reports also indicate that this period was nonetheless one of relative unease for the Fed. This was a period during which sizeable and persistent trade imbalances as well as ever higher levels of both consumer and corporate debt were causes for concern, but they were not yet understood well enough as the very source of American structural power. In this way, the Fed reports between 1985 and 1991 have a somewhat contradictory flavour: an increased awareness of how to handle and supervise greater financial innovation to the benefit of the American political economy on the one hand, and a generalized nervousness about the expansion of the debts that were the basis of the Fed's new-found capacities on the other hand. Of course, such contradictions were entirely rational given that the markets were blithely playing on the assumption that the state would forever and always operate as the lender of last resort.[10] There was, it would seem, good reason for the Fed to be uneasy.

The mid-to-late 1980s was a period during which the Fed was operating with relative ease on the international front to coordinate and manage the explosion of the debt crisis as well as to extend the logic of structural adjustment. On the domestic front, however, the Fed was more wary, working cautiously to equip itself with the kind of crisis management tools being used in facilitating the sustainability of Third World debt. The latter seems to have proved relatively easy for the Fed when compared to the difficulty it had in maintaining stability in the domestic market, complicated as it was by global banks and global flows, by non-bank intermediaries, by surges in consumer and corporate credit, by dramatic financial innovation and increasingly high levels of securitization, a persistent balance of payments deficit, and historically low domestic savings rates.

What appears to have changed after 1984 was the degree to which the Fed accepted that it could no longer hope to fight against 'fundamental market forces'. Ever-changing efforts at regulation had given way to successive rounds of 'regulatory arbitrage' through financial innovation, and the Fed had come to understand that unless it could obtain some supervisory purchase over the financial system as a whole (not just over banks), it could not hope to ensure stability and orderly behaviour in the event of a crisis. By 1985 and 1986 the reports indicate that the Fed had come to understand that it had little effective say over the quantity of credit in circulation – targeting was thus formally abandoned as an operational practice.[11] The Fed was also aware by the mid-1980s that the fight against inflation was being won, with labour militancy firmly broken. The Fed had only to figure out how to keep errant capitalists in line in what was the most dynamic market in the world.

Though the answer would not become completely clear until the subsequent period (1992–2001), when the Fed would abandon calls to resolve the US's persistent balance of payments problems, to correct domestic savings imbalances and to resurrect some revised version of Glass-Steagall, the Fed did articulate a relatively complete strategic programme between 1985 and 1991. First, the Fed looked to leverage deregulation so as to both reposition banks as primary players in financial markets and to extend its domain over non-bank financial firms that were offering facilities/instruments that were functionally the same as those that were available at commercial banks.[12] Second, the Fed looked to revamp its large dollar settlement system, 'Fedwire', so as to facilitate same-day settlement, and thereby neutralize settlement risk within the system. Third, the Fed began talking about cooperative efforts with market players to establish sound risk management tools as well as better self-regulatory programmes for market participants.

In its 1985 and 1986 reports the New York Fed did make clear that what these strategies aimed to do was empower the market to function both more smoothly and more independently. The 1987 report went a step further and attempted to clarify – though still in a decidedly oblique way – what strategic deregulation, extended supervision and stalwart cooperation would engender: something close to a self-regulating market within which the state operates only to coordinate private bail-out monies, not as their primary source. Ironically, the Fed did not, in its 1987 report, even mention Black Monday or the savings and loans crisis, but instead offered a lengthy description of how the Fed aided in the 'resolution' of the Mexican debt crisis. Yet this was also indicative of how it was no doubt envisioning the solution of crises at home:

> This was a sharp adjustment in the way the Fund normally did business. Typically, an IMF programme was negotiated on the basis of assumptions about the volume of private capital inflows. With a Fund agreement in hand, a debtor country could then work out arrangements with its lenders. But because the threat of slippage in the Mexican case was so great, the Fund had to raise the cost of non-cooperation. Because the banks would not usually commit any new loans until an adjustment plan was agreed to, the move set up a strong mutual dependence between IMF programmes and new money packages. The success of the tactic in the Mexican case created a powerful precedent. Initially, the banks were taken aback by the Managing Director's announcement. However, the Chairman of the Federal Reserve, who had been working closely with the Managing Director throughout the crisis, stressed that, 'in such cases where new loans

facilitate the adjustment process and enable countries to strengthen their economies and service their international debt in an orderly manner, new credits should not be subject to supervisory criticism ...' In effect Chairman Volcker was saying that regulators recognized that new bank lending associated with an IMF-supported adjustment programme could improve the value of outstanding bank loans. Regulators would not take special supervisory initiatives regarding such new money packages in a context in which a country remained current on its interest obligations. (FRBNY 1987: 12–13)

Generally, the reports between 1985 and 1991 indicate that what the Fed increasingly viewed as a smoothly functioning system was not at all one in which the economy unerringly grew, but one in which it could better coordinate the management of crisis by in turn coordinating primarily private debt restructuring programmes that would insulate the US state, to a greater degree than was the case before, from having to act as lender of last resort. The Fed, to put it another way, was in the midst of creating a supervisory framework that would provide a basis for stability, but leave the market to 'perform'. To be sure, the Fed has always understood itself as the ultimate backstop/source of liquidity in the event of crisis. The point here was that the Fed was developing an increasingly cooperative supervisory framework within which it could better force large private players to write off some losses in the event of crisis. The 1991 report made this logic manifest: the Fed washed its hands of any responsibility either in terms of cause or resolution for the 1990–1 recession and explained the recession as merely a market-based 'adjustment' to the 'overhangs and hangovers' of the 1980s.

However, there was still ongoing nervousness about the US's balance of payments position, domestic savings rates, the degree to which US debts were being financed by foreigners, and the erosion of Glass-Steagall. In fact, the 1988 report offered an extended discussion of the US's balance of payments deficit:

The present high level of US external debt and its persistently strong rising trend are unique for a large industrial country unaffected by war. Moreover, to appreciate the magnitude of our debt problem, we must keep in mind that the United States is not just a large industrial country but the largest economy in the world by far ... This means that our large external debt has substantial economic and political consequences not only for us but also for the rest of the world. Viewed from this perspective, the current level of our external debt and its increasing trend are much more problematic than would be the case for any other country in a similar situation. While it may be possible for the United States to live for a long time with the present or perhaps even higher levels of external debt relative to GDP, there are clearly significant and increasing costs associated with this outcome. In any event, an increasing level of external debt is not sustain-able over time and, at minimum, the external debt to GNP ratio will need to stabilize in the long run. (FRBNY 1988: 29–30)

Yet, the sheer breadth and depth of the US's credit market, premised as it was on a boom in consumer debt and debt-based securities, was seen as the lynch-pin that was arguably keeping the system together. Indeed, the attractiveness of US markets and US securities to both foreign manufactures and creditors was the basis upon which the Fed was able to establish the kind of inter-national supervisory framework that it has since attempted to consolidate through the Basel agreements.

In summary then, the reports of this period suggest that the mid-to-late 1980s were in part about transforming the way in which the Fed worked through other states, which, as Panitch and Gindin have pointed out, has been fundamental to the construction of the American empire throughout the post-war era. What the 1985 Plaza Accord and the 1988 Basel Accord can together be read to represent therefore is a move to impress both structurally and politically upon its G5 partners the need to operate a more market dis-ciplinary form of capitalism, though without the relative efficiency of the instruments that would be used in the period that immediately followed. This period was also one during which the Fed was only coming to grips with the domestic economy: with how it could, at home, both impose a dis-ciplinary form of capitalism and work with booming market forces based on conspicuous consumption.

Neoliberalism realized

A clear sign of the consolidation of neoliberalism by the beginning of the 1990s was that the Fed seemed unconcerned about the recession that rocked most of the developed world. In its 1991 report the Fed did attempt to explain the recession as a necessary correction of the 'debt overhangs' from the 1980s, the unwinding of the real estate bubble, and high corporate and household debt service costs. The Fed also explained that the corporate sector was wisely attempting to 'move to a more efficient scale of operation under existing cost structures' (FRBNY 1991: 24) by which it meant laying off workers, and often shifting production to Third World sites so as to restore profit rates. But by 1992, the reports begin to talk more plainly about central banking and the Fed in a manner that reflects the degree to which the principles of sound money and fiscal discipline evolved in the 1980s had become utterly inscribed in the Fed's institutional design and operation.[13]

The Fed had also come to understand the utility of the US's balance of payments position as a platform of economic growth. At the same time, it began to view household debt and conspicuous consumption as both functional and manageable. The Fed's confidence in its crisis management and containment strategies thus led it to take on new public relations functions aimed at building popular support for 'globalization', both at home and abroad, as well as strengthening ties with both market players and other central banks in the ongoing fight against any sign of price inflation. All of this was underscored by the Fed's embrace of New Growth Theory, and other forms of multivariate analysis that stem from both risk and portfolio management theory. While set firmly within the neoclassical frame, the adumbration of theoretical 'innovations' like 'imperfect competition' and 'imperfect information' was remarkable in that it offered the Fed a lens through which to functionally understand and model both global economic complexity and the uniqueness of the American political economy. There was, in other words, no longer a constant need to revise policy so as to better fit theoretical moulds, or to panic when outcomes failed to match expectations – if only because the amorphous and adaptive nature of new models led the Fed to assume the unexpected. So all at once the Fed was able to explain and justify the weakness of previous explanations, and further emphasize growth and inflation as, for the Fed, the only meaningful macroeconomic markers.[14]

Internationally, the maturation of neoliberalism, both theoretically and practically, was most evident in the Fed's calls for the revision of the first Basel Accord, a move that the Fed understood quite well as something that would give significant advantages to American banks. The initial Accord (1988) stipulated reserve requirements via a capital adequacy ratio (a rather straightforward formula) that provided American banks, which were more experienced in working with capital adequacy standards, with a significant advantage over their European and Japanese counterparts. However, by the early 1990s it had become increasingly clear that the formula used to develop capital adequacy levels either led to lower than needed capital provisions, or, as was more often the case, unnecessarily tied up liquidity, effectively hamstringing banks' ability to compete both nationally and internationally.[15]

These changes show a still more definitive shift from 'regulation' to 'supervision' than was evident in the preceding period. It also marks a decided shift towards a kind of 'customer service' perspective, one within which the Fed's allegiance to corporate and financial capital was stripped of its political meaning and content, and made merely a matter of sound business practice. The discursive and practical shift from 'regulation' to 'supervision' and/or 'surveillance' becomes most clear after 1992, when the Fed literally announced its preference for this kind of terminology. In 1994, New York Fed Chairman William McDonough, in a speech to bankers, put it this way:

> As somebody who was a commercial banker for twenty-two years, with responsibility for foreign exchange operations for that entire period, and a central banker for just over three years, I could not be more convinced

that you and we are in this together. The world in which we live is not only a saner one, but over time a much more consistently profitable one for you, if central bankers and market practitioners work together to make these complicated, difficult, and yet intellectually fascinating markets both sage and sound. (FRBNY 1994: 14)

By 1995, the Fed started to argue that the largest American and global banks had developed intensely complex and advanced risk management techniques and technologies, generally through the application of portfolio and econometric theories that had been developing since the 1950s. The reports of the period in turn maintained that what this meant was that banks' own internal risk controls allowed the movement of liquidity more fluidly within the organization as a whole, such that global overarching capital adequacy requirements were not really necessary. Thus, by the mid-1990s the Fed started to call for the revision of Basel, arguing that regulation should be replaced by a supervisory regime that replaced capital adequacy requirements with the frequent review of banks' internal risk management procedures. And the Fed's efforts to revise Basel were mirrored domestically, by calls to simply repeal Glass-Steagall (prior to 1992, the reports called for amendments to and the reworking of that legislation). Leveraging the power of American banks meant allowing them – and other American financial players – to run the financial gamut at home so that they could spread their wings further abroad. Because American banks had an advantage in domestic markets – which were central to global credit markets – and because new capital adequacy standards would allow banks to leverage deposits to a greater extent, American banks would become fundamental to the export of American-style banking (FRBNY 1993: 8–9).

Though the revised version of the Basel Accord is not yet in effect, Chris Rude (this volume) has demonstrated that what became known as Basel II offers significant advantages to the most capitalized banks and economies in the world, and forces banks in underdeveloped and under-capitalized parts of the world to either remain as such, or to liberalize domestic markets so as to invite global – and primarily American – finance. Of course, Basel II reflects more than just the Fed's recognition that it could revise international capital adequacy standards to the advantage of American banks; it also promises to bring the Fed closer to its 'customers' – commercial banks. By having national 'supervisors' merely verify that the risk management procedures employed at member institutions were satisfactory, instead of formally establishing capital adequacy requirements and imposing them on member institutions, the Fed: (a) forced itself to develop fluency in the operation and evaluation of dominant risk management processes and strategies; and (b) began relying very heavily on banks and other intermediaries to police themselves, to stick by whatever capital adequacy standards their risk management methodologies indicated were necessary.

Indeed, the Fed became by the second half of the 1990s increasingly committed to using in-house the kind of risk management and market analytical tools used in the private sector. The Fed even construed the LTCM crisis as a correctable problem through revising credit risk management models to account for 'highly leveraged institutions' (HLIs), like LTCM. In effect the Fed outlined a programme that would facilitate the kind of speculative business HLIs conduct, by providing some minimum prudential guidelines for banks that chose to do business with them. The 1998 report reads:

> The near collapse of LTCM underscored the need for lenders to recognize and manage the risks of interacting with highly leveraged institutions (HLIs) – risks to creditors and, under certain market conditions, to the financial system as a whole. In addition, the LTCM situation highlighted the blurring of the distinctions between the regulated and the unregulated segments of the financial marketplace. Since the LTCM episode, senior supervisory staff from the Bank have contributed importantly to the Working Group on Highly Leveraged Institutions, an international effort to analyze the risks posed by HLIs, to assess banks' risk management practices with respect to such institutions, and to evaluate potential responses to those risks. (FRBNY 1998: 16–17)

As was mentioned above, the shift towards supervision was underscored by an obvious shift away from 'public interest' type regulatory structures and towards a 'customer service' orientation (FRBNY 1993: 4–5). This was packaged as a more democratic kind of process, one that would enable the Fed's primary 'customers' in turn to respond more efficiently to the needs of their own customers. This 'customer service' orientation was further buttressed by the transformation of the Fed into a progressive and 'cutting edge' research institution, one whose staff economists were increasingly pushed to develop in-house econometric and risk management methodologies that the Fed had once borrowed from the private sector. By the late 1990s the Fed published increasingly more journal articles, arranged and participated in more and more conferences, hosted foreign central bankers at two-week training seminars, and developed, in conjunction with the BIS, a school for central bank staff. The Fed also became a principal player in what Adam Harmes (2001) has called 'mass investment culture', i.e. the popular dissemination and reproduction of financial literacy and the reinforcement of the rather individualized notion that welfare depends on an individual's market savvy. To this end the Fed in the 1990s began writing elementary and secondary school curricula, conducting community outreach educational seminars, holding a national annual high school competition, the aforementioned 'Fed Challenge' for high-school students,[16] and providing a wide array of resources and referral services for interested investors at all levels. The core elements of all this – inscribed in the design of both Basel II, as well as the development of extensive research capacities – have been augmented through unprecedented amounts of international participation. The BIS, the IMF and World Bank, not to mention the ready participation of central banks throughout the underdeveloped world, were fundamental to this process as was made perfectly clear in the 1997 and 1998 reports.

The Fed also developed into a far more adaptive and fluid institutional body itself. As a market player the Fed became more active during the 1990s, expanding, in the second half of the decade the contents of its System Open Market Account (SOMA) to include mortgage-backed securities. In fact, in 2000, the Fed, nervous about the effects of retiring government debt after the US ran the first budgetary surplus in a couple of decades, began to recognize mortgage-backed securities as acceptable reserve collateral. Previously only government-backed Treasury bills had been acceptable (FRBNY 2000: 4–5). Several of the reports from the 1990s track the formation of new research groups within the Fed, or the merging of trading functions so as to more effectively and seamlessly manage both national and international transactions coming into and out of the SOMA. In effect the Fed attempted to build in not just a series of adjustment mechanisms, but a culture of change and adaptation that has sought to enhance its 'service orientation'.[17]

The consolidation of neoliberalism

Arguably, both the intended and unanticipated effects of the Volcker shock (i.e. the disciplining of labour, the wholesale financialization of the US economy, and the ballooning and structural importance of the balance of payments deficit to both the American and global economies) set the Fed on a course to which it has become increasingly wedded. Simply put, the Fed and the American state as a whole have become dependent upon ever increasing levels of domestic labour market 'flexibility' and, simultaneously, upon ever increasing levels of consumer debt, which must be constantly revolved. This course has obvious international ramifications too – the American economy has come to depend upon the supply of cheap goods from foreign markets and upon the constant transfer of liquidity from those markets back into the US. And of course the reverse is true too – the American economy has come to be relied upon as the purchaser of first and last resort.

The Fed, it seems, understands this well. Yet various Fed documents indicate that far from considering the possibility of loosening the reins on either inflation or wages, the Fed remains devoted to maintaining the status quo and to managing emergent problems very much within the frame of the now institutionalized mode of thought. What this means is that the Fed will sooner tolerate a recession (and make such functional) or attempt to manage emergent crises by relocating inflationary pressures to the financial realm where workers are less likely to benefit, than it will consider other unorthodox options, like fiscal stimuli and other redistributional options. The evidence for this is not hard to find.

Between 1998 and 2003, the Fed's Annual Reports to Congress included a section entitled 'Goals and Objectives'. In 1998 there were three such goals: growth and price stability; stability through supervision and regulation (presumably à la Basel); and the integrity of the pricing system (Board of Governors 1998: 95–7). In the 2000 report to Congress the goals were mildly but revealingly revised – removed from the second goal was any mention of the Fed's lender of last resort function and of consumer protection (to avoid moral hazard?) (Board of Governors 2000: 165–7). And the third goal was amended in a way that indicated the centralization of authority over the Fed's settlement system, and therein the further institutionalization of a supervisory, rather than regulatory framework.[18] Aside from these changes, the triumvirate of price stability, risk management through reserve manipulation, and the integrity of the settlement system were again made clear. In 2003, the Fed gives itself five goals, the first two of which were more or less the same (Board of Governors 2003: 133–5). The final three, however, reflecting the institutionalization of credit revolution as fundamental to the Fed's agenda, read as follows:

> To enforce the consumer financial services laws fully and fairly, protect and promote the rights of consumers under these laws, and encourage banks to meet the credit needs of consumers, including those in low- and moderate-income neighbourhoods . . .
> To foster the integrity, efficiency, and accessibility of US payment and settlement systems . . .
> To provide high-quality professional oversight of Reserve Banks.

What this indicates is that the practice of monetary policy has ossified into a now routine pattern of heating and cooling investment and consumption through both the manipulation of interest rates and efforts to increase overall liquidity in credit markets, all underscored by an ever-watchful eye on inflation and wages. At issue is only the relative size of any intervention, the mechanisms used, and the players involved. And so it is that in contemplating what options were available to it in 2003, when the Federal Funds Rate entered, in real terms, negative territory, the Fed openly considered and then apparently clandestinely coordinated a 'helicopter drop' of liquidity, in conjunction with the Bank of Japan (Duncan 2005; Kohn 2007).

It should come as no surprise, then, that in seeking to maintain the neoliberal status quo the Fed has remained concerned to conclude negotiations around Basel II; has continued to popularize the fight against inflation; and has called for additional labour market flexibility and the education/production of ever larger stores of 'human capital'.[19] The Fed has, however, periodically examined the challenges that are no doubt faced in maintaining the present course of action: since the bursting of the dot-com bubble in 2001 the Fed has seemed cognizant of the contradictions implicit in ever-expanding fiscal and current account deficits, the pitfalls faced in winding those deficits down, as well as the unsettling consequences of declines in aggregate demand. And the Fed has also repeatedly expressed concern over the possibility of deflation, of repeating the mistakes made in Japan when deflationary pressures set in.

These expressions of concern have been well documented in Richard Duncan's *The Dollar Crisis: Causes, Consequences, and Cures* (2005) which reviews testimony by former Fed Chairman Alan Greenspan as well as by newly appointed Chairman Ben Bernanke and concludes that the Fed seems content to provide a basis for short-term stability by continuing to fuel financial asset price inflation. For Duncan, this will do little if anything to correct the dangerous imbalances that he sees as threatening to the sustainability of demand, and therein the sustainability of economic growth. Duncan also maintains, much as has been argued above, that corporate profit rates have been restored from their decline in the late 1970s and early 1980s by disciplining labour and simultaneously relying on household debt-based consumption. For Duncan, this course can only be maintained for a short while longer – American households cannot carry high and increasing debt loads and be expected to continue to consume unendingly. Duncan also argues that the likelihood that markets in Asia and Europe will be able to become less export-dependent rapidly enough to escape their present dependence on US consumers is small, so the possibility that the vicious cycle fuelling asset price inflation will be broken by external events is unlikely. And the likelihood that this will happen alongside sizeable increases in the demand for US manufactured goods Duncan believes is smaller still. So it is that Duncan sees the Fed's present attempts to preserve the status quo while encouraging the state and capital to slowly wind down the twin deficits as starkly contradictory and unlikely to work. But the Fed, it seems, is steadfast.

Though the full extent of the 'subprime meltdown' that began in August 2007 is not yet clear, the crisis is undoubtedly related to the supervisory framework designed by the Fed, which has allowed banks to self-regulate reserves based on in-house risk assessments; the degree to which the Fed has and continues to ply markets with liquidity in moments of crisis, and thereby effectively act as a lender of last resort; and the degree to which successive rounds of deregulation have intensified and globalized competition. In other words, banks have been both allowed and encouraged to let out risky loans, which have been packaged and resold off-balance sheet through bank-owned affiliates – structured investment vehicles – such that reserve requirements remain largely unaffected. Given the sizeable rewards involved, and the presumption of low downside costs, it should come as no surprise that a massive bubble, now in the process of bursting, was created.

Far from reconsidering its modus operandi, however, it presently appears as though the Fed, in close cooperation with the Treasury, is trying to cope with the crisis without abandoning a stalwart low-inflation, supervisory/self-regulatory framework. Until its unprecedented cutting of interest rates in January 2008, it also appeared to be willing to tolerate an economic downturn while betting on the degree to which recessionary pressures would abate over the medium term because weakness in the dollar would translate into a broad revival of the manufacturing sector.

The Fed also exhibited a clear reluctance to put public money into bailing out bank profits, while its involvement in the design of the private Master Liquidity Enhancement Conduit (M-LEC) fund as the main direct response to the crisis was nominal, perhaps signalling, at least in the short term, some reluctance by the Fed to be always counted on as a lender of last resort and indicating to financial capital that it must undergo some temporary discipline.

As for the turmoil that has occurred in global interbank markets in the wake of this crisis, it is not yet clear how far the massive interventions by the Bank of Japan, the ECB, the Bank of England and the Fed in making liquidity available were coordinated. What is clear is that none of the interventions appears to have been taken in opposition to the Fed's approach to crisis management. Indeed, the Fed's devotion to low inflation and risk management has been mirrored and mimicked with incredible alacrity. For its part, the Fed announced both a determination to continue to allow banks to evaluate risk and set reserve requirements internally and to remain stalwart in the fight against inflation even in the face of evidence that the subprime meltdown was having a deleterious effect on more creditworthy borrowers. In fact, the Fed still indicated that future policy decisions would be based on assessments of 'headline' inflation, which has tended to be a point or two higher than 'core' measures of the same, thereby signalling less, not more, interest rate flexibility (Bernanke 2007). The Fed's initial reluctance, after having cut rates in both September and October 2007, to accommodate the markets' clamouring for another cut to the Federal Funds Rate (the Fed), was indicative of the widely publicized concerns expressed by Fed Governor Kroszner (2007b): 'In the current context, I would be especially concerned if inflation expectations were to become unmoored and will watch both market-based and survey-based measures of inflation expectations closely.' When measured against the rather dreary medium-term assessment that Kroszner immediately went on to give (with much the same coming from Treasury Secretary Paulson and Fed Chairman Bernanke), it was clear that capital was being told, both literally and figuratively, that there was little the state could do to keep it from taking a temporary hit.

But when world stock markets plunged in January 2008, the Fed did finally move into emergency mode and drastically cut interest rates. Notably, as *The Economist* put it on 26 January 2008: 'It is striking that the Fed's rate cut came the day after a swoon in stock markets outside America (Wall Street was closed at the time for a holiday). America's central bankers, it seems, are more worried about tumbling shares in Europe than Europeans themselves.' This is not to say that concerns about falling US stock indexes leading to major recession in the US domestic economy were not uppermost in the minds of the Fed governors, as was indicated by their now openly signalling their determination to cut rates again if need be. But it does indicate the importance of understanding the extent to which its actions in the current crisis reflect the Fed's role as the world's central bank.

Nonetheless, what the Fed's actions in respect of the subprime debacle indicate is not the reform of neoliberalism, but rather its further entrenchment, potentially to the great long-term advantage of capital. It is noteworthy that an increasingly extensive literature has developed not only in academe but also in the BIS which has and continues to question the long-term efficacy of Basel II and the supervisory programme it recommends (Underhill et al. 2004). However, it is highly doubtful that such challenges will lead to any significant reform of the Basel Accord, at least insofar as the centrality of the dollar is concerned. Far more likely is that some guaranteed source of emergency finance will be developed that would enable developing countries to weather crises without too much domestic unrest. Still, in the long run, the potential efficacy in having the imperial structure made clear should not be underestimated, particularly in light of the seemingly intentional unwinding of the dollar's high exchange rates vis-à-vis other currencies. Though many countries are nominally following Basel II guidelines, the Accord has yet to formally come into effect, in part because of the problems identified here. Challenges may also focus around reform of the new Continuous Linked Settlement (CLS) system which is co-owned by the Fed and 71 of the world's largest banks. The CLS, which started operations in 2002, is not just a key part of the Basel supervisory programme, but is also evidence that global flows can be both tracked and, if tracked, taxed. Indeed, a case might be made that the regulatory potential of a system that can track and monitor – and facilitate – the settlement of every major transaction in the US could well be a useful tool in the development of international policies like the Tobin Tax.

More immediately, the outlook does not warrant ending this section in terms of fostering hopes about the imminent breakdown of the current system: the Fed and the US state are more than likely going to be able to continue on their present course; perhaps even make the imperial architecture sturdier. And we must consider that oppositional movements everywhere will have to deal more and more with an operationally cohesive financial sector, one which, in spite of the inevitable recurrence of crises, may – with the able coordination and direction of the US state – still be able to contain such crises, and even make them functional to both American and global capital.

Conclusion

Neoliberalism has involved the discipline of 'financial prudence' and the imposition of 'labour market flexibility' throughout the world, a programme realized in a multitude of ways and with varying degrees of efficacy. This needs to be understood in terms of the development of a specific juridical and regulatory order that recasts regulatory laws as supervisory practices, which are in turn also subject to varying levels of adherence. This includes a specific set of international institutional arrangements, centred in the Western central banks, the BIS, the G8, the IMF and the World Bank, that together facilitate discussion and contain dissent between the most important states and players in international finance; a remarkably deep and broad global securities market, premised on and benchmarked against US Treasury bills; an adaptive world central bank, the US Federal Reserve, that has cultivated solid relationships with both other central banks and the largest players in the markets; a set of cultural practices that work to recreate 'financial literacy'; and a series of theoretical and analytical practices that have made increasingly automatic a 'reflexively fellative' pattern of communication between the state and markets.

The notion of the Federal Reserve as the world's central bank has gained considerable currency in recent years, so much so that one very important paper for a Fed symposium by Alan Blinder and Ricardo Reis (2005) has even proposed changing the Fed's mandate to include such considerations as global financial market stability. Clearly, this speaks to the imperial power of the American state as well as to the nexus between the state and capital, rooted in global financial flows. The primacy of the Fed is also indicative of the degree to which finance must be dialectically understood as something both diffuse and decentred and, at the same time, immensely centralized and coordinated; global finance depends crucially upon debt-based consumption and upon the Fed's willingness to fuel such consumption by pumping and priming American financial markets without loosening the reins on labour markets. At the same time, the Fed is crucial to providing some basis for international stability, not least by providing foreign central banks with sufficient outlets (Treasury bills) so that exchange rates can, for the most part, be maintained. And then there is the issue of 'mopping up' – as Blinder and Reis have referred to the Fed's necessary actions in a post-bubble situation: the Fed is crucial to the containment and alleviation of periodic crises, and to the negotiation and construction of a juridical framework in which capital can place faith.

The issue of Fed centrality also leads to another point. Alan Greenspan's highly successful stewardship of the Fed for fully eighteen years was based on his having understood that his main role was to stand behind and enhance the Fed as the bulwark of neoliberalism. Blinder and Reis (2005: 81–5) distil Greenspan's legacy into a series of axioms that can be practised by

Greenspan's successors. All of these axioms indicate the importance of gradualism, transparency, patience and, perhaps most crucially, flexibility. The deification of Greenspan, and his popular association as *the* Fed, is fitting because he has personified neoliberal central banking and in so doing helped to mystify the institutional and structural apparatus that operated behind and underneath him. Individuals, at least in this sense, do matter.

We have seen how the Federal Reserve came to understand and then leverage the US's position as *the* destination marketplace within the contemporary world order. Fundamental to this has been a better understanding of and comfort with debt-based consumption and the global financial flows necessary to sustain such patterns in the US. Furthermore, in recognizing this, the Fed has looked to build and institutionalize a series of crisis management tools that promise to enhance its capacity to manage whatever difficulties the present modus operandi might create. The Federal Reserve has built and institutionalized its capacity: to break the back of labour; to normalize the fight against inflation and the conflation of the public good with corporate welfare; to isolate financial crises when and wherever they emerge; and to enhance its position as the global lender of last resort, as the lynch-pin in global financial markets addicted to debt-based consumption in the US. While some might argue that neoliberalism is close to its end, about to fold upon its own contradictions, the point that needs to be recognized here is that neoliberalism in the US and through much of the West is hardly suffering at the moment. On the other hand, to the extent that neoliberalism can be defined with increasing clarity and not just in terms of policy but in terms of the juridical and institutional forms that such policies take, there is reason to expect that we might begin to see the development of a resistance that rejects and confronts the principles of American structural design and leadership.

Acknowledgements

Many thanks to Sam Gindin and Leo Panitch for their time, their advice and support, and of course their comments on earlier versions of this chapter. Thanks also to Martijn Konings for his outstanding work in helping to edit this chapter. And thanks to my friend and sounding board, Travis Fast. Acknowledgement also goes to all participants in the York University Comparative Political Economy Seminar Series for their thoughtful comments on an earlier version of this chapter.

Notes

1. Peter Gowan (1999) has proposed that the Treasury is really at the centre of the 'Dollar-Wall Street regime'. While the Treasury's role should not be overlooked, it must be measured against the operational capacity of, and institutional separation from, its primary operating wing – the Federal Reserve.

2. The reports of the New York Fed, particularly those issued in its Annual Reports, can be said to be representative of the system in general on primarily three grounds: (1) New York maintains the largest research department which is heavily relied upon by the system in general; (2) New York is the operational centre of the Federal Reserve System, and thereby benefits from a perspective not necessarily available at the other regional Federal Reserve banks; and (3) all reports are vetted and approved by the Board of Governors in Washington. From 2003, when the New York Fed's Annual Reports become substantially less useful and descriptive, I have relied on the Congressional testimony, speeches and Annual Reports to Congress of the Fed's Board of Governors. For a useful overview see Fase and Vanthoor (2000).

3. Both the Smithsonian and Ramboillet agreements sought to establish ranges within which currencies would be allowed to fluctuate. The 1975 report simply omits any discussion of fixed exchange rates, and instead indicates that rates could be maintained within certain parameters so long as the G10 worked cooperatively and domestic economies were stabilized.

4. By the late 1970s, however, the Fed did indeed begin to develop a series of more effective standing SWAP arrangements, primarily with the Germans and the Swiss, many of which remain to this day.

5. In a section entitled 'The Need for Structural Reform', the 1976 Annual Report contended that 'drawings on that institution [the IMF] beyond the initial tranches have, of course, always been conditional upon the adoption of measures to reduce the borrowing countries' external deficits' (FRBNY 1976: 29). The report also includes the first mention of 'sound policies' in respect of BOP adjustment and debtor countries. Herein fiscal austerity and market liberalization are specifically mentioned. The discussion proceeds to focus on the appropriate mix between private and public flows of finance for deficit financing. In this regard, the World Bank and the IMF are, for the first time in the reports of the 1970s, mentioned as important managers, as significant to the surveillance of debtor countries, and underwriters of private flows. Helleiner (1994) usefully tracks the transformation of the World Bank and the IMF in the manner alluded to here. Arguably the experience gained in the restructuring of the British economy in 1976 was instructive here. For a detailed account of this workout see Harmon (1997).

6. The Basel process (since 1999 referred to as 'Basel') began after the failure of Bankhaus Herstatt in 1974. The initial concordat dealt exclusively with the supervision of emergent 'global' banks. The initial concordat was revised in 1983. Not until 1988, however, did 'Basel I' begin to deal more substantively with things like capital adequacy and risk – regulatory issues that have since been developed and which convey significant structural advantages to US banks. See http://www.bis.org/publ/bcbsc314.pdf and http://www.bis.org/bcbs/history.pdf for additional information.

7. The 1976 report notes that the revision of the IMF's founding Articles of Agreement (1976) expressly prevented states from lowering currency values to gain competitive advantage, a move that the US would itself undertake in 1985.

8. For the Keynesians, excess demand would press capitalists to expand production capacity ad infinitum, stabilizing the business cycle and leading to untrammelled growth at full employment. For the neoclassicals, inflation was a purely monetary phenomenon that emerged at full employment, when the productive capacity of an economy was at its limit. The confluence of inflation

and unemployment therefore had both theoretical schools stumped (for an account of Keynesian and neoclassical accounts of inflation see Shaikh (1999) (at: http://homepage.newschool.edu/~AShaikh/inflation2.pdf).

9. About the Americanization of global finance, Konings (2008: 52), himself drawing from Peter Gowan, says this: 'US liabilities had [by the 1970s] become the basis of the international monetary system, and US intermediaries had developed an extraordinary capacity to sell dollar-denominated debt. As a result, balance of payment constraints became ever less relevant. In other words, the globalization and expansion of financial markets did not render the US vulnerable to the same disciplinary pressures as other countries but largely freed it from the balance of payments constraint and increased its policy leverage.'

10. The 1986 Annual Report notes this, as does Michael Lewis (1989) in his famous book *Liar's Poker*, which documents the rise – and subsequent (if temporary) – fall of the mortgage market in the US.

11. For a useful discussion of the imposition and subsequent failure of monetary targeting in various industrialized countries, see Mishkin (2000).

12. By 'leverage' I mean an ability to force primary players within the financial system to undertake certain prudential lending practices and to absorb some level of loss in the event of some form of crisis. In its 1985 Annual Report the Fed proposed changes to federal laws that were allowing non-bank intermediaries to operate as banks without being subject to oversight and regulation by the Fed (FRBNY 1985: 15–16). In the 1986 Annual Report, the Fed proposed a system of categorization that would give the Fed the ability to manipulate reserve requirements at both commercial banks and non-bank financial firms offering facilities and services that were functionally identical to those that were available at more heavily regulated commercial banks (FRBNY 1986: 26–8).

13. In the 1992 report New York Fed Chairman Gerald Corrigan outlines the 'trilogy of central banking' as having to do with: (1) price stability; (2) the supervision of banks' own risk management techniques; and (3) the creation of a sound payments system. In other words, what appeared in 1992 was what had been stated only piecemeal to that point: a clear and consolidated vision of how to achieve stability in the system through institutional reform (FRBNY 1992: 9).

14. For excellent outlines of New Growth Theory, see Ankarloo (2002) and Ankarloo and Palermo (2004).

15. Basel I distinguished between 'market' and 'credit' risk. On the basis of this distinction, capital adequacy standards were required within each different category, rather than for each bank as a whole. Non-bank intermediaries, brokerages, etc., were not required to maintain any capital adequacy standards despite competing for much of the same business.

16. The Fed Challenge Competition asks participating high-school students to evaluate macroeconomic data and, on the basis of their analysis, to recommend appropriate policy action. At each stage participants are asked to present their findings in a 15-minute presentation that is evaluated by a panel of judges. The programme can also be used in a non-competitive environment via a module that is also provided by the Fed (see: http://www.federalreserveeducation. org/teachers/FedChallenge/FedChallenge_intro.htm).

17. In 1999 the Gramm–Leach–Bliley Act, which repealed Glass-Steagall, extended the purview of the Fed by empowering it to act as the 'umbrella regulator', overseeing the operation of immense, integrated, and global commercial and investment banks. The move came on the heels of a decades-long war against organized

labour, which capital had effectively won, and dressed up in a language that purported concern with the 'public good' and 'customer service'.

18. The third goal was also mildly amended. In 2000, the goal read: 'To foster the integrity, efficiency, and accessibility of US dollar payment and settlement systems, issue currency, and act as the fiscal agent and depository of the US government' (Board of Governors 2000: 165–8). In 2003, the third goal was changed to that of providing 'high-quality professional support to the Board in overseeing Reserve Bank operations and in fostering the integrity, efficiency, and accessibility of US payment and settlement systems' (Board of Governors 2003: 133–5).

19. Since 2003 the Annual Reports of the New York Fed have become much lighter in terms of content – they have become little more than financial statements. As a result, this section has been built through extensive reference to various resources from the Board of Governors (Annual Reports to Congress, Congressional testimony, and key speeches), alongside obvious references to the outside literature on the Fed and on the American political economy.

6
US Power and the International Bond Market: Financial Flows and the Construction of Risk Value

Scott Aquanno

The disciplinary rigidities that continue to separate the study of politics from the study of economics still stand in the way of a deeper understanding of the matrices and operation of post-Second World War global power. The crucial role of global bond markets in particular cannot be meaningfully understood without taking into account both power and product formation in financial markets.[1] This chapter attempts to pull disparate disciplinary threads together and comment on the dynamics of contemporary imperialism by tracing the post-Second World War history of the international bond market.

The global market for international bonds consists of a complex of three trading posts: the market for domestic issues (e.g. the foreign branch of the US domestic bond market); the foreign bond market; and the offshore market. The offshore market can be further subdivided into the Eurobond market and the global bond market, with the former being more developed and significant to the development of the international bond system. Also, the markets for foreign and domestic issues can be divided into a series of distinct bond markets, the most notable of which are those of major industrialized nations, particularly the United States, Japan and Switzerland.[2] Since the Second World War, offshore, domestic and foreign bond placements developed in conjunction with US imperial power – making American capital and political forces crucial to the development of the international bond market. This chapter therefore focuses on dollar-denominated placements and US-based issues.

If we are to concretely understand the history of the international bond market, conceptual tools for illuminating the mechanisms that have driven the expansion of the market must first be offered. To that end, the first section of this chapter will introduce and outline the theory of risk value. Building on this framework, the next section explores the period from 1945 to 1979, and the third the 1980s and 1990s. While this chronological division is based on the dynamics engendered by the end of Bretton Woods, we follow Panitch and Gindin (this volume) in arguing that the dichotomy between liberal and non-liberal moments of financial regulation is misleading.

Risk value and the structure of capital markets

The *General Theory of Employment, Interest and Money* (1936) still provides important insights for understanding the nature of financial markets. Keynes' idea that financial asset values fluctuate with investor sentiments identified capital markets as creatures of *psychology*, i.e. as institutions dictated by a complex of investor perceptions about future value. However, the insights of the *General Theory* sprang from a methodological approach which failed to account for the modalities of power embedded in capitalist social relations. Keynes' causal analysis displayed a lack of sensitivity to the structural aspects of economic life by overemphasizing the volatility of financial markets and largely failing to appreciate the system of power which permeates and organizes financial markets – the system that informs capital market psychology. At a deeper level, financial market trends are not simply the product of investor expectations and sentiment. Rather, they reflect a socially constructed conception of risk which expresses itself as a system of order in the financial marketplace. Underlying all global and domestic flows of funds is a notion of risk which becomes reified in the financial products that are distributed globally. For example, in its most abstract form a corporate bond derives its value from an agreed payment of future royalties to the registered holder or bearer. But the market value of this transaction is contingent on the validity of the underlying promise as perceived by financial market participants. This promise that is crucial to the bond's value thus requires unpacking at a more complex level of analysis.

As social and historical constructions, structures of risk value cannot be conceptualized in an abstract manner. Risk structures are subject to periods of strength and weakness, depending on the relationships between risk and productive capacity. When productive capacity decreases, previous ideas of risk lose force and investments move from productive to financial capital, feeding growth in speculative flows. Moreover, temporary fluctuations emerge within regimes of risk stability. A country may possess positive 'risk value' and negative 'risk premium' at the same moment; this reflects short-term expectations of value decline against a general faith in the structural viability of asset fundamentals. The valuation of US financial commodities after 1990 is a good illustration. Despite its central position within global financial markets, the US dollar possessed a negative risk premium from 1995 to 1999. This did not mean the collapse of the attractiveness of US financial assets, reflecting the continuation of positive US risk value, but it acted to temporarily reduce the popularity of US government and corporate securities. After 1999, despite growing balance of payment deficits, US risk premiums strongly rebounded to express positive overall ratios.

Contemporary risk throughout the global economy is largely measured in terms of the American dollar and indirectly through the American Treasury bill/note/bond. In the first instance, 'America's free financial ride' is a product of the psychological structures and social constructions which emanated from the Bretton Woods Agreement and, more generally, the productive capacity of US capital (Hudson 2003: 3–12). However, in contrast to the claim made by Hudson, the gains made by the US market due to its position in global debt channels has not depended on the passivity of European and Asian central bankers. While the US state has had ample opportunity to unilaterally manipulate financial flows, the circular exchange of US debt between the Federal Reserve and surplus nations has its roots in the post-Second World War logic of risk value. It is this naturalization of US risk that has facilitated the reproduction of the 'Treasury-bond standard' (Hudson 2003: 3).

The epistemic structures which sustained US risk value have changed considerably over time: whereas initially the US derived considerable substantive financial validity from the link between US debt instruments and gold, since the onset of financial globalization the management of US risk value has become based on controlling inflation and maintaining a high degree of 'moral hazard' (that is, the expectation that the Treasury and the Federal Reserve will furnish adequate liquidity at key crisis moments to prevent the bankruptcy of key financial agents). But these changing modalities of risk calculation hide a basic continuity between the two periods which stems from the way in which financial market patterns have been influenced by tacit systems of knowledge informed by a particular structure of imperial power. The transition to neoliberal-inspired fundamentals in risk assessment has been responsible not for a decline but rather for a deepening of America's financial hegemony.

International bonds and the Bretton Woods era

In important respects, the Bretton Woods system was linked to the need for independent macroeconomic management following the destruction caused by international depression and global warfare. The idea was to establish currency stability through capital controls so that countries could relatively freely manipulate domestic interest rates based on principles of domestic growth and expansion. The United States was central to this system as the dollar was established as the international monetary reference point or the global reserve asset. All other countries tied their currency to the dollar at a fixed rate of convertibility and the US guaranteed dollar convertibility with gold at US\$35 per ounce. The Bretton Woods system thus established the foundation for the dollar-centred growth of the international bond market. The new financial order created an international conception of risk which effectively eliminated concern as to the future value of the American currency. As Grabbe (1996: 12) argues, the position of the dollar as the central reserve asset instilled a generalized understanding in the international community that the dollar was a 'riskless asset'.

The idea of currency and country risk embodied in the Bretton Woods Agreement had as one of its most immediate effects the development of the so-called Yankee bond market (the market for foreign bonds placed in the US domestic market). The American dollar was unique during this period as it remained convertible into other major currencies at fixed rates. The brief experiment with sterling convertibility in 1947 only confirmed its fall from hegemonic status. The convertible nature of the American dollar greatly strengthened its role as an internationally secure store of value and made bonds denominated in US dollars and issued in the American market uniquely attractive assets.

From small beginnings in the period immediately following the war, the Yankee bond market grew impressively through the 1950s, particularly following the removal of convertibility restrictions on major European currencies. Between 1955 and 1962, foreign bond issues offered in the US totalled US$4.2 billion, approximately US$1.3 billion more than the foreign issues offered in the principal European countries combined (Mensbrugghe 1964). These capital investments helped to turn the American dollar shortage of the late 1940s and early 1950s into a dollar glut (Fisher 1979). In the 1960s the growth of the Yankee bond market exploded: from US$0.85 billion in 1960 to more than US$1.5 billion by the first half of 1963 (Fisher 1979: 18).

The growth of the foreign bond market increasingly troubled US state officials concerned about the adequacy of American gold reserves. On 18 July 1963, the Kennedy administration defied (mostly passive) Wall Street resistance and imposed an equalization tax (IET) on foreign borrowers (Helleiner 1994). The tax was designed to reduce capital outflows by taxing interest income on securities issued by foreign borrowers in the US market. The effect of the IET was to undermine the growth of the Yankee bond market. According to the US Treasury Department, sales of new foreign securities to US residents had shrunk by 75 per cent by the end of 1963. The market function that remained corresponded to issue placements that were exempt from the tax (Hays and Hubbard 1990). The international nature of the American bond market was also constricted in the 1960s and 1970s by federal regulations on the issue of securities to foreigners such as the 30 per cent withholding tax on purchases of US corporate bonds by non-residents. While the same also applied to US companies issuing Eurobonds, this restriction could be escaped if the issuing company was a subsidiary which generated 80 per cent of its income from non-US sources (Grabbe 1996).

At the same time, these developments facilitated the expansion of a European offshore market in US dollar bonds centred on London, i.e. the

Eurobond market. The structural preconditions for Europe-based capital financing had been present for some time in the guise of the London merchant bank market and the sustained sales of US Treasury debt to European banks, but growth had been very limited. The liquidity of the US bond market as well as the dollar payment chain had ensured the relative quiescence of European markets in the early 1960s. But now that capital regulations effectively closed off Yankee bond financing opportunities and encouraged US corporations to 'utilize foreign financing subsidiaries', European investors began experimenting in US dollar bond financing in their home and regional markets (Grabbe 1996: 276; Fisher 1979; Clark 2002). By the end of 1963, Eurobond issues stood at US$147.5 million and by 1964 they reached US$680.8 million (Fisher 1979). The expansion of Eurobond financing continued throughout the 1960s and 1970s so that by the end of 1977 the market issued a total of US$15.74 billion to global corporations and governments (Hays and Hubbard 1990).

The early success of the Eurobond market cannot be understood except in terms of the regulatory apparatus governing Euromarket placements. It offered an open meeting ground for international debtors and creditors of both public and private origin. Helleiner summarizes the nature of the Eurobond market appropriately as 'the most liberal international financial environment that private market operators had encountered in several decades'; a centre where 'transactions could be made in non-local currencies, especially dollars, completely free of state regulations' (Helleiner [1994] 1996: 82). Crucial here was the absence of interest rate ceilings, which meant that rates in the Eurodollar markets were higher than those in the US market. Moreover, borrowers and lenders could avoid the type of disclosure rules imposed by domestic regulators (Evans 1992). The fact that the 'identities of the bond owner did not appear in any legal record and the interest on them was payable to whomever presented the proper coupons' meant that the interest harvested from Euro-issues was non-taxable and that the offering company could pay a lower rate of interest than on similar domestic issues (Evans 1992: 44).

The Eurobond market has historically been dominated by Eurodollar bond placements. From 1963 to 1978, as the Eurobond market continued to grow, the percentage of US dollar denominated loans as a total of outstanding issues averaged approximately 60 per cent for the period (having reached a high of 88.9 per cent in 1967) (Fisher 1979). While US dollar denominated issues as a percentage of Eurobond placements fell in the 1990s in comparison with the 1960s and 1970s, the substantive validity of the dollar was not only central in driving the early development of the Eurobond market but also remains a central feature today.

While the Eurobond market was at the heart of the dynamism that characterized international securities markets in the 1960s and 1970s, two other markets – the US domestic market and the Yankee bond market – nonetheless played crucial roles in the construction of global securities connectivity during this period. Until the mid-1960s, the growth of global connectivity through US Treasury securities was relatively limited for a number of reasons, including the lower volume of US government debt, remaining capital controls in Europe and Japan, interest rate differentials with respect to the Eurobond market, and the limited industrial development and saving pools in the rest of the world. The risk value attached to the dollar was thus not fully expressed in the American market for bond issues. The market required a more mature institutional base in the form of an internationally oriented complex of primary dealers and selling groups capable of distributing issues globally.

Nevertheless, driven to an important extent by foreign investors, the public issue of US Treasury securities continued to grow through the 1960s, reaching US$369 billion by 1970 (Hays and Hubbard 1990). In fact, measured in terms of the dollar value of privately held assets, the internationalization of the US market for Treasury securities was deeper than that of the Eurobond market at the end of the 1960s. The aggregate value of Eurobonds outstanding in 1970 totalled roughly US$13.5 billion, whereas foreigners held US$19.8 billion in US Treasury securities by the end of the same year (US Census Bureau 1989; Hays and Hubbard 1990). As with Eurodollar markets, the growth of the Treasury market was driven by the fact that real interest rates rose above the 'Regulation Q' ceiling.[3]

By the end of the 1960s, many of the conditions that limited the global distribution of US Treasury securities had been relieved. Also, the privatization of currency risk and commodity price volatility in the 1970s enhanced the attractiveness of US Treasury securities. This was evidenced by the reaction of capital markets following the Yom Kippur War and the subsequent oil embargo. As a result, the foreign purchase of Treasury securities, particularly bills, grew steadily throughout the 1970s, averaging US$10.5 billion per year (Sobol 1998). By 1980, foreign and international investors owned US$129.7 billion in US Treasury securities (which represented 21 per cent of privately held US public debt) (US Census Bureau 1989). By comparison, the outstanding volume of Eurobond issues by the same year was approximately US$110 billion (Hays and Hubbard 1990). The Eurobond market had displayed even more pronounced growth through the decade (expanding by 815 per cent in comparison to 655 per cent) but the foreign market for US Treasury securities still remained larger at the end of the 1970s. Thus, the international market for US Treasury securities brought global creditors – particularly those from Germany, Canada and the United Kingdom – together with US borrowers in a way that drove the internationalization of the broader securities marketplace.

If until the 1970s the international market for US Treasury debt still lacked the dynamism that it has displayed since, this should in large part be attributed to the fact that the conception of risk value embodied in the Bretton Woods Agreement showed clear signs of stress. This instability, which had its roots in the productivity decline and class antagonisms experienced by the US economy, partially depressed the capacity of the US Treasury debt to act as risk-free value. Thus, by the time that many of the conditions for the generalized expansion of foreign placed US Treasury securities were in place, the risk value of the US dollar showed a growing incongruence with the Bretton Woods standard. It was not until the late 1970s and early 1980s that the forces necessary for the explosion of the market would become fully aligned.

The development of the Yankee bond market after 1963 can be attributed, almost exclusively, to the IET's prejudicial classification of foreign investors. Two lasting exceptions were built into the framework of the IET: first, the tax did not apply to international institutions to which the United States was a member; second, investors from certain borrowing countries, most notably Canada and Mexico, were exempt from the regulations (Fisher 1979). Due to the liquidity of the US domestic market, these qualifications had the effect of sustaining the internationalization of the Yankee bond market between 1963 and 1974, after which the market enjoyed even greater prominence as the capital controls curtailing the participation of non-US borrowers were lifted. In 1974 foreign issues in the US market grew by 230 per cent to US$3.291 billion, outpacing growth in the Eurobond market which saw new issues slump to 1967 levels (Hays and Hubbard 1990). But this was more the result of fluctuations in short-term interest rates, and predictions that New York would reintegrate the Eurodollar bond market have proved to be off the mark. Between 1974 and 1978, the total value of capital raised in the Yankee bond market was US$33.4 billion, roughly US$16.6 billion less than new issue volume in the Euromarket. In important respects, the two markets remained segmented following the reversal of capital controls, appealing to different groups of international borrowers. After 1974 underwritings of borrowers previously distanced by IET stipulations continued to represent only a fraction of the total Yankee bond market through the mid- and late 1970s. Instead, issuers who were already integrated into the market continued to account for the majority of its size and growth: from 1974 to 1978, Canadian entities and international organizations represented between 60 per cent and 80 per cent of the overall market (Fisher 1979).

To summarize: even prior to the Volcker shock, the international securities marketplace was dynamic in form and function. The Eurobond market emerged to become a central source of internationalization and, in terms of growth and international connectivity, the most vibrant of the three central markets. Even if the Yankee bond market had also shown development through the 1970s and displayed a more complex global connectivity than it had in the 1960s, its place at the centre of internationalization was weakened. Finally, the US domestic securities market had slowly emerged from the late 1950s and 1960s onwards to become, in terms of total issue volume, the most significant international bond market. The international growth of this market came exclusively from the volume of US Treasury securities issued to foreign investors. Thus, this market depended on the removal of capital control programmes as well as sustained US balance of payments deficits. Following the Volcker shock, the foreign placement of US Treasury securities would expand in volume and the international arm of the US domestic market would be further extended by the removal of capital controls on US based corporations. While other markets would also expand in prominence, including the Samurai and Deutschmark market, the international primacy of the US domestic market, and specifically the Treasury bill market, would not be displaced.

The Volcker shock and after

During the early-to-mid-1970s the breakdown of the Bretton Woods system did not adversely affect America's position in the global financial system: fluctuations in the dollar did not amount to an attack on its fundamental value and the notion of risk value embedded in the post-war system continued to dictate financial flows. In part, this was helped along by the agreement between American and Arab officials to finance oil in US dollars. However, as the decade progressed, the American financial system and the dollar increasingly displayed symptoms of crisis. Global investors became less convinced that the Bretton Woods standard could cogently be applied to US financial flows. The 30 per cent decline in the value of the US dollar vis-à-vis the Deutschmark caused concern among American policy officials that the role envisioned for the US dollar under the floating rate system would be jeopardized unless action to restructure the idea of risk value was taken (Eichengreen 1996).

The appointment of Paul Volcker as Chair of the Federal Reserve Board in 1979 initiated a key turning point in the way these concerns were addressed. Opposing capital control programmes, Volcker's strategy was to impose strict limits on the annual growth of the money supply, giving priority to combating inflation and leaving the determination of interest rates to the market. His goal was to contract the domestic money supply in a way that compensated for the capacity of banks and multinational corporations to elude monetary restrictions by accessing offshore European markets (Helleiner 1994). Between the late 1970s and early 1980s, short-term US interest rates increased dramatically, reaching a high of 21.5 per cent. As a result, the US economy entered a severe recession in 1982 and inflation was brought to a halt. The Volcker shock can thus be seen as a unilateral attempt by the American state to maintain the post-war risk structure outside of the constraints of gold parity. The class realignment which followed sent a clear message to global investors that the US economy was not only open for business but capable of guaranteeing future value. Furthermore, the policies of Volcker and Reagan reshaped the power relations in global finance in a way that would allow for the spread and normalization of those policies.

The Volcker shock was a politically orchestrated attempt to maintain the risk value of the dollar previously enshrined in the Bretton Woods Agreement, by restructuring the American economy and financial system. Unlike Bretton Woods it did not attempt to redefine the concept of risk globally. In fact, it is doubtful that the Volcker shock could have generated the effects that it did if it had not sought to build upon the structural foundations previously laid by the Bretton Woods Agreement. The result of tight monetary policy and domestic neoliberal adjustment was to mend the chasm which had emerged during the 1970s between the Bretton Woods conception of value and US economic fundamentals. All of this meant that the US remained the dominant actor in foreign and offshore bond markets in terms of placements and currency denomination.

In the period following the Volcker shock, international bond placements grew exponentially, driven by growth in all of the market's primary segments. From 1980 to 1990, the total foreign ownership of US public debt securities increased from US$129.7 billion to US$458.4 billion (US Census Bureau 1989; US Department of the Treasury 1996). Republican tax policies and military expenditures – respectively aimed at neoliberal consolidation and the undermining of the Soviet Union – foddered federal budget deficits and fuelled growth in the US Treasury market. Further, the international arm of the US market received a boost from the globalization of US corporate securities: foreign purchases of US corporate bonds increased from $2.9 billion in 1980 to $39.8 billion in 1985 (US Census Bureau 1998). New issue volume in the Eurobond market was even more pronounced, increasing in volume from approximately US$18.8 billion in 1980 to over US$210 billion by the end of the decade (Hays and Hubbard 1990). The expansion of the Yankee bond market was more modest by comparison. The gross issue and placement of foreign bonds in the US domestic market grew from US$5.8 billion in 1978 to US$9.9 billion by 1990 (Fisher 1979).

The Volcker shock extended the risk free value of American Treasury debt, linking financial value to the credibility of the US Treasury and Federal Reserve. The appreciation of the dollar in the period between the Volcker shock and the Plaza Accord stimulated demand for US liabilities within the Eurobond market and the US domestic market leading to the overall expansion of these market segments (a trend that became even more fully apparent during the 1990s when the dollar was both strong and stable). Following the managed decline of the US dollar in the aftermath of the Plaza Accord, new bond issues initially moved away from dollar denomination and towards issues placed in other major currencies. In 1987 dollar denominated bonds fell to 37 per cent of the international total (from 55 per cent in 1986) while international bonds denominated in yen climbed from 10 per cent in 1986 to 15 per cent in 1987. In the same period, owing in part to currency instability, the Euromarket and the foreign bond market contracted somewhat and net annual foreign purchases of US corporate and Treasury securities declined from their highs in the mid-1980s. As the dollar gained strength near the end of the decade and interest rate differentials between the US and Japan grew, dollar denominated bonds regained their 50 per cent share of the international market and growth in the Euro and foreign bond markets 'recovered to their former peak level activity' (Das 1993: 11).

With the post-war value norms firmly in place, the US took steps to deepen internationalization by extending financial liberalization. While the US took important steps to liberalize capital flows in 1974 with the repeal of the IET, it was not until 1984 that the US removed the last of its significant capital controls on debt financing. The US relaxed the 4.25 per cent cap on interest payments for Treasury securities (Craven 1990), which laid the groundwork for the further expansion of the market. Moreover, the decision to remove the 30 per cent withholding tax on foreign purchases of non-public debt effectively facilitated the creation of a vast international market in US-placed corporate debt. In the past, US corporations had been forced to depend on foreign subsidiaries to access international capital and foreign investors were directed to US government securities (Grabbe 1996). This had stimulated offshore investment banking and added to the attractiveness of US Treasury debt but it had put limits on the internationalization of the bond market. Following liberalization, the incentive for US corporations to place securities offshore was largely removed and non-residents were given free access to both US corporate dollar bonds and government debt. Whereas in 1980 the foreign purchase of US-placed corporate bonds totalled US$2.9 billion, by 1985 this had grown to US$39.8 billion. After the contraction of the US market during the late 1980s resulted in a temporary decline in corporate bond placements, foreign purchases of US corporate debt expanded throughout the 1990s, reaching US$271.1 billion by 2003 (US Census Bureau 1998, 2004).

It was feared that the liberalization of the international market for US corporate debt would have an adverse impact on both the Eurobond market and the foreign branch of the US Treasury securities market. But in neither case have such concerns materialized. This can be explained by the changing shape of the regulatory environment outside of the US: the increased liberalization of global financial flows opened up new savings pools allowing investment financing to be a more important source of capital accumulation internationally. Following Japan's 1980 Foreign Exchange and Trade Control Law, which was viewed by US interests as a first step towards liberalization, the American state increasingly pressured other countries to undertake far-reaching liberalizing reforms (Pigeoon 2005). Access to Japanese capital was crucial as Japan had emerged as a major surplus nation by the beginning of the 1980s. The consequences of the opening up of the Japanese financial system were especially pronounced for the international bond market (Helleiner 1994).

By the start of the 1990s, the international bond market had established itself as central to the functioning of neoliberal globalization and it continued to grow apace due to the operations of institutional investors and speculators. Issue volume broke all previous records. In many ways, the groundwork for this expansion was laid by prior transformations. OECD figures report that the Eurobond market grew from US$180.1 billion in 1990 to US$735.1 billion by the end of 1997 (OECD 1992, 1998a).[4] During the same period, gross foreign bond placements nearly doubled from US$49.8 billion to US$96.5 billion. On the eve of the Asian financial crisis, the market for foreign bond placements achieved a record US$119 billion in annual gross issues. Despite a temporary decline in foreign Treasury sales commensurate with federal budgetary surpluses, internationalization was strengthened by the foreign branch of the US domestic market. In 1990 total foreign ownership of US Treasury debt by private investors amounted to US$458.4 billion or 20 per cent of outstanding public debt securities. By 1999 foreign investors held US$1.2687 trillion in Treasury debt, nearly 40 per cent of the entire US public market (US Department of the Treasury 1996, 2005). Annual foreign purchases of US corporate bonds increased from US$9.7 billion in 1990 to US$160.4 billion by 1999, a net growth of 1,653 per cent (US Census Bureau 1998, 2004).

The dynamism that characterized the 1990s was due not only to the continued growth in traditional placements, but also to the development of the global bond market. Global bonds are securities simultaneously issued in the US, Europe and Asia by a network of investment banks, meaning that they are Eurobonds that are issued immediately both in the US market and/or the market in which the issue is denominated (Amira and Handorf 2004). First unveiled in October 1989 with a US$1.5 billion offering by the World Bank, global bonds expand on the institutional framework which underlies the other segments of the international market as internationally oriented investment dealers provide the global reach and structure which ultimately bring these issues to market. As investment capital must be capable of moving internationally in order for the global bond market to function, its development required the prior liberalization and internationalization of financial markets.

In the face of a hospitable investment climate, the global bond market thrived through the 1990s, growing apace with the other segments of the international market (Amira and Handorf 2004). From 1990 to 2000, the dollar value of funds raised increased annually at a cumulative rate of nearly 45 per cent, reaching an aggregate total of US$1.634 trillion. In spite of momentary declines following the US recession in the early 1990s and the Asian and Brazilian financial crises near the end of the decade, issue volume on the global bond market grew annually at approximately 40 per cent in the same period. By 2000 a total of 2,568 global bonds, denominated in 22 different currencies, had been successfully issued to international investors. Despite this variety, the global bond market has developed as a US dollar market, following the tendency of other international markets to issue along lines of global risk value. At the end of 2000, dollar denominated placements accounted for 86.1 per cent of all global bonds issued. At 3.48 per cent of the market share, Euro denominated debt ranked a distant second in popularity. This means that bond issuers generally use global placements to raise US capital and realize international risk value.

The derivative era

There are a number of explanations which account for the growth of international bond issues in the 1990s. In good part, the proliferation of asset-backed securities (ABS) has been especially important here. Securitized bonds are financial instruments created through the bundling of traditional bank loans. The obligations tied to ABSs are funded through cash flows linked to the underlying assets with the banking institution acting as a financial conduit for the flow of funds. In response to diminishing returns on traditional services, banks have used securitization to reconfigure their liabilities and restructure their balance sheets (Mailander 1997/1998: 377). ABSs transfer risk and allow major banking institutions to deepen their participation in world debt markets. Through the mid- and late 1990s, the global market for asset-backed securities grew by about 36 per cent annually, reaching a total capitalization of US$484 billion in 1997 (Davies 1998).

Moreover, the expansion of global bond markets has been accompanied by the explosion of financial derivative contracts. Derivatives serve to render asset values commensurable across space (Lipuma and Lee 2004) and in that sense they can be said to represent a new form of capitalist money. This point is made especially well by Bryan and Rafferty (2005: 35–7), who argue that derivatives 'turn the contestability of fundamental value into a tradable commodity ... [by providing] a market benchmark for an unknowable value' and thereby create 'a means to compare all sorts of capital – a universal measure of value'. However, it is important to stress that the benchmarking and commensurability function provided by derivative contracts is not neutral in nature. Bryan and Rafferty still rely too much on the understanding of market risk/trust employed by neoclassical economics and so perpetuate to some degree the conceptual dichotomy between the nation-state and global money. But the abstract form of derivative contracts precisely serves to naturalize the particular constructions of risk value that underlie them. Derivatives may provide a 'universal measure of value', but the commensuration process is informed by nationally centred inequalities in contestability. As such, derivative money is shot through with historically grown conceptions of what constitutes legitimate and secure financial claims. The obscure world of currency and interest rate embodies the norms of the structure of US risk value.

There exists a strong mutual dependency between derivatives and bonds. Issuance placement and trading activity on international bond markets has been directly impacted by the development and vigorous expansion of financial swaps. International bonds subject investors to interest rate and currency volatility. Concerns as regards changes in currency levels and interest rates have traditionally served to reduce market dynamism – making investment in, for instance, bonds denominated in non-preferred currencies too risky. But now investors can swap floating and fixed rate obligations to obtain a risk structure that more fully matches their perception of market direction or their risk preference. By providing investors with the opportunity to transfer forms of interest rate and currency risk, swap markets reduce many of the risks associated with international bond markets. Currency swaps permit investors 'to hedge the principle and interest payments in the currency of issue against a currency preferred', while interest rate swaps enable borrowers 'to arbitrage differences between the component markets of the international bond market' (Mailander 1997/1998: 358). Thus, in controlling for cost and short-term risk, swaps have made international bond markets more attractive as outlets for global investment.

What are known in the markets as 'flavoured' and 'plain vanilla' derivative contracts have modified the relationship between risk and issue placement, but US value continues to inform financial transactions. The norms reified in US debt instruments still order the perception of international financial value in such a way that market actors base their investment decisions on the risk value of US instruments/markets. The US state and capital have been the main driving forces in the process of bond market internationalization during the post-Volcker period since 1980 just as much as they were in the post-war Bretton Woods period. The profound dynamism and steady expansion of the international bond market throughout both periods are often masked by conventional differentiations between Keynesian and neoliberal moments of finance – something that can be avoided once we perceive, as this chapter has argued, that the financial norms, knowledge and innovations underlying this dynamism and expansion cannot be understood except in terms of their relation to the structural power of the American state.

Risk value in crisis?

The 2007 credit crisis – in which asset-backed derivatives have played such a central part – has starkly raised the question of whether this system could finally be coming unstuck. Among the various dimensions of the crisis, one of the major problems in American securities markets has concerned structured investment vehicles. SIVs are investment conduits organized and managed by banks but treated as separate entities because they fund their debt independently. SIVs can be conceptualized as virtual companies; they purchase bonds, usually asset-banked securities, and finance this debt by issuing money market securities at low interest rates. Like banks, SIVs generate capital through interest rate arbitrage – profiting off the spread between short- and long-term capital – and rely on very high rating for their senior debt. Beginning in August 2007, the capital notes issued by structured investment vehicles became illiquid due to concerns about the class of debt that supports these issues; financial consumers basically lost faith that the long-term assets held by SIVs were sufficiently safe and caused an overall decline in outstanding asset-backed commercial paper that reverberated through the global financial community. The unwinding of the market for asset-backed commercial paper together with the broader crisis in structured credit has been financially significant and will likely leave questions about the assessments published by bond rating firms. For the time being, moreover, the subprime crisis may impact negatively on the demand for US greenbacks and produce the type of mini-retreat from US assets witnessed in the 1980s. But while financial turmoil has not remained contained within specific sectors, the crisis is unlikely to produce a fundamental threat to the risk value of US corporate finance.

Above all, the continuation of the Treasury standard cannot be understood apart from the role of the American state in managing US global credibility. Shortly after the credit crunch began the Treasury coordinated private capital to reshape perceptions and conceptions of risk in the asset-backed securities market in order to complement the liquidity providing operations ongoing at the Federal Reserve. The rescue plan spearheaded by Secretary Paulson and Under-Secretary Steel employed the Treasury's convening power to coordinate private sector actors with the goal of creating a super conduit (the Master Liquidity Enhancement Conduit – M-LEC) aimed at repackaging SIV debt and sponsoring new capital paper. At separate meetings in September and October, Treasury officials applied pressure for a timely and coordinated resolution which would amend the securitized debt market over the long term (Bawden and Hosking 2007). The process of restructuring risk is more complicated than providing liquidity to financial markets; which is to say that the response from US regulators has been, if historically consistent, institutionally unorthodox. To different degrees, this has been the basic recipe for remarketing and repricing financial commodities decimated by modern financial crisis in sophisticated markets. The forced conversion of Mexican tesbonos from peso to dollar denominated debt in 1994 offered one very clear illustration of this type of financial medicine: by compelling the Mexican government to change the basis of risk attached to tesbonos, US authorities were able to offer protection to speculators, effectively revaluing instruments that previously were worthless.

The important point is not that the M-LEC did not itself succeed or even become fully operational. As was the case in 1998 when the hedge fund Long Term Capital Management unravelled due to global currency mismatches following the Russian financial crisis, the US Treasury and Fed have shown a willingness to do what is required to protect the privileged position of the US capital markets. In the end this will be needed in greater measure, but especially if the Treasury's most recent interlude into American financial market value is viewed as a harbinger of further interventions which would of necessity put the full faith, security and power of the US state behind Wall Street's general functionality, this is very likely to work not only to secure American risk value but to further strengthen the risk credibility of American financial markets in the wake of the current crisis.

As for recent pressure on US dollar value, the current decline can be traced to the beginning of 2006 and is, in good part, reflective of the strength of the dollar following 2002. What is more, the decline has occurred alongside strong international demand for US dollar bonds: while the share of international bonds and notes denominated in dollars has fallen behind the Euro since 2003 in terms of annual gross issuance (as of June 2007 47 per cent of outstanding issues were denominated in Euros compared to only 36 per cent in dollars), the demand for dollar denominated international debt has been remarkably stable since 1999 (BIS 2007). More important, foreigners have continued to support inflation in US federal securities, with international ownership of US federal securities reaching US$2,036 billion at the end of 2005 and a record US$2,220 billion in June 2007 (US Department of the Treasury 2007). What has foremost precipitated the demand for alternative currencies following August has been international interest rate differentials, including the prediction of future cuts in US federal funds. Given the importance of American consumption and the overall centricity of the US economy, with a slowdown of the US economy surely precipitating a decrease in global growth and inflation, this type of interest rate disjuncture is more likely to be a short-term feature.

While the subprime collapse has surely impacted the psyche of financial markets, burdening the substantive financial validity of important market segments, the templates that have underpinned global risk since the beginning of the Bretton Woods period do not appear to be seriously in danger. The specificities of the credit crisis as it relates to international bonds are such that while US commercial and investment banks have suffered significant monetary losses, global market makers are unlikely to question the patterns of security risk attached to Wall Street in general. In good part, this is because the types of securitized assets that were widely abandoned following the unexpected appreciation of subprime delinquencies are sufficiently disconnected from the nervous system of American finance; which is to say that the collapse of counter-party risk in the market for asset-backed commercial paper has nowhere meant that global financial actors are questioning the long-term credibility of America's most prominent financial outfits. So far, the gains made by the Euro not only in 2007 but following 2003, have not overturned the strong international demand for US federal debt. Once we understand that the conditions of existence of substantive validity are volatile global markets and the social relations they mediate, annual expressions of value over the short term become meaningful only in the context of wider historical mappings. This does not guarantee the perpetuation of US risk value – the construction of financial validity remains a contingent historical process – but it does suggest the need for sober and circumspect readings of the implications of the financial crises that attend global capitalism.

Notes

1. A few important studies have taken this up, including *International Financial Markets* (Grabbe 1996), *The Eurodollar Bond Market* (Fisher, 1979) and *States and the Reemergence of Global Finance* (Helleiner [1994] pbk 1996), but they barely touch on the actual development of the international bond market.
2. Domestic placements are internationally classified only when two criteria are met: first, at least part of the investment syndicate supporting the placement must be internationally organized; and second, foreign members of the syndicate must hold the issue or distribute it to investors domestic to their country of origin. American Treasury bills issued internationally are by far the most important constituent in this market segment. A foreign bond is a debt security issued and traded by a foreign company or government in a jurisdiction outside its domestic market. Foreign bonds are usually denominated in the currency of the jurisdiction they are issued in and are labelled according to their place of issue. A bond issued by a Japanese company in the United States in US dollars would be titled a Yankee bond, while a bond issued by a US company in Japan and denominated in yen would be classified as a Samurai bond. Each issue is subject to the discipline of the securities regulator of the country of issue and distributed according to domestic bond standards.
3. Because Regulation Q did not apply to offshore interest payments on dollar deposits, it became possible for the Eurocurrency market to create disequilibrium in US domestic interest rates.
4. Reflecting different statistical measures, according to the ISMA, issue placements in the Eurobond market grew from US$160 billion in 1992 to nearly US$700 billion by the end of the decade (Clark 2002).

7
Towards the Americanization of European Finance? The Case of Finance-Led Accumulation in Germany

Thomas Sablowski

The German financial system has often been described as a bank-based system – to be contrasted with the market-based systems of the United States or Great Britain. Social scientists have conceived this bank-based financial system as a cornerstone of the so-called 'model Germany'. In the past, it had often been admired by external observers because the long-term relations between banks and industrial firms and the prevalence of 'patient capital' not oriented towards short-term profit maximization seemed to be the basis for competitive strategies focused on innovation and product quality, enabling high growth rates and a top position in the international division of labour (see Zysman 1983; Edwards and Fischer 1994; Deeg 1999). Even during the 1970s and 1980s, when the exhaustion of the Fordist regime of accumulation became apparent and the pressure for restructuring mounted, Germany seemed to do relatively well in comparison to the Anglo-Saxon countries. The 'intellectual and moral turnaround' announced by the Christian-Democratic Chancellor Helmut Kohl in March 1983 did not immediately bring such radical change as 'Thatcherism' in Britain or 'Reaganomics' in the USA. Many observers stressed the continuity of 'model Germany'.

However, after the collapse of 'really existing socialism' and the crisis of the early 1990s the situation changed. In the US neoliberal restructuring seemed to pay off in the rise of the 'New Economy' while in Germany growth rates further declined and unemployment increased. At this juncture, the relatively underdeveloped state of German financial markets came to be seen as a competitive disadvantage by politicians and economists at home and abroad. The Kohl government introduced a number of laws aimed at strengthening the German capital market, and this policy was continued by the 'red-green' government of Gerhard Schröder, as well as the 'grand coalition' of Angela Merkel. Beneath the legislative level, moreover, a multitude of processes have contributed to fundamentally change the systems of finance and corporate

governance in Germany. The traditional, relatively 'cosy' financial environment for banks has altered dramatically. As Bernd Fahrholz, the former CEO
of Dresdner Bank, Germany's third largest bank, put it: 'no stone has been
left unturned' (cited in Hackethal 2004: 71).

There is little agreement among social scientists about the consequences
of these changes. Some still stress the continuities of 'coordinated' or
'Rhineland' capitalism (e.g. Vitols 2004) while others emphasize the rup-
tures (e.g. Lane 2003). But almost all such assessments limit themselves to
descriptions of the changes and continuities in German capitalism and often
give no clear account of the driving forces of this change and continuity.
Often 'globalization' is presupposed as the driving force of change (treated
like a *deus ex machina*)[1] while the rather ambiguous and somewhat tautolog-
ical concept of 'path dependency'[2] serves to explain continuities. I share the
view that a transition from a bank-based system to a market-based system
is on the way in Germany. This trend, I argue, is likely to continue despite
the bursting of the stock market bubble in 2000–2 and the current financial crisis because there are more fundamental driving forces at work. The
transition to a market-based financial system is not confined to Germany.
It is taking place in other developed capitalist countries as well. I want to
argue in this chapter that it has to be explained in relation to the long-run
tendencies of capital accumulation, especially as these dynamics are shaped
by the restructuring of American capitalism and the changing policies and
capacities of the American state. American capital markets serve as a model
for the restructuring of the German financial system and American firms and
financial investors are important actors in the German financial system. We
can talk about Americanization to the extent that the US still incarnates the
most advanced state of capitalist development: the more developed shows
to the less developed the image of its own future, as Marx (1990: 91) once
put it.

The relation between industrial capital and financial capital

To properly address the relation of the financial system to capital accumulation, it is necessary to clarify the concepts of industrial and financial capital,
not least because they are often used with different meanings even within the
Marxist tradition. Marx showed that under the capitalist mode of production
all forms of capital are ultimately related to the exploitation of labour and
the appropriation of surplus value in the process of production. However,
as potential capital, money itself becomes a commodity. More precisely, the
potential function of money as capital is 'sold' only for a certain time; money
is lent. Interest is the 'price' the borrower has to pay for the potential capital
(in mainstream economics referred to as 'cost of capital'). The payment of
interest presupposes that potential capital is really converted into productive
functioning capital, because the interest ultimately has to be paid out of the

surplus value produced by industrial capital. To put it differently, industrial profit is divided into interest paid to the lender and business profit remaining in the hands of the productive functioning capitalist.

The division between interest and business profit becomes a basis for capitalist calculation even if a productive capitalist uses only equity capital and no outside capital. Interest appears to be the fruit of the mere ownership of capital, while business profit appears to be the fruit of the activity of the productive capitalist. So the opposition between the owner of money and the productive businessman overlays and disarticulates the opposition between labour and capital. Moreover, Marx called interest-bearing capital the most fetish-like form of capital because it appears to presuppose no production at all. Or to put it differently, money seems to have the immediate capability to produce more money. Similarly, regular money revenues can appear to be the interest on a capital, even if they do not arise from a real capital valorized through the exploitation of labour (cf. Marx and Engels, *Werke*, various years, Vol. 25: 482). This observation leads Marx to introduce the concept of *fictitious capital*. Bonds, shares and other forms of securities can be regarded as fictitious capital because they represent merely legal claims on future revenues. As these claims can be bought and sold, they seem to have a value on their own and represent capital independently from real capital.

The forms of interest-bearing capital and fictitious capital together constitute financial capital, as opposed to industrial capital (cf. Guttmann 1994: 37ff.).[3] The relation between industrial capital and financial capital is generally contradictory. On the one hand, financial capital contributes to the expanded reproduction of industrial capital. With the development of credit money, the investment fund for capital accumulation is no longer confined to previously realized surplus value. In other words, the expansion of credit relations is shifting the limits to capital accumulation, allowing the expanded reproduction of industrial capital to occur on an ever larger scale. On the other hand, as an *ex ante* validation or pseudo-validation of social labour, credit cannot be expanded without limits (see Lipietz 1985). The development of credit money is accompanied by its own forms of structural crisis: creeping inflation expresses the precarious relation between credit money and social labour. The systemic insecurity is expressed in credit risks and financial instability. Furthermore, the accumulation of financial capital relies on a redistribution of income that is produced in the circuit of industrial capital. There are also contradictions between the different forms of financial capital. For instance, a corporation's operating profit, its return on equity and the earnings per share can be increased by running into more debt, increasing leverage. However, dividends can only be paid from the net profit after interest payments. The higher the interest payments are the lower is the share of the profit that can be distributed to shareholders or accumulated in the corporation. Thus, the expanded reproduction of capital can be accompanied by an expanded reproduction of the contradictions between financial and industrial capital.

Although the forms of capital discussed so far should not be identified with concrete actors, they nonetheless tend to give rise to different interests, allowing for an analysis of the contradictory relations between different capitalist class fractions. Hilferding, writing in an era when German and Austrian bank capital played a leading role within the industrialization processes of these countries, coined the concept of 'finance capital', a relatively unified form of capital that he saw as emerging from the merger of industrial capital and bank capital under the dominance of the latter. This concept was popularized by Lenin and became enormously influential in Marxist theory and communist politics. However, it was also deeply problematic. The unitary concept of finance capital closed the space for an analysis of the contradictions between the different functional forms and fractions of capital. First, credit relations constitute a real division in society between creditors and debtors. Banks and industrial firms often both act as creditors and debtors at the same time, but it is still important to take into consideration the different interests and contradictions that arise from these functions. Second, in the contradictory relationship between creditors and debtors or between banks and industry there is interdependence and not just a one-sided dependence. Industrial firms depend on the banks' credit supply, but banks depend also on industrial firms' credit demand (cf. Sandleben 2003: 32ff.). Third, the emphasis on how banks establish close links with industrial firms through long-term investments in capital ties and supervisory board mandates to monitor their development ignores the evidence that banks can also have a strong interest in avoiding close relations with industrial firms and to seek more liquid and mobile alternatives (cf. Guttmann 1994: 40f.). Even in Hilferding's time the relations between banks and industry varied substantially across countries.

In the late 1960s and 1970s, Nicos Poulantzas tried to develop a theoretical framework for the analysis of political processes in which the contradictions within capital and the bourgeoisie played a central role. He argued that the 'merger' of banking capital and industrial capital 'that gives rise to finance capital is, beneath its legal appearance, a divergent and contradictory process; finance capital is not an integrated capital, but refers to the mode of functioning of the capitalist fractions in their growing interdependence, and to the relations between them in this process'. And while he insisted that throughout capitalism's history 'the reproduction of total social capital is determined by the cycle of productive capital, which alone produces surplus value', he also pointed out that 'this does not directly indicate which fraction of capital...plays the dominant role in the economy, and, according to the conjuncture, enjoys political hegemony' (Poulantzas 1975: 130–2). Thus, Poulantzas brought back a conceptual complexity to Marxist analysis that had been destroyed through the notion of finance capital as a unified entity, dominated by banking capital.

The changing regime of accumulation and the transformation of the financial system

The long-run development of capitalism has been characterized by an ever more comprehensive development of credit relations. The securitization of credits, the development of interest rate derivatives and credit derivatives indicate a growing socialization of credit risks and enable further growth of the credit system. In this sense the development of financial markets is not accidental or conjunctural but rather an essential aspect of capitalist growth. This is something that critical accounts of globalization tend to overlook. Critical scholars often attribute the enormous growth of financial markets since the 1970s to the crisis of Fordism and the over-accumulation of capital. To some extent this is certainly correct. When the profitability of industrial capital declined in the 1970s, the owners of money capital began to search for other investment opportunities. This increased the pressure to deregulate and liberalize financial markets. Furthermore, the breakdown of the Bretton Woods system, the shift towards flexible exchange rates and the increasing competition between key currencies led to an enormous expansion of currency markets. The growing volatility of exchange rates meant that the demand for safeguarding against currency risks also increased, leading to the development of currency derivatives. The development of currency derivatives in turn implied new opportunities for speculation. When controls of capital movements were abolished and national financial markets were deregulated in the 1980s, further sources of instability were introduced into the system. All in all, with the development of financial markets the investment opportunities for money capital were enlarged significantly.[4] However, 'big' structural crises like the crisis of Fordism and 'smaller' crises like the recent burst of the stock market and housing bubbles[5] are precisely the forms through which the long-run trends of capitalist accumulation and the expansion of financial markets develop. This includes the possibility of short- and medium-term setbacks. There is of course no linear development of these trends.

How can the expanded reproduction of capital take place in the medium and long run, given its internal contradictions? In order to understand this, we need to draw on the conceptual apparatus developed by the French Regulation School (see Aglietta 1979; Lipietz 1985, 1987; Boyer 1990), above all their distinctions between regimes of extensive versus intensive accumulation, extroverted versus introverted accumulation, and accumulation dominated by industrial capital versus accumulation dominated by financial capital (modified from Becker 2002: 64–77). This helps us to see that accumulation has historically taken place in different forms. A regime of accumulation is not a self-reproducing entity. It is shaped by the strategies of a multitude of actors facing the constraints and contradictions emerging from capitalist social relations. It depends upon the political compromises resulting from the shifting balance of forces in social struggles. Institutional forms of regulation can be complementary and coherent and thus support a regime of accumulation; but they can also be subverted by the dynamics of accumulation and prove to be dysfunctional.

We can distinguish between regimes of predominantly *extensive* accumulation and predominantly *intensive* accumulation. Extensive accumulation is based on the production of surplus value through the expansion of the number of wage labourers or through the extension of their labour time (absolute surplus value). Intensive accumulation is based on the production of relative surplus value through the parallel transformation of the labour process and the wage labourers' way of life. Extensive accumulation is limited by the number of potential workers, the physical limits of the extension of labour time, as well as the continued presence of non-capitalist forms of production (that is, extensive accumulation works through the destruction of non-capitalist forms of production). The limits of intensive accumulation are less obvious than the limits of extensive accumulation. Intensive accumulation depends first on rises in labour productivity through the introduction of new technologies and changes in the organization of work. Secondly, it depends on the formation of a norm of consumption for wage labourers: real wages and consumption have to grow more or less in line with the increase in labour productivity or else the tendency towards overproduction is reinforced.

The advent of Fordist methods of production effected a shift away from the regime of extensive accumulation that had prevailed until the early twentieth century towards a regime of predominantly intensive accumulation based on the parallel development of mass production and mass consumption that became the basis of expanded reproduction during the post-Second World War 'golden age' of capitalism. However, with the slowdown in productivity increases (see Glyn et al. 1990: 44), the crisis of Fordism in the 1970s and the subsequent turn to neoliberal policies, extensive accumulation has become more important once again. The share of wages in the GDP has declined in the EU since the mid-1970s (see Huffschmid 2002: 143) and privatization policies are opening up new areas for capital accumulation. At the level of the world economy as a whole the process of destruction of non-capitalist forms of production has experienced a big push forward with the collapse of 'really existing socialism' and the processes of globalization.

Indeed, the limits of accumulation appear different when we look at the level of the world economy as a whole or when we look at single spaces of accumulation within the world economy like nation-states or regions. A barrier to accumulation within the borders of a nation-state can be overcome through the internationalization of capital. For the world economy as a whole this is not possible. The internationalization of capital is shifting the limits of accumulation that exist within a national or regional space. This is an aspect of what David Harvey (1982: chapter 13) has called a 'spatial fix'.

Thus, the regime of accumulation within a nation-state or a region can be more or less *extroverted* or *introverted*.

The development of capitalism in Germany in the present period is characterized by a pattern of increasingly extroverted accumulation. The export orientation has always been strong in Germany. However, the link between export-oriented development and development of the internal market which characterized German capitalism during the Fordist period has become precarious. In line with the resurgence of extensive accumulation strategies under neoliberalism, it seems that the tremendous export success of German firms is increasingly based on wage and investment restraint. German exports increased in relation to GDP from 22 per cent in 1970 to 40 per cent in 2005, while the share of investment in GDP declined in the same period from 29 per cent to 17 per cent. Wages lag behind productivity: while the index of gross value added at current prices per hour worked increased from 1 in 1996 to 1.42 in 2005 in the German manufacturing industry, the index of compensation per employee hour worked increased only from 1 to 1.23 in the same period. This means that the index of real unit wage costs per employee hour worked declined in that period from 1 to 0.87 (my own calculations based on figures of the *Statistisches Bundesamt*).

This can only be understood, however, in combination with the shift from accumulation dominated by industrial capital to accumulation dominated by financial capital. As I said before, this shift cannot be attributed only to the crisis of Fordism and the instability inherent to capitalist globalization. The growing importance of market finance is also a secular moment of capitalist development. Global financial markets represent a higher development of the credit system. Securitization and the development of new financial instruments like credit derivatives are not only necessary as an 'insurance' against risks in an increasingly unstable and volatile international economy, they are also difficult to reverse because they serve to overcome barriers to capital accumulation inherent to former regimes of accumulation. Even during the Fordist 'golden age' the reconstruction of the world economy and the further development of credit money and financial markets took place (see Panitch and Gindin, this volume). The crisis of Fordism only accelerated these developments. Thus, the development of global financial markets transforms the regime of accumulation: the accumulation of financial capital tends to grow faster than the accumulation of industrial capital; and fictitious capital tends to grow faster than ordinary credit. This is illustrated by Figure 7.1, which shows the development of private credits, bond market capitalization and stock market capitalization in relation to the GDP in Germany since 1990.

The relative decline of private bond market capitalization in Germany since the year 2000 seems to contradict my thesis at first sight. However, this does not signify that bond financing has become less important for German firms. Bond financing takes place at an international level. While bond market

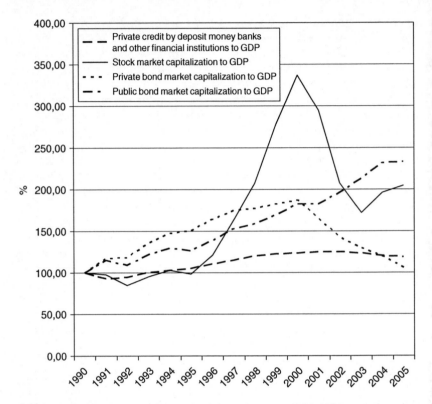

Figure 7.1 The structure of the German financial system, 1990–2005
Source: World Bank, Financial Structure Database.

capitalization in relation to GDP has stagnated in Germany, France, Japan and the UK, it has steadily increased in the USA (Figure 7.2). It seems that private bond financing has become concentrated more and more in the US. European and Japanese firms are using the American bond market as well, because it is still the most liquid market. Emission volumes are much higher in the American capital market.

With regard to the increased importance of the stock market, Germany is no exception. If we compare the development of stock market capitalization in relation to GDP in the US, Japan, Germany, France and Great Britain, we see the same characteristic development.[6] That the stock market capitalization was and still is lower in Germany and in France than in the US and Great Britain corresponds to the expectations bred by the discourse on the 'varieties of capitalism'. However, the developmental tendency is the same in the major economies (Figure 7.3).

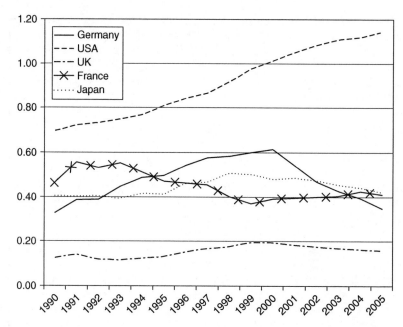

Figure 7.2 Private bond market capitalization in relation to GDP, 1990–2005
Source: World Bank, Financial Structure Database.

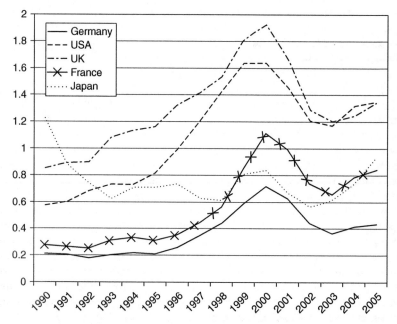

Figure 7.3 Stock market capitalization in relation to GDP, 1990–2005
Source: World Bank, Financial Structure Database.

It is not just a *quantitative* shift which is taking place in the relation between industrial capital, interest-bearing capital and fictitious capital. Capitalist relations of production are *qualitatively* transformed because new forms of institutional ownership of capital develop in this process. This transformation is described by the concept of finance-led accumulation or accumulation dominated by financial capital.

The transformation of the German accumulation regime

Capital markets have become more and more important for big firms in the last decades. What started in the US in the 1980s with the wave of leveraged buy-outs and the introduction of shareholder value concepts spread to European countries after the economic crisis of the early 1990s. While the reasons for the proliferation of the shareholder value orientation and the increasing importance of the capital market are manifold at first sight, we first of all have to take into account *changes in the structure of ownership*, namely the rise of institutional investors as powerful agencies of the centralization of money capital. These institutional investors usually are not 'patient' shareholders but aim at short-term profit maximization. Shareholder involvement and activism ('voice') becomes the exception, and the threat to sell a company's stock if it fails to deliver the expected return ('exit') becomes an increasingly important means to exert pressure on corporate managers. In order to prevent a hostile takeover, publicly traded companies have to keep their share price as high as possible. Indeed, giant corporations increasingly use their stock as a takeover currency (that is, mergers and acquisitions (M&A) often involve the exchange of stock). The *function of the stock market as a market for corporate control* has become more important because national oligopolies have been broken open with the crisis of Fordism and the growing internationalization of capital. Competition in product markets has intensified, giving rise to waves of mergers and acquisitions. As a consequence, international oligopolies are developing.

The *financing function of the stock market* generally plays a secondary role for established companies. Self-financing through accumulated profits and credit-financing via loans or bonds is more important in quantitative terms than raising new capital in the stock market. Taking on debt or issuing new shares produces new claims on the future profits of a company. Thus, in contrast to self-financing, it might restrict managerial discretionary powers. Furthermore, the issue of new shares has the effect of diluting the shares of previous owners if the latter are not willing or able to participate in the increase of capital. Especially owner families and other major shareholders are often reluctant to agree to increases of capital because they increase the likelihood of a hostile takeover. So, there might indeed be a hierarchy of preferred forms of financing, with self-financing at the top, followed by less risky forms of debt, more risky forms of debt and increases of share capital (Myers and Majluf 1984). Even if financing through increases of share capital is not as important as is often thought, the share price is indirectly connected with the company's self-financing capacity and its access to credit as it influences shareholders' dividend demands (i.e. high capital gains allow for lower dividend pay-outs) as well as the monitoring of the company by analysts (which determines a company's access to external credit).

Comparing the second half of the 1970s and the first half of the 1990s, Huffschmid (2002: 27ff.) has shown that, due to the increase of profits since the 1980s and the comparatively slower growth of investment, companies' demand for external finance has declined in relation to self-financing in the G7 countries. But while self-financing has remained the most important form of financing, we have to differentiate between small and medium-sized companies on the one hand and large companies on the other hand. For large companies, financing through the capital market is especially important: they can take on more debt through capital markets than they ever could through ordinary bank credit. By exploiting the opportunities opened up by international capital markets, industrial companies have also become more independent from banks. That is why the development of international financial markets is not only fostered by banks or institutional investors but also by industrial firms.[7]

Since the 1970s a so-called disintermediation has taken place. Banks reacted to the relative decline of their traditional business by expanding their activities in the capital market which became more and more profitable during the 1980s and 1990s. Investment banking became more attractive than commercial banking for different reasons. First, the restructuring of industrial capital was mediated through the capital market. In the US it was driven by a wave of hostile takeovers and leveraged buy-outs during the 1980s. Banks participated in the financing of these activities with high yield bonds ('junk bonds'). These takeovers seemed to be especially lucrative where the market value of the targeted companies had fallen below their book value, as had happened in a number of cases during the crisis. Conglomerates were crushed, and their parts were either closed down or restructured and sold with a profit to other companies or to investors via the stock market. Another wave of mergers and acquisitions was fostered by the stock market bubble of the late 1990s. During these waves of centralization of capital, advising on M&A became the most important and profitable branch of investment banking.

Nor was it only large industrial firms that used the advantages of direct access to financial markets; savers also realized that they could earn higher interests by investing their money in securities instead of savings deposits on ordinary bank accounts. Moreover, privatization in many countries offered another lucrative business for investment banks organizing the initial public offerings (IPOs) of formerly state-owned enterprises.[8] The fiscal crises of states and their growing indebtedness in general provided great business opportunities for banks acting as intermediaries between states and investors.

Furthermore, asset management had become more important with the accumulation of middle-class savings since the Fordist 'golden age' and with the growing income inequality under neoliberalism. Last but not least, the 'New Economy' bubble in the late 1990s fuelled the IPO business.

The move towards investment banking changed the structures of financial systems in many countries. In the US, the big commercial banks tried successfully to circumvent the legal separation between commercial banking and investment banking that had been instituted after the Great Depression in the 1930s with the Glass-Steagall Act. The division between commercial and investment banking became more and more blurred, and ultimately the separation was also abolished legally. Because the biggest commercial banks like City Group, Chase Manhattan Bank or the Bank of America were much bigger than most investment banks, the former could easily take over the latter.

In Germany, where legal restrictions on banking like those in the US had never existed, the shift towards investment banking nevertheless caused a rupture of the traditional relations between banks and industry. Close relationships and interlocking directorates between the big private banks and the major industrial companies can be traced back to the time when the German nation-state was founded during the war of 1870–1 against France and industrialization took off in Germany. Compared to other countries, the national market had developed late, and it was difficult to mobilize enough capital for the development of the new heavy industry at a time when capitalism's centre of gravity had already shifted from textiles to railways and other sectors. The foundation of private universal banks like Deutsche Bank (1870), Commerzbank (1870) and Dresdner Bank (1872) solved this problem of German industry. Whereas industrialization in the UK and the US was dominated by self-financing entrepreneur families and the successive enlargement of the capital base via the distribution of shares, credit financing in Germany was important from the very beginning.[9] The business model of the new universal banks turned out to be a big success. At the beginning of the First World War, German banks were among the biggest in the world.

These banks acted as 'patient shareholders' providing long-term finance and a certain investment security for industrial firms. Because the banks had been acting primarily as creditors for the industrial firms, their interest in monitoring their clients closely could be realized best through controlling shares and supervisory board mandates to the end of their long-run profitable development. And because the banks had close relations to many industrial firms, they also had an interest in regulating competition among their clients. So they actively promoted the development of cartels, which were destroyed in Germany only after the Second World War. In the US, antitrust policy meant that cartels were dissolved early, and the concentration and centralization of capital had to find other channels, primarily through vertical integration and later through diversification. Unlike in the US (after banking regulation introduced during the New Deal), in Germany universal banks were always allowed to be active in commercial banking and investment banking alike, but as they drew their profits mainly from ordinary credit relations they had relatively little interest in the type of investment banking that developed in the US. Until the 1980s neither German banks nor German industry seemed to have much interest in that aspect of the capital market. Indeed, due to the processes of concentration and centralization of capital, the number of corporations listed at the German stock exchange declined from 636 in 1963 to 436 in 1983 (Beyer 2003: 124).

However, the profitability of the ordinary credit business declined during the 1970s and 1980s as financial markets began to expand rapidly. In this context, investment banking became more attractive for the German banks, too. As they had little experience in this business, they had to acquire British or American investment banks to become important players in this field. With the shift towards investment banking, the close relationships with certain industrial firms became an obstacle for the German banks. Specifically, if banks want to arrange mergers and acquisitions, including hostile takeovers, they need the trust of their customers and a solid reputation. Ties with specific industrial firms might then easily cause conflicts of interest between the bank's roles as consultant and owner.

That is why the big banks, led by the Deutsche Bank since the beginning of the 1990s, started to retreat from their former relationships with single industrial companies. The number of interlocking directorates declined, and capital ties began to dissolve. For instance, in 1980 directors of Deutsche Bank, the biggest German bank, had supervisory board mandates in 40 of the 100 largest German firms. By 1998, this number had declined to 17. Taken together, from 1992 to 1999 the banks' share of chairmanships in the supervisory boards of the 40 largest companies fell from 44 per cent to 23 per cent (Höpner 2001). And in March 2001 Deutsche Bank announced it would no longer take any chairmanships in supervisory boards of other firms (Beyer 2003: 131f.). The Deutsche Bank wants to avoid the impression that it aims at controlling other firms, shifting remaining shareholdings to a separate holding company and putting more emphasis on the medium- rather than long-term return of its shareholdings. By now, Deutsche Bank has sold most of its big industrial shareholdings and other big private banks have made similar moves.

Meanwhile, Allianz, the biggest German insurance company (and besides Deutsche Bank the most important power centre in the network of cross-shareholdings and interlocking directorates of German capitalism) shifted its investment strategy, first from Germany to Europe starting in the 1970s and then in the mid-1990s from Europe to the whole world. From a 'shareholder value' point of view it is not rational anymore to invest primarily in German companies or to hold shares in the case of shrinking returns. On the other hand, Allianz is trying to become an integrated financial group offering all

Table 7.1   The transformation of relations of ownership in Germany, 1995 and 2005: percentage of share ownership by group

	1995 (%)	2005 (%)
Private households and non-profit organizations	18.2	12.5
Non-financial businesses	44.0	27.8
State	4.2	2.8
Banks (including home loan banks)	12.9	10.7
Mutual funds	6.2	13.7
Insurance companies	6.3	12.4
Foreign investors	8.2	20.1
Total	100.0	100.0

Source: Deutsche Bundesbank (2006: 111).

kinds of financial services (*Allfinanz-Konzern*). So it is acquiring shares in financial companies and selling shares in industrial companies.

By the turn of the century, the network of capital interlinkages between the giant corporations and banks which was typical for German capitalism had been already hollowed out significantly (Wójcik 2001). Just how much the relationship between banks and industry had changed became apparent when Vodafone-Airtouch tried to acquire Mannesmann in 1999. Mannesmann was a leading German firm in the steel and machinery industry, but Vodafone was interested only in Mannesmann's fast-growing mobile communications business. Vodafone could only succeed in its attempt at a hostile takeover because the leading German banks, Mannesmann's biggest shareholders, accepted it in the end. This first successful hostile takeover of one of the core companies of German capitalism was widely seen as a turning point (Höpner and Jackson 2001, 2006). It indicated that the dense network between financial and industrial firms could dissolve and that a market for corporate control like in the US or in Great Britain could develop.

With the expansion of the financial markets, institutional investors like mutual funds and insurance companies as well as foreign investors have gained more and more influence (see Table 7.1). These institutional investors engage in active portfolio management. They often shift their assets and have no interest in strategic long-term relationships with industrial firms. Even if, compared to other countries, the role of the new institutional investors is still limited, the large banks and insurance companies in Germany have set up their own investment companies which are pursuing the same short-term shareholder value orientation as Anglo-Saxon institutional investors. Table 7.2 shows that the biggest mutual funds in Germany are owned by the major banking groups and insurance companies. So, the big banks did not lose power with the change of their strategies and structures.

Table 7.2 The ten biggest mutual fund groups in Germany in 2006

	Owner	Assets in million €	Share of all funds (%)
DWS-Group	Deutsche Bank	202,804.0	14.7
Allianz Global Investors Deutschland Group	Allianz	191,133.1	13.9
Deka-Group	Deka-Bank (top organization of federal state banks and savings banks)	157,345.7	11.5
Union Investment-Group	Cooperative banks	135,054.6	9.8
AMB Generali Group	Assicurazioni Generali	74,912.3	5.5
Universal Investment Gesellschaft mbH	Four private banks and Landesbank Baden-Württemberg	67,986.1	5.0
Cominvest-Group	Commerzbank	52,635.7	3.8
Internationale Kapitalanlagegesellschaft mbH	HSBC	50,789.5	3.7
Pioneer Investments Kapitalanlagegesellschaft mbH	Unicredit	47,868.1	3.5
MEAG MUNICH ERGO Kapitalanlagegesellschaft mbH	Münchener Rück	36,948.6	2.7

Note: Assets refer to securities only, excluding real estate.
Source: BVI (2007).

The transformation of political regulation

The transformation of the German financial system has been part of the liberalization and integration of European financial markets. This in turn is related to European political integration which can be conceived as a political form of the internationalization of capital. Since its beginning in the 1950s, it was based on a convergence of the interests of American and European capital. European integration was increasingly in the interest of the big European firms who were coming up against the limits of national markets. At the same time, political integration was in the interest of US multinational corporations because it allowed them to sell their commodities across the European Economic Community.

With the crisis of Fordism European integration gained new momentum, first of all in the area of exchange rate policy. When the US government terminated the Bretton Woods Agreement, European governments considered cooperation as necessary to stabilize exchange rates in the face of increasing economic instability and exchange rate volatility. However, each attempt to stabilize exchange rates in the European community created new contradictions and presented governments with the alternative of falling back into unilateral national politics or moving towards deeper integration. Thus, the European 'currency snake' installed in 1972 was replaced in 1979 by the European Monetary System, and the latter was replaced by the European Economic and Monetary Union at the end of the 1990s. European integration was pushed forward in the 1980s when competition among firms from Europe, the US and Japan intensified and the pattern of slow growth and high unemployment was conceived as 'Eurosclerosis'. In the face of the rise of Japan to technological and export leadership as well as renewed dynamism in the US economy, by the mid-1980s European leaders turned to the creation of a single European market as a way to restructure the European economies.[10] The liberalization and deregulation of financial markets was a cornerstone of this plan (Bieling 2003, 2006). Financial companies from the member states were allowed to offer their services and to establish subsidiaries in the whole European Community based on the rules of their home country. However, the creation of a single financial market also required some basic common rules which were set out in a number of directives in the late 1980s.

The fact that this still left European financial markets fragmented in many respects was increasingly seen as a problem in the second half of the 1990s as the US profited from the 'New Economy' boom and huge capital inflows. Businessmen, neoliberal economists and politicians regarded the relative underdevelopment of capital markets in Europe as a central cause of lower growth and higher unemployment. According to this view, a centralized European monetary policy could only be effective if the transmission channels between monetary policy and economic activity in the financial system were free of all barriers. The Financial Services Action Plan (FSAP), released in 1999 (European Commission 1999), comprised 42 measures aiming at the completion of a unified financial market for corporate clients, the development of open and secure markets for financial services for private households, the guarantee of financial market stability and the removal of tax barriers (Fröhlich and Huffschmid 2004: 88f.). The FSAP can be regarded as part of the Lisbon strategy 'to become the most competitive and dynamic knowledge-based economy in the world capable of sustainable economic growth with more and better jobs and greater social cohesion' (European Council 2000: 2). By the 2005 deadline for the completion of the FASP, 41 of the 42 measures had been implemented.[11] In the same year the European Commission released the White Paper 'Financial Services Policy 2005–2010' which outlines the planned measures after the completion of the FSAP.

Central to these developments at the EU level has been the German state's active promotion of a stronger capital market and a new type of corporate governance. Since the beginning of the 1990s a series of laws have been passed to these ends, partly implementing EU directives and partly going beyond them (see also Lütz 2002; Vitols 2004). The 'first law for the promotion of the financial market' (*Erstes Finanzmarktförderungsgesetz*) in 1990 abolished the tax on stock market turnover among other things. Thus, a big barrier to trading in secondary capital markets was removed. The 'second law for the promotion of the financial market' (*Zweites Finanzmarktförderungsgesetz*) in 1994 made insider trading a criminal offence, established a new agency for the supervision of the securities trade (*Bundesaufsichtsamt für den Wertpapierhandel*) equivalent to the US Securities and Exchange Commission (SEC), and deregulated financial investments through changes of various laws while introducing a new form of regulation of money market funds. On the eve of the 1998 federal elections the 'third law for the promotion of the financial market' (*Drittes Finanzmarktförderungsgesetz*) was introduced, giving investment companies more room for manoeuvre, lowering the taxes for equity investments and introducing new regulations for pension funds. In the same year the 'law for control and transparency in the area of companies' (*Gesetz zur Kontrolle und Transparenz im Unternehmensbereich – KonTraG*) allowed corporations to repurchase their stock and to establish stock option programmes for employees; while the 'law to facilitate raising capital' (*Kapitalaufnahmeerleichterungsgesetz – KapAEG*) allowed corporations to choose to produce their financial statements according to the German commercial code (*Handelsgesetzbuch – HGB*), International Accounting Standards (IAS) or US Generally Accepted Accounting Principles (GAAP).

The new Social Democrats and Green coalition did not change political direction when it came to promoting the development of financial markets in Germany. In 2000, it introduced one of the most important legal changes: the exemption of sales of blocks of shares, previously tied up in cross holdings, from tax payments (a major concern for companies like Deutsche Bank and Allianz). The German ministry of finance explicitly stated that this company tax reform was aimed at encouraging foreign investors to buy shares in German companies, and to break up the tight structure of cross shareholdings between a few corporations which had been characteristic of 'model Germany'. And even when the 'fourth law for the promotion of the financial market' (*Viertes Finanzmarktförderungsgesetz*), passed in 2002 amidst the stock market crash and a series of financial scandals, tightened some regulations so that outside investors were protected against insiders, it proceeded with deregulation in a number of other areas.

Furthermore, the neoliberal policy of privatizing public services has contributed to the reconfiguration of the relations of ownership. The partial privatization of the German state's telecommunications network via the IPO of Deutsche Telekom in 1996 induced many people with small savings to become 'shareholders'. The stock market hype of the late 1990s was further promoted not only by new business journals but also by news broadcasts on public television, which suddenly included comprehensive stock market reports. The number of direct stockholders in Germany increased from 3.8 million in 1996 to 6.2 million in 2000, while the number of owners of shares in investment funds increased from 2.3 million in 1997 to 9.8 million in 2001 (DAI 2003: 08.3-Zahl-D). The stock market boom stimulated all manner of ideological illusions: Germany would become a 'shareholder democracy' or a 'people's capitalism'. However, the proportion of capital assets in the hands of ordinary workers has always remained insignificant (see Priewe 2001), and when the 'New Economy' bubble burst, the number of direct stockholders began to decline. By 2006, only 4.2 million Germans held stocks directly while the number of owners of shares of investment funds declined to 7.9 million (DAI 2007: 1).

In 1997 the German stock exchange (which itself had been transformed into a joint stock company in 1990) installed the 'New Market' (*Neuer Markt*) for small joint stock companies. With the NASDAQ as its role model, the New Market was expected to improve the financing of high-technology start-up companies. Technological innovation and high-technology competition with other countries, especially the US and Japan, became (and remained) an obsession of many businessmen, economists and politicians in Germany.[12] In 2000, more than 300 companies were listed at the New Market, but after the burst of the bubble many went bankrupt so that by July 2001, there were over forty 'penny-stocks' at the New Market. There were also a number of spectacular cases of insider trading and fraud. All this was quite similar to what was going on in the US, but while NASDAQ survived the collapse of the 'New Economy', the New Market did not. The value of the Nemax index fell from an all-time high of 9666 points on 10 March 2000 to a mere 318 points on 9 October 2002. Thus, within two and a half years 96 per cent of a fictitious capital of over €200 billion had been destroyed. In 2003, the New Market was closed.

While the New Market failed, the obsession with high-technology start-ups and venture capital remained. Again, Germany followed the American trend. When investors shifted more and more money from the stock exchange to hedge funds and private equity funds, German politicians discovered that these forms of capital had been underdeveloped in Germany as well. In 2003 the German government loosened the rules for investment funds and the use of derivatives and admitted hedge funds. This meant that riskier investments were promoted at a time when the returns from conventional financial investments were shrinking. When the chairman of the Social Democratic Party (SPD) criticized Anglo-Saxon hedge funds and private equity funds as 'locusts' during the electoral campaign in 2005, this hypocritical electoral manoeuvre did little to increase its popular support, and in fact the SPD continued to support the development of financial markets after the election.

New measures are scheduled to promote private equity funds and venture capital. Real Estate Investment Trusts (REITs) have been admitted in 2007, reflecting and further promoting the bubble in the real estate market which developed after the burst of the stock market bubble. The possibilities for issuing mortgage backed bonds (*Hypothekenpfandbriefe*) have also been extended in 2005. Whereas previously only public banks and special mortgage banks could issue such mortgage-backed bonds, now all banks can. This change in regulation also reflects the huge accumulation of capital in the real estate and mortgage markets. Thus, the policies of the German government are based on the principle that new forms of capital developed in Anglo-Saxon capital markets should also be promoted in Germany.

Although this was of course not their publicly declared goal, reforms of the pension system also served to strengthen the German capital market (see Christen et al. 2003: 46ff.; Beckmann 2007: 169ff.). Already since 1978, the financial problems of the public social insurance system (a result of the changing balance of forces between capital and labour, increasing unemployment, stagnating wages and demographic changes) had motivated a number of pension reforms. However, until the 1990s these reforms did not attack the main principles of the pension system: they merely tried to limit the necessary increase of the rates of contribution by cutting down pension levels and restricting entitlements. Despite several cuts, Norbert Blüm, the conservative minister of labour and social security from 1982 to 1998, frequently stated that the pensions would be secure. The public discourse changed completely in the late 1990s. Demographic change and globalization were now presented as hard constraints forcing the government to fundamentally reform the pension system. This was highly ideological and misleading since other relevant factors influencing distributable wealth (like increases in labour productivity) were completely ignored.

Yet there remains a broad consensus among the established parties that further radical pension cuts are necessary and that the public social insurance system will no longer be able to guarantee social security for the elderly. Wage earners are pressured to save money for their retirement on a private basis. The government's aim is to strengthen private pension schemes while further cutting down on public pensions. The real change occurred under the Social-Democratic minister of labour Walter Riester in 2000, who drastically cut pay-as-you-go pensions and introduced huge public subsidies and tax incentives for private pension schemes. Employers were relieved to some extent from mandatory pension contributions while wage earners have to pay more for their retirement than before when they used the supplementary private retirement savings schemes. Essentially, the reforms channelled parts of workers' wages to the financial markets. At the end of 2006, eight million workers had signed the new private retirement savings contracts subsidized by the state. On the one hand, this figure shows that private retirement savings have become an important source for the accumulation of financial capital. On the other hand, it shows that about 80 per cent of the working population in Germany still have not bought into subsidized private retirement savings contracts. The retirement income of the broad majority of the working population still depends on public pay-as-you-go pensions, and some of these workers also have additional company pensions.

However, the latter have also run into crisis with the burst of the stock market bubble in 2001–2. As companies had to devalue their financial assets with the downturn of stock prices, their pension benefit plans were suddenly severely underfunded. Instead of increasing their reserves to provide the necessary funding, a number of companies abolished or reduced their pension benefits. The *form* of the remaining company pension benefit systems is also changing. In the past, company pension benefits were often paid directly from deferred wages which were accumulated within the firm. But by now a number of leading companies have set up their own pension funds. It is attractive for companies to change the form of their retirement benefit system because the investment rules for pension funds are less restrictive than the rules for the older types of company benefit systems, especially since investment rules were liberalized to permit riskier investments. Companies hope to lower the necessary level of contributions for a given benefit plan by shifting the money to pension funds, thereby reinforcing the detrimental effects of the overall structural changes in the German pension system in terms of lower and increasingly insecure retirement incomes, greater social inequality and growing poverty among the elderly, and a regressive shift in pension contributions to wage earners from employers – all of which are the result of the capitalization of retirement savings fuelling the expansion of financial capital.

Conclusion

The transformation of a bank-based financial system into a market-based financial system under way in Germany is not a linear process free of contradictions. Nor is it anywhere near completion. Political controversies arise not only along the lines of different class interests, but also along the lines of competition between firms, industries, fractions of capital and states as bearers of capitalist interests. A good example of the divergence of the different capitalist interests is the long struggle about the regulation of takeovers of companies in the EU.

Preliminary work on a directive regulating takeovers began in 1987, a time characterized by the emergence of 'new financial capitalists' like Kohlberg Kravis Roberts (KKR), a wave of leveraged buy-outs and unfriendly takeovers in the United States (see Blair 1993; Baker and Smith 1998). However, it was only in July 2001 that the directive was put to the vote in the European Parliament – at which point it was turned down. What made it so controversial was the question as to which strategies the board and management of a target company should be allowed to use in order to avert an unfriendly takeover. On the one hand, from the perspective of financial investors such measures are illegitimate because they prevent the legal owners of the company from realizing the value of their assets (including a takeover bonus). On the other hand, legal measures to prevent unfriendly takeovers and to limit the influence of the stock market have historically served to guarantee the stability of ownership of national corporations. This had been in the interest of single owner families, managers, workers and national governments alike. The conflict over the abolition of measures against unfriendly takeovers was emblematic of the contradiction between industrial and financial capital as well as the increasing competition among EU countries. The takeover directive of the EU in principle aimed at liberalizing takeover regulations and banning anti-takeover measures. However, the draft of the takeover directive ruled out only certain defence mechanisms; others were left untouched. In particular, politicians from Germany and some other countries feared disadvantages for 'their' companies and criticized the directive for not creating a level playing field. At the same time as the directive was rejected at Strasbourg, the German government reacted to the pressure of financial capital with its own law on takeovers (*Wertpapiererwerbs- und Übernahmegesetz*). The law expressed a certain balance of forces between the different interests. On the one hand, some rules aimed at protecting the interests of bidders and minority shareholders. On the other hand, the law allowed defence measures of the management of target companies under certain conditions.

The proponents of a free market for corporate control did not accept their defeat at the EU level. Following further attempts to support the interests of bidders and financial investors at EU level, in 2004 an EU takeover directive came into force. Once again the directive included a ban on defence measures against takeovers. However, a consensus had only been possible after a modification of the draft which made member states responsible for the implementation of this ban. The directive also offered different options to companies affected. In the end, the directive institutionalized the kind of compromise seen in the German law. It reflected the unequal development of the balance of forces between classes and class fractions within the different member states as well as within different companies. Nevertheless, the thrust of the directive was to support the interests of financial investors and the centralization of capital, and it has become more difficult for single member countries or corporations to justify deviations from this line. The directive was supposed to be implemented at the national level by May 2006 and most countries have done so. Yet the whole case shows that the transition towards finance-led regulation characterized by the dominance of financial capital and American-style capital markets is not a linear and harmonious process. Thus, the process cannot be understood in a functionalist or teleological way. Contradictions give rise to struggles and counter-tendencies. However, these struggles have not completely changed or reversed the direction the development has taken in the last decades.

Summing up these developments, we can say that bank-based financial systems are increasingly replaced by market-based financial systems where the evaluation of economic activities takes place in a different way. The internal monitoring process within the credit department of a bank is replaced by a more or less public evaluation of companies with rating agencies, investment banks, financial analysts, and financial information brokers as important intermediary actors. Institutional investors like pension funds and mutual funds are gaining influence, exerting considerable pressure on industrial companies to generate 'shareholder value'.[13] It has to be emphasized, however, that it would be wrong to see industrial companies as mere victims of the pressure of financial investors. Industrial companies are important actors within financial markets both on the demand side and on the supply side.

However, the process is unlikely to be reversed. It is not confined to Germany, but it is a European, and to some extent a global process. If the expansion of financial markets were just the result of neoliberal ideology and politics or of a crisis of over-accumulation, it could be reversed with a change in the balance of class forces and with the development of a different growth regime. However, the shift towards market finance is a necessary element of the long-run development of capitalism. Securitization, the development of derivatives and new financial instruments represent a growing socialization of risks and allow for an expansion of the credit system which in turn fosters the accumulation of industrial capital. Thus, the *contradiction* between industrial and financial capital should not be confused with a simple *opposition*. The transition to a market-based financial system is linked with the growing dominance of financial capital and in particular fictitious capital within the regime of accumulation. However, this development does not run against the interests of industrial capital in general. On the contrary, industrial firms are themselves interested in using the possibilities of financial markets to refinance themselves and to realize additional profits by investing idle money in financial markets. Especially the big multinational corporations have been important actors in the development of financial markets.

The transition from a bank-based financial system to a market-based financial system can indeed to some extent be considered as an 'Americanization' of the German financial system and European finance more broadly. The capital market has been relatively more important and more developed in the US for a long time. However, the American financial system is changing too. For instance, the separation of investment banking and commercial banking which had been institutionalized after the Great Depression of the 1930s has been abolished. Thus, it could be argued that the US has followed the German model with the return to universal banking. However, there can be no doubt that the influence of the United States on the German financial system is much stronger than vice versa. The transformation of the German financial system clearly followed the model of the American capital market. German businessmen, economists and politicians tried to emulate US developments because they perceived it as necessary in order to survive in competition.

American hegemony has certainly experienced its ups and downs. The collapse of the 'New Economy' and the financial scandals of Enron and other companies seemed to have stalled the 'Americanization' of the German system of corporate governance and finance for some time.[14] Of course, the stock market euphoria of the late 1990s has disappeared. However, the crisis has not brought about any fundamental political change. On the contrary, the processes outlined here have continued in recent years. Of course 'Americanization' does not mean that all differences between the countries will vanish. There will always be varieties of capitalism due to the existence of the international state system, the fragmentation of the world economy, the processes of uneven development and the importance of domestic political struggles. Nevertheless, despite all remaining differences, very similar developments take place in different countries.

Any analysis has political implications. If I am right here about the international character of the transformation of the financial system, the objective necessity and basis for *international* political strategies is much stronger than proponents of the 'varieties of capitalism' perspective believe. And if I am right about the relation between the transformation of the financial system and the long-run development of capital accumulation, any attempt just to 're-regulate' financial markets will probably fail unless it is part of a strategy to transform the capitalist mode of production as a whole.

Notes

1. Susanne Lütz, for instance, treats globalization as an 'independent variable and given phenomenon' in her account of the changes of the financial systems of Germany, Great Britain and the US (Lütz 2002: 44).
2. For a critique of the concept of path dependency see Scherrer (2005).
3. Financial capital defined in this sense is not synonymous with Hilferding's (and Lenin's) concept of finance capital. See below.
4. Different scholars have analysed different aspects of these developments within different theoretical frameworks. The empirical and theoretical work of Aglietta and Rebérioux (2005), Boyer (2000), François Chesnais (1994, 2004), Froud et al. (2002, 2006), Krippner (2005) and many others on 'financialization', the emergence of a finance-led regime of accumulation, and new forms of corporate governance associated with the rise of institutional investors and the ideology of shareholder value can easily be reinterpreted within the framework outlined here.
5. When I finished this chapter, the consequences of the bursting of the housing bubble and the following crisis in the money market were still not completely clear.
6. The development in Japan is different only in the sense that a major speculative bubble burst there at the end of the 1980s, followed by a long deflation, so that the New Economy bubble in the second half of the 1990s was less striking.

7.   Industrial firms as actors are often neglected in critical accounts of the development of financial markets. For instance, when Huffschmid (2002) talks about the actors behind the markets, he confines his presentation to banks and institutional investors (pension funds, mutual funds, insurance companies).

8.   The amount of capital raised from privatization in OECD countries increased from US$24 billion in 1990 to US$104 billion in 1999; in the EU countries it increased from US$15 billion in 1990 to US$61 billion in 1999 (Bieling 2003: 221). According to Bieling (2003: 221f.), in Italy, Spain and Portugal privatized companies accounted for more than half of the total market capitalization.

9.   Just to give an example of the close relations between banks and industry in early German capitalism: the first director of Deutsche Bank was Georg von Siemens, member of the Siemens family, the owner of one of the largest industrial firms in Germany.

10. The Single European Act in 1986 established the plan to create the single market by 1992, comprising the free movement of goods, services, labour and capital, mainly by the mutual recognition of the various national regulations – albeit on the basis of the harmonization of only basic rules, given that earlier attempts to harmonize national regulations had failed (Fröhlich and Huffschmid 2004: 86).

11. The exception being the proposed 14th Company Law Directive on the Cross-Border Transfer of Registered Office. This directive would make it possible for companies to transfer their legal headquarters to somewhere else in the EU. Until now this was either not possible at all or required the company to be liquidated in its country of origin before it could be re-founded with its registered office in the new country. On 21 November 2006, Commissioner McCreevy announced that he planned to come forward with a proposal for a directive on the cross-border transfer of seat in the spring of 2007. See European Commission (2006, 2007a, 2007b).

12. The books written by Konrad Seitz (1990, 1998) are a good example of this obsession. Seitz was for many years a leading official in the German foreign office and German ambassador in India, Italy and China. See also Steinmeier and Machnig (2004) as a representative example from the era of the 'red-green' government.

13. I have analysed the consequences of the shareholder value orientation in different industries, and its influence on the restructuring of production in former studies. It is not possible to repeat this here. See Menz et al. (1999) and Sablowski (2003a, 2003b, 2005a, 2005b). See also Dörre and Brinkmann (2005).

14. For instance, in November 2003, one of the most dedicated proponents of stock market development in Germany, Rüdiger von Rosen, head of Deutsches Aktieninstitut (the lobby organization of stock market actors in Germany), argued that US corporate governance was no shining example any more. He criticized that 'in old Europe the US system had been praised always almost pontiff-like as the only blessing' (von Rosen 2003: 5). He argued that it had been a mistake to present the clear separation between executive board and supervisory board in the German system of corporate governance as inefficient and outdated. He pointed to the fact that even US experts like John Snow and Paul Volcker had advocated a separation between the position of the Chairman and the position of the Chief Executive Officer of a corporation in the wake of the financial scandals.

8
Accounting for Financial Capital: American Hegemony and the Conflict Over International Accounting Standards

Thomas Sablowski

The history of accounting is closely linked to the history of capital accumulation. Accounting fraud has been part of every major crisis in capital accumulation, as have attempts to re-establish investor trust. Accountants are structurally caught in the contradiction of corporations' interests and investors' interests. At times their role is to help companies make their books look as rosy as possible; yet they have to keep the trust of financial investors. The development of accounting institutions and accounting standards is a reflection of this contradiction. The economic crisis and financial scandals of the 1930s led the accounting industry to promote public trust in the profession by formalizing (i.e. guaranteeing the consistency and transparency of) accounting procedures. Similar developments accompanied the crisis of Fordism in the US with the creation of the Financial Accounting Standards Board (FASB). It is one of the paradoxes of such institutions that after a few years they might act and function in a way that is completely opposed to the original intentions behind their creation. Although the FASB was originally established because the accounting practices of some companies were regarded as problematic, in practice the development of new accounting standards had the effect of eliminating many restrictions and facilitating the use of accounting as a weapon in economic competition. The logic that resulted can be said to have culminated in the financial scandals of Enron, Worldcom and other companies – a series of events that triggered new institutional reforms such as the Sarbanes–Oxley Act.

The development of accounting standards in Germany and the European Union reflects the transition from a bank-based financial system to a market-based financial system and is in many ways directly constitutive of it. Until 1997 the financial reporting of all companies in Germany was based on the rules of the German commercial code (*Handelsgesetzbuch* or HGB). In 1997 the German stock exchange required companies listed in the 'New Market'

(*Neuer Markt*) to produce financial reports based on International Accounting Standards (IAS) or US Generally Accepted Accounting Principles (US GAAP) – which are broadly similar to one another. In 1998 all companies listed in the German stock market were allowed by law to choose between IAS, US GAAP and the rules of the HGB for their financial disclosures. Since January 2005 companies operating in the EU capital market are required to use International Financial Reporting Standards (IFRS, as the IAS were renamed in 2001).

Accounting for financial markets

A comparison between the rules of the HGB and IFRS reveals interesting differences (see Table 8.1; see also Nölke and Perry 2005; Perry and Nölke 2006). The 'philosophy' behind the two sets of rules is quite different. The rules of the HGB primarily aim at the protection of creditors. This is expressed in the principle of 'cautious representation' of a company's income, assets and liabilities. It reflects the traditional preponderance of banks and credit financing in the German financial system. In a financial system based on bank credits liquidity is secured by the legal obligation to repay credits and savings deposits, and by the role of the central bank as a 'lender of last resort'. The creditworthiness of a debtor is usually checked through an internal monitoring process where the creditor has access to internal accounting information of the debtor's business. The primary interest of a creditor is not that a borrowing firm should maximize its profits but that its profits should be high and stable enough to repay the credit plus interest. Preventing the debtor's bankruptcy thus becomes a paramount concern. So, the creditor will support the internal accumulation of capital by the debtor rather than the distribution of high dividends. The rules of the HGB support precisely such strategies.

By contrast, IFRS primarily reflect the interests of financial investors operating in securities markets. Liquidity is obtained through securitization: liabilities are converted into commodities which can be purchased and sold in financial markets. A market-based financial system depends on the continuous influx of money in capital markets. Risks are limited by the diversification of portfolios. Contrary to creditors, investors in financial markets do not need to develop long-term relations with debtors. They are interested in short-term profitability rather than in the long-term viability of the firms they are investing in. The (external) monitoring of firms by financial investors relies to a large extent on public financial information. So, first and foremost, they need accurate information about companies' cash-flow, income and balance sheet. This is reflected in the IFRS principle of the 'fair and true representation' of a company's situation.

When we compare the HGB rules and IFRS, it becomes immediately clear that accounts are social constructions. In a number of ways the principle of 'true and fair representation' in IFRS tends to produce higher profits than the principle of 'cautious representation' in the HGB. For instance, future expected profits can be accounted according to the IFRS but not the HGB rules. Depreciations are set at higher levels within the framework of the HGB which means in turn that profits are lower (because profits are basically cash-flows minus depreciation allowances). The same is true for the different presentations of a company's assets. In some respects, assets tend to be higher under IFRS than under the HGB. For instance, immaterial assets can be recognized according to the IFRS (under certain conditions) but not according to the HGB. Expenditures for research and development are considered costs in the HGB framework while they should be viewed as investments according to IFRS rules. The revaluation of fixed assets is forbidden according to the HGB while it is possible according to IFRS.

In general, accounting is mainly based on historical costs or the lowest possible values under the HGB while it is rather based on current market prices or a 'fair value' derived from theoretical price models under IFRS. This difference becomes all the more important because the weight of fictitious capital and derivatives in the balance sheets of companies is increasing. The changes in the field of accounting standards are not just reflections of structural changes in the economy. The former are also constitutive of the latter because accounting standards provide an incentive structure for specific practices. Some strategies pay off in balance sheets, and others do not. In the end, 'mark to market' and 'mark to model' practices tend to produce virtually higher profits.

The internationalization of accounting as Americanization

The development of IFRS followed the model of Anglo-American accounting. The internationalization of accounting standards can also be interpreted as a process of Americanization that originated in the crisis of Fordism in the early 1970s. It is interesting to note that new accounting institutions were formed in the US and at the international level at the same time – and partly by the same actors. The American Institute of Certified Public Accountants (AICPA) and the US government established the Financial Accounting Standards Board (FASB) in 1973. It was founded because the accounting practices of some corporations were responsible for growing doubts among investors. The creation of the International Accounting Standards Committee (IASC) in the same year can be traced back to an initiative by professional accountancy bodies in the United Kingdom, the US and Canada (see Botzem and Quack 2005: 7f.). According to Hopwood (1994) British accountants instigated the foundation of the IASC to protect their profession from the possible consequences of Britain's accession to the European Economic Community (EEC) in 1973. The European Commission had proposed a draft of an accounting directive in 1971 which reflected continental European rather than British accounting

Table 8.1   Selected differences between HGB and IFRS

	HGB	IFRS
Primary purpose	Protection of creditors Regulation of taxation	Information of investors
Basic principle	Cautious representation	'Fair' representation
Disclosure requirements	Limited	More extensive
Unrealized profits	May not be recognized	Must be recognized
Immaterial assets produced by the company	May not be recognized	Must be recognized under certain conditions
Research & development	Treated as costs	Treated as assets
Goodwill from asset deals	Can be recognized	Must be recognized
Depreciation	Many possibilities based on tax law	Usually linear, longer than under HGB
Revaluation of fixed assets	Forbidden	Possible
Valuation of investments, financial assets	Based on historical costs or lower value	Rather based on 'fair' value
Retirement benefit obligations	Expected wage increases may not be recognized	Expected wage increases are recognized
Tax base	Congruent with financial statement	Not necessarily congruent

principles. In contrast, the character of the IASC was from the beginning primarily shaped by Anglo-American accounting culture. The members of the IASC board came primarily from the big accounting firms based in the UK and the USA, from professional accounting bodies and university accounting departments. It was not only the delegates from Australia, Canada, the US and Britain that shared the Anglo-American accounting approach; even accountants from other countries did because they often worked for one of the big accounting firms which were all headquartered in the US and the UK (Martinez-Diaz 2005: 8f.). According to Martinez-Diaz (2005: 8) many observers in continental Europe perceived the IASC as 'a Trojan horse which conceals the Anglo-American accounting enemy inside a more respectable international façade' (Nobes 1994: 21).

However, the IAS developed by the IASC had little impact on the accounting practices of firms in the major capitalist countries during the 1970s and 1980s (Martinez-Diaz 2005: 10). On the one hand, companies usually were obliged to use the specific accounting standards of their home country. On the other hand, US GAAP often were accepted internationally. In France for instance, only *statutory accounts* were regulated nationally in the 1970s. National standard-setters had released non-binding recommendations for *consolidated accounts* in 1968, but compulsory regulation did not exist.[1] Thus, major French multinational corporations began to use US GAAP from the early 1970s (Touron 2005: 582).[2]

With the accession of Denmark, the UK and Ireland in 1973, the balance of forces within the European Community shifted slowly in favour of Anglo-Saxon accounting philosophy. During the negotiations of the Fourth Council Directive on accounting, Denmark, the UK and the Netherlands insisted on the inclusion of the 'true and fair view' of a company's assets, liabilities, profits and losses. This was in contradiction with the prudence principle which prevailed in German accounting rules. Ultimately, the Fourth Council Directive[3] in 1978 required that limited liability companies across the EEC would provide annual reports with a 'true and fair view' of their financial position. It became a cornerstone of European accounting policies (Botzem and Quack 2005: 6). However, at that time it was only possible to reach a compromise in the EEC by incorporating a number of optional treatments which allowed for a considerable variety of national implementations of the basic principles. In particular, the 'true and fair' principle was interpreted in different ways. Well into the 1980s, the conflicting views and the lack of mechanisms to reconcile these views prevented the emergence of harmonized accounting standards in the EEC (Botzem and Quack 2005: 7).

In the meantime the IASC tried to link up with other collective actors. In 1976 the 'Group of Ten' bank governors at the Bank for International Settlements (BIS) agreed to collaborate with the IASC in the development of financial reporting standards for internationally active banks. In 1979 the IASC met with an OECD working group that had started to publish Guidelines for Multinational Enterprises including voluntary disclosure standards. One year later the IASC took part in the first meeting of a new United Nations Intergovernmental Working Group on Accounting and Reporting. Developing countries had proposed to establish an international accounting standard-setting body within the UN. However, this proposal was turned down by industrialized countries in 1983. Shortly afterwards the OECD supported the IASC's demand that the UN should leave standard-setting to the IASC. In 1981 the IASC began to meet with national standard-setters and formed a working group on deferred taxes with standard-setters from the Netherlands, the UK and the US. In 1984 a first official meeting with the US Securities and Exchange Commission (SEC) took place. The successive co-optation of other organizations led to a transformation of the organizational structure of the IASC. The IASC gained decisive support towards the end of the 1980s. When in 1987 the IASC and the International Organization of Securities Commissions (IOSCO) started to work jointly on the comparability and improvement of accounting standards, Anglo-Saxon accounting principles gained progressively more influence. In 1988 the FASB joined the consultative group of the IASC which had been installed in 1981 to discuss the organization's projects and priorities twice a year. At the same time the FASB joined the IASC board as an observer. The European Commission followed the FASB in 1990 and also became a member of the consultative group and an observer at the IASC board (Botzem and Quack 2005: 10f.; Martinez-Diaz 2005: 9f.).

During the 1990s the demand for the international harmonization of accounting standards grew for a number of reasons. Most important was the growth in cross-border stock exchange listings – a process clearly dominated by the centrality of the US capital market. The number of new foreign firms registering with the SEC increased from 45 in 1990 to 160 in 1998. At the same time, the capital raised by foreign firms in US securities markets increased from US$8 billion in 1990 to US$170 billion in 1998 (Martinez-Diaz 2005: 12). 'The volume and liquidity of American capital markets made them increasingly attractive for investors from other countries. This explains why American accounting rules (US GAAP) gained global importance. As guardians of the financial reporting standards that enabled access to the world's leading capital markets, the American standard setter, the FASB, and the SEC became key players in the regulatory field' (Botzem and Quack 2005: 12).

Major German and European corporations were interested in a listing on the US stock market in order to raise capital more easily, to develop their reputation as 'global' companies and to facilitate mergers with US companies. However, the move to the US capital market created substantial problems for the European companies in the field of accounting. These foreign firms often had to prepare two sets of accounts. In the US they were required to comply with SEC rules and to use US GAAP for financial reporting, while in their home countries they were required to use the accounting standards of the respective countries. This often led to considerable differences between the accounts of one and the same firm for one year. For instance, Daimler-Benz AG was the first German company to become listed at the New York Stock Exchange (NYSE) in 1993. The German accounting rules had allowed Daimler-Benz to average out reported earnings over the business cycle to a large extent. In the 1980s high reserves had been built up that could be drawn down during the years of crisis in the early 1990s. Thus, in 1993 Daimler-Benz AG was still able to report a net income of 615 million Deutschmarks according to HGB rules while it had to report a loss of 1.8 billion Deutschmarks according to US GAAP (Bea et al. 1997: 93). These huge differences gave rise to considerable uncertainty with regard to the informational content of a company's accounts. The credibility of accounting was weakened by the use of a double standard. Thus, it is not surprising that major European corporations were demanding harmonized international accounting standards.

The second reason for the increasing demand for the harmonization of accounting standards was the growing competition among stock exchanges seeking to attract (international) listings. Thus, NYSE Chairman Richard Grasso became an advocate of international accounting standards. He thought that the SEC would hinder international listings by requiring foreign firms to use US GAAP (Martinez-Diaz 2005: 13). European stock exchanges also hoped to attract international investors and companies and to increase their liquidity and thus were in favour of the internationalization of accounting standards. 'As demand for international accounting standards grew, supporters of harmonization began to exert political pressure on regulators in Washington and Brussels. In the United States, pressure on the SEC to back international accounting standards came mainly from American stock exchanges hoping to capitalize on a new wave of foreign listings' (Martinez-Diaz 2005: 14).

However, the FASB and the SEC were reluctant to accept International Accounting Standards instead of US GAAP. They regarded US GAAP as superior and insisted that it should remain mandatory for all companies listed on US stock exchanges. US regulators were only ready to accept the 'convergence' of US GAAP and IAS to the extent that the IAS were adapted to US GAAP and not vice versa. However, the interests of the US regulators could only become so dominant because they coincided with the interests of financial market actors in general.

> Professional representatives of continental European and other countries diverging from the Anglo-Saxon model came increasingly under pressure to give up their accounting principles in order to raise the acceptance of IAS among financial market actors. Above all, the precautionary measure aiming at protecting creditors was perceived as incompatible with financial market expectations. Another controversial item was the treatment of reserves, which are closely tied to issues of taxation. In many cases it had to be accepted that continental European options would be subordinated and only treated as allowed alternatives to the preferred Anglo-Saxon benchmark options or eliminated altogether from IAS. (Botzem and Quack 2005: 13)

The dominance of the SEC became apparent when the IOSCO decided not to approve the revised IAS in 1993 although it had collaborated with the IASC in the Comparability and Improvement Project. 'While most European members were in favour of instant endorsements of the 14 standards considered acceptable in 1993, the position of the SEC was to recognize and endorse IAS only after a complete set of core standards would be developed. This led to a second round of revisions' (Botzem and Quack 2005: 13). In 1995 the European Commission published a document titled *Accounting Harmonisation: a New Strategy Vis-à-Vis International Harmonisation*. There it described the problem as follows:

> Accounts prepared in accordance with the [European Company Law] Directives and the national laws which implement them do not meet the more demanding standards required elsewhere in the world, notably by the Securities and Exchange Commission in the United States. The result of this last problem is that large European companies seeking capital on the international capital markets, most often on the New York Stock Exchange,

are obliged to prepare a second set of accounts for that purpose. This is burdensome and costly and constitutes a clear competitive disadvantage. Producing more than one set of accounts also causes confusion. Moreover, it involves companies in conforming with standards (US Generally Accepted Accounting Principles or GAAP) which are developed without any European input. As more and more Member States are implementing important privatisation programmes and as the capital needs of the companies concerned are increasing, the number of companies facing this problem is growing. (European Commission 1995: 2)

The reference to privatization policies in Europe shows that the European Commission also wanted to attract US investors, hoping to sell them shares of privatized European companies. The same document states: 'The most urgent problem is that concerning European companies with an international vocation. The accounts prepared by those companies in accordance with their national legislation, based on the Accounting Directives, are no longer acceptable for international capital market purposes...There is a risk that large companies will be increasingly drawn towards US GAAP. They and the Member States are looking to the Union for a solution that can be implemented rapidly' (European Commission 1995: 4).

Thus, the European Commission recognized the growing international influence of US GAAP but was not ready to accept American 'accounting imperialism' (Martinez-Diaz 2005: 15). At the same time the Commission realized that an exclusively European standard-setting had become impossible and that the only solution to this problem was to put

the Union's weight behind the international harmonization process which is already well under way in the International Accounting Standards Committee (IASC). The objective of this process is to establish a set of standards which will be accepted in capital markets world-wide. The Union must at the same time preserve its own achievements in the direction of harmonization, which are a fundamental part of internal market law. It therefore needs to take steps to ensure that existing international standards (IAS) are consistent with the Community's Directives and that IAS which remain to be formulated remain compatible with Community law. (European Commission 1995: 2)

In October 1996 the US Congress passed the National Securities Markets Improvement Act. In Section 509 (4) it was stated that the SEC 'should enhance its vigorous support for the development of high-quality international accounting standards as soon as practicable'. The SEC was obliged to report to Congress within one year on its progress in harmonizing accounting standards. In 1997, the G10 accepted the IASC's monopoly on producing international accounting standards (Martinez-Diaz 2005: 13, 15).

The Asian crisis further increased the interest in International Accounting Standards because underdeveloped accounting standards and auditing practices were seen as catalysts of the crisis. In May 1998, the G8 ministers of finance agreed on the necessity to develop international accounting and auditing standards. In October of the same year the G7 finance ministers and central bank governors called on the IASC to 'finalize by early 1999 a proposal for a full range of internationally agreed accounting standards' (Declaration of G7 finance ministers and central bank governors, quoted from Martinez-Diaz 2005: 13). The IMF also suggested the adoption of IAS as a part of the attempt to strengthen the 'international financial architecture' after the Asian crisis, while the World Bank started to ask its borrowers to use IAS in their disclosures. In 2000, the Basel Committee on Banking Supervision (BCBS) reviewed fifteen IAS but accepted only seven. The IASC responded by setting up a joint BCBS-IASC committee to address the Basel Committee's concerns (Martinez-Diaz 2005: 14).

In the meantime some EU countries began to change their accounting regulations. When, following the example of the NASDAQ, Germany's 'Neuer Markt' was institutionalized in 1997 to support high-tech start-up companies, listed companies were required to use IAS or US GAAP – and not the German accounting rules of the HGB. In 1998 German joint-stock corporations were generally allowed to use IAS or US GAAP instead of the HGB rules to prepare their annual reports. Five years later practically all DAX companies[4] were using US GAAP or IAS.

If the problem of double standards seemed to be solved for German corporations, it turned out that this solution was only temporary. Conflicts remained not only between regulators in the USA and in the EU but also between the EU and the IASC. The SEC was still not ready to accept IAS which it considered inferior to US GAAP. So, on the one hand US regulators agreed to negotiate with the IASC to achieve the harmonization of accounting standards. On the other hand, US regulators tried to increase their influence within the IASC and to shape it based on the model of the FASB. At the same time they reserved their right to reject any international standard running counter to their national standards. While the European Commission followed a similar strategy, it soon turned out that the IASC was inclined to follow American preferences and standards. For instance, the IASC accepted segment reporting requirements which were common in the USA but not in Europe. In 1997 it announced that it would use parts of US GAAP as building blocks for the further development of IAS. In general IAS reflect the Anglo-American rather than the continental European accounting tradition. This is reflected for instance in the growing importance of fair value accounting as opposed to historical cost accounting (cf. Perry and Nölke 2006).

In 1999, discussions took place within the IASC about a restructuring of the organization. The European Commission suggested transforming the Consultative Group of the IASC into a decision-making organ which should select the IASC's trustees. The commission also proposed that the IASC's members should be national standard-setters rather than private-sector professionals. The European Commission's concern was to increase the legitimacy of the IASC. 'The proposal would have stripped the accounting profession and its private associations from control over the IASC' (Martinez-Diaz 2005: 18). The European Commission's proposal met resistance by the SEC which proposed a two-tiered structure (trustees and board) similar to the FASB. According to the SEC the group of trustees should consist of investment analysts, academics and accounting professionals. The board should consist of full-time members drawn from national standard-setters and always include representatives of the largest economies and the biggest capital markets. Representatives of smaller economies should have rotating seats.

In December 1999, when the new structure was approved by the board, it became clear that the SEC had prevailed on all key points. The Consultative Group was renamed the Standards Advisory Council and left without decision-making power.[5] The group of trustees was formed by six representatives from North America, six from Europe, four from Asia Pacific and three from any region. The trustees would appoint twelve full-time and two part-time board members based on technical expertise, not geographical representation. Paul Volcker, former chairman of the US Federal Reserve Board, was chosen as the new chairman of the Board of Trustees (Martinez-Diaz 2005: 18f.). Nevertheless, the SEC did not fully approve the IASC's work. In May 2000, the IOSCO – of which the SEC is a member – recommended allowing multinational issuers to use the thirty core standards of the IAS to prepare financial statements for cross-border offerings and listings. But the IOSCO's resolution also included the possibility of rescinding single standards if they contradicted national or regional regulation.

From the collapse of the 'New Economy' to the recognition of IFRS

US regulators began to move more quickly only when, after the collapse of the 'New Economy' boom and the financial scandals of Enron, Worldcom and other companies, the American system of accounting and corporate governance came under pressure. The accounting scandals called into question the rules-based approach of US GAAP. The Sarbanes–Oxley Act in 2002 directed the SEC to undertake a study on the adoption of a principles-based accounting system. The Sarbanes–Oxley Act also required the FASB to work towards the international convergence of accounting standards. In the same year a 'memorandum of understanding' (the so-called 'Norwalk Agreement') was reached between the IASB and the FASB to foster the convergence of IFRS and US GAAP (see Eaton 2005; Cox 2007).

The European Commission endorsed all available International Financial Reporting Standards in September 2003, with the exception of IAS 32 and

IAS 39 (accounting for financial instruments). Companies listed on an EU stock exchange were to use IFRS for their financial disclosures from 1 January 2005. This ruled out the alternative use of US GAAP in EU countries which was widely practised among major German corporations since 1998. It is currently being discussed in the EU whether even European companies not listed in the capital markets should be required to use IFRS for their financial reporting. According to a survey by PriceWaterhouseCoopers and DIHT, the top organization of the German chambers of commerce, 79 per cent of the German companies participating in the survey dislike switching from HGB to IFRS.

On the other hand, large transnational corporations' interest in accounting harmonization is still strong. Since 2005, corporations listed in US and EU capital markets are obliged to prepare two sets of accounts: in the EU they have to use IFRS, while in the United States they have to use US GAAP or at least they have to reconcile their IFRS accounts to US GAAP. The problem became even more urgent because in the wake of the collapse of the 'New Economy' bubble and the ensuing crisis a number of European corporations were planning to pull out of US capital markets. On 9 February 2004, eleven European industry associations wrote a letter to SEC Chairman William Donaldson asking for a change in the US financial reporting rules. They stated that

the U.S. rules make it difficult, and in some cases impossible, for a European company to terminate its reporting obligations...Most of our member companies that have securities listed in the United States entered the U.S. market to achieve specific objectives, such as developing a liquid trading market for their securities in the United States, using their securities as acquisition currency in the United States, raising capital in the U.S. market on a rapid basis, or enhancing their reputation in the United States and internationally...Some of our member companies, however, have not realized the benefits they sought to achieve, or have changed their business strategy since their U.S. listing...In this context, a number of our member companies have re-evaluated the benefits of a U.S. listing compared to the substantial costs involved...They have been advised that, while they can withdraw their securities from U.S. exchanges, they must continue to file reports with the Commission [the SEC] so long as there remains even *de minimis* U.S. investor interest in their securities...To terminate or suspend a reporting obligation, a company must have fewer than 300 U.S. resident security holders...If a company has ever made a public offering in the United States or engaged in certain business combinations, its U.S. reporting obligation can never be terminated. At best, the company can eliminate its reporting obligation one year at a time, always remaining subject to renewed reporting if, without any action on its part, its U.S. shareholder base increases. (EALIC et al. 2004)

In June 2004, the SEC's Chief Accountant Donald T. Nicolaisen suggested that 'if things continue as they have been going – if the IASB operates as a strong independent standard-setter, if the commitment to quality application of IFRS remains, and if good progress is made in accounting convergence and the development of an effective global financial reporting infrastructure – then "in this decade", the SEC will be able to eliminate the reconciliation' with US GAAP required from foreign firms listing in US capital markets and producing accounts based on IFRS (Nicolaisen 2004). In April 2005, Nicolaisen suggested a 'roadmap' to eliminate the reconciliation requirement by 2009 (Nicolaisen 2005).

In May 2005, Olaf Scholz, the leader of the Social Democratic Party's parliamentary group, articulated the desire among most German corporations to have 'uniform standards to avoid the expensive production of two sets of accounts', and expressed the widespread dissatisfaction with slow progress in this area (*Börsen-Zeitung*, 17 May 2005). The German Parliament started to check whether and how it could influence the development of IFRS more strongly. It seems that the Parliament recognized that it had lost any influence over the development of accounting standards. But this insight has come rather late.

In February 2006, SEC Chairman Christopher Cox explicitly affirmed the 'roadmap' suggested by Nicolaisen the year before (SEC 2006). One year later, Cox remarked: 'Once unveiled, the Roadmap took on a life of its own. Governments, regulators, and standard setters around the world have been relying on it to determine their actions.' He also affirmed that the SEC would 'not expect to see total convergence or even a specific level of convergence' of IFRS and US GAAP 'before eliminating the reconciliation requirement. Instead, there must be a robust and active process in place for converging IFRS and U.S. GAAP. If the process is in place, then the current differences will be minimized in due course' (Cox 2007). This meant 'that IFRS and U.S. GAAP would someday compete freely in America's capital markets . . . at least until the process of convergence concludes with actual convergence' (ibid.). However, the SEC was still concerned that foreign companies often fail to use IFRS as specified by the IASB and instead use a modified set of IFRS more in accordance with home country regulations. SEC Commissioner Roel Campos said in March 2007: 'Now, we certainly understand why a jurisdiction may wish to adopt its own version of IFRS. However, one goal of the roadmap was to . . . have only two versions of robust standards developed by independent standard setters in the U.S. capital markets – one U.S. GAAP and one IFRS – not thirty different versions' (Campos 2007). Thus, the SEC wants to rule out that the EU or individual nation-states modify the IFRS or recognize them only partially.

However, the public pressure to facilitate listings of foreign firms in US capital markets increased. While the number of foreign firms listed in US stock exchanges had increased from 328 in the year 1990 to 960 in 2000, it actually decreased to 866 in 2005 (Doidge et al. 2007: 48). This has sparked a discussion as to whether US stock exchanges have become less competitive and whether this has been the case because of the costs involved for firms to comply with the new rules of the Sarbanes–Oxley Act on auditing (see Committee on Capital Markets Regulation 2006; McKinsey & Co. 2006; Paulson 2006; Commission on the Regulation of US Capital Markets in the 21st Century 2007; Doidge et al. 2007). Treasury Secretary Henry M. Paulson stated in a speech on the competitiveness of US capital markets in November 2006:

> One important feature of the IFRS accounting system is that it is principles-based, rather than rules-based. By 'principles-based', I mean that the system is organized around a relatively small number of ideas or concepts that provide a framework for thinking about specific issues. The advantage of a principles-based system is that it is flexible and sensible in dealing with new or special situations. A rules-based system typically gives more specific guidance than a principles-based system, but it can be too rigid and may lead to a 'tick-the-box' approach. (Paulson 2006)

Several capital market actors demanded that the requirement to reconcile accounts based on IFRS to US GAAP should be abolished earlier than 2009 and that American companies should also be free to choose between IFRS and US GAAP (Nazareth 2007). According to Paulson, talks between US and EU regulators not only aimed at eliminating the reconciliation requirement in the US, but also at 'continuing to permit listings in the EU on the basis of statements prepared according to GAAP' (Paulson 2006). In June 2007 the SEC finally decided to issue a 'Proposing Release' to allow the use of IFRS in financial reports filed by foreign firms registered in US capital markets (SEC 2007a). One month later the SEC went one step further and proposed to allow all US issuers of securities to prepare their financial statements using IFRS (SEC 2007b).

In 2008, the IASC Foundation will undergo a new constitution review. In this context, the trustees of the foundation announced some proposals to strengthen its public accountability and funding on 6 November 2007 (IASC Foundation 2007). These proposals are not very concrete so far; however, they aim at establishing stronger formal and informal contacts between public securities regulators and the trustees of the IASC Foundation. It is no coincidence that the European Commission, the SEC, the IOSCO and the Financial Services Agency of Japan issued a combined statement one day later, suggesting 'the establishment of a new monitoring body within the governance structure of the IASC Foundation to reinforce the existing public interest oversight function of the IASC Foundation Trustees ... The monitoring body would, together with the IASC Foundation Trustees and in consultation with the trustee appointments advisory group, participate in the selection of Trustees. The monitoring body would also be responsible for the final approval of Trustee nominees and would have the opportunity to review the Trustees' procedures for overseeing the standard-setting process and ensuring the IASB's proper funding' (SEC 2007c). Thus, the struggle for the control of the standard-setting process between the various public and private 'stakeholders' of the IASB is ongoing.

Conclusion

What can we learn from the internationalization of accounting standards with regard to questions of imperialism, hegemony and the state? Can the conflicts over accounting be understood in terms of imperialist rivalries between the US and its European competitors? Does the internationalization of accounting standards reflect the emergence of a transnational ruling class, a transnational state or a transnational empire (cf. Hardt and Negri 2000; Robinson 2004)? Does it support arguments on the decline of US hegemony (cf. Arrighi 2005) or the continuing vibrancy of American empire (cf. Panitch and Gindin 2005a)? Does the EU challenge American hegemony in this field? It is certainly not possible to draw general, far-reaching conclusions from such a limited case study. However, the empirical evidence presented here can at least contribute to our understanding of these theoretical and political problems.

To sum up, it seems fair to say that US and UK standard-setters 'have historically dominated the IASC/B's governance structure' (Martinez-Diaz 2005: 4). They enjoyed a 'first mover advantage' because of the dominant position of the US and the UK within the global financial system. 'Harmonization has been driven in this case by decentralized market forces, primarily the desire to access the world's most established equities markets', as Simmons (2001: 611) noted. In this process 'the IASC has provided the cover of multilateral legitimacy to mostly US standards. In doing so, the IASC has provided a focal point that bears a close resemblance to SEC rules' (ibid.). However, the 'IASC did not automatically become a focal point for US preferences, and the US regulator decided to endorse IASs only after lengthy negotiations and qualifications that even today have not been fully resolved. In sum, US regulators were not willing to let the world adapt to hegemonic standards without a fairly heavy guiding hand' (Martinez-Diaz 2005: 6). So far, the 'convergence' of US GAAP and IAS/IFRS has primarily taken place as the remodelling of the latter after the example of the former.

Of course, there are still differences between the two sets of standards: US GAAP are 'rules-based' whereas IFRS are 'principles-based', for instance. However, these standards are clearly more similar to each other than to former continental European accounting standards like those of the German HGB. The internationalization of accounting standards has taken place as their Americanization. The collapse of the New Economy and the series of financial scandals in the US have certainly led to a temporary crisis of the

American system of accounting and corporate governance. With the stock market crash, huge sums of capital have been moved from US capital markets to Europe and other locations. The crisis has led to a more serious debate about the advantages and disadvantages of various systems of accounting and corporate governance. However, when measured by market capitalization, US GAAP were still used for the presentation and evaluation of more than half of global corporate capital in 2005 (Tafara 2005).

The recent debate about the declining competitiveness of US exchanges and the critique that it would be too costly to comply with the Sarbanes–Oxley Act for foreign companies is not necessarily a sign of an ongoing crisis. It rather shows that investors and corporations try to loosen regulations and to return to business as usual. In any case, a retreat of foreign companies from US exchanges should not be confused with a crisis of hegemony of US capital. This retreat partly reflects the fact that the stock market crash in 2000–2 was not confined to US capital. A number of European multinationals have experienced symptoms of 'overstretch' in the last few years. The retreat from US exchanges is partly a sign of *their* crisis, too. On the other hand, it also signifies that US financial capital is more active in Europe and that getting access to American capital no longer requires European corporations to go onto US exchanges.

For the time being, not one but two accounting standards are widely used in the world: US GAAP and IFRS. It remains to be seen whether complete convergence will take place. However, both sets of standards have a number of characteristics in common – like the growing pre-eminence of fair value accounting which reflects the predominance of financial markets and the growing importance of fictitious capital within capitalist reproduction. The transformation of European accounting regulation indicates a transformation of bank-based financial systems into more market-based financial systems. This is in line with the growing global dominance of financial capital. Thus, it could be argued that the internationalization of accounting standards has taken place as their Americanization because US standards were most suitable for an emerging global regime of accumulation dominated by financial capital and particularly fictitious capital.

Perry and Nölke (2006) have stressed the rise of transnational private authority in European accounting regulation. If we do not understand the state in narrow, juridical terms but follow Gramsci's concept of the expanded or integral state as the unity of civil society and political society, the IASB could well be understood as an emerging transnational state apparatus. However, this transnational state apparatus does not completely replace national actors and state apparatuses in the regulation of accounting. On the one hand, the IASB is itself composed of actors rooted to some extent in national contexts. On the other hand, the development of IFRS by the IASB does not take place in isolation, as we have seen. So, the development of international accounting standards is rather the product of a network of actors and state apparatuses, with the IASB as a central node, but also including American state apparatuses and organizations like the SEC and the FASB. Trade unions are completely absent in this process so far (Perry and Nölke 2006: 580). The emerging new form of accounting regulation can be interpreted as the result of a shift in the social balance of forces to the disadvantage of the working classes. The formation of accounting standards has become further isolated from democratic control. Perry and Nölke (2006) rightly emphasize that the content of international accounting standards is also to the disadvantage of labour as the paradigm of fair value accounting enables the capitalization of future profit expectations at an extended scale and thus contributes to a growing inequality in the distribution of wealth.

Notes

1. Statutory accounts refer to the corporation as a legal entity. Consolidated accounts refer to the entity considered as a group (the parent company and its affiliates and subsidiaries).
2. Saint Gobain in 1970 was the first French multinational which adopted US GAAP. Pechiney followed in 1972, Rhône-Poulenc in 1973 (Touron 2005).
3. Fourth Council Directive 78/660/EEC of 25 July 1978 based on Article 54 (3) (g) of the Treaty on the annual accounts of certain types of companies.
4. The DAX is the most important German stock market index and comprises the quotations of 30 out of the 35 most important German corporations in terms of market capitalization and stock turnover.
5. Incidentally, the International Confederation of Free Trade Unions (ICFTU) had been a member of the Consultative Group. With the restructuring the representation of trade unions in the standard-setting bodies ceased to exist (Müller 2004: 6).

9

From Bretton Woods to Neoliberal Reforms: the International Financial Institutions and American Power

Ruth Felder

The last decade has seen numerous debates about the performance and the future of the International Monetary Fund (IMF) and the World Bank as well as many proposals for reform. Some have criticized the international financial institutions (IFIs) for creating problems of moral hazard and have argued that their original mandates have been gradually distorted and overextended. Others have condemned the narrow theoretical framework behind structural adjustment programmes or the narrow focus on business interests and the disregard for civil society. Although such critiques are inspired by different assumptions and political orientations, many of them are characterized by a tendency to isolate the IFIs' operations from the dynamics of the capitalist relations of which they are part. More substantial critiques of the IFIs must locate their discourses and policies in the context of the neoliberal transformation of the economies and societies of the global South – a process that involves the liberalization of trade and finance, the creation of opportunities for accumulation through the privatization and commodification of public goods, the protection of foreign direct investments and the building of domestic institutional structures of accountability to international financial markets. Indeed, over the past decade the role of the IFIs has been extended from the enforcement of these reforms to the management of their adverse effects (such as impoverishment, social dislocation, expropriation of public goods, regressive distribution of wealth and environmental degradation). Their new focus on poverty, governance and transparency was meant to shore up their legitimacy and to enhance their capacity to manage the conflictual and contradictory development of neoliberal globalization and contain the spread of the disruptive effects of crises.

Cammack's (2002a, 2002b, 2003) comprehensive review of the World Bank's recent intellectual production reveals that its attention to institutional and social issues is driven primarily by the aim to establish the structural conditions for the global governance of capitalism, especially the creation and maintenance of an exploitable and disciplined global proletariat.

He links this to the IMF's ongoing effort to strengthen the international financial architecture, arguing that both institutions have assumed the role of guardians of global capitalism in a way that transcends the particular interests of countries and capitalists. Similarly, Fine (2001: 10–15) argues that the World Bank's (and to some extent also the IMF's) turn to a more positive view of the state and a greater concern with poverty since the late 1990s suffers from serious conceptual flaws but has served to legitimate the IFIs' intervention in borrowing countries beyond economic policies to broader dimensions of governance and social reproduction. In a similar vein, Bond (2001: 437–8) has shown that World Bank and IMF initiatives to bring issues such as the environment, participation and debt relief onto the agenda have been subordinated to the aim of enforcing neoliberal structural adjustment.

These important contributions shed light on the connections between economic and institutional reforms, governance and social discipline, and reveal the lines of continuity that run between the pro-market orthodoxy of the Washington Consensus and the apparently more social post-Washington Consensus. But to fully appreciate all this, more attention must be paid to the IFIs' relation to American imperialism and its political project aimed at the creation and reproduction of the institutional conditions for neoliberal globalization. This is especially important today because the questions that have been raised in mainstream economic and political circles about the effectiveness of the IMF and the World Bank have resulted in a new American agenda for keeping their policing role intact while streamlining their organizational structure, reasserting control over their bureaucracies and addressing problems of multiple and incoherent goals.

To assess the current institutional crisis of the IFIs properly it is necessary to go beyond the mainstream focus on the institutional and organizational dimensions of the IFIs. These dimensions are certainly not unimportant but they are by themselves inadequate to grasp the complex nature of the IFIs and of their successive crises and redeployments. The discourses and strategies of these institutions, the connections among them and their relationships with both donor and borrowing states need to be conceptualized in the context of the historical balances of forces, including their relationship to the imperial power and the way it has historically used them as enforcers of capitalist discipline.

In order to appreciate the role the IFIs have come to play in establishing the conditions for neoliberal globalization, this chapter will attempt to put them in proper historical perspective. Moreover, since the IMF and the World Bank are not identical twins, their actions and theoretical premises have undergone periods of divergence as well as convergence, and as they have responded to different political and social demands, the coordination between them has not been automatic. It is necessary, therefore, to review their histories separately.

The IMF: from regulating exchange rates to policing neoliberal global integration

The Bretton Woods Agreement of 1944, which gave birth to the IMF, established an organizational structure and procedures that guaranteed a pro-American bias in the goals and operation of the new institution. To join the Fund and get support in the event of balance of payments problems, countries had to commit to peg their currencies to the dollar (which alone was pegged to gold) and to remove exchange controls and discriminatory practices affecting current transactions. To be sure, concessions were made that would relax this discipline in some respects. First, it was accepted that countries could control current transactions during a transitional period. In addition, a scarce currency clause (which has never been invoked) was included in the IMF's Articles of Agreement that allowed discrimination against exports from a country with a large balance of payments surplus whose currency had been declared scarce (Block 1977: 48–9).

The IMF's voting system is based on a country's quota subscriptions and its governing bodies reflected the uneven balance between core and peripheral countries and, especially, the unmatched power of the US.[1] This has been accentuated by the fact that some important decisions require a special 85 per cent majority, giving the US effective veto power. The subsequent evolution of the requirement of special majorities has helped the US to extend its influence. The number of categories of decision that require these majorities has gradually increased from nine to sixty-four and includes decisions about the adjustment of quotas, the creation of a council, the allocation of the IMF's own international reserve asset, the Special Drawing Rights (SDRs) and, since 1977, all political decisions (Woods 2000a: 833). However, the US has not often needed to resort to its veto power. Consensus among the major shareholders is usually reached through informal channels, which allow the US Treasury to exercise influence on the IMF's executive directors and staff[2] (Thacker 1999: 41; Babb 2003: 16–17; Smaghi 2004: 233, 242). The strength of this influence depends on US decisions to ensure large disbursements and on the fact that managers will not make recommendations that risk American rejection, so that sensitive issues would be 'run past' the US Treasury before being presented to the Board (Woods 2003: 107).

During the early years of the post-war period the US state, pushed by Wall Street bankers (who had gained considerable influence in the Truman administration) (Helleiner 1994: 52), worked to reshape the IMF – an institution ostensibly created to protect countries from the potentially deleterious effects of untrammelled financial markets and capital flows – into a guardian of the integrity of financial markets (Frieden 1987: 61–5). Orthodox economists and 'old-fashioned' financiers took important positions in the institution and set the basis for its strong anti-inflationary culture and its tendency to take price stability, financial responsibility and the repayment of debts more seriously than other economic problems even in the context of the Keynesian policy climate of the time (Babb 2003: 20). By imposing restrictive lending criteria, the US ensured that the institution would work to create the same discipline the gold standard had imposed in the past. In this context, the international liquidity shortage of the period increased the need for US private and public investments and generally inclined countries to offer a better climate for business (Block 1977: 113).

The American preference for restrictive assistance became operational in the Fund's lending in the years to follow. The US prevented European countries receiving assistance under the Marshall Plan from getting IMF assistance. It also put pressure on the IMF Executive Board to make lending conditional on the borrower's efforts to overcome balance of payments problems. Even though European and other members of the Board initially rejected this conditionality, it was finally accepted as the only way to overcome the IMF's initial deadlock and make its resources widely available. The US's capacity to impose its criteria was enhanced by the fact that this pattern was established at a time when only weak peripheral countries – those most likely to accept conditionality – were applying for assistance. During the 1950s, and especially after the fall of the prices of raw materials that followed the Korean War prompted peripheral countries to apply for IMF assistance on a regular basis, the principle of conditionality became institutionalized. Conditions included quantitative performance clauses which limited public expenditures. Disbursements were often 'phased', i.e. spread over time contingent on performance (Harmon 1997: 26; Babb 2003: 10).

The IMF's first crisis

After the return to convertibility of European currencies in the late 1950s, the Fund responded to the challenges posed by the rapid growth of private financial activities by expanding the resources available for financing used to offset capital flows (especially against the pound sterling). To deal with the potentially disruptive effects of the growth of the Euromarkets without turning to trade restrictions or capital controls, Managing Director Peer Jacobson proposed an increase in the quotas subscribed by member countries and the establishment of a line of credit with governments and banks (the General Agreement to Borrow) that would enable the IMF to provide additional funds to meet the needs of countries in periods of crisis (Helleiner 1994: 96), while at the same time enforcing conditionality on all the IMF's standby loans – including those to a core country like the UK (Harmon 1997: 27–9).[3]

In spite of its additional financial resources and its expanded disciplinary power, the Fund did not play a meaningful role as the crisis of the fixed exchange rate system developed through the 1960s. Indeed, it became marginalized and cut off from the major decisions that reshaped international monetary relations (Kahler 1990: 98–101). The IMF's proposal to defend the fixed exchange rate system through the strengthening of cooperative capital controls got the support of Europe and Japan but foundered on US opposition (Helleiner 1994: 104–5). The marginalization of the Fund undermined US domestic support for the institution and showed other member countries and Fund officials that 'the organization's status and role in the world economy would depend upon the uses to which the United States would put it' (Woods 2003: 94). The US's unilateral ending of the fixed exchange rate system of the Bretton Woods Agreement made the IMF's regulation of exchange rates meaningless while lending and surveillance became less important in the context of growing international liquidity and capital flows to peripheral countries. As the number of loans consequently decreased dramatically and conditionality was relaxed, the decline of the IMF seemed unavoidable (Babb 2003: 13).

This dire prospect changed in the 1970s, starting with the first oil crisis, when the balance of payments deficits of non-oil producing countries ushered in a new area of IMF intervention (Peet 2003: 67–72). Initially, new lending facilities with longer repayment periods and looser conditionality were created to assist countries that were suffering a substantial deterioration in their current accounts. The principles underlying these facilities involved 'sharing the deficit' and providing for medium-term financing, rather than rapid adjustment. This ran against the preferences of the US Treasury for more orthodox adjustment policies similar to those followed by core countries and for recycling petrodollars through financial markets without the mediation of the Fund. This divergence, however, came to an end in 1976, when the IMF aligned itself behind the US's rejection of the financing of disequilibria and greater loan conditionality – and moreover applied it very stringently to the 1976 standby loan to the UK (under pressure from the US and Germany). Since then, core countries have avoided recourse to its assistance, as the British loan 'fostered the belief that a conditional Fund standby was politically costly and something to be avoided if at all possible' (Harmon 1997: 233). This reluctance, combined with the availability of non-conditional private lending for middle-income peripheral countries, seemed to confine the IMF to assisting its poorest members in Africa and Asia that could not get private credit and to providing a 'seal of approval' for policies that offered guarantees to private investors. In what seemed to prefigure a new role in development financing, the Fund became a permanent monitor of countries (on the behalf of lenders), rather than an adviser helping them to overcome temporary imbalances (Kahler 1990: 102).

Accompanying the reformulation of the IMF's roles and tasks, the 1978 amendment of its Articles of Agreement recognized countries' right to define their exchange rate policy (reflecting US efforts to liberalize the exchange of goods, services and capital), and redefined surveillance in vague terms that would pave the way for expanding the number of economic issues that could be subjected to scrutiny (Fieleke 1994: 21–2; Helleiner 1994: 110; Bradlow

2006: 6). The Guidelines on Conditionality released in 1979 ratified the expanded surveillance power by authorizing the Fund to 'pay due regard to the domestic social and political objectives, the economic priorities, and the circumstances of members'. This also laid the basis for the conditionality associated with structural adjustment that would accompany IMF assistance from the early 1980s (Pauly 1999: 415). These modifications expressed and catalyzed a trend that has made the Fund more influential in a broad range of developing countries while reducing its influence in industrialized countries.

The debt crisis and structural adjustment

The debts accumulated during the 1970s by peripheral countries turned problematic when it became apparent that economic growth was not sufficient to allow for the servicing of the loans; and the problem became critical when the Federal Reserve increased interest rates with the Volcker shock of 1979. After the 1982 Mexican debt crisis, debt management allowed the Fund to reassert its role as the guarantor of the stability of the international financial system. Its assistance to indebted countries became conditional on the implementation of structural adjustment programmes that reshaped their domestic economies and prioritized debt repayment. The IMF also played an important role in coordinating the actions of private banks that were seeking to reduce their exposure in the countries affected by the debt crisis. By threatening to withhold credit unless banks cooperated, the IMF prompted them to contribute their own funds to bail-outs, thereby expanding its command over resources beyond its own reserves (Peet 2003: 75–6). In this way, its intervention put the burden of the crisis on debtors while enforcing the collective interest of bankers. Not surprisingly, this soon led to a reversal of the initial hostility of the Reagan administration towards the Fund (Kahler 1990: 103–7).

Even though the IMF succeeded in preventing the debt crisis from turning into a major dislocation of the international financial system, its interventions prompted serious criticisms. When it became apparent that the crisis was not a mere problem of liquidity, the Fund was blamed for pushing countries into recession and postponing necessary systemic reforms (Bird 2001: 828). As a response to this impasse, in October 1985 US Treasury Secretary James Baker announced a debt restructuring plan whereby a group of highly indebted countries[4] would obtain additional lending from private banks and the international financial institutions conditional on fiscal, financial and monetary reform monitored by the IMF. Although the plan failed to attract new private lending and to reduce the burden of indebtedness, it was a turning point in that it recognized the structural nature of the debt crisis and encouraged the IMF to formulate 'growth-oriented' adjustment programmes (Killick 1995: 7).

In 1989, in the wake of the failure of the Baker plan, Nicholas Brady, the Treasury Secretary under the Bush administration, announced a new debt restructuring scheme that would increase collectability, diversify risk and improve debtors' creditworthiness through the reduction and securitization of existing debts with commercial banks in countries willing to implement IMF-sponsored structural reforms. As part of this new strategy of debt management, the Fund's intervention went even further in transcending its traditional focus on domestic credit, budget deficits and currency devaluation and promoting radical structural 'reforms' deemed necessary for the success of adjustment, based on more detailed assessment of the allocation of resources and specific budget cuts (Killick 1995: 25). Hence, the Brady plan created the conditions for the Fund to catalyze the infusion of new private credit to indebted countries while assisting them with adjusting to the imperatives of free capital markets through a more intrusive intervention in their domestic economic management.

Crisis management and surveillance

By the early 1990s, when many peripheral countries were engaged in structural reforms and regained access to international financing, the 'Tequila crisis' in Mexico threw into question the neoliberal promise of crisis-free development. Complementing US bilateral assistance, the IMF disbursed the largest loan in its history to prevent the crisis from spreading. The US imposed its view on the Executive Board despite the opposition of the European members who argued that the loan weakened the liquidity of the institution and contradicted the catalytic role of the Fund (Riesenhuber 2001: 58). The IMF also followed the US's lead in understanding the crisis as the result of mismanagement on the part of the Mexican government and made its assistance conditional on fiscal austerity and further financial deregulation (Soederberg 2004: 52–4). As in 1982, its intervention was instrumental in directing the impact of the crisis away from investors to the poor majority of the Mexican population.

The IMF's response to the 1997–8 East Asian crisis, in line with the US priorities, involved pushing governments further in the direction of free capital mobility (Soederberg 2004: 133–6). IMF Managing Director Michel Camdessus saw the crisis as a 'blessing in disguise' that created room for introducing substantial policy changes in exchange for financial assistance that national governments would not otherwise have adopted. Blaming crony capitalism and the structural weakness of the economies of the region, the Fund took the opportunity to demand floating exchange rates, fiscal and monetary discipline, trade openness and financial liberalization (Medley 2000: 381).

The IMF's role was central to the strategy crafted by the US Treasury and the Federal Reserve, bringing together the G7, the Asian Development Bank and the World Bank to rule out a regional alternative of the creation of an Asian Monetary Fund which had been mooted by Japan, and which the US especially saw as a threat to the Fund's capacity to enforce conditionality and financial discipline (Riesenhuber 2001: 126). Even more than its previous interventions, the Fund's performance in the East Asian crisis fuelled intense debates. The US Congress initially refused to increase the US quota to the IMF on the grounds that it was handing 'good money to bad people', but it soon relented, mollified by US Treasury Secretary Larry Summers' reassurances that the IMF was 'the cheapest and most effective way' to promote the American interest in world-wide financial stability (Riesenhuber 2001: 125).

Yet the crises also triggered the IMF's own recognition of the problems associated with the process of liberalization. New emergency facilities to assist countries affected by international crises were created, and the New International Financial Architecture (NIFA) process was launched at the 1995 G7 summit in Halifax. It was decided that IMF surveillance would be expanded beyond a given country's macroeconomic position or its foreign exchange reserves to include the financial structure (especially the debt and foreign debt ratios) of their major companies and banks (Harris 1999: 207–8). The IMF established standards of 'good practices' and used its leverage to encourage all countries to adhere to the General Data Dissemination Standard to provide information on economic, fiscal, financial, external and socio-demographic issues following specific guidelines that guarantee its quality, periodicity and timeliness. Participation in this would be 'voluntary' but non-participation would have a significant impact on countries' access to financial markets. In addition, the Fund, in conjunction with the World Bank, started compiling Reports on the Observance of Standards and Codes (ROSCs) that assess the national level of implementation of information codes and standards (Langley 2004b). Moreover, the IMF instituted a new series of Press Information Notices (PINs) through which its assessment of a member country may be made known to the public. 'In this way the Fund's dissatisfaction with a country's progress in adhering to the Fund's principles of "good governance" can be a very credible threat and result in capital flight or investment strikes' (Soederberg 2001: 859).

At the same time, some crucial institutional and political dimensions of structural reforms came into focus when the IMF decided that assistance would be withheld from countries with poor 'governance' (e.g. ad hoc decision-making, rent seeking, preferential treatment of individuals and organizations). In what seemed to be a recognition of the social costs of 'disembedded liberalism', Managing Director Horst Köhler not only spoke of the need to alleviate the costs of globalization and to fight global poverty, but also advanced a new form of conditionality in which agreements between the IMF and client countries should be based on the domestic 'ownership' of the reforms. This meant that governments should assume responsibility for adjustment programmes and civil society should support such structural reforms. In Fine's (2001: 12) blunt terms, ownership means 'doing what the World Bank/IMF would do but also appearing to do it by yourself and willingly'. This has translated into the widely advertised debt-relief initiative for Heavily Indebted Poor Countries (HIPC) implemented through the Poverty Reduction Strategy Papers (PRSPs) tailored to the specific circumstances of each country (Lee 2002; Peet 2003: 95–7). The IMF's emphasis on governance and institutional arrangements and more recently on ownership and poverty alleviation involves the acknowledgement of the limitations of universal recipes and of the importance of recognizing the specific situation of any given country. However, as Best (2003: 374) suggests, national variations seem to be treated as 'temporary deviations from the true direction of the international regime – the universal liberalization of finance'.

Nevertheless, not only left-wing but also right-wing critics have increasingly raised their voices against the IMF in this context. The Meltzer Report authored by the US Congress International Financial Institution Advisory Commission criticized the IMF's excessive lending, declaring it responsible for aggravating situations of moral hazard, and proposed its transformation into a short-term lender for countries that had already qualified for assistance. The Clinton administration rejected the conclusions of the report and only favoured minor changes that would not alter the role of the Fund in the governance of the international financial system (Langley 2004b: 79). On the other hand, the new Bush administration favoured a narrower role for the institution concentrated on early intervention for crisis prevention, streamlined conditionality and the fight against money laundering (Munk 2001: 405; Lee 2002: 290). The Bush administration's unwillingness to back IMF assistance to Argentina in order to avoid default on its sovereign debt in 2001 was an important expression of this new approach. The hostility to IMF bail-outs and the preference for 'market solutions' to crisis provided the discursive context in which the Fund adopted a more aggressive style in the negotiations.

The search for a new sense of mission in line with this 'streamlined' agenda underlay Managing Director Rodrigo de Rato's call to define a clear focus on surveillance and financial assistance for the Fund after a decade of being 'pulled in too many new directions' (IMF 2005: 2). Rato's successor, Dominique Strauss Kahn, has made gestures to restore the confidence of peripheral countries in the IMF in a context in which the relevance of the institution seemed to be at stake as several middle-income countries made efforts to free themselves from conditionality, and as East Asian countries amassed large amounts of reserves so as to deal with a potential crisis without the Fund's assistance (Woods 2006: 2). Similarly, several Latin American countries cancelled their debt with the IMF in advance, which freed them from the policy conditions and surveillance associated with its lending programmes. These decisions not only weakened the IMF's leverage but also deprived it of loan charges and interest from large borrowers that constitute a major source of its income (Kapur and Webb 2006: 14).

This historical account has revealed an institution that has overcome previous crises and has recently helped to translate neoliberal globalization into concrete blueprints for structural reform which redirect the potentially disruptive effects of financial turmoil away from creditors and financial actors towards workers and the poor in peripheral countries. It has also revealed why it is that any purely institutional history does not suffice to explain the role of the IMF: the adaptation to diverse historical situations and the IMF's changing roles and power have depended on economic scenarios and political dynamics that go far beyond the boundaries of the institution itself and have everything to do with US global power.

The World Bank: the successive strategies of social engineering

Unlike the IMF, the International Bank for Reconstruction and Development (IBRD) – the agency in charge of financing reconstruction and development – did not receive much attention at Bretton Woods. It was mostly a US creation meant to facilitate the flow of private investment to finance European reconstruction. Development goals were included in its Articles of Agreement mainly so that Latin American countries would agree to join the IMF – which was made a condition of qualifying for development loans (Williams 1994: 103). In its six decades of existence, the World Bank Group that emerged from the IBRD would gradually grow into an ambitious institutional complex providing technical assistance and policy advice to governments, financing private investments, offering guarantees to investors in peripheral countries and facilitating the settlement of investment disputes between governments and foreign investors. Its own lending capacity has come to exceed by far that of other IFIs, and its intellectual production has become central to the academic and political development agenda (Stone and Wright 2006: 2).

The governing and organizational structures of the Bank are similar to those of the IMF in that the shares of each country determine its voting power.[5] Decisions about the rules that regulate its activities required a special majority of 80 per cent, which gave the US, with more than 20 per cent of the votes, a veto power; in 1989 when the US share fell to 17 per cent, the majority required for amendment was increased to 85 per cent (Gilbert and Vines 2000: 20). As the IBRD's ability to float bonds depended on Wall Street when it was created, it was decided that a US citizen chosen by the US government should lead it, and with only a few exceptions the World Bank's presidents have been chosen from the private financial sector (Kahler 2001: 43). Since the 1960s, the number of Bank officials from developing countries has grown but approximately 80 per cent of its economists have been trained in the UK or North America (Berger and Beeson 1998: 493).

Beyond these formal mechanisms of control, US influence is exercised in several informal ways. First, the Bank staff have rarely advanced loans and promoted policies that were not backed by the US for consideration to the Board (Woods 2000b: 134). In addition, the US is the only Bank member to check all loan proposals in detail and Treasury officials are in daily contact not only with the US executive director but also with other Bank officials. More generally, US influence is grounded in the Bank's dependence on world financial markets, New York's central position as a global financial centre, and the close alignment of the interests of key financial actors with those of US foreign policy (Berger and Beeson 1998: 493).

The IBRD quickly became entwined in the power relations of the Cold War. US government aid through the Marshall Plan rather than Bank lending became the main source of financial assistance for reconstruction. This left the Bank lacking quality projects to be financed and unable to offer good investment opportunities. In 1948, after gaining the confidence of the US financial market under the leadership of its second president, John McCloy, a Wall Street lawyer (Rich 1994: 68), the Bank began lending to Latin America. It further positioned itself as a source of development financing in the 1950s when the process of decolonization created a new group of clients with an agenda of rapid growth and development (Gilbert and Vines 2000: 14). In this context, its financial assistance was a critical instrument in drawing the decolonizing third world into the logic of a bipolar world order. Reflecting the Keynesian and Cold War consensus on liberal developmentalism (expressed in the rise of classical modernization theory), its lending concentrated on infrastructure, transportation and energy projects that would foster industrialization, import substitution and exports (Berger and Beeson 1998: 488). Its intervention was conceived in terms of addressing capital market failures and overcoming the tension between the short-term horizon of private financing and the long-term horizon of infrastructure investments (Gilbert and Vines 2000: 15).

During the 1950s the IBRD began to collaborate with governments in identifying projects – or, as Rich (1994: 74) puts it, it worked to create the demand for development financing. To build up technical and planning skills among its potential borrowers, in 1956 it created the Economic Development Institute (EDI) that served to train administrators from peripheral countries in the formulation of development plans.[6] With considerable financial support from the Ford and Rockefeller Foundations, the EDI offered courses in the theory and practice of development for senior officials from borrowing countries. It later also ran training programmes on World Bank project appraisal and country programming. In the words of its first director, Sir Alexander Cairncross, students at the EDI 'would carry with them ideas that were more congenial to the Bank when they went back to their own country'. He added that by the late 1970s, 'EDI graduates "more or less ran" South Korea, and in Pakistan there were "a great many ex-EDI men who quite consciously were pulling together and having an influence on development"' (Berger and Beeson 1998: 492–3).

The Bank's pursuit of a universal model of development based on the assumptions of modernization theory did not prevent US strategic interests from becoming a deciding factor in the Bank's lending policies. While Yugoslavia received loans in 1948 after its break with the Soviet bloc, loan applications from post-war Poland and Czechoslovakia were turned down when the US made it clear to the staff that it would vote against such loans if presented to the Executive Board. Similarly, negotiations for a World Bank loan to build the Aswan Dam in Egypt were suspended when US Secretary of State John Foster Dulles decided to refuse financing for the project. Conversely, Somoza's Nicaragua and the Shah's Iran – both seen as especially helpful anti-communist allies to the US – obtained a disproportionate number of loans (Payer 1982: 42–3; Kapur et al. 1997: 500; Woods, 2003: 105).

From the beginning of the 1960s, amidst growing concerns that poor peripheral countries would succumb to communist ideology, the International Development Agency (IDA) (in charge of concessional lending for basic social services in the poorest countries) was established. Positioning the struggle against poverty as its main focus, the World Bank justified its lending more and more in terms of the requirements of the development process rather than capital market failures (Gilbert and Vines 2000: 15). In this context, Robert McNamara, former Ford CEO and US Defence Secretary under Kennedy and Johnson, reformulated the Bank's notion of development, taking the position that poverty could be eradicated through direct policy intervention and that managerial competence was more important than ownership. This translated in a greater role for governments in development (Peet 2003: 118–20). Lending grew at unprecedented rates and was redirected towards projects of rural development, urban infrastructure, education and health that were said to target the needs of the poor (Pieper and Taylor 1998: 40; Gilbert and Vines 2000: 15). This major shift was accompanied by a process of institutional expansion in which research and long-term planning gained in importance (Rich 1994: 84–5).

The focus on poverty and the creation of the IDA produced frictions between the Bank and the Nixon administration. But even so, there was no major departure from the US's geopolitical priorities. The Bank refused to lend to the democratically elected governments of Goulart in Brazil and Allende in Chile but did lend to the subsequent dictatorships in both countries. Similarly, it had not lent to Indonesia during Sukarno but it did lend to Suharto after the anti-communist bloodbath he perpetrated (Rich 1994: 103). Also Turkey, Mexico, Iran and the Philippines, among other countries with a record of corruption, human rights violations and failure to meet the conditions associated with loans, received 'close and generous treatment from the World Bank' with the support of the US Treasury and the State Department (Woods 2000b: 146). But even in this geopolitical context, the failure to alleviate world poverty to any significant extent, and changes in development thinking that generally weakened US support for foreign aid, increasingly put in jeopardy the Bank's new agenda and soon led to a reversion to its more traditional areas of action (Gwin 1994; Peet 2003: 120).

The shift to structural adjustment lending

When the prospects of development and modernization were thrown into question by the international economic slowdown of the 1970s, private banks needing to recycle large amounts of liquid funds took the lead in extending loans to several peripheral countries, thereby creating the conditions for the accelerated growth of their external debt. This coincided with the declining importance of official financing in peripheral countries and with US calls for their governments to focus on inflation, the reduction of the external deficit and the adjustment of economic policies in line with market forces. This was an inauspicious context for the World Bank's efforts to increase lending.

The Bank was slow to recognize and respond to the changes. Only after the second oil shock in 1979–80 did it begin to issue public warnings about the limited ability of the international financial system to recycle funds sufficient to maintain import levels and economic growth rates in peripheral countries. Also, the deflationary policies implemented by neoconservative governments in core countries were responsible for its more pessimistic assessment of growth prospects. The Bank responded by prioritizing macroeconomic intervention over its traditional project lending (Chahoud 1991: 35). Debt management and 'adjustment with growth' policies in middle-income indebted countries became its new priorities. Structural adjustment lending (SAL) – previously seen as an instrument only used in exceptional situations – now became common. By making loans conditional on the implementation of structural reforms, the Bank expected it would be able to persuade governments to change their economic policies so as 'to put their houses in good economic order' (Mosley et al. 1995: 33).

The appointment of the former president of the Bank of America, Alden Clausen, as the World Bank's president in 1981 marked the virtual elimination of the fight against poverty from its agenda and a decisive turn to neoliberalism. The Bank's goals were now about ensuring efficient prices, reducing tariffs and subsidies, eliminating regulations and barriers to financial activities, deregulating labour markets, privatizing public assets and reducing state intervention (Pieper and Taylor 1998: 44–5). This shift occurred in the context of pressures from the Reagan administration to reduce multilateral aid and to make US support to the IFIs conditional on the implementation of policies aimed at advancing market-oriented reforms. While the Bank assumed that adjustment required substantial financing, the US – with the Treasury explicitly threatening to withhold support for capital increases and IDA replenishments – made it clear that it wanted the Bank to serve as a lender of last resort and pushed for a reduction in its lending levels (Gwin 1994: 62–3).

Although the Bank had focused on sustaining the payment position of indebted countries and preventing default since the early stages of the debt crisis, it was only after US Treasury Secretary James Baker launched his proposal for debt restructuring that the Bank developed a comprehensive strategy and took on a key role in debt management (Williams 1994: 117; Gilbert and Vines 2000: 16). The US administration in this context came to see the World Bank's structural adjustment lending as a useful instrument, one that could respond to the debt crisis and advance market liberalization at the same time, and one that could give a multilateral appearance to a strategy essentially framed by the US Treasury. This reversed the US opposition to a capital increase for the Bank and to replenishments for the IDA (Gwin 1994: 42–3; Williams 1994: 120).

But the Baker plan failed either to solve the debt crisis or to deliver on its promise of 'adjustment with growth'. As structural adjustment lending came under attack for its destabilizing consequences the World Bank's shift from project financing to policy-based lending and closer collaboration with the IMF began to draw considerable criticism. Under Clausen's successor, Barber Conable, poverty alleviation, distributional issues and governance would become central objectives of the Bank's lending activity (Kapur et al. 1997). This was accompanied by an institutional reorganization in which the Research Department (where a group of neoliberal ideologues had congregated during the 1980s) was eliminated (Berger and Beeson 1998: 491). The gradual incorporation of the political and social dimensions of adjustment and the relaxation of the rigid neoclassical orthodoxy of the 1980s paved the way for an apparent revolution in the World Bank's thinking and lending policies and for heated debates about its role in the tumultuous international developments of the mid-1990s.

A 'post-neoliberal' agenda?

The substitution of non-performing loans with the so-called Brady bonds during the early 1990s provided a new rationale for World Bank interventions. When the US Treasury changed its debt management strategy, the Bank's research into debt relief helped to define the new orientation (Woods 2000b: 142). In spite of serious objections from major shareholders, it also contributed resources to support debt reductions (Gwin 1994: 45). When private lending resumed, the Bank's interventions were justified in terms of the need to create the appropriate environments for capital and to ensure that investments contributed to growth and poverty reduction (Gilbert and Vines 2000: 18). The Bank thus came to play a major role in the development debate of the 1990s regarding the institutional underpinnings of globalizing markets. Recognizing that structural adjustment had been only partly successful even on its own terms, and that neoliberal reforms needed legitimacy and had to be protected from social pressures, the anti-state view of the 1980s gave way to prescriptions regarding the proper role of the state in market-oriented economies.

The World Bank's 'rediscovery' of the state was widely interpreted as a break with the neoliberal era. But the consolidation of a consensus on the free-market orientation of development made the new concessions in the direction of state intervention relatively harmless politically. Moreover, the Bank's new institutionalist arguments did not alter the rational-choice foundations of its understanding of development, which resulted in what Berger and Beeson (1998: 481) describe as 'a highly mechanistic approach to the dynamics of political and economic change in the various countries which the researchers at the Bank sought to understand'.

The 1994 crisis in Mexico occurred in spite of its faithful adherence to neoliberal prescriptions. This was especially remarkable when set alongside the fact that the 'Asian miracle' had been based on a strategy that departed from such prescriptions, and this dealt a major blow to the World Bank's premises for reform and development. When President Lewis Preston resigned in 1995, the US Treasury, the State Department and the White House joined forces in the search for a candidate who could define a new role for the Bank and rebuild its legitimacy (Kahler 2001: 46). The new President, James Wolfensohn, accompanied by Chief Economist Joseph Stiglitz, led a theoretical renewal that further stressed the non-economic dimensions of development, articulated a positive role for the state in orienting and regulating markets, and raised new concerns about sustainability, equity and accountability. This set the stage for the expanded intervention of the Bank in member countries through projects aimed at strengthening institutions, fighting poverty, and empowering civil society actors through training, consultation and technology transfers – all aimed at creating reliable political actors in borrowing countries. The definition of new areas for the World Bank's intervention was formalized in new guidelines for financial assistance that sought to replace conditionality with the domestic 'ownership' of the reforms – the Comprehensive Development Framework (CDF) launched in 1999. Countries were now required to show their record of good policies and institutional environments to be eligible for financial aid (Pender 2001: 408).

This World Bank response to the tensions associated with neoliberal reforms was incorporated into its lending, policy advice and intellectual production, with the purpose of remoulding economies, institutions and societies in a more coherent fashion. This was straightforwardly expressed in the 1999–2000 *World Development Report*, which encouraged countries to create national regulatory structures designed to attract foreign capital; reduce the potential for financial crises by controlling short-term capital movements most likely to destabilize the economy; hold sufficient foreign reserves; and establish an orderly liberalization of the capital account

(Coleman 2002: 509). Likewise, the turn towards a 'social vocabulary' and domestic 'ownership' has been part of an attempt to make local conditions compatible with the Bank's own comprehensive operational standards (Woods 2006: 3) as well as to depoliticize social and distributional issues (Hatcher 2006: 202). The inclusion of political and social dimensions of reforms and the emphasis on ownership helped to reshape the World Bank's image as a partner engaged in dialogue and exchange of ideas with client countries (Harrison 2001: 540; Pender 2001: 409). This was reinforced by the priority given, under Wolfensohn's leadership, to the systematic production, collection and diffusion of knowledge about development (Gilbert et al. 1999: 608–10).

In the wake of the crises of the 1990s, the Bank's renewed agendas have sparked intense academic debates and political controversies. As in the case of the IMF, criticism has not just come from the left and social movements; mainstream commentators have also criticized World Bank intervention (Stone and Wright 2006: 5; Vetterlein 2006: 127). In what may be interpreted as a response to these criticisms as well as a realignment with the new Bush administration's agenda, the Bank stressed the idea in its 2003 Annual Review of Development Effectiveness that lending should be limited or postponed in the absence of a good policy environment (Hatcher 2006: 194–5). The appointment of the former US Defence Secretary Paul Wolfowitz as World Bank President was accompanied by a wave of 'self-criticism' and by efforts to redefine the scope of intervention in more modest terms. The Bank's internal evaluation of its institutional performance resulted in a very critical assessment of the poor quality of its research, to the chagrin of many of its staff. The rapid ouster of Wolfowitz after a corruption scandal that further damaged the Bank's reputation has left its future role more uncertain than ever.

Conclusion: does Argentina foretell the future of the IFIs?

In the context of the institutional crisis that had enveloped both the Bank and the IMF by the turn of the century, the fact that many blamed the IFIs for the economic and social turmoil that affected Argentina in 2001 (which culminated in the Argentinian state's default on its debt) was bound to shake both institutions to their core. The new government's subsequent decision to pay off the entire debt with the IMF drew further international attention and triggered intense debates about the possible 'demonstration effect' of the Argentinian strategy and the future of the IFIs. These concerns have been reinforced by proposals for coordinated regional financial arrangements in Latin America that are explicitly designed as an alternative to the IFIs' tendency to privilege the interests of external creditors and that celebrate the Argentinian decision as a remarkable break with the neoliberal past. Mainstream analyses have also accepted that the IFIs' earlier role in enforcing neoliberal reforms in Argentina has severely damaged their reputation, effectiveness and prospects but view the rift between the Argentinian state and the IFIs as an alarming sign of a resurgent populism.

However, Argentina's adoption of the neoliberal strategy of development and international integration has been a highly complex process that goes far beyond the 'mistakes' or even the 'evil nature' of the IFIs. The decision to pay off the debt with the IMF cannot simply be understood as an unambiguous act of emancipation on the part of the Argentinian government or as a clear sign of the loss of authority and reputation of the IFIs. Whether other countries will follow in Argentina's footsteps cannot be deduced from the institutional links between countries and the IFIs but depends, among other things, on the broader picture of their economic policies, their location within the global economy, their relation to the American empire, and the constellation of domestic and international social forces still marked by the effects of neoliberal reforms.

In the early 1990s, Argentina emerged from a long crisis to become the 'poster child' of neoliberalism for its audacious process of state restructuring and macroeconomic stabilization. As those reforms translated into lower rates of inflation and massive capital inflows, the IFIs began to see the country as the showcase of the effectiveness of the neoliberal reforms. Their blessing was expressed in technical, financial and political support (under the Brady plan, among other projects) for the further privatization of public assets, the deregulation of the economy, the reform of public administration and the restructuring of the country's public debt.

But the combination of financial deregulation and a macroeconomic stabilization scheme based on a fixed exchange rate regime gradually eroded Argentina's international competitiveness and made the country extremely vulnerable to the international financial crises of the 1990s. For several years, lending from the IMF and the World Bank helped the government to compensate for capital outflows, to finance budget deficits and to respond to growing social demands – in exchange for a commitment to deepen fiscal discipline and expand the neoliberal reforms to a wide range of areas of state action. The country recovered from the Mexican and the Asian crisis but was hit hard by the recession that followed the Russian and Brazilian crises of 1998. The Fund disbursed several emergency loans to improve the international financial position of the country, while blaming the Argentinian government for its lack of political will to deepen the reforms and enforce fiscal discipline. The government committed itself to meeting the IMF's requirements, maintaining its fixed exchange rate regime and honouring the public debt. By the turn of the century, this led to an explosive combination of economic depression, uncontrollable growth of the public debt, social unrest and loss of international confidence in the Argentinian economy.

Even though IMF staff began to express doubts about the effectiveness of multilateral lending in addressing the crisis, financial assistance was maintained, helping to postpone the explosion of this crisis and giving economic actors time to transfer enormous amounts of money out of the country. This lasted until late 2001 when, in line with the hostility of the Bush administration towards international bail-outs, the IMF put an end to its leniency with regard to the non-fulfilment of conditions associated with its assistance programme. The IMF thus cancelled its disbursements to Argentina, expecting that this would enforce a restructuring of the public debt. Without the support of the Fund, the government renewed its efforts to reduce public spending and meet its financial commitments but failed to prevent or contain the explosion of political and social unrest that led to the resignation of the President, the announcement of unilateral default on the public debt and the abandonment of the fixed exchange rate regime in a context of growing economic instability.

These measures were followed by fierce struggles over the distribution of the costs of the crisis. The IMF actively intervened to prevent the reversal of the reforms and to protect the interests of international investors and creditors. Arguing that assistance should not precede but follow sound policies, it demanded an orthodox fiscal adjustment and further structural reforms without releasing new loans. At the same time, Managing Director Köhler pleaded guilty to not having paid enough attention to the institutional and fiscal weaknesses of the country, and justified the refusal to give additional financial assistance by asserting that 'the roots of the evil are in Argentina, therefore, if Argentina does not do anything about it the IMF cannot do it' (Zaiat 2002).

After months of unsuccessful negotiations with the Fund, by late 2002 the Argentinian government started to challenge some of the orthodox policies demanded by the institution. A combination of capital controls, taxes on exports and regulation of the exchange rate created the conditions for a gradual recovery of the economy. In this context, Néstor Kirchner won the presidential election and took power in May 2003. His discourse blamed neoliberalism for the crisis and rejected the pressures from the IMF, the World Bank and the G7 to deepen structural adjustment and to prioritize debt payment over growth. Amidst hostile negotiations and mutual accusations, an agreement with the IMF was reached in September 2003 with the support of the US, but against the opposition of the Europeans and Japanese who saw the agreement as excessively lenient. The government announced a restructuring of the defaulted debt that proceeded without the support of the IFIs and the G7 and was concluded in early 2005 with a high rate of acceptance among bondholders. Unlike the debt with private creditors that suffered a 'haircut', the debt with the IMF and the World Bank was not restructured, in an unsuccessful attempt to gain their support. In August 2004, the Fund cancelled its assistance programme on the grounds that the country had not made any progress with the necessary reforms. Since then, the government has not attempted to negotiate a new assistance programme. By late 2005, after more than three years of sustained growth and very favourable external and fiscal balances, Kirchner announced the decision to pay off the entire debt owed to the Fund to free the country from external discipline and surveillance. Likewise, the number of active programmes and the debt with the World Bank were considerably reduced and the government has rejected the Fund's offer to mediate in the debt negotiations between Argentina and the Paris Club of creditor states.

The Argentinian government's rejection of the IMF's deflationary blueprint and the demands of international creditors were key to its economic recovery. This in turn strengthened the official discourse that blamed neoliberalism and the IFIs for the previous crisis. This was the context in which the government took its controversial decision to fully repay the debt with the IMF. On the one hand, the IMF was aiming at reducing its exposure in Argentina, expecting to see the entire debt repaid by 2011 (Nudler 2004). This casts doubt on the Argentinian government's presentation of its decision as a bold assertion of its sovereignty. Critics have also argued that fiscal surpluses could have been, but were not, used to alleviate the situation of a huge mass of impoverished people in the country. On the other hand, the break with the Fund effectively gave the Argentinian state more room to regulate several macroeconomic variables and intervene in the economy in a way that would have been unthinkable in the context of traditional IMF programmes. The state has actively manipulated the exchange rate to improve the competitiveness of Argentinian exports, controlled the prices of privatized public utilities and refused to meet the demands of the public debt 'holdouts' – all this in the face of IMF antipathy to these forms of state activism and against the interests of capitalist fractions fiercely defended by the Fund. The government has also rejected the IMF's recommendations to prioritize the fight against inflation over growth.

Undoubtedly, Argentina has gained a degree of autonomy to make decisions about the use of its public resources, but this does not necessarily constitute a reversal of the previous structural transformation of the state and economy and of the patterns of distribution of power and wealth associated with it. Rather, the Argentinian government's antagonism towards the IMF and the World Bank should be located within a political strategy that centres on restoring the legitimacy of the political system while enlarging the room for manoeuvre for the state to recreate the conditions for capitalist accumulation. The strategy has paid off: as President Kirchner put it during a state visit to Germany, 'there is life after the IMF and it is a very good life' (Kirchner, 2005, quoted by González 2005). GDP has been growing at impressive rates, the 'endemic' fiscal and external deficits have been reversed and foreign currency reserves are at record levels after having plummeted in 2002. Yet, the recovery of profitability and competitiveness has been based on the revival of exports and has been premised on low wages (whose purchasing power has been further eroded by inflation), precarious labour relations, the persistence of high levels of poverty and inequality, and the maintenance of a regressive tax structure. Even though the Argentinian government has been highly vocal in its criticisms of the IFIs and neoliberalism, it has maintained fiscal discipline and hoarded large amounts of foreign reserves to respond to financial problems in the future. Ultimately, these safeguards are aimed at protecting the system in the event of a financial crisis rather than challenging the interests of its dominant groups (Katz 2007).

But the effects of the clash between Argentina and the IMF have heady international implications. The debt with the IMF was cancelled in the context of a growing social rejection of neoliberalism in Latin America, the coming to power of progressive, centre-left or left political forces in several of the region's countries, and new regional political and economic alliances that could grow into alternative regional financial institutions. Venezuela has backed Argentina's financial position by buying its public bonds (Swann 2007) and both countries, together with Brazil, Bolivia, Ecuador, Paraguay and Uruguay, have agreed on the creation of the regional Bank of the South, which will initially finance regional infrastructure projects. The new institution is intended to at least partly supplant international lenders and avoid their policy conditions. Some countries have announced a more radical break with the IFIs. In May 2007, Bolivia, Venezuela and Nicaragua withdrew from the World Bank's International Centre for the Settlement of Investment Disputes (ICSID), arguing that this institution, in charge of solving conflicts between countries and international private investors, favours the interests of transnational capital over the sovereignty of countries. Also, Venezuela announced its decision to leave the IMF and the World Bank, which (in the words of Venezuelan Finance Minister, Rodrigo Cabezas, quoted by BBC Mundo on 14 April 2007) 'are controlled by US hawks'.

These political initiatives have emerged in an international context marked by the ample availability of liquidity and high market prices for the commodities exported by Latin American countries; both of these factors have made them less dependent on lending from the IFIs. The question is whether this will be a lasting trend catalyzing development strategies independent from the IFIs or if, when external circumstances take a turn for the worse, countries will again agree to conditionality in order to get financial assistance. Alternative regional financial institutions, if realized, might play a role in guaranteeing credits and offering rapid-disbursement loans but their success or failure will ultimately depend on which of these broader political choices prevails. Without changes in the subordinated integration of the countries that make up these new Latin American initiatives within the global capitalist hierarchy, regional institutions will hardly be able to replace the IMF whose effectiveness is based on its capacity to reassure global investors by strengthening the accountability of borrowing countries. To put it differently, the fate of an alternative regional financial architecture will depend on the transformation of the historical forms of global integration that are at the origin of the recurrent crises in Latin America.

As for the IFIs, their capacity to adapt themselves to changing conditions has not only neutralized some critical views but has also given them more refined tools to expand and sustain their historical agendas. Notwithstanding this adaptability and the important differences between the modernization view of the 1950s and 1960s, the radical anti-statism of the 1980s and the more recent concern about the institutional, social and political dimensions of global capitalism, their tendency to locate the source of development problems in the domestic features of countries rather than in their position in the hierarchy of the international capitalist economy has remained unchanged.

When the IFIs came into existence, they were able to frame their policies in technical terms. But as early as the 1960s, the differential treatment of core and peripheral countries and the alignment with the Cold War cleavages raised questions about the IFIs' presentation of their programmes in neutral, technocratic terms. Later, the end of the fixed exchange rate drastically changed the nature of the environment in which the IFIs operated. Initially, both the IMF and the World Bank seemed to lose their purpose and became marginalized from the transformation of the international economy. The hostility of the US administration was crucial in this apparent loss of significance. But it was also one of the key factors behind the IFIs' repositioning with the neoliberal revolution. On the one hand, the IFIs very openly aligned themselves with the US by committing themselves to the imposition of economic discipline after the Volcker shock. On the other hand, the debt crisis led the Reagan administration to relax its initial preference for strictly market-based solutions to crises, thereby creating new opportunities for the IFIs to act as enforcers of discipline. In the process of bringing about neoliberal adjustments in indebted countries, they polished and repolished theoretical frameworks and technical instruments to respond to changing situations and to the 'secondary effects' of their own intervention. In this trial-and-error adaptation process, the IFIs have effectively translated the initiatives of the US Treasury into operational blueprints and procedures for domestic reform.

Although their involvement in the debt crisis and structural reform was effective in containing the damage to the international financial system, the serious economic and social impacts of adjustment meant that the IFIs became targets of social anger. Growing criticism, as well as the emergence of an awareness that the expansion of neoliberal globalization requires international and domestic institutional networks, has fuelled reformulations of the orthodox neoliberal recipes for reform and widened the scope for intervention by the IFIs under the banner of good governance, market imperfections and domestic 'ownership' of reforms (Fine 2001: 12). The IFIs' policies in the international financial crises of the 1990s and the disruptive consequences of their intervention in many peripheral countries damaged their legitimacy world-wide. The Argentinian default, followed by its successful restructuring of its public debt, has thrown into question the conventional neoliberal premise that indebted countries are powerless vis-à-vis international capital (Cooper and Momani 2005: 309-13), although it is still very much an open question as to whether the moves that have been made by some Latin American countries under recent conditions of ample international liquidity and relative regional prosperity will be sustained or amount to a really substantial challenge to the IFIs.

Recent years have also seen many proposals to reform the IFIs by strengthening their social accountability and creating space for peripheral countries to secure a more equitable participation in their decision-making bodies and for more pluralist views to be expressed in the research that backs IFI interventions. Undoubtedly, these social demands have forced the IFIs to search for new forms of legitimacy and have limited some of the most disruptive effects of their programmes. But many of these proposals have tended to assume that civil society actors in core and peripheral countries and governments in borrowing countries share a straightforward agenda for the democratic reform of the IFIs. Moreover, the very idea of democratic reform is based on assumptions about the nature of the multilateral institutions, and the possibility of altering the hierarchy of the international economy through institutional reform, that cannot be taken for granted. The complex networks of international and domestic forces which have historically embedded the actions of the IFIs in the American imperial project of global neoliberalism still remain firmly in place today.

Notes

1. Around 45 per cent of the shares are held by the G7 countries, which gives them the strongest voice in determining the Fund's policies. The highest decision-making body is the Board of Governors, comprising the finance ministers and central bank governors of all member countries. But most of its powers are delegated to the Executive Board comprising 24 Executive Directors appointed by its five major shareholders (the US, Japan, Germany, France and the UK) or elected by groups of countries according to their quotas.
2. The IMF's Managing Director is always a European citizen. But when the post of Deputy Managing Director was created in 1949 it was accepted that the position would be filled by a US Treasury nominee, which ensured a close watch on IMF operations by the US (Kahler 2001). While the staff have very diverse national backgrounds, they have mostly been trained in US, British or Canadian universities (Woods 2003: 109).
3. Helleiner (1994: 96–7) explains that Jacobson's initiative changed the long-term interpretation of the IMF's Articles of Agreement that prevented it from lending to offset capital movements. However, the IMF's decision-making procedures made the quick disbursement of large sums to respond to speculative flows difficult. The

more flexible Bank for International Settlements became the preferred institutional setting to organize the response to speculative attacks.

4. The countries involved were Argentina, Bolivia, Brazil, Chile, Colombia, Costa Rica, Ecuador, Ivory Coast, Jamaica, Mexico, Morocco, Nigeria, Peru, the Philippines, Uruguay, Venezuela and Yugoslavia.

5. The highest formal decision-making body is the Board of Governors composed of the finance ministers of its member countries. Most of its powers are delegated to the Executive Board. The five largest shareholders appoint one director each and another 19 are elected by groups of countries. The Executive Board is chaired by the President, who is also the chief of the staff.

6. Also in 1956, the International Financial Corporation (IFC) was created to support potential private investors in developing countries. Complementing its lending, the IFC also gives technical assistance, encourages business alliances and gives advice to governments with regards to the creation of a sound environment for private investment, the formation of capital markets, direct private investments and privatizations.

10
The Role of Financial Discipline in Imperial Strategy

Christopher Rude

Financial instability has been a consistent feature of neoliberal global capitalism, and when this instability has taken the form of a major financial crisis, as it did in East Asia in 1997, the consequences for the economies involved have been severe. Economic contractions, leaving economies in ruin and populations traumatized by increases in unemployment, poverty and inequality, have been the typical results. The liberalization and internationalization of capitalist production relations have created an economic system in which recurrent financial crises set the pace and rhythm of economic activity and change within the centre as well as at the periphery. This chapter examines this financial and economic turmoil and the role that it plays under neoliberalism. It also explores the role that the state plays in regulating, but not eliminating, the turmoil. Some readers may find the argument surprising. It is that the financial instability and the economic hardship that it creates play an essential role in reproducing capitalist and imperial social relations. The financial instability is functional. It disciplines world capitalism.

We begin with a theoretical analysis. We argue that the financial turmoil is not a surface phenomenon but an expression of the way the law of value operates under neoliberalism; second, that the liberalized global financial system is not the source of the instability but has the task of managing and containing the deep-seated uncertainties that today disrupt the global accumulation process; and, third, that the financial and economic turmoil, as managed by the global financial system, reproduces capitalist and imperial social relations by disciplining and punishing subordinate classes and nations. The reproduction of capitalism and imperialism via persistent financial and economic instability is risky. If capitalism and imperialism are to be reproduced through financial turmoil, the global banking and financial system must be resilient enough to survive its own disorder, so that the subordinate classes bear the burden of the turmoil, and the banking and financial systems higher up the 'imperial chain' of national banking and financial systems must be more resilient than those lower down, so that subordinate nations and regions bear the cost. This is where the state comes in. The various national banking and financial systems are regulated and supervised and, where appropriate, supported by injections of official liquidity, in such a way that the damage caused by the turmoil is directed away from the dominant classes and the centre towards the subordinate classes and the periphery.

After examining the core features of the supervisory and regulatory regime organized under continued US domination by the early 1990s to ensure that financial and economic turmoil is managed so that it extends and reproduces global capitalism, we then turn specifically to the 1997 Asian and 1998 Long-Term Capital Management (LTCM) crises to see how they affected the policies of the authorities – the G10 central banks, G7 ministries of finance, IMF, BIS, and other related bodies – that were responsible for managing the global economy.[1] The reforms that these authorities implemented in response to the two crises – a 'New International Financial Architecture' taking final form in a New BIS Capital Accord – did not change anything essential. The policy-makers continued to believe in the rationality and efficiency of financial markets, reasserted their desire to create a fully internationalized global economy, and renewed their efforts to maintain the profitability of banking and finance. On the other hand, the Asian and LTCM crises did affect their views on the nature of neoliberal capitalism in significant ways. In particular, the policy-makers came to see that financial crises were an inevitable feature of the neoliberal regime they had created and thus that the focus of their reforms should be on controlling rather than eliminating them. Contrary to those who believe neoliberalism implies a lack of regulation, moreover, the reforms that they implemented increased rather than decreased regulatory oversight over the global financial system, albeit in a decidedly neoliberal manner. In this, the authorities followed an old pattern: the liberalization and internationalization of capitalist production relations during the neoliberal period have always been accompanied by nearly continuous re-regulation of the global financial system in response to its recurrent financial crises.

The banking regulation, supervision and lender-of-last-resort policies that have been in place since the early 1990s, and that were strengthened in the wake of the Asian and LTCM crises, have played a role in maintaining global capitalism under US domination as important as the role played by local police forces, or by the US military in Kosovo, Afghanistan, Iraq and elsewhere. And it is precisely because of the central role the US financial authorities in the making of these policies as well as because the US banking and financial system is the strongest and most resilient in the world that, as we note in conclusion, the US not only has the capacity to sustain its own massive current account deficit but also to reproduce its position at the top of the imperial chain.

Theoretical considerations: financial turmoil, risk management and neoliberal discipline

Financial crises and the economic contractions that follow are not haphazard events. Financial crises occur because imbalances build up between the financial system and the underlying macroeconomy – imbalances between stocks of financial assets and liabilities, on the one hand, and flows of national income, on the other – and they occur when these macroeconomic financial stock/income flow imbalances become unsustainable.[2] The 'function' of financial crises and the economic contractions that they create is to remove these imbalances between the financial system and its macroeconomic 'monetary base'. Under neoliberalism, there is a greater tendency for imbalances of this sort to appear. Stating the issue in classical Marxist terms, since the equity and debt instruments that make up the financial system exist as fictitious capitals – as discounted future expected profit streams – the financial and economic turmoil that characterizes neoliberal global capitalism expresses itself, in the first instance, in an increase in the tendency for the financial markets to over- and underestimate future profits. The damage caused is not just economic bubbles but also the misallocation of capital.

But why has this occurred?[3] The internationalization of the circuits of capital has created a truly global economy, but not abolished the nation-state. Due to the continued existence of a system of territorially sovereign national states and thus the continued use of different national currencies as mediums of exchange within each national territory, intrusions of essentially local factors – national currencies affected by domestically determined interest rates – disrupt the movement of capital through its global circuits. Regardless of whether it exists in its money, commodity or productive form at the time, a capital is denominated in the currency of the nation whose space it occupies for the moment and thus must change its currency denomination as it moves from one national territory to the next. The point we are making is simple. A US multinational corporation operating a factory in Brazil, for example, pays its local labour force and purchases any locally produced intermediate products using *real*. Not only that: the whole enterprise is accounted for in *real*, including the depreciation of the capital stock. Inputs produced in another nation are accounted for in the currency of that nation. Products sold locally earn *reais*; those sold elsewhere earn the local currency. A factory operating in another country is accounted for in the currency of that country. One of the tasks of the Treasury Department of the home office in the United States is to translate the foreign activities of the firm into US dollars in such a way as to maximize the firm's profits on a global basis. The financial assets that trade on the Euro and other external financial markets are the sole exception to this 'local currency' rule. But this is why they were created: they exist to help multinational corporations hedge their exposures and thus maximize their global profits in their home currencies.

Due to the uneven movement of capital through its global circuits, moreover, these nationally specific monetary/financial obstacles are different in different parts of the globe and changing. The financial obstacles that disrupt the global circuits of capital are themselves discontinuous as a result, because they are contingent and uncertain. Their contingency and uncertainty, in turn, makes the movement of global capital through its circuits contingent and uncertain. In the new neoliberal global economy there is thus no longer a single money commodity, as there was under the nineteenth-century gold standard, functioning as a universal standard of value throughout the global economy. Nor is there a single state-backed national currency that can fulfil the same role, as the US dollar did under the Bretton Woods system until the early 1970s. Instead, there is a multiplicity of different national currency commodities that circulate internationally at changing rates of exchange against each other, and a parallel multiplicity of domestically determined and constantly changing interest rates – and this manifold of changing exchange and interest rates is itself continually being restructured by the foreign exchange and interest rate derivatives that make up the global money market.[4] As a result, the transformation of socially necessary labour time into prices of production has become a radically contingent process, since the monetary values in terms of which economic value is measured are different in different parts of the globe, change relative to one another across monetary areas as well as over time within each monetary space, and are also being continually transmuted through the use of derivatives. Deep-seated, persistent financial and economic turmoil is therefore a characteristic feature of neoliberal global capitalism because of the resulting increase in the uncertainty of the global accumulation process – which in turn increases the uncertainty of the profits of capital as a whole.

These contingencies and uncertainties exist because of the particular way in which capitalism became organized towards the end of the twentieth century as a world economic system divided into nation-states, organized into three imperial or sub-imperial blocs, centred on the economies and currencies of the United States, Europe and Japan.[5] As the internationalization of the circuits of capital has taken place primarily among the countries of the centre, these contingencies and uncertainties arise chiefly in the centre rather than in the periphery: a capital faces greater uncertainties as it moves between any of the three major imperial-currency blocs than it does when it circulates within a single imperial-currency bloc.[6] But we must not hold the 'liberalized' global financial system itself primarily responsible for the financial turmoil that this situation tends to produce. The opposite is in fact the case: the global financial system has the responsibility for managing and containing the financial contingencies and uncertainties that disrupt the global accumulation process.

This last point is very important. The financial system still has to intermediate between savers and investors, and to that end, global financial capital continues to fulfil the traditional tasks of collecting the idle monies in the hands of individual capitals, of bringing these individual money capitals together to form what David Harvey (1999: 284) has called the 'common capital of the capitalist class', and of allocating them to the most profitable investment outlets wherever they may be. Today, however, the financial system also has to manage the spatial and inter-temporal financial uncertainties that intrude into the operation of the law of value. The financial contingencies that global capital has to contend with as it moves through its circuits call for the use of the risk management techniques that the global financial system now provides, and the success of the risk management strategies employed affects the performance of the underlying economy fully as much as the way the aggregate global social capital is allocated.

The resulting transformation of the day-to-day operation of domestic and international financial markets has been profound. Indeed, most of the features of the global economy today that are alluded to under the rubric of 'financialization' can be explained in terms of the competitive struggle between individual capitals to profit from the global economy's need to hedge against the financial contingencies that would otherwise disrupt the international circulation of capital. These include dramatic increases in the trading volumes of both exchange-traded and over-the-counter securities; securitization (the transformation of mortgages and other apparently non-marketable assets into marketable securities); the extensive use of derivatives; hedge funds; increases in the financial activities of ostensibly non-financial corporations; the rise of the large multinational financial conglomerates that now dominate the global financial system; and the increase in the proportion of the social surplus transferred to finance.

Trading activity has risen in the stock, bond, foreign exchange and money markets in every country because trading allows an individual company to pass on to another company a risk that it does not want to assume, and thus permits the spreading of the risk to whomever wishes to bear it. The advantages of securitization are similar. Securitization permits a bank to exchange the mortgages, car loans, credit cards, etc. it creates for cash or other securities. Derivatives – securities whose values are defined in terms of the performance of other securities – are used extensively because they allow a company to bridge the gaps between different spatial and inter-temporal uncertainties and thus allow it to restructure these exposures in any way it sees fit. Hedge funds exist to absorb the risks that the large multinational financial conglomerates do not want to bear. Multinational non-financial corporations engage in financial activities to manage their own exposures because it is less costly for them to do it themselves. In addition to other factors making for the concentration and centralization of capital, large financial conglomerates dominate the global financial system because their size and global scope allow them to transfer and so diversify their risks internally, using their own risk measurement and allocation systems to do so as efficiently as possible. And finance absorbs so much of the social surplus simply because its risk management activities are needed.

Several factors, however, limit the capacity of the international financial system to manage the risks of the global accumulation process. First, financial crises no longer function, as they did under the gold standard or the Bretton Woods system, fully to remove the imbalances that arise between a country's financial system and its monetary base. Since there is no stable monetary unit of value against which the fictitious capital values can be measured, the manner in which a financial crisis is resolved depends on the response of the monetary base. Changes in exchange rates and interest rates can alter the underlying macroeconomy so as to lessen or intensify a crisis or to keep it contained in a particular part of the globe – or they can create a financial contagion that spreads the turmoil elsewhere. The financial and economic turmoil thus never really disappears but assumes an essentially protean form, so that one crisis transmutes into the next. Second, the spatial and inter-temporal discontinuities that disrupt the international circulation of capital have a particularly profound effect on the circulation of global financial capital itself. The international financial system has to manage its own uncertainties as well as those of commercial and industrial capital – uncertainties that in any case essentially are irresolvable. Third, the competition between individual capitals to profit from the global economy's risk management needs cannot but lead to misallocations of these risks that increase the uncertainty of the accumulation process. Financial institutions can and do underestimate the risks they are assuming and thus take on too much risk relative to their capacity to manage it. The search for profits tempts them to underestimate the risks in whole regions of the globe and thus to misallocate their capital. Global financial capital therefore has a task that it will inevitably mismanage. This is why financial crises appear. Imbalances arise between the financial system and the underlying macroeconomy because the financial system cannot always contain the risks it is supposed to contain, and because competition leads individual financial capitals to take on risks they cannot bear.

Here is where the state comes in. The international economic system through which global capital moves as it completes its circuits is not just discontinuous; it is also fundamentally hierarchical. The national monetary spaces through which a capital circulates exist in relations of domination and subordination. The multiplicity of national currencies and domestically determined interest rates that disrupt the circulation of capital form a strict hierarchy, an 'imperial chain' of more powerful and less powerful national banking and financial systems. The liberalization and internationalization of capitalist production relations have not abolished the hierarchical and antagonistic relationships that exist between the centre and the periphery of the world economy, between the imperial powers within the centre, and between capital and labour world-wide. They have simply altered the way in which these structures of domination manifest themselves.

The introduction of financial contingencies into the operation of the law of value has created a capitalism characterized by a deep-seated and persistent financial and economic turbulence, and in doing so, it has changed the way in which capitalism reproduces itself. The turmoil is not just an economic phenomenon. It both shapes and is shaped by the capitalist and imperial social relationships that constitute the world economy system and is thus essentially political. The turmoil maintains and restructures capitalist and imperial social relationships by disciplining and punishing the subordinate classes or nations involved just as surely as do the local police and the military. The weapons deployed are not billy clubs and bombs but financial crises and the ensuing stagnations.

Neoliberalism is not just an effort to privatize the reproduction of capitalist and imperial social relations of production. It is an attempt to turn over to the private sector many functions that had previously been considered legitimate functions of the state and thus a truly radical project. Its goal is to establish a kind of social control very different from that employed during the 'golden age' of Keynesian economics and US 'New Deal' imperialism. The discipline used during the golden age is probably best understood in terms of Gramsci's concept of hegemony, which he defined as consent plus force. This was a structure of domination where the dominant classes (in the centre if not in the periphery) and the dominant imperial power (the United States) were willing to make sacrifices of an 'economic-corporatist' kind. The subordinated classes and nations could consent to their subordination provided they could believe their short-term material interests would be met. State violence was still used when the consensus broke down, but as long as the consensus was maintained, the struggles that did occur were protracted political/ideological/cultural wars of position that took place in the first instance within the institutions of civil society.[7] The neoliberal project establishes a different form of domination, one where financial instability and economic insecurity replace compromise and consensus. The mechanisms of social control are much more direct. Global capital, under continued US domination, can maintain the subordination of the dominated classes and nations using what amounts to a financial and economic violence, backed up by militarized police action when economic intimidation breaks down. The manipulation of cultural symbols by the global mass media can fill any residual need for legitimacy.

The introduction of new financial contingencies into the operation of the law of value has therefore given the global financial system new responsibilities. As the financial infrastructure of a capitalist and imperial world system, it must manage financial and economic risk and turmoil in such a way that they reproduce the hierarchical relations between the centre and periphery, between the imperialist powers within the centre, and between global capital and global labour. The global financial system must therefore have the crisis management capacities needed to contain and shape risk, and to calm and shape turmoil when it erupts into financial crises and recessions, and it does these things in very specific ways. The imperial chain of national banking and financial systems that make up the global financial system must be so organized as to reproduce itself through recurrent financial crises. In this way, the burden of a crisis will not be borne by financial capital in the form of lower profits, bank failures and insolvencies as much as it is by the subordinate classes in the form of unemployment, poverty and greater inequality. This also means that the banking and financial systems higher up the imperial chain must have greater risk management capacities than those lower down. The 'ideal' neoliberal global economy is one where all of the harm caused by the instability is transferred to the dominated classes and the periphery.

Capital's regulatory regime

The policy regime, which capital established in the 1990s, that accomplishes all this is surprisingly simple. The core features of neoliberal global capitalism's supervisory and regulatory regime are, first, internationally uniform risk-based capital standards, developed by the BIS's Committee on Banking Supervision, that permit the large multinational financial conglomerates that dominate the international financial system to set their own capital requirements based on their own internal risk models; second, the principle, also promulgated by the Basel Committee, that home countries in the centre and not host countries in the periphery have the supervisory, regulatory and lender-of-last-resort responsibilities for multinational financial conglomerates; and third, a division of labour between the IMF and the central banks in the centre according to quite different principles than the first two, whereby the IMF resolves financial crises in the periphery by imposing austerity, while the major central banks resolve financial crises in the centre by easing credit.[8]

The US authorities took the initiative in the development of the BIS capital standards. The initiative was taken in response to the difficulties that the Latin American debt crisis caused to the US banking system, and in keeping with the specific nature of this crisis, the capital requirements were initially designed to protect a bank against its credit risks. According to the original 1988 Basel Capital Accord, all internationally active banks, regardless of where they are headquartered, must maintain a capital reserve fund equal to 8 per cent of their risk-adjusted assets. The amounts of capital that a bank must hold in reserve to back up its particular portfolio of investments increase with the credit risks associated with its investments: the credit-risk weights of each of the bank's assets are determined by prescribed formulas, and off-balance sheet as well as on-balance sheet investments are subject to the capital requirements.[9] Since less creditworthy assets have a higher risk-weight, the capital requirements force financial institutions to allocate their capital according to the credit risks of their investments. Banks are penalized for making risky investments and rewarded for making safe investments.

The banks must also maintain capital reserve funds sufficiently large to insure them against insolvency in the event that their counterparties are unable to honour their commitments. The capital requirements thus aim to make each financial institution strong enough to survive its own risk-taking.

The capital requirements under the 1988 Capital Accord went into effect at the end of 1992. The Accord was amended in 1996 to incorporate the market risks arising from banks' open positions in foreign exchange and traded debt securities, equities, commodities and options.[10] In the amended Capital Accord, banks must hold capital against both their credit and their market risks, and the overall minimum capital ratio remains at 8 per cent. An important aspect of this amendment was that, subject to strict quantitative and qualitative standards and the approval of their supervisors, banks could use their own internal risk models for measuring their market risk, but not their credit risk, capital requirements. The amended Accord thus created a two-tiered system of banks. The large multinational financial conglomerates that have the resources to set up and run their own internal risk-measurement and risk-management systems are allowed to determine their own market risk capital requirements, and are expected to set aside a capital reserve fund sufficiently large to protect them from their market risk at a predetermined probability. If properly enforced, the amended capital standards also imply that the supervisory and regulatory authorities of the major capitalist states work 'hand-in-glove' with their multinational financial conglomerates on a daily basis to monitor how the conglomerates measure and thus allocate their global market risks. The smaller and less sophisticated banks, which cannot quantify their survivability in this way, have their market risks determined by the 'standard measurement method' specified in the amendment to the Accord, and consequently receive less attention – and help – from the regulators. Many of these smaller and less sophisticated banks are of course headquartered in the periphery.

As for 'prudential supervision and regulation', in the aftermath of the failure of the Bankhaus Herstatt in 1974, the G10 central banks determined that the home country, and not the host country central bank has the ultimate responsibility for the foreign branch of an internationally active bank (BCBS 2001: 1). Until this time, the G10 central banks had not determined how they should share the responsibility for resolving international financial crises. The first major decision of the Basel Committee concerned how these responsibilities should be discharged under a 'Concordat' (made public in 1983) that established that no foreign banking establishment should escape supervision, that the supervision should be adequate, and that the home country rather than the host country should be responsible for supervising the foreign branch. The agreements reached in the Concordat were subsequently revised and strengthened to become the 'home country rule' of international banking supervision, according to which the home country has the supervisory, regulatory and lender-of-last resort responsibilities, on a global consolidated basis, for the internationally active banks that are headquartered there. Thus, the authorities of the imperial powers in the centre of the global economy, who have the greatest crisis prevention and management capacities and in whose countries the multinational financial conglomerates are headquartered, have the responsibility for supervising, regulating and maintaining the liquidity of their multinational banks and investment houses no matter where they may do their business. The authorities in the centre are thus responsible for the behaviour of the branches of their banks in the periphery and so indirectly responsible for the banking and financial systems of the periphery insofar as the interests of their banks are involved. The regulators in the periphery are responsible only for their own banks and the few foreign branches these banks may have.

This prudential supervision and regulation aspect of the Basel Accord is related as well to the division of labour mentioned above whereby the IMF stabilizes a crisis in the periphery through a structural adjustment programme, while the major central banks stabilize a crisis in the centre by a monetary easing. The purpose of the IMF's austerity in the periphery is to prevent the turmoil that originates there from spreading to the centre. The purpose of the monetary easing in the centre is to end any turmoil that may appear there – regardless of its origin. This division of labour was not the product of a formal agreement, but originated informally in the 1980s during the Latin American debt crisis, for this was when the IMF was redesigned in order to impose structural adjustment programmes on the debtor nations, and strengthened when the authorities in the United States learned to ease or extend state credit to troubled firms to counter the 1987 stock market crash and resolve the ensuing US savings and loans crisis.

The G10 central bankers who set up the BIS capital requirements in 1988 and revised them in 1996 were certainly not thinking in terms of the law of value as they tried to cope with the uncertainties and contingencies that intrude into its operation today. Still, it is no mere coincidence that the risk-based capital requirements encourage risk taking and risk management on the part of market participants. By forcing all internationally active financial institutions to allocate their capital according to the risks of their investments, internationally uniform risk-based capital requirements have created a global financial system designed to manage the risks of the accumulation process. Internationally uniform risk-based capital requirements also require every internationally active financial institution to hold a capital reserve sufficiently large so that it can survive its own risk taking. By thus laying the ground for the solvency of every financial institution by means of rules intended to relegate bank failure to a low level of probability, the BIS Capital Accord designed a global financial system that is at least in principle resilient enough to survive its own disorder.

The G10 central bankers gave the global financial system another noteworthy property: risk-based capital requirements force financial institutions to cut back on their lending during a financial crisis. Since equity makes up the largest part of a bank's capital, the total value of its capital is largely determined by the value of its equity in the stock market and thus will fall sharply in any financial crisis that includes a stock market crash. Meanwhile, according to the formula set up by the Basel Committee, the volatility of a financial crisis increases the measured market risks of the financial conglomerates that use their own internal risk models to determine their own capital requirements.[11] During a financial crisis, therefore, the capital requirements become more burdensome just when the available capital is most likely to decline. To meet the capital requirements, the large financial conglomerates must decrease their investments, i.e. cut back on their extensions of credit. In creating a global financial system designed to manage the risks of the global accumulation process and to be resilient enough to survive its own disorder, the G10 central bankers designed a global banking and financial system that in stabilizing itself, destabilizes the underlying macroeconomy.

The imperial chain of national banking and financial systems is thus maintained by way of two-tiered market risk capital requirements, the home country rule principle, and the contrasting crisis-management policies of the IMF and the major central banks. A multinational financial conglomerate headquartered in the centre of the global economy is able to use its own internal risk models to set its own market risk capital requirements, is supervised on a global consolidated basis by a stronger and more resourceful regulator, who will work with the multinational firm daily to increase the efficiency of its risk measurement and allocation methods, and can count on injections of official liquidity should the bank, despite all this, need it. A smaller and less sophisticated financial institution headquartered in the periphery, by contrast, must set its market risk capital requirements using the rule-based 'standard methodology', is supervised by a weaker (and perhaps very weak) regulatory authority, and will face an IMF-imposed structural adjustment programme should a financial crisis hit its country. The discipline created by this system is obvious: the bank headquartered in the periphery is placed at a competitive disadvantage relative to the multinational financial conglomerate.

The Asian and LTCM financial crises as turning points

The amended Capital Accord went into effect at the end of 1997, just as the Asian crisis was reaching its climax. That crisis and the LTCM crisis that followed in 1998 were not the first financial crises of the neoliberal period. Federal Reserve Chairman Volcker's 1979 monetary policy shock did not just end the 1970s inflation; it also precipitated a Latin American debt crisis which would burden the US financial system and the Latin American economies throughout the 1980s. The debt crisis was followed by the US stock market crash in 1987, the US savings and loans crisis of the late 1980s, the meltdown of the Japanese financial system and economy in the early 1990s following the bursting of the Japanese stock market and real estate bubbles, the European Monetary System's crises of 1992 and 1993, and the Mexican peso crisis of 1994–5. The Asian and LTCM crises were turning points in the history of neoliberal global capitalism, however, for at least four reasons.

First, because of their intensity and global scope. The financial turmoil that began with the devaluation of the Thai *baht* in July 1997 spread swiftly from Thailand to Malaysia, the Philippines, Indonesia and the Republic of South Korea (the other countries at the centre of the crisis), leaving economic devastation in its wake.[12] By the end of 1997, the Asian financial panic pushed these economies into a steep contraction, with Indonesia experiencing the largest decline. In doing so, the Asian crisis brought to an end what had hitherto been one of the longest periods of rapid growth ever to occur in the periphery: the 'Asian miracle' of the 1980s and early 1990s.

The Asian financial panic also reduced the profits of the multinational banks and investment houses that had invested heavily in South-East Asia and South Korea. Japanese banks were hit particularly hard. Already burdened by the non-performing loans that had appeared on their books due to the collapse of the 'bubble economy' in the early 1990s, Japanese banks had attempted to consolidate their investments world-wide by concentrating their foreign exposures in the countries that were now at the centre of the crisis. The losses they experienced on their investments there added to their already considerable burdens. The effect was to push any recovery of the Japanese economy well into the future. The harm that the Asian crisis did to the profits of the large multinational financial conglomerates also led them to reduce their exposure to the periphery more generally, and this, in turn, had an immediate adverse effect on emerging market economies worldwide – an effect made worse because the authorities in the periphery were forced to adopt contractionary fiscal and monetary policies to counter the downward pressure on their currencies. By early 1998, signs of acute financial and economic stress began to appear in Russia, Brazil and Argentina.

Following a period of calm in the spring and early summer of 1998, the financial turmoil resurfaced in the autumn when, following the Russian default in August, the collapse of the LTCM hedge fund led to panic in the very heart of the world financial system. The unwinding of the fund's highly leveraged derivative positions caused the otherwise very liquid US Treasury market, positioned at the very apex of the hierarchy of global financial markets, to freeze up, causing a potential threat to the foundation of the entire system. For a moment in the autumn of 1998, therefore, with the financial systems of the periphery already in crisis and the US Treasury market, typically the deepest and most liquid financial market in the world, in disarray, the global financial system really did seem on the verge of collapse.

Second, the Asian and LTCM crises were turning points because they were the first financial crises fully to reveal the neoliberal nature of the turmoil.

In contrast to the 1980s Latin American debt crisis, the countries at the centre of the Asian crisis were following policies entirely in keeping with the precepts of neoliberal thinking. Tight fiscal and monetary policies, low inflation, and high private sector saving and investment rates characterized all of the crisis countries before the crisis broke. They had also recently liberalized both their domestic financial systems and their capital accounts, thus dismantling the mechanisms that had previously allowed them to pursue activist industrial policies without interference from the international financial system. The proximate causes of the 1980s Latin America debt crisis, the 1993 EMS crisis, and the 1994–5 peso crisis were specific actions on the part of national governments in the centre of the global economy: the 1979 Volcker money supply shocks, the high interest-rate policy adopted by the recently reunited Germany, which was inconsistent with existing EMS parities, and another round of tightening by the Federal Reserve in 1994. The Asian crisis, by contrast, was a purely private sector phenomenon, an endogenously determined asset boom–bust cycle, involving lending by G10 banks – mostly in the form of increasingly short-term bonds – to private borrowers in the crisis countries, who, in turn, had used the monies for increasingly speculative purposes. Unlike previous financial crises, which were widely anticipated, the Asian crisis also caught international investors by surprise, and when they suddenly became aware of the size of their impending losses, they withdrew their capital from the region in a panic. In the first half of 1997, foreign capital had continued to flow into the crisis countries on a massive scale; the swing from a capital inflow to an outflow in late 1997 was over 10 per cent of the GDP of the countries involved. In contrast to previous periods of acute financial turmoil, once the Asian crisis started to unfold and spread, it took on a dynamic of its own, which no authority, the IMF included, could stop or control until it had run its course – that is, until the imbalances that had built up between the financial systems of the afflicted countries and their underlying macroeconomies had been removed.

The neoliberal origins of the LTCM crisis are equally obvious. Ahead of the Russian default the LTCM hedge fund had reportedly adopted a set of very large and highly leveraged trading strategies, mostly through the use of derivatives, that assumed credit spreads would narrow, equities would rise, and the volatility of the financial markets would fall. In taking on these positions, the firm was not attempting to guess the future direction of the market or the underlying macroeconomy. Instead, based on a presumably rigorous statistical analysis of past price movements, LTCM's strategy aimed at arbitraging price discrepancies: it purchased securities its theoretical model suggested were underpriced and sold and 'shorted' securities its model suggested were overpriced. The large banks and investment houses that were on the other side of LTCM's trades welcomed its complex arbitrage strategies. Before the appearance of LTCM, they had used other firms to unload their risks. However, due to its reputation for high standards and sophisticated risk-management systems, as well as to its size and global reach, LTCM came to play a very special role in the international financial system: it became the place where the multinational financial conglomerates believed their most complex risks would be most expertly managed.

Following the Russian default, however, when global financial markets began to move simultaneously in the same direction, with credit spreads widening, equity markets falling, and volatility increasing in every market, LTCM began to experience losses on every front. As the firm tried to reduce its exposures, it found that the attempt to do so aggravated its difficulties. The LTCM's counterparties made its situation worse by attempting to unwind their own positions. Soon the liquidity of the credit derivative, interest rate swap, US Treasury and other fixed income markets where LTCM had been most active began to disappear. The crisis came to a head when LTCM reportedly could not make the margin call on a large losing 'short' position in the Treasury bill futures market. Had LTCM actually defaulted, the futures market clearing house might have collapsed, in which case the Treasury bill market would have become illiquid. Under these circumstances, the Federal Reserve Bank of New York organized a private support operation for the firm in late September 1998, as it had clearly taken on more risks than it could bear. However, the global financial system did not regain its ability to manage the risks of the accumulation process until the Federal Reserve restored the system's liquidity by easing interest rates in October.

The third reason why the Asian and LTCM financial crises were historical turning points was that the turmoil they unleashed is still very much with us. Though the LTCM-related turmoil in the centre quickly abated following the Federal Reserve's interventions, the Fed's actions had little effect on the forces that the Russian default and LTCM's demise had set in motion in the periphery, forces that would eventually lead to the floating of the Brazilian *real* in January 1999 and to Argentina's depression and subsequent default in December 2001. Moreover, the interest rate reductions that ended the LTCM turmoil helped fuel what Federal Reserve Chairman Greenspan had already called the 'irrational exuberance' of the US stock market. The consequences were the stock-market-bubble-driven recovery of the US in the late 1990s and hence the recession that occurred when the 'dot-com' bubble burst in 2000. Due to decisive counter-cyclical action on the part of the Federal Reserve, this time in the form of another round of interest rate reductions, the ensuing recession in the United States was mild. But the Fed's easing did little to end the imbalances that continued to exist between the US banking and financial system and its underlying macroeconomic base. Instead, it allowed the financial turmoil to transmute into yet another stock market/housing bubble, whose collapse at the time of this writing in the autumn of 2007 in the form of a global credit market crisis threatens the world economy with a recession.

Finally, the Asian and LTCM crises were turning points because of their political effects. The crises did succeed in reproducing existing class and imperial social relations. By bringing the Asian miracle to a halt and post-poning any recovery in Japan for years, the way the Asian crisis was resolved reinforced the economic victory of the United States over Japan that was ini-tially accomplished with the collapse of Japan's 'bubble economy'. If there was an economy besides the United States that benefited from the Asian crisis, it was mainland China. With the end of the 'miracle' in South-East Asia and South Korea and with Japan mired in stagnation, China became the centre of capital accumulation in Asia, even as millions of Chinese workers and peas-ants became 'redundant'. But by increasing unemployment, inequality and poverty throughout the periphery, the Asian crisis put downward pressure on wages worldwide, thus increasing the global rate of exploitation. Meanwhile, the Federal Reserve's quick and decisive action, first to organize a private sup-port operation for LTCM and then to lower interest rates, brought the LTCM crisis to a halt well before it could have any adverse effects on the position of the United States in the global economy.

On the other hand, the Asian and LTCM crises, and the Asian crisis in par-ticular, caused many to question the merits of the neoliberal order. Due to its severity, global scope and obvious neoliberal nature, the Asian crisis delegit-imized neoliberalism as a historical project for many individuals throughout the globe, and in doing so, helped to launch the 'anti-globalization' move-ment. As combined with the subsequent LTCM crisis, it also led many of the policy-makers who were responsible for managing the global financial system, and who had hitherto been advocates of neoliberalism, to express doubts about the viability of their previous efforts. The crises destroyed any lingering beliefs they may have had that the neoliberal order was not crisis-prone, and for a time made them doubt their ability to prevent and manage the crises they now believed would inevitably occur. In view of its failure to contain the contagion stemming from the Asian crisis, they questioned in particular the crisis prevention and management capacities of the IMF.

In this atmosphere, policies that previously had been seen as either irrele-vant or radical were taken seriously. Capital controls, Tobin taxes, regulations placing quantitative restrictions on financial institutions' borrowing and lending, and other similar policies that earlier had only been discussed by the critics of neoliberalism suddenly had currency. For a time, as well, calls for a new and different regulatory institution, including a 'World Finan-cial Authority', and for an international lender-of-last-resort received serious attention.[13] As the effects of the Asian and LTCM crises receded into the back-ground, however, with the recovery of the US economy in the late 1990s, policy-makers regained confidence both in neoliberalism and in their crisis management capacities. They lost interest in more radical and far-reaching reforms and began to devise measures that would instead strengthen rather than change the existing policy regime. By the time of the G7 summit meet-ing in Köln, in June 1999, the essential features of the reforms that would be implemented under the rubric of the 'New International Financial Architecture' had already been largely agreed upon. They were conservative. In the end, the authorities would be content to renew the existing supervisory and regulatory regime in the form of a New BIS Capital Accord.

The 'New International Financial Architecture'

Six principles governed the reform measures that the G7 leaders endorsed at that time (see Group of Seven Finance Ministers 1999). They were, first, that improved transparency and better codes of conduct would reduce the severity of future financial crises; second, that more extensive banking and financial market regulation would have the same effect; third, that the more serious informational and regulatory lapses lie in the periphery rather than in the industrialized centre; fourth, that the economies of the periphery should continue liberalizing their capital accounts, albeit subject to its proper sequencing; fifth, that the integration of the same economies into international capital markets requires them to pursue austere monetary and fiscal policies; and sixth, that the steps that had already been taken to improve the available crisis management facilities and policies were sufficient to handle future financial crises.

Central to the reform measures endorsed by the G7 at the Köln summit meeting was the belief that insufficient information contributed significantly to the Asian and LTCM crises, and thus that 'improved information will help [financial] markets adjust more smoothly to economic developments, minimize contagion and reduce volatility' (Group of Seven Finance Ministers 1999: paragraph 16). To this end, the authorities took steps to make more timely and reliable information, mostly about developing countries, available to investors, and advocated the development and implementation of codes and standards of good practice for economic, financial and business activities. They covered codes of good practice on fiscal transparency and in monetary and financial policy, as well as the codes and standards necessary for the proper functioning of the private financial system, including accounting and auditing, bankruptcy, corporate governance, insurance, payment and settlement systems, and the organization of securities markets.

The G7 also stressed the need for improved regulation and supervision of the monetary and financial systems in both the centre and the periphery to deal with specific problems that the two crises had revealed. In the centre, the focus was on banks' dealings with hedge funds and similar operations in commercial and investment banks (proprietary trading desks) as well as on the regulation of offshore financial centres. The authorities also advocated measures to improve the management of lending to the periphery, especially of a short-term nature, to contain the foreign financing of risky investments there. For the periphery itself, measures were adopted concerning the need to manage the risks associated with the rapid growth of domestic credit, currency and maturity mismatches of assets and liabilities, the accumulation of large short-term borrowings in foreign currency, and the valuation of collateral during episodes of asset inflation.

The proposals adopted at Köln reflected the G7 governments' commitment to financial market internationalization and liberalization. 'Recent events in the world economy', they argued, 'have demonstrated that a strengthening of the system is needed to maximize the benefits of, and reduce the risks posed by, global economic and financial integration.' By affirming the need for further internationalization and liberalization, the G7 saw the problem of reforming the international financial architecture as largely one of filling in certain gaps in the provision of information, implementation of codes and standards, and regulation and supervision of financial markets and institutions. They shifted the burden of reform, however, away from the industrial countries to the developing world, for this was where the more serious informational and regulatory gaps supposedly were, and where greater openness to the international capital markets was still required. To this end, 'capital account liberalization should be carried out in a careful and well-sequenced manner, accompanied by a sound and well-regulated financial sector and by a consistent macroeconomic policy framework.' Though 'the use of controls on capital inflows may be justified for a transition period as countries strengthen the institutional and regulatory environment in their domestic financial systems', more comprehensive controls on inflows 'may carry costs and should not in any case be used as a substitute for reform'. Controls on outflows, the G7 emphasized, 'can carry even greater costs'. The same commitment also shaped the kind of macroeconomic policies they stressed developing and emerging-market economies should adopt. Because of increasing international capital mobility, they warned, 'weak macro-economic policies and financial infrastructures [in developing markets] can be penalized more severely and more suddenly by investors' (Group of Seven Finance Ministers 1999: paragraphs 1, 30). The recommendation was strong: developing and transition economies should have tight monetary and fiscal policies leading to low wage and final goods inflation and exchange rate policies that lead to sustainable current account deficits and external debt burdens.

The depth and severity of the Asian turmoil, coupled with the apparent inability of the authorities to contain it or its contagion, led to the recognition that the Asian crisis was new, and thus that the policies that had been designed to manage 'current account' crises in the periphery were inappropriate to deal with the 'capital account' crises that were the product of internationalized financial markets. The IMF introduced new and expanded lending facilities, and advocated orderly 'standstill' and 'workout' agreements for debtor countries and their creditors. To increase the involvement of the private sector in the prevention and management of emerging-market financial crises, the G7 also advocated 'the use of market based tools ... aimed at facilitating adjustment to shocks through the use of innovative financial arrangements, including private market-based contingent credit lines in emerging countries and roll-over options in debt instruments'. They also stressed the importance 'of collective action clauses in sovereign debt contracts, along with other provisions that facilitate creditor coordination and discourage disruptive action' and encouraged 'efforts to establish sound and efficient bankruptcy procedures and strong judicial systems'. Finally, they warned that the resolution of a financial crisis in the periphery might require sacrifice on the part of foreign creditors to the periphery. The G7 were quite explicit about the risks involved. They indicated that 'reducing net debt payments to the private sector can potentially contribute to meeting a country's immediate financing needs and reducing the amount of finance to be provided by the official sector'; and that since in 'exceptional cases, it may not be possible for the country to avoid the accumulation of arrears, IMF lending into arrears may be appropriate if the country is seeking a cooperative solution to its payment difficulties with its creditors'; and that in such exceptional cases, 'countries may impose capital and exchange controls as part of payments suspensions or standstills in conjunction with IMF support for their policies and programs, to provide time for an orderly debt restructuring' (Group of Seven Finance Ministers 1999: paragraphs 41, 43, 45, 50).[14]

Certain features of the not-so-well-hidden imperial agenda of the G7's reforms are easy to decipher. One does not have to believe that increased transparency and better codes of conduct will reduce the severity of financial crises to see that global capital would benefit from more accurate and timely information about the economies in the periphery or from uniform codes of conduct for the private financial systems there. Nor should the benefits that the countries involved would obtain from improved banking and financial market regulation and supervision blind us to the fact that capital would benefit from these as well. The interests of global capital are also clearly represented in the strong overall condemnation of capital controls, especially on outflows, and the requirement that the governments in the periphery adopt restrictive fiscal and monetary policies, as these will lead to low wages and inflation. It is not so obvious, however, why the authorities went out of their way to warn investors about the risks of lending to the periphery, or why they took steps to 'involve' the private sector in the resolution of future financial crises there. Especially, given the severity of the LTCM crisis, it is also not clear why the authorities decided that the more serious lapses lay in the periphery and not in the centre.

An important BIS document on the Asian crisis released around the time of the Köln summit contains the following statement about the regulatory framework that allowed the banks in the centre of the global financial system to weather that period of extreme turmoil:

> While significant risks existed, there were also significant risk mitigants that played an important role regarding banks' ability to limit the negative

effects of the Asian crisis. Solvency [capital] requirements of G10 bank supervisors and regulators allowed banks to better weather the problems associated with Asian risks with fewer fears of insolvency than in the earlier debt crisis. For example, US banks' total cross-border claims accounted for 500% of their capital in 1982; in June 1997, total cross-border claims represented 108% of capital. Moreover, the foreign claims of G10 banks were also much better diversified than in past crises, in terms of both countries and types of counterparties.

Disclosure of risks by G10 banks in some countries improved compared with past emerging market crises, but the G10 countries had a diversity of experience in the quality of their banks' disclosures. For those market participants that made their risks more transparent, they and their supervisors were better able to judge risks and temper their actions accordingly ...

Prudential supervision and regulation also assisted in protecting G10 banks from the Asian crisis. In particular, guidance by supervisory authorities on internal controls, risk management systems, lending limits and country risks aided G10 banks in managing their Asian exposure. Those banks with sound country risk, market risk and liquidity risk management systems appear to have been able to avoid significant loss. Regulators and supervisors themselves took away lessons from the 1980s debt crisis, and applied them to their respective banks. (BCBS 1999c: 15–16)

In its analysis of the LTCM crisis released a few months later, the BIS goes on to suggest that policy-makers should learn the following 'tentative lessons from this experience':

> Foremost is the realisation that the first line of defence at a time of market stress is sound risk management by market participants, which in turn requires a regulatory and monetary policy environment ensuring that market discipline effectively governs credit decisions and risk-taking. Policymakers should also appreciate that the fallout from last year's financial market strains was less pronounced on real activity in the industrial countries because a healthy commercial banking system was able to act as a substitute means of intermediating funds. (Committee on the Global Financial System 1999: 2)

Several themes run though these statements. They are, first, the importance that the G10 central bankers gave to risk taking and risk management by market participants; second, the view that the more robust and resilient a nation's banking and financial system, the more able it is to survive and function in a financial crisis; and third, the confidence the central bankers showed in the regulatory framework in place within the advanced capitalist nations ahead of both crises, a framework they believed had allowed their banking and financial systems to withstand the Asian and LTCM turmoil without too much damage. The implications of the statements are clear. The authorities warned investors about the risks of lending to the periphery and took measures to 'involve' the private sector in the resolution of future financial crises there to encourage risk taking and risk management. And they determined that the more serious lapses lay in the periphery and not in the centre because of their confidence in the crisis management capacities of the regime they had already put in place in the centre.

The confidence that the G10 central banks had in the then-existing policy regime was not just verbal. In June 1999, the Basel Committee took advantage of the calls for reform that prevailed in the aftermath of the Asian and LTCM crises to issue a proposal for a new capital requirement to replace the 1988 Capital Accord. This proposal was refined over the next six years, culminating in the release of a New BIS Capital Framework in June 2004 (BCBS 2007).[15]

Basel II builds upon Basel I in three ways. First, the 1988 Accord's rule-based methodology for measuring a bank's credit risk is replaced by a more flexible methodology that reinforces the two-tiered system created by the 1996 amendment and effectively privatizes the setting of banks' regulatory capital. Subject, once again, to strict quantitative and qualitative standards and the approval of their supervisions, the New Accord permits banks to use their own internal risk models for measuring their credit as well as their market risks. The large multinational financial conglomerates, working closely with the authorities of the advanced capitalist nations in which they are headquartered, can thus use their own risk measurement systems to set their own market and credit risk market capital requirements and so are given free rein to use their own internal risk management and capital allocation systems to shape both their market price and counterparty exposures as they please. Other less sophisticated banks that do not have the resources to set up such systems have their market risks, as before, determined by predetermined rules and, in the New Accord, their credit risks determined by a risk-weighting system where the credit-risk weights for their assets are determined by the ratings that the major credit rating agencies give to them: higher-rated assets have lower risk weights than lower-rated assets. And as before, these banks, many of which are headquartered in the periphery, need and so receive less regulatory oversight: their required market risk capital is determined by clear rules; unregulated credit rating agencies determine their required credit risk capital.

Second, in the New Capital Accord, capital requirements are but the first of the 'Three Pillars' of a more comprehensive regulatory framework that includes, besides regulatory capital, two other pillars – market disclosure and discipline, and prudential supervision and regulation.[16] The emphasis is placed on the capital requirements that permit the use of financial institutions' internal risk management systems. Market discipline is second. The authorities de-emphasize the traditional activities of official regulators and supervisors, who actively enforce externally determined regulations. The 8 per cent capital requirement is a minimum capital ratio. A bank's supervisor may require it to maintain a higher one. But the authorities may have no need to enforce any requirement that a bank have a higher capital ratio, due to market discipline. Since a bank's capital ratio is made public, it functions as a quick and easy measure of the bank's soundness. Banks with high capital ratios have easy access to both capital and credit. The markets punish banks with low capital ratios.

Third, in the new regime, what supervision the authorities do provide is no longer considered to be the responsibility solely of the central banks or other agencies having direct oversight over the depository institutions headquartered within their national territories. The 'home country rule' principle still applies, with all of its imperial implications, but the web of regulatory control is now more complex and denser. Central bank supervision is exercised in cooperation with a variety of other national and international institutions: ministries of finance, regulators of securities firms and investment banks, agencies that oversee insurance companies, and the IMF and World Bank, who work to ensure compliance in the periphery. This is a system designed to monitor multinational financial conglomerates. There is little place for small firms in this regime.

The effect of the New Basel Capital Accord on the international financial system is threefold. First, in redefining regulatory credit risk, the New Accord precipitated a virtual revolution in how financial institutions manage their credit exposures and thus in the entire practice of credit markets everywhere. The use of credit derivatives, including credit default swaps, and issuance of asset-backed securities, including collateralized debt obligations and asset-backed certificates of deposit, are now commonplace, and the trading of credit risk is today as sophisticated and complex as, if not more sophisticated and complex than, the trading of market risk. Second, Basel II intensified the pro-cyclicality in the provision of credit. Institutions' measured market and credit risks both decrease during a boom just when the value of their capital is likely to be rising in the equity markets; both risks increase during a crisis just when their capital's value is likely to be falling. Third, the new capital requirements have encouraged concentration and centralization and thus the consolidation of the global financial system under the control of a few huge multinational financial conglomerates. Basel II reinforces financial discipline: in creating a global financial system dominated by a few large banks and investment houses resilient enough to survive their own risk-taking, the G10 central banks, in cooperation with the IMF, World Bank and the other related bodies, designed a global banking and financial system that in being so controlled destabilizes the underlying international macroeconomy, thus disciplining subordinate classes and nations.

Can the centre hold?

But is the confidence that the financial authorities showed in the status quo in first devising and then implementing Basel II justified? There is a widely held belief, not confined to the left, that a crisis of the dollar is now unavoidable, threatening the dominance of the US financial system and the imperial power of the US state that stands at the centre of the global financial order. At the root of the problem, according to this view, is the US current account deficit. The deficit is unsustainable, the argument goes, because every quarter's current account deficit means an equivalent increase in the United States' net debtor position, which is already massive. Eventually, foreign investors will get tired of purchasing US assets, and this will lead to a run on the US dollar. If this view were correct, the argument of this chapter would be problematic, to say the least. It would be hard to maintain, as we have, that neoliberal global capitalism is a world economic system wherein the financial and economic turmoil is distributed internationally depending on the strength and resilience of the national banking and financial systems that make up the imperial chain, and in which persistent financial and economic instability reproduces capitalist and imperialist social relations by punishing and disciplining subordinate classes and nations.

But, in fact, the view that the US current account deficit must result in a dollar crisis is mistaken. The relationship between the US current account deficit and the net change in the US net debtor position used in the argument is an accounting identity and has no explanatory power. What matters to foreign investors is not the total size of their investments in the United States relative to the total size of US investments abroad, which is what the US net foreign asset position measures. What matters to them is the share of their US investments in their portfolios and the expected returns on the various components of their portfolios. Standard portfolio theory implies that foreign investors will reduce the relative US share in their investment portfolios if and only if the risk-adjusted expected rate of return on US investments declines relative to the risk-adjusted rates of returns on their investments elsewhere; and that they will reduce their investments in the United States if and only if they anticipate losses on their dollar exposures.

This does not mean, and it is very important to understand this, that the United States is immune from financial crisis, that its status as a debtor will not complicate the effects of a crisis, and that a falling dollar will not play a powerful role in perpetuating and deepening a financial crisis once it has appeared. As of this writing in the autumn of 2007, the United States is undergoing an acute financial crisis, one centred on its credit markets; its foreign creditors are threatening to reduce their dollar exposures; and a falling dollar is exacerbating the situation. But these events only reinforce our point.

The argument is simply that one should not see in the United States' status as a net debtor a potential cause of turmoil: crises originate in national – domestic – financial systems. In the case of the crisis at hand, its cause is a collapsing domestic housing bubble: falling housing prices are creating turmoil in the market for mortgage-backed securities, and this turmoil is spreading to other credit markets and thus to the international financial system more generally.[17]

The US national banking and financial system, like any national banking and financial system, is crisis prone. Nonetheless, it is the strongest and most resilient one of all and thus sits at the top of the imperial chain. This is why foreign investors, like US investors, are willing to hold dollar assets, even to increase their holdings of dollar assets when they and the dollar are under pressure. The market that truly matters here is not the US stock market or the market for mortgaged-back securities, but the US Treasury market. The US Treasury market is the deepest and most liquid market in the world because US Treasuries have the lowest credit risks. It is the market in which the Federal Reserve operates, and Treasury bills, notes and bonds have the 'full faith and credit of the government of United States'. For these reasons, the US Treasury market is the foundation of the international financial system. This both reflects and gives the United States tremendous power. For if the argument we have presented here has any validity, it implies that the effects of global economic and financial instability are shifted everywhere away from the United States. Investors' faith in US Treasuries reflects the global political power of US capital, which is why investors today are fleeing mortgages for the safety of the market for US sovereign debt.

No proper understanding of the international economic system can be had today without an understanding of the nature of imperialism today. Neoliberal globalization is a historically radical capitalist project, an attempt to discipline subordinate classes and nations through economic intimidation. But since the attempt to maintain and extend capitalist social relations through recurrent financial and economic crises is an inherently risky venture, neoliberal capitalism is also a dangerous, even a radically absurd, historical project: the global financial system is a chaotic system that if left to its own devices might well collapse. This is why the centralizing, organizing and coercive activities of the capitalist state, and above all of the US imperial state at the centre of the system, continue to play such an essential role. If financial instability is a means by which capital disciplines world capitalism, capital has to find a way to regulate and control it, to make a liberalized global financial system not just resilient enough to survive its own disorder but also resilient in such a way as to maintain its fundamental hierarchical structure. The capitalist state, and especially the US imperial state, disciplines the financial discipliners.

Notes

1. This is largely based upon primary sources, above all the reports and working papers of the BIS's Basel Committee on Banking Supervision (herein cited as BCBS) from 1979 to the present.

2. This is how Marx understood financial crises. See Harvey (1999: 292–6). It is also one of the major themes in Taylor (2004).

3. The analysis of the way in which the law of value operates in the neoliberal period presented in the following paragraphs takes its lead from Rafferty et al. (2000). Though their work is an attempt to give a labour theory of value interpretation of financial derivatives, the implications of their analysis of the spatial and inter-temporal discontinuities that disrupt the international circulation of capital are quite general. A theoretical justification for this approach can be found in Foley (1998).

4. Local national currencies are clearly obstacles to the international circulation of capital, but why interest rates? In a system of variable interest and exchange rates, interest rates and exchange rates are intrinsically linked by way of the interest rate parity condition, according to which the difference between the interest rates of two currencies is equal to the expected change in the relevant exchange rate. In the real world, any sharp distinctions between the obstacles caused by interest rates verses exchange rates are dissolved in the global foreign exchange and money markets.

5. On this, see Albo (2004). China, however, may be taking over the leadership of the Far Eastern bloc.

6. If there is more uncertainty in the centre than the periphery, why are interest rates higher in the periphery than in the centre? Is not what is normally called a 'risk premium' on the assets of the periphery actually an 'imperial premium'?

7. The argument that Gramsci's hegemony has a material basis is taken from Przeworski (1985). He applied it to class compromises, but the same argument can be applied to imperial compromises, with the Cold War undoubtedly structuring this cultural war.

8. Kapstein (1989, 1994) was one of the first to recognize the importance of the BIS and the Basel Committee in the governance of the global economy, although in his exploration only the implications of the capital requirements and the 'home country rule' principle, and not the division of labour between the major central banks and the IMF, are analysed.

9. The 1988 Accord is described in BCBS (1988). In the 1988 Accord, each of a bank's assets has a prescribed risk weight and the 8 per cent capital minimum requirement applies to the value of the asset as this value is adjusted by its risk weight. A bank's claims on OECD central governments, for example, have a zero risk weight and the capital requirements pose no cost to the banks in terms of capital they can't lend out and make money from. A fully secured residential mortgage has a 50 per cent risk weight and thus a 4 per cent cost – in bankers' language this is known as a 'capital charge'. Claims on non-OECD central governments have a 100 per cent risk weight and thus an 8 per cent 'capital charge'. The 'capital charges' for $1,000,000 in US Treasury bonds, a $1,000,000 residential mortgage, and a $1,000,000 loan to the government of Brazil are $0, $40,000 and $80,000, respectively.

10. The amended Accord is described in BCBS (1996). A bank using its own internal risk model to measure its market risk capital requirements does so using a 'value-at-risk' model that measures the losses that the bank can incur at a predetermined probability level. For a bank using the 'standard methodology', each of the bank's assets is given a risk-weight similar to that used in the initial Accord, except that the risk-weights used here are designed to measure the market risk of each of the bank's assets.

11. Since a bank's capital requirements are determined by the probability distribution of the returns of its assets over the past year, the volatility of a recent financial crisis will increase the variance of the bank's probability distribution and thus increase its 'value-at-risk'.

12. The account of the Asian crisis presented here is taken from Rude (1999). The account of LTCM troubles relies upon the BIS reports on the matter (BCBS 1999a, 1999b; Committee on the Global Financial System 1999), Mehrling (1999) and market sources.

13. For a description of the World Financial Authority proposal, see Eatwell and Taylor (2000).

14. Most large international loans are syndicated loans. In the event of a default of an international loan, the problem frequently arises therefore as to how to coordinate the interests of the many creditors involved. Collective action clauses in loan contracts prevent creditors from negotiating with the debtors individually and thus facilitate the orderly work-out of non-performing loans for the creditors as a whole.

15. The language agreed upon in June 2004 is available in BCBS (2004). BCBS (2006) provides a comprehensive version of the New Capital Accord. This document is a compilation of the June 2004 Basel II Framework, the elements of the 1988 Accord that were not revised during the Basel II process, the 1996 Amendment to the Capital Accord to Incorporate Market Risks, and a November 2005 paper on 'Basel II: International Convergence of Capital Measurement and Capital Standards: a Revised Framework'.

16. The role of the 'Three Pillars' of the Capital Accord is explained in BCBS (2003). These distinctions are also discussed by William White (1999, 2000), the BIS's chief economist.

17. As of this writing, the best account of this crisis can be found in BIS (2007).

Part III
Conclusion

11
The Politics of Imperial Finance

Martijn Konings and Leo Panitch

The purpose of this concluding chapter is not to summarize the previous chapters but to draw together some of the lines of argument presented in the various essays and to reflect on some of their broader implications in terms of political contestation, crisis and democracy both historically and today. It does so by analysing the relationship between American empire and global finance along three fundamental axes: (i) the distinctive interaction between class and finance in the American social formation; (ii) the mutually constitutive relationship between the state and financial markets; and (iii) the processes of financial internationalization that have entailed not only the *externalization* of American financial forms and practices but also the *internalization* of a variety of heterogeneous and geographically dispersed practices and relations into spaces structured by American rules and institutions.

Whereas most accounts of US financial power take the world of global finance and its dramatic expansion since the 1970s as their point of departure and then try to locate the US state within this system, the contributions to this volume have tried to outline the gradual, decades-long build-up of America's financial power, both at home and abroad. In doing so, they have painted a fuller picture of the historical, social and political sources of American financial strength than has so far been available in the literature. The chapters here show that the roots of the highly distinctive institutions and forms of American finance stem in large part from the fact that America's financial engagement with the world was preceded by a long period of domestic, inward development. This point should not be overstated of course, in light of the international dimensions of American development, all the way from the connections between British and American merchants based on transatlantic trade, to the use of dollar diplomacy in Latin America to open up new economies for American exports and investment in the early twentieth century, to the involvement of American bankers in the financing of Germany's post-First World War reparation payments as well as the American FDI that flowed into Europe by the 1920s. But it is important to recognize how even these externalizations of US finance were accompanied by a series of internalizations whereby foreign systems and credit relations were sucked into the American financial system. This included the way the inflows of financial capital that helped to finance industrialization and railroad construction during the nineteenth century were both employed and transformed by the distinctive domestic dynamics of class and state formation in the US. This determined that at the same time as Britain was at the high point of its international power during the late nineteenth and early twentieth centuries, the United States was able to engage in a process of relatively autonomous and unprecedented continental expansion.

One key factor in this process of internal development was the role of farmers: unlike pre-modern European farmers, American yeoman farmers were closely connected to market relations and as a result financial relations and institutions proliferated rapidly (Kulikoff 1989). But farmers' financial demands were specific to their socio-economic position: their need for mortgage credit and populist fears of financial concentration clashed with attempts by mercantile and financial elites to model America's financial system on the British system (based on short-term, trade-related credit and supported by a central bank functioning as lender of last resort), and as a result the antebellum US financial system often failed to generate sufficient liquidity for banks to be able to function properly (Hammond 1934). Thus, whereas in Europe the development of finance was seen as removed from daily life and divorced from social struggles (*haute finance*), in the US, political contestations articulated class and finance from the very beginning, and this has had a lasting impact on the nature of America's financial institutions (Goebel 1997). Precisely because American financial institutions were so hotly contested they ended up incorporating a much wider variety of interests.

The state's role in constituting financial markets, especially from the time of the Civil War onwards, was crucial in turning this into a strength rather than a weakness of US finance. As a number of the chapters here have shown, in order to help fund war debts, the Northern government created a national banking system that served to centralize funds from all over the country in New York banks, which were faced with a scarcity of liquid assets and had great difficulty investing their funds. This set in motion a veritable transformation of the mechanisms of financial intermediation that had emerged with the growth of commerce in sixteenth-century Europe and then developed with the industrialization and commercialization of England. The defeat of a stagnant, undynamic system of hyper-exploitation in the American South (which had been highly compatible with the existing system of transatlantic financial linkages under British hegemony) required and promoted the development of a more coherent, centralized system of financial practices and institutions. American banks after the Civil War turned away from classical commercial and mercantile banking and towards what by the turn of the twentieth century was already identified as a distinctive form of 'financial banking' (Youngman 1906), based on the investment of funds in the stock market and other speculative markets through which American banks had invented new ways to create and access liquidity (Myers 1931).

The direct borrowing and lending through the trading of financial instruments which remains to this day the hallmark of the American financial system can in part also be seen to result more directly from farmers' continuing engagement with financial institutions in the post-Civil War era. The institutions created to organize and run agricultural commodities exchanges over time became so sophisticated and diversified that they would eventually give birth to today's massive financial derivatives markets. The Chicago Mercantile Exchange, the world's central futures market in livestock long after the slaughterhouses were gone from Chicago, invented the futures market in currencies after the collapse of the Bretton Woods system of fixed exchange rates; and the Chicago Board of Trade, the world's centre of trade for wheat, corn and soya futures long after grain was no longer stored in Chicago, soon followed by launching the futures markets in US Treasury securities. As the head of the CME, Leo Melamed (who initiated the process in 1971 with the help of Milton Friedman) put it: 'without the cadre of traders who left the known risks of the cattle, hog and pork belly pits for the unknown dangers of foreign exchange ... [the financial futures revolution] could not have been implemented' (Melamed 1993: 43).

The fact that the new system of financial intermediation established in the US in the latter part of the nineteenth century was highly market-based and characterized by a self-reinforcing dynamic of speculative expansion also gave rise to a relationship between finance and industry that was rather different from the one that prevailed in Europe. The extraordinary growth of the American domestic market propelled a wave of mergers that was responsible for a tremendous and lasting concentration and centralization of capital (Roy 1997). Yet the result was not a system of uncompetitive monopoly capitalism: the increasingly large firms remained intensely competitive with one another within the giant domestic market. Key here was the fact that the mergers were financed and organized through the institutions that had been built around the stock market, which grew from $500 million to $7 billion from 1893 to 1903. To be sure, American investment bankers were a key driving force behind these developments and the process was accompanied by the growth of interlocking directorships across finance and industry. But these bankers were nonetheless very different creatures from the German *Grossbanken*, who were much better positioned to take controlling interests in a number of firms, and to function as the glue among them.

Hilferding's theory of 'finance capital' (1981, first published in 1910) – the institutional combination of industry and banking under the dominance of the latter to limit competition – was premised on the same developments occurring in the US as in Germany. Yet, in the US such a structural restriction of financial competition never solidified. To a large extent, this was due to the intense populist hatred of corporate collusion and the political clout of the antitrust movement. But by the early twentieth century this was backed up by the institutional fact that the relations between industry and finance were based on what was in principle a publicly accessible open market. While more direct ways of exercising influence were available, the principal relations between finance and industry were mediated by the stock market. The role of bankers was first and foremost in handling corporations' sale of their own stocks and bonds to raise capital or take over other firms. The concentration of capital thus went hand in hand with intense financial competition. In early twentieth-century America, capital accumulation was not dependent on the restriction of competition in the financial sector; nor was it still primarily dependent on the geographical extension of the domestic market. Rather, what became a key source of growth was the deepening of the market – a process facilitated and sustained by the very same market-based financial institutions and practices that prevented a Germany-style organized capitalism.

With the defeat of the late nineteenth-century challenges that had emerged from what was then the most industrially militant working class in the capitalist world as well as from the radicalized farmers' populist movement, US capitalism entered the twentieth century demonstrating a remarkable capacity to integrate and subsume small business, professionals, middle-class strata and working-class consumers (Sklar 1988). On this basis, the US developed the industrial innovations that became identified by the first decade of the twentieth century with Taylorism and Fordism – both of which reorganized mass production so as to make a high-wage proletariat functional to industrial capitalism. These organizational changes were not confined to the organization of the corporation and the workplace but penetrated the household and personal lifestyle. By the late 1920s one in five Americans owned a car, and 60 per cent of these cars were bought on instalment credit. Edwin Seligman's *The Economics of Installment Selling* in 1927 captured the ethos of Fordism in the new mass consumer age. He extolled credit-based marketing for increasing 'not only consumers' capacity to save but also the desire to save; indeed, [t]he family with car payments to make would be forced to work hard to make the payments' (Calder 1999: 252). This was crucial in the overall explosion in demand for consumer durables that transformed the retail sector with the aid of a massive advertising industry, whose expenditures at the end of the 1920s were five times what they had been before the First World War.

The specificities of American finance's engagement with labour, capital and the state were such as to give rise to an unprecedented expansion of the financial system. The rise of consumerism, the corporate revolution in American industry and the exponential increase in government expenditure (induced by war and the regulatory imperatives created by an industrializing society alike) fuelled a demand for credit and financial services that banks and other intermediaries were in an excellent position to meet. The federal government was both market participant and regulator in this process. The constitutive relation between state and financial markets was especially seen in the creation of the Federal Reserve as an attempt to manage the expansionary but volatile dynamics of the financial system. While it would take the better part of the century for the Federal Reserve to become the uniquely powerful actor that it is today, from the beginning it changed the institutional configuration of American finance – not least, as Sarai's chapter points out, by amplifying the power of the Treasury far beyond the role of the government's bookkeeper and fundraiser. With the Federal Reserve's policy instruments enlisted in the service of the Treasury's funding operations, the dramatic growth of government debt over the course of the twentieth century gave domestic US financial markets a huge boost.

While economists tend to think of government borrowing in terms of its tendency to 'crowd out' private financial activity and lending, in the US the financial operations of the government have always been a key element in the expansion of financial markets at large. This meant that as the twentieth century progressed it saw the construction of an ever denser network of organic (if often contradictory and conflictual) institutional linkages between the American state and financial markets. As the chapters here show, market depth and liquidity are not created by the autonomous operation of markets but are constructed through very specific institutional arrangements and agents.

The institutional configuration of the Federal Reserve and the Treasury with private financial intermediaries was crucial in this regard. This is not say that this relationship was a stabilizing one for the economy – as was abundantly proved with the 1929 crash. As the current Chairman of the Federal Reserve, among many others, argued in his academic work (Bernanke 1983, 2000), the Federal Reserve and Treasury's aggravation of its consequences significantly contributed to the Great Depression both in the US and internationally. The New Deal's stabilizing financial reforms, even while emerging out of the class conflict that resulted from working-class mobilization in the wake of the disappointment of their expectations fostered by the 'American dream', once again showed the intricate interplay between class and finance in the US. The New Deal was marked by the idea that the expansionary dynamics of American finance needed to be actively managed, rather than suppressed. It put limits on competition and speculation, but the objective and effects of this were not the general suppression of finance but precisely the fortification of key financial institutions and so an enhanced capacity to regulate the dynamics of expansion. Thus, while the New Deal was certainly a progressive response to social instability and discontent, it should not be conceptualized primarily in terms of the Polanyian re-embedding or social-democratization of American capitalism. Indeed, the New Deal reforms were oriented towards promoting (rather than reducing) the working classes' integration into and dependence on the financial system. This was most conspicuous in – but by no means limited to – the creation of the Federal National Mortgage

Association (Fannie Mae), charged with securing the availability of cheap mortgage credit through the securitization of mortgage loans. Together with the expansion of government debt and corporate debt during the 1930s, this meant that American finance was in full motion by the time the Second World War started. Moreover, the war itself gave a huge further boost to these dynamics.

The New Deal was in turn crucial to the nature of the imperial project embodied in the post-Second World War US state. As several of the chapters here have argued, we can only fully understand the dynamics of post-war international finance – including the nature of the neoliberal era – if we have a proper understanding of the transformation of the American state during the New Deal and the war. They have underlined how crucial it is to understand this transformation in a more profound way than is the norm, not least in most IPE work with its standard conceptualization of markets versus states. The transformation of the American state was far more complex than can be captured in such general, stylized terms, and thus requires an understanding of some of the basic historical features and dynamics of the American financial system. The wartime American state, strengthened by the capacities it had developed through the New Deal, effectively rewrote the rules of global finance as part of its planning for the post-war world. Insofar as the Treasury's Keynesian economists took the lead in this, this involved no little tension with Wall Street. But the compromises that emerged, even in the Bretton Woods Agreement itself, let alone its subsequent application, need to be understood in the context of what the New Dealers themselves called the overall 'grand truce with business' (Brinkley 1995: 89–90). A resilient US financial capital was not external to the constitution of the post-war Bretton Woods order: it was embedded within it and determined its particular character.

This crucial dimension of the reconstruction of the international financial order after the Second World War has received too little attention in the IPE literature on American financial power. The notion of 'embedded liberalism' in particular fails to capture what made these market structures and institutions qualitatively different from those that had prevailed during the previous wave of globalization under British hegemony. Moreover, embedded liberalism has served as the foundation of an overly stylized periodization of the half century after the Second World War into two highly distinct orders, as if the Bretton Woods era and the era of neoliberal globalization had nothing in common. The chapters in this volume show instead how much the two eras were linked via the evolution of the American informal empire and the development of financial capital under its aegis. With the system of private international payments largely defunct, the US used governmental capital flows outside the Bretton Woods system as a lever to influence the European pattern of post-war reconstruction. Thus, during the first years after the Second World War the penetration of European economies by US capital worked primarily through the institutions of the nation-state: the diffusion of American imperial power occurred through the internationalization of national states. IPE has always taken the prominent role of the national state in the immediate post-Second World War period as evidence of the limits to economic and financial globalization. But it is much more accurately viewed as indicating a particular *form* of imperial globalization. National economies and capitalist elites depended to an ever greater degree on states whose key institutions and capabilities had already been internationalized and whose functions were profoundly imbricated with the reproduction of American empire (Panitch and Gindin 2004). The inward national development model was grafted onto American methods of production in polities reconstructed under American auspices, facilitated by the provision of American funds that helped pay for crucial imports. In other words, internationalization should not be opposed to the Fordist model of nationally oriented development; instead, it occurred to a significant degree *through* that model.

If the 'liberal' aspect of the concept of 'embedded liberalism' leads to a failure to capture important aspects of the internationalization and Americanization of European economies, so does the notion of 'embeddedness' fail to capture important dimensions and sources of American financial power. For one thing, the dollar was the only convertible currency and New York was the only open financial centre, so foreigners wishing to float bonds had little choice but to turn to the US. More to the point, however, by the time European countries had recovered sufficiently to restore convertibility, the American financial system had already gone through almost two decades of domestic financial growth – propelled by industrial recovery, heavy government lending and the progressive integration of ever more layers of the American population into the financial system. The role of the Federal Reserve was crucial in facilitating the expansion of credit to keep up with the demand generated by Fordist patterns of consumption, production and government spending, further making ordinary people not less but more dependent on the capitalist system.

The dramatic post-war expansion of American financial markets effected a degree of continental integration hitherto unseen, and this contrasted starkly with the situation in Europe until the late 1950s. The origins of the changes that took place in Europe from that time on are best understood not so much in terms of the sudden re-emergence of 'global finance', but rather as part of a process through which the dramatic expansion of American finance began to assume international dimensions. It was the externalization of American practices and institutions that during the 1960s began to transform a conservative system of international payments into an integrated system of expansionary financial markets. Moreover, the arrival of American MNCs and the ideology of consumerism that came with them proved to be crucial supplements to the post-war welfare state reforms in integrating the European working classes. The attraction of an American economy that was 'universally recognized as the fountainhead of modern consumer practices' was well-captured by Donald Sassoon in his book on the practice of European socialist parties: 'how to achieve the European version of the American society was the real political issue of the fifties' (Sassoon 1997: 207).

To be sure, the enormous growth and export capacity of the European and Japanese economies that the US had sponsored, coincident with military expenditures, foreign aid and the outflow of foreign direct investment from American MNCs to the European market, began to have contradictory effects on the US itself, as a deteriorating US balance of payments produced pressures on the dollar (Odell 1982). This became the central issue of international finance during the 1960s, and it was notable that even when the Bretton Woods system was finally made operative with the return to currency convertibility at the end the 1950s, the IMF and World Bank, which had not been able to play much of a role in addressing the dollar shortage of the previous period, now found that the new problems entirely overwhelmed their capacities. It was the Treasury, the agency principally responsible for the external position of the US and for the status of dollar, which now emerged as a central player in international finance. This became especially significant towards the end of the 1960s as the Treasury became increasingly aware that the imbalances created by the deteriorating balance of payments and the growing Eurodollar market were not primarily America's own problems, and that the options available to the Europeans and Japanese were very limited. It was in this context that the US broke the dollar's link with gold, and came to recognize that its real challenge was not to fight off imperial contenders but precisely to manage the gyrations of an ever more dynamic and encompassing financial system with New York as its pivot.

Many academics and political commentators saw the end of the Bretton Woods system of fixed exchange rates and dollar–gold convertibility as the beginning of a new era of American policy irresponsibility and hegemonic decline that could, in the worst-case scenario, lead to unbridled economic rivalry and a breakdown of the world economy just as it had in the interwar period. Such perceptions were reinforced by the fact that the American state was indeed increasingly preoccupied in the 1970s with questions of domestic economic and financial management (Cargill and Garcia 1985). It was once again the distinctive class relations within the American state that proved especially salient in this. The inflationary pressures to which all the capitalist states were subject at the time had little prospect of being stifled in the US via the types of incomes policies secured through trade union cooperation with social-democratic parties in Europe. This left the militancy of a new generation of workers in the US relatively unbridled and enabled them to cash in on productivity increases and drive up wages in line with rising prices. This contradiction was aggravated, moreover, by the volatile mixture of financial innovation and securitization, as the growth of private pension funds combined with the liberalization of financial services, rising interest rates and the speculative opportunities offered by floating exchange rates. The savings of ordinary people were increasingly invested in mutual funds, and the US government used securitization techniques to promote the extension of mortgage credit. As the tension between inflation and financial expansion played itself out over the course of the 1970s, jeopardizing economic growth and producing pressure on the dollar, both industrial and financial capitalist forces within the US were increasingly drawn towards policies that entailed a drastic restructuring of the American economy of a kind that might bring about a fundamental shift in the balance of class forces in their favour.

While the coalition of forces that came to sustain a protracted period of Republican rule in the US was motivated by a broad variety of concerns and prejudices, the changes they effected were spearheaded by a dramatic move at the seemingly technical level of monetary policy-making. Monetarism as a theory had existed for some time, but until the late 1970s it had not been taken very seriously by academics and policy-makers. Paul Volcker, appointed by Carter as Federal Reserve Chairman to shore up his anti-inflation credibility, saw monetarism as offering a useful ideological cover for raising interest rates to a level that would break the back of inflationary pressures by changing the balance of class forces. This was highly effective in bringing inflation down, but this did not happen in classical textbook fashion. The innovation strategies of American financial intermediaries trumped attempts to restrict the creation of money and credit. Rather, the high interest rates – in combination with the opportunities opened up by neoliberal deregulation and trade union concessions and repression – meant that financial markets began sucking in economic activity. American finance exploded as growing government, corporate and household debt were financed by the inflows of massive amounts of funds, most of which came from abroad.

One of the main contributions of this volume is that it presents a substantially new picture of the rise of neoliberalism and monetarism and of their role in the restructuring of American imperialism. In sharp contrast with prevailing ways of understanding this shift, the chapters here have analysed the turn to neoliberalism and monetarism as a key moment in the constitution of American imperialism. As we pointed out in the Introduction, theories in IPE rely on an external understanding of the US state vis-à-vis global financial markets, and from this perspective neoliberalism and monetarism can only appear as the American state's admission of weakness or, at best, an acceptance of external discipline vis-à-vis international financial markets. The understanding of neoliberalism and monetarism presented here, by contrast, emphasizes the fact that it reconfigured the institutional parameters of American finance in a way that allowed the American state to regain a considerable degree of control over financial markets. Over the course of the post-Second World War period the externalization of American financial practices and institutions had created so many dense linkages between global financial markets and the American state that the latter possessed an extraordinary degree of pulling power – and this remained operative in the course of the transition from the Bretton Woods era to the neoliberal era that succeeded it.

The dynamics of the neoliberal era tend to confuse most of the spatial metaphors that political economists use to describe processes of imperial integration. Many of the analyses presented in this volume have, implicitly or explicitly, relied on the idea of externalization, which serves to draw our attention to the process of Americanization. Yet even this fails to capture some of the dynamics that emerged following the monetarist shock and neoliberal deregulation – which in a sense represented the obverse side of such externalization. The post-Volcker shock pattern of financial globalization also needs to be understood in terms of a renewed and much advanced instance of the process of internalization, as a vortex-like process whereby foreign systems and credit relations are sucked into the American financial system. These concepts can be used to highlight two aspects of globalization processes. First, externalization means that globalization operates as the extension of the constitutive forms of one state and their penetration into other polities and economies, and so creates a dense network of linkages between global processes of socio-economic expansion and the imperial state. Second, these linkages have the effect of heightening the policy leverage enjoyed by the imperial state, of increasing its 'pull'. Externalization, in other words, can create conditions that allow for internalization.

Moreover, the vortex metaphor suggested by the notion of internalization can be used to highlight yet another aspect of the specific nature of American empire: the global expansion of American finance has not only been shaped by the nature of its domestic institutions, but it also exists in a perennial relationship of functional interdependence with its domestic dynamism. In stark contrast with the case of British hegemony, the international expansion of American finance always has been and continues to be inextricably connected with its domestic expansion. In an important sense, the growth of US international power occurs through the internalization of foreign financial practices and credit relations into the dynamics of American finance. Especially in the neoliberal era, American financial imperialism functions by drawing in a variety of heterogeneous and geographically dispersed practices and relations and concentrating them into a space structured by American rules and institutions. This vortex-like quality is what underlies the non-territorial, network-like power of American financial imperialism. Of course, ultimately all metaphors have limits as guides to understanding and it is important not to stretch them beyond what they can accommodate. In particular, none of the above is meant to suggest that the turn to neoliberalism did not involve an imposition of financial discipline. But this was not a discipline imposed by depoliticized international financial markets on the US state, but rather by the US state and its ruling coalitions on the American subordinate classes. This was a crucial condition for the generalization of such discipline internationally by other states and ruling classes in the neoliberal era.

Crisis and democracy

The fact that American finance had attained a new degree of hegemony did not mean that it had become immune to instability, nor did it mean that the financial volatility that came with neoliberalism did not matter to the American state. Even if it had solved the problems of inflation and insufficient capital inflows, it was still experiencing considerable difficulty in managing the dynamics it had unleashed. The debt crisis, the savings and loans crisis and ultimately the 1987 crash of the stock market raised the question of how destabilizing the consequences of accelerating financial expansion would be and threw into doubt the ability of the American state to regulate this instability. Moreover, as more and more states inserted their economies into the dynamics of financial globalization and opened their socio-economic spaces to be structured by American rules and practices, this created new sources of instability. For a time it seemed that the US had bought some short-term relief from the pressure of global financial markets at the expense of its own and the world's economic health. This was the heyday of predictions of imperial decline (e.g. Kennedy 1987) and many felt that the passing of America's international power to Japan was just a matter of time.

But such perspectives were rather oblivious to the flexibility that the US state displayed in addressing these problems and laying the basis for a regulatory regime more appropriate to the new financial dynamics. The Treasury became more active not only in opening up but also regulating financial markets, and it did so in close consultation and cooperation with the IMF and the World Bank. Since the demise of Bretton Woods, the IFIs had been redefining their role and by the 1980s had morphed into more or less responsible agents of the neoliberal project as well as of American imperial power. At home, repeated US government interventions and bail-outs amounted to an acknowledgement of the US state's responsibility for the soundness of the financial system and created a pattern of stabilizing expectations for the future. It also introduced a major element of moral hazard into the system, which promoted more financial innovation and risk. The Basel Accord response to this by creating regulatory standards for the banks' risk and liquidity-management strategies, as a number of the chapters here have shown, sought to stabilize global financial markets while reinforcing the structural pro-American bias embedded in their legal framework.

By the early 1990s the expansionary dynamics of American and global finance had been consolidated into a regime that possessed more coherence than most commentators had imagined possible during the previous decade. Domestically, the regulatory fragmentation of the New Deal framework was not so much replaced as reproduced with a broad neoliberal remit, overseen by the Federal Reserve and the Treasury. Internationally, this regime became known as the Washington Consensus, indicating the degree to which the strategies of the IFIs were informed by US interests. In most of the major international crises of the 1990s the US played a key role, partly in bringing on the crisis in the first place, partly in organizing and financing the rescue operations that contained the damage, and above all in writing the rules for the restructuring of states and economies that followed (Burke 2001). All this indicated the financial management capacities the American state had been able to develop.

Throughout the 1990s, the most serious threats to financial stability under the imprint of the Washington Consensus seemed to be external, stemming from the inability of developing countries or emerging markets to shoulder the discipline needed to participate in a fully liberalized world order. But by the turn of the century, the tendencies to instability were increasingly visible at home as well. The stock market had ridden on the internet boom, and the effects of the dot-com meltdown ramified through American and international financial markets. Critics now charged that the growth of the stock market and the record profits of investment banks had been a result of the artificial inflation of asset prices and that the growth of consumer debt, typically justified in terms of the wealth effect of rising stock market and real estate prices, was also built on quicksand.

However, to insist that the dot-com boom amounted to nothing but a massive build-up of fictitious capital is to ignore the extent to which financial expansion was itself structurally and materially grounded as a key part of the economic system. In fact, the speculative functions of American finance increasingly became imbricated, not least through the venture capital component of the dot-com boom, with its more productive roles. Thus, while the bursting of the bubble itself represented a major problem, this did not negate the tremendous profits that had been made and the opportunities opened up by it, many of which continued to play themselves out in other parts of the economic system – not least as the continued growth of consumer debt had as its very real material basis the dramatic increase in levels of inequality.

But a new crisis struck in the summer of 2007: the credit crunch that beset global financial markets occurred in the wake of a party of speculation, easy consumer credit and takeover activity that was spawned by the liquidity that the Federal Reserve, in conjunction with other central banks (especially the Japanese), had pumped into the system to prevent a recession after the dot-com bubble burst and through the post-9/11 political conjuncture. It originated in the subprime sector of the American mortgage market and therefore struck at the heart of the imperial financial system: the possibility of converting illiquid mortgage loans into standardized, easily tradable financial assets has always been crucial in improving the ability of American intermediaries to extend mortgage credit. As such, it has been a key driving force behind the growth of American finance in this decade as well as the ever deeper penetration of financial relations into American society – especially as many subprime mortgage lenders found their way into poor, largely African-American neighbourhoods that traditionally had been of little interest to more established full-service commercial banks (Bajaj and Fessenden 2007). Not surprisingly – and reflecting the continuing racial inequalities so endemic to American society and working-class formation – many of these underlying assets turned out to be much less secure than even the rating agencies thought. Given how centrally involved American banks had been in the packaging and sale of these mortgage securities, and how eager many foreign (especially European) banks had been to purchase them, the effects of uncertainty were rapidly transmitted through the inter-bank market and the crisis spread rapidly to other parts of the global financial system.

This has led many to conclude, once again, that the current situation has exposed the shaky foundations of the American financial system, reliant as it is on a mountain of virtual money and paper-debt without the real income streams and wealth-generating capacity to back it up. While we will make no attempt to predict the outcome and long-term effects of the current situation, the understanding of the historical evolution and present state of the American financial system and its global role advanced in this volume leads us to view with some scepticism strong claims concerning the disastrous outcome of the current liquidity crunch for the structural dynamism of the global system of finance and America's position in it. From this perspective, several things are worth observing. For one, investors' response to the liquidity crunch has been a classic 'flight to quality': investors' aversion of risk has meant a huge flow of funds to Treasury securities, a virtually riskless financial asset that nonetheless yields an income stream. Moreover, the effects of the crunch were immediately seen to be quite severe outside the US. While several US banks eventually had to write off significant losses, the British bank Northern Rock had to deal with long lines of people seeking to withdraw their savings funds in scenes reminiscent of the Depression era. Similarly, the crisis seriously hit the German Landesbanken (regional banks charged with overseeing the German system of local savings banks and operating with effective public guarantees), which had considerable amounts of funds tied up in subprime debt. At the end of the day, therefore, the German state will foot part of the subprime bill, while the British state found the only way to save Northern Rock was to nationalize it.

In a number of important ways, the present crisis affirms some of the main arguments of this book. Most fundamentally, the current situation represents at least a conjunctural interruption of American capitalism's ability to functionally integrate ordinary people's activities and aspirations into the financial system, and this has had global as well as domestic consequences. Within the US, the effects of the crisis have been contained through the extension of a range of implicit government guarantees to American financial intermediaries. And this is where we encounter what is probably the most important aspect of the current situation: the credit crunch has not resulted in any significant delegitimation of key financial institutions, despite (or perhaps because of) the 'beheading' of the CEOs of some of the most prominent US banks. The public discussion following the onset of the crisis has been largely technical and instrumental, focused on what can be done to contain the fallout of the crisis and to prevent similar events in the future. The notion that the crisis is bound up with the failure of financial institutions to address and integrate the concerns and ambitions of poor people has found its way into the public debate mainly insofar as it is also a source of worry for investment banks and hedge funds.

In terms of its international effects, while there is nothing automatic about imperial reproduction, the way this crisis is playing out suggests that it will be contained within the mechanisms through which American financial hegemony is constructed rather than result in challenges from imperial contenders. As we have argued, the hegemonic integration of most layers of the American population into the financial system has been a major source of strength for the various institutions of American empire. And as long as this pillar, fuelling the mutually reinforcing expansion of American finance at home and abroad, remains intact, instability will be treated as a technical problem rather than as a deep social crisis. It will spark reforms and adjustments but of a kind that are not likely to lead to any fundamental realignment of financial power in the capitalist world order. Thus, the main upshot of the current situation is that the American state finds itself with a peculiar and unanticipated new problem of imperial management: a fairly small amount of bad debt has managed to produce considerable turmoil in the global financial system, just because no one seems to know who is holding it. Risk, in other words, has been converted into genuine uncertainty. But it is not unlikely that this could once again turn out to be a major opportunity for financial innovation. This would work to the advantage of those firms that are capable of upgrading their risk management techniques within a reasonable amount of time, as well as spur the growth of largely privatized (and almost exclusively American) mechanisms of credit-rating and market governance. Notably, European states have called for a further refinement of the Basel II measures, and this would provide the US with an outstanding opportunity to reinforce the asymmetrical dynamics of the financial system.

It is important to emphasize here that capital inflows into the US are very much motivated by the self-interest of foreign investors. Whereas in much political economy literature such flows are theorized as meeting the functional requirements of a hegemonic power suffering balance of payments problems (which assumes an implausible degree of systemic oversight on the part of investors), we have emphasized how the construction of hegemonic power can only be understood in terms of the concrete mechanisms and institutional linkages through which US power is organically embedded in the global economy. The trade deficit that caused so many to worry about the sustainability of US power and liberal world order since the 1960s constituted a problem for the US state, but the capital inflows that financed these deficits proved less erratic, ephemeral or fundamentally unsound than many had predicted. As Panitch and Gindin argue in their opening essay to this volume, capital inflows were 'mainly the product of investors being attracted by the comparative safety, liquidity and high returns that come with participating in American financial markets and the American economy'.

Similarly, it is our claim that in the present conjuncture, even as the American financial system is rocked by large amounts of bad debt, and despite a decline in the value of the dollar, most key aspects of this framework of institutional linkages between US power and the world of global finance remain intact. Of course, the declining value of the dollar reflects investors' concerns with regard to the state of American financial markets. But the dollar is still unrivalled as an official reserve currency, as a transactions currency and as the denomination of choice for issues of bonds and stocks. More to the point, however, it is the distinctive characteristic of modern imperialism that America's financial problems are not just its own problems. That is to say, foreign investors cannot engage in a wholesale dumping of dollars on to the world market without destabilizing the system as a whole and doing serious damage to their own interests in the process. For the foreseeable future, therefore, the question is not so much how the US state will ward off an external threat but rather how it will manage and stabilize global financial markets – on behalf of domestic and foreign capital. The illiquidity that hit the Eurozone bond market in the wake of the US subprime credit crisis stands as a sharp reminder that when the US financial market sneezes, international financial markets catch a cold. As for the much inflated talk that the Euro is about to replace the dollar as the core international currency, the comment of a Bank of America economist at the height of the credit crisis deserves to be heeded: 'Regardless of short-term cyclical fluctuations, the long-term demographic and economic prospects for the US economy and currency are better than for the eurozone. Once the dollar has hit its cyclical bottom, talk of the euro dethroning it will die down' (Holger Schmieding, quoted in Atkins 2007).

Before the onset of the credit crisis, Robert Mundell, the Nobel economist laureate for his work on the relationship between capital flows, exchange rates and monetary policy, who is sometimes known as the 'father of the Euro' for his work on optimal currency zones, went so far, in a speech in China quoted in the *Wall Street Journal* (9–10 June 2007), as to say: 'I think the dollar era is going to last a long time ... perhaps another hundred years.' Whether this proves to be so will much depend on the capacity of the US state, which significantly hinges, as we have argued throughout, on the domestic integrity of the American financial system, and this is closely bound up with the issues of political legitimacy. This always stands in need of continuous renegotiation in the US, where democratic institutions reflect and mobilize populist sentiments unconstrained by the more relatively autonomous bureaucracies of other capitalist states. This is by no means to suggest that American institutions allow for a greater degree of popular sovereignty than those in other countries. Rather, the relative openness of the American political system to social interests has always implied a strong need for ideological mechanisms of integration – and these have in turn provided a very sturdy foundation for the capacities of the American state. As such, legitimacy does not result in the restoration of a self-regulating market at the expense of state power, but rather enhances the capacity of the government institutions that sit at the pinnacle of the institutional linkages between state and society.

This is quite the opposite of common notions in International and Comparative Political Economy that the American state lacks political capacity – that it is a 'weak state'. To the contrary, the American state has developed an extraordinary ability to refract popular discontent and misgivings and redirect them in such a way as to promote hegemonic integration and legitimacy. And nowhere has this been clearer than in the history of American finance, where a tradition of widespread suspicion vis-à-vis the world of high finance coexists with a network of ever denser linkages between Main Street and Wall Street. Indeed, as Moran (1991: 37) has argued, 'scandal and crisis' have been a crucial driving force behind regulatory change in the US. Far from buckling under the pressure of popular disapproval, financial elites have proved very adept at not only responding to these pressures but using them in such a way as to create new regulatory frameworks that have laid the foundations for the further growth of business.

In other words, the popular protest and discontent triggered by scandals, far from undermining the institutional and regulatory basis of financial expansion, have repeatedly been pacified through the processes of further 'codification, institutionalization and juridification' (Moran 1991: 13). Such scandals have often been the object of Congressional investigations, and Congress is a crucial mediator in the relation between popular opinion and the regulation of the financial system. '[T]he potential capacity to legislate, coupled with Congressional oversight of the executive agencies, makes the legislature a key place of struggle between the competing interests in the financial services industry' (Moran 1991: 24). This was as much the case with the establishment of the New Deal regulatory framework that governed the expansion of American finance from the 1930s to the 1970s as it was in the transition to the neoliberal regulatory framework of our own time. As emphasized at several points in this volume, the New Deal cannot be understood in terms of the standard categories of state and market. It imposed a massive set of rules on American financial actors, but served to promote financial expansion and the ever deeper extension of financial relations into American life. Nor can the turn to neoliberalism be understood as a means of subordinating the American state to the dictates of financial markets. The neoliberal era has seen an increase in the sheer number of rules as well as the authority of some key regulators, and the American state has, right up to the present day, proven capable of re-regulating financial dynamics when the need arose.

Once again, it is important to put this in proper historical perspective. American finance in the early twentieth century was characterized by highly expansionary and poorly regulated dynamics: instability and the concentration of financial power were widely seen as a consequence of financiers' ability to gamble recklessly with massive amounts of 'other people's money' (in the phrase used by progressive lawyer Louis Brandeis (1967 [1914]). The Pujo Congressional Committee was charged with investigating the practices of what had become known as the 'New York Money Trust'. Generating great public interest, it uncovered monopolistic practices, a high degree of concentration, a web of interlocking directorates and outright corruption. A couple of decades later, after the Federal Reserve had proved itself incapable of balancing the dynamics of American finance and curbing its excesses, the Pecora Congressional Committee uncovered a range of shady financial practices and connections (Weldin 2000). Indeed, Wall Street bankers' intimate relations with the New York branch of the Federal Reserve System seemed to work primarily to further their interests. Nor did the revelation that J. P. Morgan himself had not paid any income tax during the two preceding years do much to improve the public's opinion of New York financiers' moral character.

But the New Deal reforms did as much to protect the financial services sector from these popular sentiments as they responded to democratic pressures for reform. The regulatory system that was imposed after the New Deal made the financial services sector much more transparent and accountable, but this increased accountability was organized through bodies representing financial capital's various sectional interests. The New Deal restrained competition and the excesses of speculation not so much by curbing the power commanded by finance but rather by promoting professional self-regulation and vesting private actors with quasi-public authority. In this way, self-regulation became a means to not merely shield financial markets from democracy but to make it positively serviceable to them. That is, the New Deal legislation and regulations reassured the American public that technical matters were now in safe, professional hands, and this faith was an important factor driving the growth in public participation in financial markets.

This new regime contained in-built dynamics of expansion. The fragmentation of the regulatory landscape meant that regulatory competition became a crucial promoter of financial expansion and the sheer density of semi-public regulatory authority meant that institutional reform became a key dimension in strategies of financial innovation and the construction of competitive advantage. Moreover, as we have argued, the changes in the global and American financial system since the late 1960s are best viewed not as a resurgence of the 'high finance' that governed financial globalization under British hegemony, but rather as a process of finance coming down to earth, marked by the ever deeper penetration of financial relations into new layers of society. These characteristics of the American financial system had already driven its steady growth from the 1930s to the 1960s.

It was in the latter decade that the dynamics of financial growth began to strain against the New Deal framework. This meant that the patterns of hegemonic socialization and integration and the ideological mystifications used to justify self-regulation devised with the New Deal state came under pressure. The opening up of the financial system also meant that, in certain respects, it – and the many problems generated by self-regulation – became more transparent. New and often powerful financial actors raised questions about the functioning of self-regulatory institutions which served the interests of older, more established actors, and these new actors began publicizing the woes plaguing their competitors and playing up the 'scandals' that beset the New Deal system as financial activity outside the self-regulatory structures continued to grow, and as the institutions of New Deal regulation experienced growing difficulty both in performing their technical tasks and their ability to keep outsiders out.

This all came to a head in the late 1960s as the growth of trading volume on the NYSE gave rise to the 'back office crisis': the NYSE members' offices handling the paperwork were collapsing under their growing workload, resulting in the failure of several houses and large financial losses for investors. This made it clear that Glass–Steagall did not provide sufficient protection and sparked a Congressional investigation that attracted considerable media attention and provided the liberalization lobby – spearheaded by pension and mutual funds and insurance companies and supported by retail-oriented investment firms such as Merrill Lynch – with a forum to make its case. Under pressure, the SEC responded with a shift away from its support for the cartel-like structures of brokers, investment banks and corporate managers that had dominated capital markets for several decades (Seligman 2003). In 1975 the SEC abolished the system of fixed-rate brokerage commissions (which had worked to the disadvantage of institutional investors) (Lütz 2002: 208). In the same year Congress passed amendments to the Securities Acts which strengthened the SEC's regulatory authority by giving it more instruments to intervene in the structures of self-regulation and to enforce competitive market structures, promote market transparency and target insider practices.

The opening up of the securities sector intensified the imperatives of competition in the financial sector to such an extent that banks too embarked on a campaign for deregulation. And they too could link up with the American ideology of the small saver and thus count on considerable popular support to push the programme of neoliberal deregulation further than the administrations of the 1970s had wanted to go. Reagan's neoliberal revolution was a prime example of how financial elites can channel social discontent into their drive for regulatory change. During the 1970s, these business interests funded conservative lobby groups and think-tanks, so fomenting and capitalizing on a popular backlash amongst the white suburban middle and working classes (Lyons 1998). The right's particular strength was to portray economic problems (such as unemployment, high levels of inflation, the predicament of the savings and loan sectors and the dangers it posed to the home building industry, financial volatility and the declining dollar) as the inevitable result of the excessive regulation of the New Deal framework. But deregulation was in fact re-regulation. Indeed, the neoliberal programme was accompanied by a dramatic enhancement of the US state's control over financial markets. The main piece of legislation was the 1980 Depository Institutions Deregulation and Monetary Control Act: it aimed not only to lighten the burden of regulation, but also to re-regulate the system and so to improve the mechanisms of monetary control (Cargill and Garcia 1985). In Moran's terms, deregulation occurred in conjunction with heightened institutionalization, codification and juridification.

Crisis, scandal and re-regulation are more pronounced at certain times than others, but they are nonetheless more or less permanent, recurring features of American capitalism: the dynamics of financial expansion destabilize existing norms and practices when they penetrate into new areas of social life, and the resulting popular consternation becomes the occasion for re-regulation. Indeed, it is no exaggeration to say that this dynamic became the organizing principle of a neoliberal regulatory regime that was increasingly pre-emptive in nature, not in the sense that this regime is premised on the illusion that financial crises can be entirely prevented, but rather in the sense that measures can be taken that may limit their intensity and their spread. Few crises involved such a wide swathe of US society as the savings and loans crisis, but a whole range of crises – such as the debt crisis, the 1987 stock market crash, the LTCM crisis and the bursting of the dot-com bubble – contained a clear potential for widespread instability, unrest and scandal.

The role of Congress remained crucial in all this, especially in such major scandals as were revealed in the savings and loans crisis. But the difference between the political conjuncture of the 1960s and 1970s and that of the 1980s and 1990s was evident from the enhanced autonomy that government bodies other than Congress had acquired in addressing the problem of financial instability. Whereas before these actors were hamstrung by a web of New Deal regulations that they could do little to revise or overturn, after the neoliberal turn, and especially by the 1990s, they wielded their enhanced institutional capacities to great effect. Indeed, in cases where Congress was deemed to be unhelpful – such as the 1994 Mexican peso crisis, when the Treasury perceived a clear threat to the stability of global and American financial markets – they would even boldly bypass Congress without running into much trouble for doing so.

To say that the neoliberal regulatory regime was increasingly pre-emptive in nature means that the US state had come to recognize the potentially dramatic consequences of a major crisis for the legitimacy of the system at large so that its actions were no longer primarily reactive or dependent on the anxiety experienced by Members of Congress seeking re-election. But far from trying to contain financial expansion within specific parameters, it dedicated itself to constructing a regime that would exercise stabilizing effects on such accelerating expansion, or at least guaranteed rapid government intervention as soon as financial crises erupted. The Basel agreement on capital requirements was important here: as financial innovations had made a mockery of traditional ways of controlling the creation and extension of credit – notably the manipulation of reserve requirements by reserve banks – the US (in cooperation with the UK) promoted the attempt to create new international capital standards that would serve to formalize and codify risk. In addition to benefiting the US in a quite direct way (US Treasury bills were classified as the most liquid assets), this regime had the simultaneous effect of promoting financial expansion and appearing to put it on a more secure footing. Uncertainty was operationalized as risk and while this was now justified in prudential terms, it also opened up a wealth of opportunities for well-positioned American intermediaries (Seabrooke 2001).

The construction of a new international regime of capital standards was accompanied by the creation of a set of more flexible institutional capacities. Key here was the ability to marshal massive amounts of stand-by funds in a short period of time to reassure the market. The Treasury and Federal Reserve repeatedly acted to bail out financial intermediaries in trouble and this created expectations for the way in which monetary authorities would deal with the imminent failure of such intermediaries in the future. Thus, what was at least as important as the build-up of a set of material capacities was the institutionalization of a pattern of expectations that the US state would take responsibility for the difficulties of private financial actors. As we have said, it also did much to exacerbate the problem of moral hazard, which in turn reinforced the pursuit of financial innovation and risk and kept re-regulation on the political agenda.

The bursting of the dot-com bubble in 2001 brought an end to a decade or more of relatively smooth domestic financial expansion in the US. It meant a return to full-blown financial scandals. During the late 1990s the upper echelons of companies like Enron had become engaged in highly creative accounting practices to sustain the upward trajectory of their stock prices. With the bursting of the bubble, it took little time for this to be exposed: a relatively small group of upper-level executives had collaborated with supposedly independent auditor firms and analysts to engage in fraudulent bookkeeping and sustain deceptive stock prices of which they themselves were the prime beneficiaries. The public outcry was enormous and in the best tradition of American populism: the collusive practices of a tight-knit circle of financial elites were widely seen not as an outcome inherent in the logic of an empire built on capital but precisely as negating and undermining the virtues of hard work and free enterprise. The executives involved received treatments that probably had never featured in J. P. Morgan's worst nightmares. Publicly named and shamed by powerful erstwhile friends, they were unceremoniously prosecuted as criminals and some received lengthy prison sentences.

In July 2002 Congress adopted the Sarbanes–Oxley bill. Its central objective was to make corporate governance practices more accountable and transparent to investors and so to secure the American public's faith in financial markets. It established a Public Company Accounting Oversight Board and put serious penalties on corporate fraud and conflicts of interest. White-collar crime was no longer considered an innocent, victimless crime – so was the central message. These measures seem to have been fairly effective, if only in the sense that, after the fall-out of the dot-com crash had worked its way through the system, the American financial system has not been rocked by scandals on the scale of Enron or WorldCom. To be sure, American corporate and financial elites have frequently complained that Sarbanes–Oxley imposes unreasonable costs and restrictions and greatly hampers the dynamism and competitiveness of American business. While it is always advisable to understand the statements of the business community in terms of their political efficacy rather than their truth-content, such sentiments do echo a real concern that Sarbanes–Oxley might have stifled some of American finance's traditional strengths. New York bankers and their political representatives have certainly been concerned that the reforms have impeded some of their business relative to other financial centres. This was noticeable especially in the decline of the number of Initial Public Offerings at the New York Stock Exchange and a slowdown in the mergers and acquisitions business. London in particular was well positioned to profit from the slowdown of business in New York, and recent years have seen several campaigns to adopt some of the City of London's 'principle-based' regulatory practices that involve less intrusion by public regulators. In earlier years, with the birth and expansion of the Eurodollar market, London's lenient regulatory climate had been a crucial factor in the externalization of American finance; recent years have seen attempts to selectively appropriate and internalize these regulatory principles on Wall Street.

But despite its drawbacks, Sarbanes–Oxley did what it was supposed to do. It improved the quality of corporate reporting to investors, while only scratching the surface of the bountiful benefits that American financial elites can reap from their connections and privileged access to information. By addressing a concrete problem, it created legitimacy for the economic and financial practices that had given rise to those problems in the first place. The restoration of legitimacy in this classically American way – involving small popular gains produced through an elaborate public spectacle – reinvigorated the capacity of America's key financial state institutions, allowing them to continue deepening and extending the reach of US financial markets.

Inevitably, such developments will give rise to new bouts of instability and crisis. Whether the US state will continue to develop the institutional capacities needed to deal with these situations will depend on the degree of legitimacy American finance still enjoys and on whether further rounds of re-regulation can retain the character of a technical, neutral 'learning' process. And this is probably one of the most noteworthy features of the current crisis: even though the crisis is intimately bound up with the financial plight of America's subordinate classes, the threat of mass foreclosures on mortgages is dealt with as a technical problem of financial management; its purely financial implications have been much more prominent than its social aspects. In other words, legitimacy has translated into the considerable autonomy enjoyed by American financial authorities in dealing with the current crisis as they engaged in one intervention after another to try to bring it to an end during the autumn and winter of 2007–8. To change this would require a far more radical and coherent challenge to the 'interactive embeddedness' of state and finance in the US than has so far appeared on the political agenda.

The politics of political economy

This volume's interpretation of American empire and finance not only addresses fundamental analytic issues but also has important political implications. The two literatures – International Political Economy and Comparative Political Economy – that this volume has theoretically engaged with reflect different aspects of the contradictions and dilemmas of progressive politics in the era of capitalist globalization. IPE largely has reflected the shifting political perspectives of liberal internationalism while CPE has reflected the political orientation of social democracy. The former has been inclined towards extolling multilateral international institutions as the best means of attenuating external pressures on states, while the latter has devoted itself to demonstrating the continued resilience of national models so long as these are based on a democratic-corporatist attenuation of domestic class conflict. The intellectual division of labour between these two branches of contemporary political economy has in some ways reflected the intractable nature of the contradictions produced by the confrontation of national welfare states and global capital, as well as the absence of any real-world political propensities to work through these contradictions. It is crucial in this respect to realize that these literatures represented opposite poles of a Polanyian understanding of markets as characterized by an expansionary, disembedding logic, and of institutions as society's instruments to embed the market and subordinate it to social and political purposes. For it is only on such an understanding that the division of labour between IPE and CPE is plausible, with the one focused on the international regulation of disembedded capital flows and the other on the national institutions responsible for keeping capital embedded.

However, it can be argued that IPE's focus on the regulation of international payments and capital flows and CPE's focus on the role of national institutions in promoting growth and employment both represent very restrictive, partial conceptions of the role of financial relations. The very reason that the 'varieties of capitalism' perspective and the politics of models it fostered acquired so much plausibility with the onset of neoliberalism was that it operated with IPE's very thin conception of financial globalization. In other words, the kind of globalization that both IPE and CPE focused on was only the tip of the iceberg. What completely disappeared from view were those aspects of financial globalization that are not so easily described through IPE's focus on payments systems and international capital flows. What did not feature in either IPE's or CPE's conception of globalization was the kind of financial expansion that was itself highly dependent on the formation of a range of new private and public institutions. In other words, the 'market and state' discourses of IPE and CPE are much too superficial to conceptualize processes of market expansion that are profoundly dependent on the construction of a range of new institutions that precisely facilitate and promote the expansion of financial relations.

With the exception of its more cynical realist strand, the discipline of IPE is overwhelmingly liberal internationalist in orientation, i.e. driven by a belief that the key to a well-regulated global order is to be found in institutions that derive their legitimacy as much from their normative force as from their insertion into a particular set of power relations. Such idealism can be traced back to Keynes: while far from oblivious to the national interests at stake in the reconstruction of the post-Second World War financial system, he nonetheless viewed as Bretton Woods' primary function the guarantee that the destructive spirits of speculators would be kept at bay and the world economy could expand on the basis of the classic liberal principle of free trade. Modern IPE emerged when Bretton Woods had come under threat and the instrumental way the US state treated it had become apparent. Against the grain of historical events, IPE scholars adopted what was at its core the same idealized understanding of Bretton Woods as had underlain the hopes that accompanied its creation. This is what has motivated the incessant search for a functional alternative to the role of the US as the guardian of liberal international institutions. Even in 1982, when the debt crisis was in full swing, and structural adjustment conditionality was already clearly in the works as a response, Ruggie (1982) expressed the hope that the IMF would assume the responsibilities for the reproduction of embedded liberalism that the US was no longer willing to shoulder. And the present search for functional institutions of 'governance' represents a similar disregard for the power relations that have always gone into the making of global finance.

As for Comparative Political Economy, Hilferding's old idea of 'finance capital' as the functional imbrication of finance with productive capital has been the key point of reference – as it once had been for European social democracy. But its meaning has been transformed in a subtle way: finance capital is no longer viewed in terms of problematic concentrations of power and influence. The Marxist social-democratic theorists of the Second International had seen this in terms of capitalist socialization processes preparing the way for a gradual transition to socialism. Modern social democracy has rather celebrated it as a specific 'non Anglo-American' form of capitalist coordination capable of reconciling competitiveness and equity. That is, the configuration of institutions and actors identified by Hilferding – i.e. a concentration of economic power among nationally embedded and closely connected industrial, financial and state elites – changed from an opportunity for social transformation into a putatively desirable situation that is seen to allow for the construction of corporatist class compromises and economic competitiveness within the confines of a national capitalist society. Financial systems are evaluated primarily in terms of their ability to organize the channelling of society's savings into productive investments that serve to make a national economy more competitive in the global market for manufactured exports.

There are three key points to appreciate here. First, external openness is only one dimension of the processes of financial globalization; conceived in a broader sense, global financial expansion also involves processes of financial innovation, growing market depth and the penetration of financial relations into ever more social spheres. Second, the notion that all credit creation that cannot be directly related to productive activities is merely a speculative distraction from real production is misleading and in many ways incorrect. Third, the dynamics of financial globalization have their roots in the way US finance has developed, and continue to be driven and shaped by the development of American capitalism. What stands out about the development of American finance is how its financial system has never resembled a system of finance capital in Hilferding's sense, and this has been reflected in the financial globalization that has taken place under the imprint of the American empire.

In recent years, the dynamics of financial expansion have been captured through the concept of 'financialization' (Langley 2004a; Krippner 2005; Montgomerie 2006). This literature, formulated to a large extent in response to IPE's adherence to the language of states and markets and the limits to its understanding of the precise mechanisms of market globalization, concentrates on the mechanisms of market innovation and private governance that emerged during the 1970s and were a crucial component of the expansion of global finance. Financialization thus tends to be conceptualized in terms of the emergence of a new type of capitalist regime with institutions and mechanisms of its own rather than a dysfunctional divergence from the more fundamental conditions of economic growth. However, the financialization literature does not view this phenomenon as something specifically American with historical roots that go much further back into history than the 1970s and institutional roots that are embedded deeply in the fabric of American society. That is, it tends to understate the historical role played by financial innovations and techniques in the construction of America's domestic hegemony. Nor does it pay much attention to the ways in which financialization trends are related to the more formal institutions of the American state. And it is precisely in the articulation of these institutions with their broader social bases that we can find the sources of American imperial power. Thus, what is given short shrift is the way financialization is connected to the domestic and global constitution of empire, i.e. class and international power.

Once we enrich our understanding of financial globalization in this way, the 'politics of national models' loses much of the plausibility that it enjoyed on the basis of its presentation of itself as an alternative to IPE's conception of globalization. That is, in order to fully understand how global financial expansion is related to issues of class power and international power, we need to appreciate that, while in Europe the growth of international financial flows from the 1960s seemed a novel phenomenon that challenged the internal coherence of class compromise, the idea of 'finance against social integration' reflected a profoundly European perspective (often shared by progressive American academics) that was never really applicable to the US situation, and has become increasingly inapplicable to the European reality.

The history of finance in the US, so qualitatively different than in most of Europe, has always provided much less room for the 'institutions vs. markets' perspective. While in nineteenth-century Europe industrialization produced intense struggles over the existence, nature and terms of the wage relation, in the US the political efforts of farmers bent on retaining their yeoman independence were primarily focused on the organization of the monetary and financial system. While populism as a political programme was defeated at the end of the nineteenth century, the struggles around the financial system nevertheless had a constitutive impact on the nature of the financial system as this emerged by the early twentieth century. In particular, it was much more dynamic and capable of integrating the ambitions of ordinary working people, linking the worlds of high and low finance in a way that European finance did not. But European finance has also changed over the past fifty years as part and parcel of the tendency of American finance to take on international dimensions. As we have argued, it was not so much global capital as American capital that came knocking on the European door in the 1960s, propelled by and drawing great strength from its deep domestic rootedness.

Once we realize that American finance is *more rather than less* socially embedded than European finance, and that this does not indicate the restraint of markets but rather their facilitation, the politics of models and its academic literature seems more like a social-democratic rearguard battle against processes of neoliberal globalization that have already rendered the old models increasingly unviable. Indeed, it often seems as if the threat that

American financial practices pose to the institutional integrity of coordinated market economies is more a matter of concern for progressive academics than for the social groups supposed to have an interest in preserving the welfare state and staving off neoliberal globalization. Right-wing parties in the 1980s had fewer problems getting elected, and social-democratic lamentations concerning the declining power of politics vis-à-vis financial globalization did not stop voters from abandoning these parties en masse. Moreover, when, by the mid-1990s, most European countries had once again put in place social-democratic governments, they readily promoted continued financial liberalization. Popular apathy towards the finer details of financial regulation was important in their ability to do this, but in cases where political entrepreneurs found themselves able to break through this wall of apathy, public opinion was mobilized as a significant force behind the further liberalization of financial markets. What energy European citizens had to resist neoliberalism went into protesting the dismantling of the welfare state and employment protection.

Of course, a distinct American ideology – whereby there is no financial reform, it often seems, that cannot be pursued in the name of the small saver or the small investor – was associated with the legitimation of financial expansion. Part and parcel of the penetration of European financial systems by American institutions has been the adoption of such sentiments by more and more Europeans themselves. For instance, since the late 1980s, many European countries with large capitalized pension funds have lifted the regulatory restrictions on the activities of these funds and been in the forefront of the opening up of financial markets at large. One major source of pressure for this was public opinion, which grew increasingly indignant at the state's nerve to impose restrictions on the investment freedom of pension fund managers, resulting in low rates of return. Deregulation has meant a dramatic shift in the investment strategies of pension funds: instead of investing in low-yield, domestic government obligations, they now put large and continuously growing amounts of money in foreign (primarily American) financial markets for corporate equity, asset-backed securities and hedge funds and private equity funds – with much higher (if more volatile) returns.

At the same time, it is important to appreciate that such structural convergence of attitudes towards financial expansion is incomplete. Especially in recent years, we have seen the re-emergence in European politics of the classic images of the rentier and the financier. To continue with the example of pension funds: while ordinary people benefited from the liberalization of pension funds in their capacity as investors, in a much more indirect way, i.e. in their capacity as workers, they often suffered the consequences. The liberalization of financial markets left their domestic equity markets ever more open to penetration by foreign financial actors. Increased competition for pension fund capital has meant that European companies are under growing pressure to adopt Anglo-Saxon corporate governance practices and standards, and the strategies of American private equity funds and investment firms have meant an even more direct intervention in European industry, often with hostile takeovers and job losses as a result. In recent years, this has led some social democratic politicians to resurrect the classic image of the financier and rentier, castigating them as benefiting from unproductive financial engineering and speculative practices. Yet the public denouncements of hedge funds and private equity funds have remained largely rhetorical and peculiarly inconsequential.

Moreover, while the imperialist transformation of material interests formed the basis of the steady continuation of liberalization and deregulation, the politics of models was instrumental in defusing residual discontent. Especially during the 1990s it had morphed into a 'Third Way' strategy according to which economic globalization should not be resisted but could be positively used as an opportunity to combine equity and efficiency and to improve competitiveness in a socially progressive manner (Zuege 2000; Albo 2004). This signified a further stretching of the relation between the transformation of European political economies and the ideological representations of that process. In important ways, therefore, social democracy's relationship to finance mirrors its encounter with the state: however much it has pushed for policies premised on the achievement of state autonomy from capitalist classes and markets, it has for just as long embraced the state's ideological appearances, seduced by its promises of neutrality and instrumentalism.

This is not to say, of course, that social democracy's belief in the state has been nothing but an illusion: the state's ideological appearances are always anchored in the reality of its need for legitimacy, and the relationship that developed between organized labour and the state over the twentieth century can only be described as a Janus-faced process, improving the material lives of working-class people while depoliticizing their ambitions and demobilizing their political capacities. Social democracy's relationship to finance has been characterized by a similar mixture of suspicion and inaction. As a consequence, it has become expert in denouncing finance without really engaging it. This persists until the present day: the activities of hedge funds and private equity funds have drawn repeated condemnations by European politicians on the left, but these have failed to spawn any regulatory or legislative measures that might seriously restrict the behaviour of these actors. In that sense, social-democratic parties actually present one of the main obstacles to an awareness of the contours, and an effective political response to, imperial globalization.

Of course these developments have not gone unchallenged. While social-democratic parties remained incapable of looking beyond ways to make their respective states more competitively successful within the framework of globalization, and while liberal internationalists called for reforms of the IMF and World Bank, an 'alter-globalization' movement emerged that disdained these limited 'alternatives'. Inspired by local and regional resistances, from

IMF riots to indigenous peoples' rebellions, it garnered much global attention at the dawn of the new century. Yet by focusing as it did on the World Bank, the IMF, the WTO and the MNCs, it failed to sufficiently register or target the American imperial power in particular, and the associated power of states more generally, that underlay the globalization process. To a significant extent, it was a mirror image of those who had painted globalization as all about bypassing states: its enemies were the supranational institutions, and its heroes were the radical and oppressed elements of civil society that promised to change the world without changing the state. This posture has changed with the very open face the Bush–Cheney regime gave to US imperialism in recent years, and with the challenges that have been issued to both neoliberalism and imperialism by new radical political leaders especially in Latin America. This points to the need for a fundamental transformation in class relations within states, to a radical democratization of both public and private economic institutions as part of this, and to a thoroughgoing reconstruction of 'international relations' based on strategic reciprocity and material solidarity. It is to be hoped that the kind of scholarship this book represents can help inform this kind of politics and play a role in its further development.

Bibliography

Aglietta, M. (1979) *A Theory of Capitalist Regulation*, London: Verso.
Aglietta, M. and A. Rebérioux (2005) *Corporate Governance Adrift: a Critique of Shareholder Value*, Cheltenham, UK: Edward Elgar.
Albo, G. (1997) 'A world market of opportunities: capitalist obstacles and left economic policy', in L. Panitch et al. (eds), *The Globalization Decade*, London: Merlin.
Albo, G. (2004) 'The old and new economics of imperialism', in L. Panitch and C. Leys (eds), *Socialist Register 2004*, London: Merlin.
Amira, K. and W. C. Handorf (2004) 'Global debt market growth, security structure, and bond pricing', *Journal of Investing*, 13(1).
Anderson, C. J. (1965) *A Half-century of Federal Reserve Policymaking, 1914–1964*, Philadelphia: Federal Reserve Bank of Philadelphia.
Ankarloo, D. (2002) 'New institutional economics and economic history', *Capital & Class*, 78.
Ankarloo, D. and G. Palermo (2004) 'Anti-Williamson: a Marxian critique of new institutional economics', *Cambridge Journal of Economics*, 28 (May).
Arrighi, G. (1978) 'Towards a theory of capitalist crisis', *New Left Review*, 111.
Arrighi, G. (1994) *The Long Twentieth Century: Money, Power, and the Origins of Our Times*, London and New York: Verso.
Arrighi, G. (with J. Moore) (2001) 'Capitalist development in world historical perspective', in R. Albritton, M. Itoh, R. Westra and A. Zuege (eds), *Phases of Capitalist Development*, New York: Palgrave Macmillan.
Arrighi, G. (2003) 'The social and political economy of global turbulence', *New Left Review*, 2(20).
Arrighi, G. (2005) 'Hegemony unraveling', Part 1, *New Left Review*, 2(32); Part 2, *New Left Review*, 2(33).
Arrighi, G. (2007) *Adam Smith in Beijing: Lineages of the Twenty-first Century*, London: Verso.
Atkins, R. (2007) 'Dollar safe from challenge of the Euro', *Financial Times*, 23 November.
Babb, S. (2003) 'The IMF in sociological perspective: a tale of organizational slippage', *Studies in Comparative International Development*, 38(2).
Bajaj, V. and F. Fessenden (2007) 'What's behind the race gap?', *New York Times*, 4 November.
Baker, A. (2006) *The Group of Seven: Finance Ministries, Central Banks and Global Financial Governance*, New York: Routledge.
Baker, G. P. and G. D. Smith (1998) *The New Financial Capitalists: Kohlberg Kravis Roberts and the Creation of Corporate Value*, Cambridge: Cambridge University Press.
Bank for International Settlements (BIS) (1979) *Annual Report*.
Bank for International Settlements (BIS) (2001) *The Changing Shape of Fixed Income Markets: a Collection of Studies by Central Bank Economists*, BIS Papers No. 5, Basel, Switzerland: Monetary and Economic Department.
Bank for International Settlements (BIS) (2005) *OTC Derivatives Market Activity in the Second Half of 2004*, Basel, Switzerland: Monetary and Economic Department.
Bank for International Settlements (BIS) (2007) *BIS Quarterly Review September*, Basel, Switzerland: Monetary and Economic Department.

Battilossi, S. (2002a) 'Introduction: international banking and the American challenge in historical perspective', in S. Battilossi and Y. Cassis (eds), *European Banks and the American Challenge: Competition and Cooperation in International Banking under Bretton Woods*, Oxford: Oxford University Press.

Battilossi, S. (2002b) 'Banking with multinationals: British clearing banks and the Euro-markets' challenge, 1958–1976', in S. Battilossi and Y. Cassis (eds), *European Banks and the American Challenge: Competition and Cooperation in International Banking under Bretton Woods*, Oxford: Oxford University Press.

Bawden, T. and P. Hosking (2007) 'Regulators didn't have clear enough visibility with what was going on...', *The Times*, 16 October, World Business.

BCBS (1988) 'International convergence of capital measurement and capital standards', Basel: BIS.

BCBS (1996) 'Overview of the capital accord to incorporate market risk', Basel: BIS.

BCBS (1999a) 'Banks' interactions with highly leveraged institutions', Basel: BIS.

BCBS (1999b) 'Sound practices for banks' interactions with highly leveraged institutions', Basel: BIS.

BCBS (1999c), 'Supervisory lessons to be drawn from the Asian crisis', Working Papers, Number 2, Basel: BIS.

BCBS (2001) 'History of the Basel Committee and its membership', Basel: BIS.

BCBS (2003) 'Overview of the new Basel Capital Accord', Basel: BIS.

BCBS (2004) 'Basel II: international convergence of capital measurement and capital standards: a revised framework', Basel: BIS.

BCBS (2006) 'Basel II: international convergence of capital measurement and capital standards: a revised framework – Comprehensive Version', Basel: BIS.

BCBS (2007) 'History of the Basel Committee and its membership', Basel: BIS.

Bea, F. X., A. Kötzle, K. Rechkemmer and A. Bassen (1997) *Strategie und Organisation der Daimler-Benz AG*, Frankfurt am Main: Peter Lang.

Becker, J. (2002) *Akkumulation, Regulation, Territorium: Zur kritischen Rekonstruktion der französischen Regulationstheorie*, Marburg: Edition Sigma.

Beckmann, M. (2007) *Das Finanzkapital in der Transformation der europäischen Ökonomie*, Münster: Westfälisches Dampfboot.

Bensel, R. F. (1990) *Yankee Leviathan: the Origins of Central State Authority in America, 1859–1877*, New York: Cambridge University Press.

Berger, A. N. and A. K. Kashyap et al. (1995) 'The transformation of the U.S. banking industry: what a long, strange trip it's been', *Brookings Papers on Economic Activity*, 2.

Berger, A. N. and G. F. Udell (1993) 'Securitization, risk, and the liquidity problem in banking', in M. Klausner and L. J. White (eds), *Structural Change in Banking*, Homewood: Business One Irwin.

Berger, M. and M. Beeson (1998) 'Lineages of liberalism and miracles of modernisation: the World Bank, the East Asian trajectory and the international development debate', *Third World Quarterly*, 19(3).

Bernanke, B. (1983) 'Nonmonetary effects of the financial crisis in the propagation of the Great Depression', *American Economic Review*, 73 (June): 257–76.

Bernanke, B. (2000) *Essays on the Great Depression*, Princeton, NJ: Princeton University Press.

Bernanke, B. (2007) 'Federal Reserve communications', speech delivered at the Cato Institute 25th Annual Monetary Conference, Washington, D.C., 14 November.

Best, J. (2003) 'From the top-down: the new financial architecture and the re-embedding of global finance', *New Political Economy*, 8(3).

Beyer, J. (2003) 'Deutschland AG a.D.: Deutsche Bank, Allianz und das Verflechtungszentrum des deutschen Kapitalismus', in W. Streeck and M. Höpner (eds), *Alle Macht dem Markt? Fallstudien zur Abwicklung der Deutschland AG*, Frankfurt am Main/New York: Campus.

Bieling, H.-J. (2003) 'Social forces in the making of the new European economy: the case of financial market integration', *New Political Economy*, 8(2).

Bieling, H.-J. (2006) 'EMU, financial integration and global economic governance', *Review of International Political Economy*, 13(3).

Bird, G. (2001) 'A suitable case for treatment? Understanding the ongoing debate about the IMF', *Third World Quarterly*, 22(5).

Blair, M. M. (ed.) (1993) *The Deal Decade: What Takeovers and Leveraged Buyouts Mean for Corporate Governance*, Washington, D.C.: Brookings Institution.

Blinder, A. S. and R. Reis (2005) 'Understanding the Greenspan Standard', paper prepared for the Federal Reserve Bank of Kansas City Symposium, The Greenspan Era: Lessons for the Future, Jackson Hole, Wyoming.

Block, F. L. (1977) *The Origins of International Economic Disorder*, Berkeley: University of California Press.

Board of Governors of the Federal Reserve System (1998) 85th Annual Report to Congress, http://www.federalreserve.gov/boarddocs/rptcongress/annual98/ann98.pdf

Board of Governors of the Federal Reserve System (1999) 86th Annual Report to Congress, http://www.federalreserve.gov/boarddocs/rptcongress/annual99/ann99.pdf

Board of Governors of the Federal Reserve System (2000) 87th Annual Report to Congress, http://www.federalreserve.gov/boarddocs/rptcongress/annual00/ar00.pdf

Board of Governors of the Federal Reserve System (2001) 88th Annual Report to Congress, http://www.federalreserve.gov/boarddocs/rptcongress/annual01/ar01.pdf

Board of Governors of the Federal Reserve System (2002) 89th Annual Report to Congress, http://www.federalreserve.gov/boarddocs/rptcongress/annual02/ar02.pdf

Board of Governors of the Federal Reserve System (2003) 90th Annual Report to Congress, http://www.federalreserve.gov/boarddocs/rptcongress/annual03/ar03.pdf

Board of Governors of the Federal Reserve System (2004) 91st Annual Report to Congress, http://www.federalreserve.gov/boarddocs/rptcongress/annual04/ar04.pdf

Board of Governors of the Federal Reserve System (2005) 92nd Annual Report to Congress, http://www.federalreserve.gov/boarddocs/rptcongress/annual05/ar05. pdf

Bond, P. (2001) *Strategy and Self-activity in the Global Justice Movements*, Foreign Policy in Focus, Discussion Paper No. 5, retrieved 9 March 2007, http://www.fpif.org/papers/gjm.html

Botzem, S. and S. Quack (2005) *Contested Rules and Shifting Boundaries: International Standard Setting in Accounting*, Social Science Research Center Berlin, Discussion Paper SP III 2005-201.

Boyer, R. (1990) *The Regulation School: a Critical Introduction*, New York: Columbia University Press.

Boyer, R. (2000) 'Is a finance-led growth regime a viable alternative to Fordism?' *Economy and Society*, 29(1).

Bradlow, D. (2006) 'The changing role of the IMF in the governance of the global economy and its consequences', Washington: New Rules for Global Finance, retrieved 12 January 2007, http://www.new-rules.org/docs/imfreform/bradlow_brown060906.htm

Brady, S. (1995) 'Opportunities in the Yankee market', *Corporate Finance*, July.

Brandeis, L. D. (1967 [1914]) *Other People's Money and How the Bankers Use It*, New York: Harper & Row.

Brawley, M. R. (1999) *Afterglow or Adjustment? Domestic Institutions and Responses to Overstretch*, New York: Columbia University Press.

Brendsel, L. C. (1996) 'Securitization's role in housing finance: the special contributions of the government-sponsored enterprises', in L. T. Kendall and M. J. Fishman (eds), *A Primer on Securitization*, Cambridge, MA and London: MIT Press.

Brenner, R. (2002) *The Boom and the Rubble: the US in the World Economy*, New York and London: Verso.

Brinkley, A. (1995) *The End of Refom: New Deal Liberalism in Recession and War*, New York: Alfred A. Knopf.

Broesamle, J. J. (1973) *William Gibbs McAdoo: a Passion for Change, 1863–1917*, Port Washington, NY: Kennikat Press.

Brown, J. R. (1994) *Opening Japan's Financial Markets*, New York: Routledge.

Broz, J. L. (1997) *The International Origins of the Federal Reserve System*, Ithaca, NY: Cornell University Press.

Broz, J. L. (2005) 'Congressional politics of international financial rescues', *American Journal of Political Science*, 49(3).

Broz, J. L. and M. Hawes (2006) 'Congressional politics of financing the International Monetary Fund', *International Organization*, 60(2).

Bryan, D. et al. (2000) 'Financial derivatives and Marxist value theory', School of Economics and Political Science Working Paper, University of Sydney, December.

Bryan, D. and M. Rafferty (2005) *Capitalism with Derivatives: a Political Economy of Financial Derivatives, Capital and Class*, Basingstoke: Palgrave Macmillan.

Burk, K. (1992) 'Money and power: the shift from Great Britain to the United States', in Y. Cassis (ed.), *Finance and Financiers in European History, 1880–1960*, Cambridge and Paris: Cambridge University Press and Editions de la Maison des Sciences de l'Homme.

Burke, M. (2001) 'The changing nature of imperialism: the US as author of the Asian Crisis of 1997', *Historical Materialism*, 8.

BVI – Bundesverband Investment und Asset Management (2007) *Investment 2007: Daten, Fakten, Entwicklungen*, Frankfurt am Main.

Calder, L. (1999) *Financing the American Dream: a Cultural History of Consumer Credit*, Princeton: Princeton University Press.

Cammack, P. (2002a) 'Attacking the poor', *New Left Review*, 2(13).

Cammack, P. (2002b) 'The mother of all governments: the World Bank's matrix for global governance', in R. Wilkinson and S. Hughes (eds), *Global Governance: Critical Perspectives*, London and New York: Routledge.

Cammack, P. (2003) 'The governance of global capitalism: a new materialist perspective', *Historical Materialism*, 11(2).

Campos, R. C. (2007) *Speech by SEC Commissioner: Remarks Before the Association Française des Entreprises Privées*, Paris, retrieved 8 March 2007, http://www.sec.gov/news/speech/2007/spch030807rcc-2.htm

Cargill, T. F. and G. G. Garcia (1985) *Financial Reform in the 1980s*, Stanford: Hoover Institution Press.

Carosso, V. P. (1970) *Investment Banking in America*, Cambridge, MA: Harvard University Press.

Chahoud, T. (1991) 'The changing roles of the IMF and the World Bank', in E. Altvater (ed.), *The Poverty of Nations: Guide to the Debt Crisis from Argentina to Zaire*, London: Zed Books.

Chandler, L. V. (1971) *American Monetary Policy 1928–1941*, New York: Harper & Row.

Chao, E. L. (2003) 'A chartbook of international labour comparisons: United States, Europe, Asia', US Department of Labor, May.

Chernow, R. (1990) *The House of Morgan: an American Banking Dynasty and the Rise of Modern Finance*, New York: Simon & Schuster.

Chesnais, F. (1994) *La mondialisation du capital*, Paris: Syros.

Chesnais, F. (2004) 'Das finanzdominierte Akkumulationsregime: Theoretische Begründung und Reichweite', in C. Zeller (ed.), *Die globale Enteignungsökonomie*, Münster: Westfälisches Dampfboot.

Christen, C., T. Michel and W. Rätz (2003) *Sozialstaat: Wie die Sicherungssysteme funktionieren und wer von den 'Reformen' profitiert*, Hamburg: VSA.

Clark, C. (1990) *The Roots of Rural Capitalism: Western Massachusetts, 1780–1860*, Ithaca: Cornell University Press.

Clark, E. (2002) *International Finance*, 2nd edn, London: Thomson.

Cleveland H. v. B. and T. F. Huertas (1985) *Citibank 1812–1970*, Cambridge, MA and London: Harvard University Press.

Coates, D. (2005) 'Paradigms of explanation', in D. Coates (ed.), *Varieties of Capitalism, Varieties of Approaches*, New York: Palgrave Macmillan.

Cohen, B. (1986) *In Whose Interest?*, New Haven: Yale University Press.

Cohen, L. (2003) *A Consumers' Republic: the Politics of Mass Consumption in Postwar America*, New York: Alfred A. Knopf.

Cohen, S. D. (1970) *International Monetary Reform, 1964–69: the Political Dimension*, New York: Praeger.

Cohen, S. D. (2000) *The Making of United States International Economic Policy: Principles, Problems, and Proposals for Reform*, 5th edn, New York: Praeger.

Coleman, M. (2002) 'Thinking about the World Bank's "accordion" geography of financial globalization', *Political Geography*, 21.

Commission on the Regulation of US Capital Markets in the 21st Century (2007) *Report and Recommendations*, US Chamber of Commerce, March 2007, http://www.capitalmarketscommission. com/NR/rdonlyres/eozwwssfrqzdm3hd5sio gqhp6h2ngxwdpr77qw2bogptzvi5weu6mmi 4plfq6xic7kjonfpg4q2bpks6ryog5wwh 5sc/0703capmarkets_full.pdf

Committee on Capital Markets Regulation (2006) *Interim Report*, 30 November 2006, http://www.capmktsreg.org/pdfs/11.30Committee_Interim_ReportREV2. pdf

Committee on the Global Financial System (1999) 'A review of financial market events in Autumn 1998', Basel: BIS.

Conybeare, J. A. C. (1988) *United States Foreign Economic Policy and the International Capital Markets: the Case of Capital Export Countries, 1963–1974*, New York: Garland.

Coombs, C. A. (1976) *The Arena of International Finance*, New York: Wiley.

Cooper, A. and B. Momani (2005) 'Negotiating out of Argentina's financial crisis: segmenting the international creditors', *New Political Economy*, 10(3).

Corbalán, A. (2002) *El Banco Mundial: Intervención y Disciplinamiento. El Caso Argentino, Enseñanzas para América Latina*, Buenos Aires: Editorial Biblos.

Costigliola, F. (1984) *Akward Dominion: American Political, Economic, and Cultural Relations with Europe, 1919–1933*, Ithaca and London: Cornell University Press.

Cox, C. (2007) *Speech by SEC Chairman: Chairman's Address to the SEC Roundtable on International Financial Reporting Standards*, Washington, D.C., 6 March 2007, http://www.sec.gov/news/speech/2007/spch030607cc.htm

Cox, R. W. (1987) *Production, Power, and World Order: Social Forces in the Making of History*, New York: Columbia University Press.

Craven, B. (1990) 'Debt management in the United States of America', in D. Gowland (ed.), *International Bond Markets*, New York: Routledge.

DAI (Deutsches Aktieninstitut) (2003) *Factbook*, Frankfurt am Main.

DAI (Deutsches Aktieninstitut) (2007) *Abwärtstrend der Aktienakzeptanz gebremst: Wiederanstieg im zweiten Halbjahr 2006*, DAI-Kurzstudie 1/2007, Frankfurt am Main.

Das, D. K. (1993) 'Contemporary trends in the international capital markets', in D. K. Das (ed.), *International Finance: Contemporary Issues*, New York: Routledge.

Davies, S. (1998) 'Myriad possibilities', *Financial Times*, 1 May.

de Cecco, M. (1984) *Modes of Financial Development: American Banking Dynamics and World Financial Dynamics*, European University Institute Working Paper, No. 84/122.

de Cecco, M. (1987) 'Inflation and structural change in the Euro-dollar market', in M. de Cecco (ed.), *Monetary Theory and Economic Institutions*, Basingstoke: Macmillan.

Deeg, R. (1999) *Finance Capitalism Unveiled: Banks and the German Political Economy*, Ann Arbor: University of Michigan Press.

Degen, R. A. (1987) *The American Monetary System: a Concise Survey of its Evolution since 1896*, Massachutts and Toronto: D. C. Heath and Co. and Lexington Books.

Destler, I. M. and C. R. Henning (1989) *Dollar Politics: Exchange Rate Policymaking in the United States*, Washington, D.C.: Institute for International Economics.

Deutsche Bundesbank (2006) *Ergebnisse der gesamtwirtschaftlichen Finanzierungsrechnung für Deutschland 1991 bis 2005*, Statistische Sonderveröffentlichung 4. Juli, Frankfurt am Main.

Dickens, E. (1990) 'Financial crises, innovations and Federal Reserve control of the stock of money', *Contributions to Political Economy*, 9.

Dickens, E. (1995) 'The great inflation and U.S. monetary policy in the late 1960s: a political economic approach', *Social Concept*, 7(1).

Dickens, E. (1996) 'The Federal Reserve's low interest rate policy of 1970–72: determinants and constraints', *Review of Radical Political Economics*, 28(3).

Dickens, E. (1997) 'The Federal Reserve's tight monetary policy during the 1973–75 recession: a survey of possible interpretations', *Review of Radical Political Economics*, 29(3).

Dickens, E. (1998) 'Banking influence and the failure of US monetary policy during the 1953–54 recession', *International Review of Applied Economics*, 12(2).

Dodd, R. (2005) 'Derivatives markets: sources of vulnerability in U.S. financial markets', in G. Epstein (ed.), *Financialization and the World Economy*, Cheltenham, UK: Edward Elgar.

Doidge, C., G. A. Karolyi and R. M. Stulz (2007) *Has New York Become Less Competitive in Global Markets? Evaluating Foreign Listing Choices Over Time*, Ohio State University, Fisher College of Business WP 2007-03-012.

Dooley, M. P., D. Folkerts-Landau and P. Garber (2004) *The US Current Account Deficit and Economic Development: Collateral for a Total Return Swap*, NBER Working Paper 10727.

Dörre, K. and U. Brinkmann (2005) 'Finanzmarkt-Kapitalismus: Triebkraft eines flexiblen Produktionsmodells?', in P. Windolf (ed.), *Finanzmarkt-Kapitalismus: Analysen zum Wandel von Produktionsregimen, Kölner Zeitschrift für Soziologie und Sozialpsychologie*, Sonderheft 45.

Drainville, A. (2004) *Contesting Globalization: Spaces and Places in the World Economy*, London: Routledge.

Duménil, G. and D. Lévy (2002) 'The profit rate: where and how much did it fall? Did it recover? (USA 1948–2000)', *Review of Radical Political Economy*, 34.

Duménil, G. and D. Lévy (2003) 'Neoliberal dynamics – imperial dynamics', Cepremap, Modem, Paris.

Duménil, G. and D. Lévy (2004) *Capital Resurgent: Roots of the Neoliberal Revolution*, Cambridge, MA and London: Harvard University Press.

Duncan, Richard (2005) *The Dollar Crisis: Causes, Consequences, and Cures*, Hoboken, NJ: Wiley.

Dupont, D. and B. Sack (1999) 'The Treasury securities market: overview and recent developments', *Federal Reserve Bulletin*, 85.

Eaton, S. B. (2005) 'Crisis and the consolidation of international accounting standards: Enron, the IASB, and America', *Business and Politics*, 7(3).

Eatwell, J. and L. Taylor (2000) *Global Finance at Risk: the Case for International Regulation*, New York: New Press.

Edwards, F. R. (1996) *The New Finance: Regulation and Financial Stability*, Washington, D.C.: AEI Press.

Edwards, J. and K. Fischer (1994) *Banks, Finance and Investment in Germany*, Cambridge: Cambridge University Press.

Egnal, M. (1988) *A Mighty Empire: the Origins of the American Revolution*, Ithaca and London: Cornell University Press.

Eichengreen, B. (1996) *Globalizing Capital: a History of the International Monetary System*, Princeton, NJ: Princeton University Press.

Ennis, H. M. (2004) 'Some recent trends in commercial banking', *Federal Reserve Bank of Richmond Economic Quarterly*, 90(2).

Epstein, G. A. and J. B. Schor (1995) 'The Federal Reserve–Treasury Accord and the construction of the postwar monetary regime in the United States', *Social Concept*, 7(1).

European Association for Listed Companies (EALIC) et al. (2004) *Letter to SEC Chairman William H. Donaldson*, 9 February.

European Commission (1995) *Accounting Harmonisation: a New Strategy Vis-à-Vis International Harmonisation*, Communication COM 95 (508), Brussels.

European Commission (1999) *Financial Services: Implementing the Framework for Financial Markets: Action Plan*, COM 232 final, 5 November, Brussels.

European Commission (2006) *Single Market in Financial Services Progress Report 2004–2005*, Commission Staff Working Document SEC (2006) 17, Brussels.

European Commission (2007a) *Single Market in Financial Services Progress Report 2006*, Commission Staff Working Document SEC (2007) 263, Brussels.

European Commission (2007b) *FASP Evaluation, Part I: Process and Implementation*, Internal Market and Services DG, Financial Services Policy and Financial Markets, Financial Services Policy, retrieved from: http://ec.europa.eu/internal_market/finances/docs/actionplan/index/070124_part1_ en.pdf

European Council (2000) 'Presidency conclusions', Lisbon, 23 and 24 March, EU official document.

Evans, J. S. (1992) *International Finance: a Markets Approach*, Orlando, FL: Dryden Press.

Fabozzi, F. J. (1990) *The Handbook of U.S. Treasury & Government Agency Securities: Instruments, Strategies, and Analysis*, rev. edn, Chicago: Probus.

Fase, M. M. G and W. F. V. Vanthoor (2000) 'The Federal Reserve System discussed: a comparative analysis', *Société Universitaire Européenne de Recherches Financières*, Vienna.

Federal Reserve Bank of New York, Annual Reports 1970–2006.

Ferguson, T. (1984) 'From normalcy to New Deal, industrial structure, party competition and American public policy in the Great Depression', *International Organization*, 38(1).

Fieleke, N. (1994) 'The International Monetary Fund 50 years after Bretton Woods', *New England Economic Review*, September.

Fine, B. (2001) 'Neither the Washington nor the Post-Washington Consensus: an introduction', in B. Fine, C. Lapavitsas and J. Pincus (eds), *Development Policy in the 21st Century: Beyond the post-Washington Consensus*, London and New York: Routledge.

Fink, L. D. (1996) 'The role of pension funds and other investors in securitized debt markets', in L. T. Kendall and M. J. Fishman (eds), *A Primer on Securitization*, Cambridge, MA and London: MIT Press.

Fisher III, F. (1979) *The Eurodollar Bond Market*, London: Euromoney Publications Limited.

Fleming, M. J. (1997) 'The round-the-clock market for U.S. Treasury securities', *FRBNY Economic Policy Review*.

Fleming, M. J. (2000) 'Financial market implications of the Federal debt paydown', *Brookings Papers on Economic Activity* 2.

Foley, D. (1998) 'Asset speculation in Marx's theory of money', in R. Bellofiori (ed.), *Marxian Economics: a Reappraisal. Essays on Volume III of Capital, Volume 1: Method, Value and Money*, New York: St. Martin's Press.

Forsyth, J. H. (1987) 'Financial innovation in Britain', in M. de Cecco (ed.), *Changing Money: Financial Innovation in Developed Countries*, Oxford and New York: Basil Blackwell.

Fortune Magazine (1942) 'An American proposal', May: 59–63.

Frankel, J. A. (1988) 'International capital flows and domestic economic policies', in M. Feldstein (ed.), *The United States in the World Economy*, Chicago and London: Chicago University Press.

Frieden, J. A. (1987) *Banking on the World: the Politics of American International Finance*, New York: Harper & Row.

Fröhlich, N. and J. Huffschmid (2004) *Der Finanzdienstleistungssektor in Deutschland*, Düsseldorf: Hans-Böckler-Stiftung.

Froud, J., S. Johal and K. Williams (2002) 'Financialisation and the coupon pool', *Capital & Class*, 78.

Froud, J., S. Johal, A. Leaver and K. Williams (2006) *Financialization and Strategy: Narrative and Numbers*, London and New York: Routledge.

Funabashi, Y. (1988) *Managing the Dollar: From the Plaza to the Louvre*, Washington, D.C.: Institute for International Economics.

Gaines, T. C. (1962) *Techniques of Treasury Debt Management*, New York: Free Press of Glencoe.

Gayer, A. D. (1935), 'Notes and memoranda: the amended U.S. Federal Reserve Law: the Banking Act of 1935', *Economic Journal*, 45(180).

Geisst, C. R. (1990) *Visionary Capitalism: Financial Markets and the American Dream in the Twentieth Century*, New York: Praeger.

Geisst, C. R. (1997) *Wall Street: a History*, New York: Oxford University Press.

Germain, R. D. (1997) *The International Organization of Credit: States and Global Finance in the World Economy*, Cambridge: Cambridge University Press.

Gilbert, C., A. Powel and D. Vines (1999) 'Positioning the World Bank', *Economic Journal*, 109.

Gilbert, C. and D. Vines (2000) 'The World Bank: an overview of some major issues', in C. Gilbert and D. Vines (eds), *The World Bank: Structure and Policies*, Global Economic Institutions, Cambridge and New York: Cambridge University Press.

Gill, S. (1998) 'New constitutionalism, democratisation and global political economy', *Pacifica Review*, 10(1).

Gill, S. (2003) *Power and Resistance in the New World Order*, New York: Palgrave Macmillan.

Gill, S. and D. Law (1989) 'Global hegemony and the structural power of capital', *International Studies Quarterly*, 33(4).

Gill, S. and D. Law (1993) 'Global hegemony and the structural power of capital', in S. Gill (ed.), *Gramsci: Historical Materialism and International Relations*, Cambridge: Cambridge University Press.

Gilpin, R. (1987) *The Political Economy of International Relations*, Princeton: Princeton University Press.

Glaser, D. and A. J. Szubin (2007) 'Joint Testimony of the Deputy Assistant Director for Terrorist Financing and Financial Crimes and the Director of Foreign Assets Control', House of Representatives, Foreign Affairs (Subcommittee on Terrorism, Nonproliferation, and Trade) & Financial Services (Subcommittee on Domestic and International Monetary Policy, Trade and Technology), 110th Congress (18 April), Washington, D.C.

Glyn, A., A. Hughes, A. Lipietz and A. Singh (1990) 'The rise and fall of the Golden Age', in S. A. Marglin and J. B. Schor (eds), *The Golden Age of Capitalism: Reinterpreting the Postwar Experience*, Oxford: Oxford University Press.

Goebel, T. (1997) 'The political economy of American populism from Jackson to the New Deal', *Studies in American Political Development*, 11 (Spring).

Goha, K., D. Pimlott and B. White (2007) 'U.S. Fed cool on long-term growth forecast', *Financial Times*, 21 November, http://www.ft.com/cms/s/0/39a8cb3a-97d4-11D.C.9e08-0000779fd2ac.html

Golding, T. (2001) *The City: Inside the Great Expectations Machine*, London: Pearson Education.

González, F. (2005) 'Hay Vida después del FMI y es una Muy Buena Vida' Retrucó Kirchner', *Clarín*, Buenos Aires [Argentina], 17 April, retrieved 29 May 2007, http:// www.clarin.com/diario/2005/04/17/elpais/p00401.htmhttp://www.clarin.com/diario/2005/04/17/elpais/p-00401.htm

Goodfriend, M. (1997) 'Monetary policy comes of age: a twentieth century odyssey', *FRB of Richmond, Economic Quarterly*, 83(1).

Goodhart, C. A. E. (1969) *The New York Money Market and the Finance of Trade, 1900–1913*, Cambridge, MA: Harvard University Press.

Gowa, J. S. (1983) *Closing the Gold Window: Domestic Politics and the End of Bretton Woods*, Ithaca: Cornell University Press.

Gowan, P. (1999) *The Global Gamble: Washington's Faustian Bid for World Dominance*, New York: Verso.

Grabbe, O. J. (1996) *International Financial Markets*, 3rd edn, Englewood Cliffs, NJ: Prentice Hall.

Grahl, J. (2001) 'Globalized finance', *New Left Review*, 2(8).

Grahl, J. (2002), 'Notes on financial integration and European society', paper presented to 'The emergence of a new Euro-capitalism?' conference, Marburg, 11–12 October (published in M. Beckmann, H.-J. Bieling and F. Deppe (eds), *Euro-Kapitalismus und globale politische Okonomie*, Hamburg: VSA Verlag, 2003).

Grant, J. (1992) *Money of the Mind: Borrowing and Lending in America from the Civil War to Michael Milken*, New York: Noonday Press.

Greenspan, A. (1997) 'Rules vs. discretionary monetary policy', Stanford University, Stanford, California, 5 September, retrieved from http://www.federalreserve.gov/boarddocs/speeches/1997/19970905.htm

Greenspan, A. (1999) 'Mr. Greenspan asks whether efficient financial markets mitigate financial crisis', Remarks before the Financial Markets Conference of the Federal Reserve Bank of Atlanta, Sea Island Georgia, *BIS Review*, 114, http://www.bis.org/index.htm

Greider, W. (1987) *Secrets of the Temple: How the Federal Reserve Runs the Country*, New York: Simon & Schuster.

Group of Seven Finance Ministers (1999) 'Strengthening the International Financial Architecture', Report of the Finance Ministers to the Köln Summit Meeting, 18–20 June.

Guha, K. (2007) 'Treasury duo push private sector solution', *Financial Times*, 16 October.

Guttmann, R. (1994) *How Credit-money Shapes the Economy: the United States in a Global System*, Armonk and London: M. E. Sharpe.

Guzzini, S. (1993) 'Structural power: the limits of neorealist power analysis', *International Organization*, 47(3).

Gwin, C. (1994) *U.S. Relations with the World Bank, 1945–1992*, Washington: Brookings Institution.

Hackethal, A. (2004) 'German banks and banking structure', in J. P. Krahnen and R. H. Schmidt (eds), *The German Financial System*, Oxford: Oxford University Press.

Hall, P. A. and D. Soskice (eds) (2001) *Varieties of Capitalism: the Institutional Foundations of Comparative Advantage*. Oxford: Oxford University Press.

Hammond, B. (1934) 'Long and short term credit in early American banking', *Quarterly Journal of Economics*, 49(1).

Hardt, M. and A. Negri (2000) *Empire*, Cambridge, MA: Harvard University Press.

Hardy, C. O. (1932) *Credit Policies of the Federal Reserve System*, Washington, D.C.: Brookings Institution.

Harmes, Adam (2001), 'Mass investment culture', *New Left Review*, 9: 103–24.

Harmon, M. (1997) *The British Labour Government and the 1976 IMF Crisis*, New York: St. Martin's Press.

Harrington, R. (1987) *Asset and Liability Management by Banks*, Paris: OECD.

Harris, L. (1999) 'Will the real IMF please stand up: what does the fund do and what should it do?', in J. Michie and J. Grieve Smith (eds), *Global Instability: the Political Economy of World Economic Governance*, London and New York: Routledge.

Harrison, G. (2001) 'Administering market friendly growth? Liberal populism and the World Bank's involvement in administrative reform in sub-Saharan Africa', *Review of International Political Economy*, 8(3).

Harvey, D. (1982) *Limits to Capital*, London: Verso.

Harvey, D. (1999) *Limits to Capital*, 2nd edn, New York: Verso.

Harvey, D. (2005) *A Brief History of Neoliberalism*, Oxford: Oxford University Press.

Hatcher, P. (2006) 'Partnership and the reform of international aid: challenging citizenship and political representation?' in D. Stone and C. Wright (eds), *The World Bank and Governance: a Decade of Reform and Reaction*, Oxford and New York: Routledge.

Hausmann, R. and F. Sturzenegger (2005) 'U.S. and global imbalances: can dark matter prevent a Big Bang?' *Kennedy School of Government Working Paper*.

Hawley J. P. (1984) 'Protecting capital from itself: US attempts to regulate the Eurocurrency system', *International Organization*, 38(1).

Hawley, J. P. (1987) *Dollars and Borders: US Government Attempts to Restrict Capital Flows, 1960–1980*, New York: M. E. Sharpe.

Hays III, S. L. and P. M. Hubbard (1990) *Investment Banking: a Tale of Three Cities*, Boston, MA: Harvard Business School Press.

Hedges, J. E. (1938) *Commercial Banking and the Stock Market before 1863*, Baltimore: Johns Hopkins University Press.

Helleiner, E. (1994) *States and the Reemergence of Global Finance: From Bretton Woods to the 1990s*, Ithaca: Cornell University Press, paperback edn 1996.

Henning, C. R. (1994) *Currencies and Politics in the United States, Germany, and Japan*, Washington, D.C.: Institute for International Economics.

Henning, C. R. (1999) *The Exchange Stabilization Fund: Slush Money or War Chest?*, Washington, D.C.: Institute for International Economics.

Henwood, D. (1997) *Wall St.*, New York: Verso.

Hetzel, R. L. and R. Leach (2001) 'The Treasury–Fed Accord: a New Narrative Account', *Federal Reserve Bank of Richmond Economic Quarterly*, 87(1).

Hidy, M. (1951) 'The capital markets, 1789–1865', in H. F. Williamson (ed.), *The Growth of the American Economy*, Englewood Cliffs, NJ: Prentice-Hall.

Hilferding, R. (1981) *Finance Capital: a Study of the Latest Phase of Capitalist Development*, London: Boston and Henley.

Hobsbawm, E. J. (1994) *Age of Extremes: the Short Twentieth Century, 1914–1991*, London: Michael Joseph.

Höpner, M. (2001) *Corporate Governance in Transition: Ten Empirical Findings on Shareholder Value and Industrial Relations*, Discussion paper 2001/5, Max-Planck-Institut für Gesellschaftsforschung, Cologne.

Höpner, M. and G. Jackson (2001) *An Emerging Market for Corporate Control? The Mannesmann Takeover and German Corporate Governance*, Discussion Paper 2001/4, Max-Planck-Institut für Gesellschaftsforschung, Cologne.

Höpner, M. and G. Jackson (2006) 'Revisiting the Mannesmann takeover: how markets for corporate control emerge', *European Management Review*, 3(3).

Hopwood, A. G. (1994) 'Some reflections on "The harmonization of accounting within the EU"', *European Accounting Review*, 3(2).

Hudson, M. (1977) *Global Fracture: the New International Economic Order*, New York: Harper & Row.

Hudson, M. (2003) *Super Imperialism: the Origin and Fundamentals of U.S. World Dominance*, 2nd edn, London: Pluto Press.

Huertas, T. F. (1990) 'US multinational banking: history and prospects', in G. Jones (ed.), *Banks as Multinationals*, London and New York: Routledge.

Huffschmid, J. (2002) *Politische Ökonomie der Finanzmärkte*, 2nd edn, Hamburg: VSA.

Hybel, A. R. (2001) *Made by the USA: the International System*, New York: Palgrave Macmillan.

IASC Foundation (2007) 'Trustees announce strategy to enhance governance, report on conclusions at trustees' meeting', Press Release, 6 November, http://www.iasb.org/NR/rdonlyres/D3F8A7DA-B979-462E-BF43- 32F2581BEE37/0/PRonTrusteesmeet061107final.pdf

Ingham, G. (1994) 'States and markets in the production of world money: sterling and the dollar', in S. Corbridge, R. Martin and N. Thrift (eds), *Money Power and Space*, Oxford and Cambridge, MA: Blackwell.

International Monetary Fund (2005) *The Managing Director's report on the Fund's Medium Term Strategy*, Washington: International Monetary Fund, retrieved 22 January 2007, http://www.imf.org/external/np/exr/ib/2006/041806.htm

International Monetary Fund (n/d (a)) *General Data Dissemination System (GDDS)*, Washington: International Monetary Fund, retrieved 14 March 2007, http://dsbb.imf.org/Applications/web/gdds/gddshome/

International Monetary Fund (n/d (b)) *Dissemination Standards Bulletin Board: Special Data Dissemination Standard*, Washington: International Monetary Fund, retrieved 16 March 2007, http://dsbb.imf.org/Applications/web/sddsdatadimensions/

Itoh, M. and C. Lapavitsas (1999) *Political Economy of Money and Finance*, Basingstoke: Palgrave Macmillan.

James, J. A. (1995) 'The rise and fall of the commercial paper market, 1900–1929', in M. D. Bordo and R. Sylla (eds), *Anglo-American Financial Systems: Institutions and Markets in the Twentieth Century*, Burr Ridge, NY: Irwin Professional Publishing.

Johnson, P. A. (1998) *The Government of Money: Monetarism in Germany and the United States*, Ithaca and London: Cornell University Press.

Kahler, M. (1990) 'The United States and the International Monetary Fund: declining influence or declining interest?', in M. Karns and K. Mingst (eds), *The United States and Multilateral Institutions: Patterns of Changing Instrumentality and Influence*, Boston: Unwin Hyman.

Kahler, M. (2001) *Leadership Selection in the Major Multilaterals*, Washington: Institute for International Economics.

Kahn, T. K. (1993) 'Commercial paper', *Federal Reserve Bank of Richmond, Economic Quarterly*, 79(2).

Kaplan, J. J. and G. Schleiminger (1989) *The European Payments Union: Financial Diplomacy in the 1950s*, Oxford: Clarendon Press.

Kapstein, E. B. (1989) *Governing the Global Economy: International Finance and the State*, Cambridge, MA: Harvard University Press.

Kapstein, E. B. (1994) 'Resolving the regulator's dilemma: international coordination of banking regulations', *International Organization*, 43(2).

Kapur, D., J. Lewis and R. Webb (1997) *The World Bank: its First Half Century*, Washington: Brookings Institution.

Kapur, D. and R. Webb (2006) *Beyond the IMF*, Washington: Center for Global Development, retrieved 12 January 2007, http://www.cgdev.org/content/publications/detail/10246/

Katz, C. (2007) *El Giro de la Economía Argentina: El Curso Neo-Desarrollista*, Buenos Aires: Instituto Argentino para el Desarrollo Económico, retrieved 29 May 2007, http://www.iade.org.ar/modules/noticias/article.php?storyid=1373

Kennedy, P. M. (1987) *The Rise and Fall of the Great Powers: Economic Change and Military Conflict from 1500 to 2000*, New York: Random House.

Keohane, R. O. (1984) *After Hegemony: Cooperation and Discord in the World Political Economy*, Princeton: Princeton University Press.

Keynes, J. M. (1936) *The General Theory of Employment, Interest and Money*, London: Macmillan and Co. Limited.

Khademian, A. (1992) *The SEC and Capital Market Regulation: the Politics of Expertise*, Pittsburgh, PA: University of Pittsburgh Press.

Khoury, S. J. (1997) *U.S. Banking and its Regulation in the Political Context*, Lanham and Oxford: University Press of America.

Killick, T. (1995) *IMF Programmes in Developing Countries: Design and Impact*, London and New York: Routledge.

Kindleberger, C. P. (1965) 'Balance-of-payments deficits and the international market for liquidity', *Princeton Essays in International Finance*, 46.

Kindleberger, C. P. (1973) *The World in Depression, 1929–1939*, Berkeley: University of California Press.

Kindleberger, C. P. (1981) *International Money: a Collection of Essays*, London: Allen & Unwin.

Kindleberger, C. P., W. Salant and E. Depres (1966) 'The dollar and world liquidity: a minority view', *The Economist*, 6 February.

Kinley, D. (1893) *The Independent Treasury of the United States and its Relations to the Banks of the Country*, Washington, D.C.: GPO.

Klein, L., C. Saltzman and V. Duggal (2003) 'Information, technology and productivity: the case of the financial sector', *Survey of Current Business*, August.

Klein, N. (2007) *The Shock Doctrine: the Rise of Disaster Capitalism*, Toronto: A. Knopf Canada.

Kohn, Donald L. (2007) 'Financial stability: preventing and managing crises', remarks at the Exchequer Club Luncheon, Washington, D.C.

Konings, M. (2006) 'The rise of American finance: agency, institutions and structural power from colonial times to the globalization era', PhD thesis, York University.

Konings, M. (2007) 'Monetarism in the US: the development of new forms of institutional control over banks and financial markets', in L. Assassi, D. Wigan and A. Nesvetailova (eds), *Global Finance in the New Century: Beyond Deregulation*, New York: Palgrave Macmillan.

Konings, M. (2008) 'The institutional foundations of US structural power in international finance: from the re-emergence of global finance to the monetarist turn', *Review of International Political Economy*, 15(1).

Kosterlitz, J. (1999) 'Is there life after debt?', *National Journal*, 31(28).

Krahnen, J. P. and R. H. Schmidt (eds) (2004) *The German Financial System*, Oxford: Oxford University Press.

Krasner, S. (1982) 'Regimes and the limits of realism: regimes as autonomous variables', *International Organization*, 36 (Spring).

Krippner, G. R. (2003) 'The fictitious economy: financialization, the state, and contemporary capitalism', PhD thesis, University of Wisconsin–Madison.

Krippner, G. R. (2005) 'The financialization of the American economy', *Socio-Economic Review*, 3(2).

Krippner, G. R. (2007) 'The making of US monetary policy: central bank transparency and the neoliberal dilemma', *Theory & Society*, 36(6)

Kroszner, R. S. (2007a) 'Implementing Basel II in the United States', speech delivered at the Standard & Poor's Bank Conference 2007, New York, 13 November.

Kroszner, R. S. (2007b) 'Risk management and the economic outlook', speech delivered at the Conference on Competitive Markets and Effective Regulation, Institute of International Finance, New York, 16 November.

Kulikoff, A. (1989) 'The transition to capitalism in rural America', *William & Mary Quarterly*, 3rd ser., 46(1).

Lacher, H. (1999) 'Embedded liberalism, disembedded markets: reconceptualizing the Pax Americana', *New Political Economy*, 4(3).

Lane, C. (2003) 'Changes in corporate governance of German corporations: convergence to the Anglo-American model?', *Competition & Change*, 7(2–3).

Langley, P. (2002) *World Financial Orders: an Historical International Political Economy*, London and New York: Routledge.

Langley, P. (2004a) 'In the eye of the "perfect storm": the final salary pensions crisis and the financialisation of Anglo-American capitalism', *New Political Economy*, 9(4).

Langley, P. (2004b) '(Re)politicizing global financial governance: what's "new" about the "new international financial architecture"?', *Global Networks*, 4(1).

Lee, S. (2002) 'Global monitor: the International Monetary Fund', *New Political Economy*, 7(2).

Lenin, V. I. (1967) 'Imperialism, the highest stage of capitalism', in V. I. Lenin, *Selected Works in Three Volumes*, International Publishers.

Levich, R. M. (1988) 'Financial innovations in international financial markets', in M. Feldstein (ed.), *The United States in the World Economy*, Chicago and London: University of Chicago Press.

Lewis, M. (1989) *Liar's Poker*, New York: Penguin.

Leys, C. (1985) 'Thatcherism and British manufacturing: a question of hegemony', *New Left Review*, 151.

Li, P. (2005) 'International committee introduces German pfandbrief', *New York School of Security Analysis*, www.nyssa.org

Lipietz, A. (1985) *The Enchanted World: Inflation, Credit and the World Crisis*, London: Verso.

Lipietz, A. (1987) *Mirages and Miracles: the Crises of Global Fordism*, London: Verso.

Lipuma, E. and B. Lee (2004) *Financial Derivatives and the Globalization of Risk*, Durham, NC: Duke University Press.

Litan, R. E. and J. Rauch (1998) *American Finance for the 21st Century*, Washington, D.C.: Brookings Institution Press.

Livingston, J. (1986) *Origins of the Federal Reserve System: Money, Class, and Corporate Capitalism, 1890–1913*, Ithaca: Cornell University Press.

Ludlow, P. (1982) *The Making of the European Monetary System: a Case Study of the Politics of the European Community*, London: Butterworth Scientific.

Lutz, B. (1984) *Der kurze Traum immerwährender Prosperität*, Frankfurt am Main and New York: Campus.

Lütz, S. (2002) *Der Staat und die Globalisierung von Finanzmärkten, Regulative Politik in Deutschland, Grossbritannien und den USA*, Frankfurt and New York: Campus Verlag.

Luxemburg, R. (1951) *The Accumulation of Capital*, London: Routledge & Kegan Paul.

Lyons, M. N. (1998) 'Business conflict and right-wing movements', in A. E. Ansell (ed.), *Unraveling the Right: the New Conservatism in American Thought and Politics*, Boulder, CO and Oxford: Westview.

Maddison, A. (2001) *The World Economy: a Millennial Perspective*, Paris: OECD.

Mailander, C. (1997/1998) 'Financial innovation, domestic regulation and the international marketplace: lessons on meeting globalization's challenge drawn from the international bond market', *The George Washington Journal of International Law and Economics*, 31(3).

Martinez-Diaz, L. (2005) 'Strategic experts and improvising regulators: explaining the IASC's rise to global influence, 1973–2001', *Business and Politics*, 7(3).

Marx, K. (1990) *Capital*, Volume I, London: Penguin Books.

Marx, K. and F. Engels (various years, cited as MEW), *Werke*, Berlin: Dietz Verlag.

Mayer, M. (1974) *The Bankers*, New York: Weybright and Talley.

McCauley, R. N. (2002) 'International market implications of declining Treasury debt', *Journal of Money, Credit and Banking*, 34(3).

McCoy, D. R. (1980) *The Elusive Republic: Political Economy in Jeffersonian America*, Chapel Hill: University of North Carolina Press.

McKinsey & Co. (2006) *Sustaining New York's and the US' Global Financial Services Leadership*, available at http://www.senate.gov/~schumer/SchumerWebsite/pressroom/special_reports/2007/NY_REPORT%20_FINAL.pdf

Medley, J. (2000) 'The East Asian economic crisis: surging U.S. imperialism?', *Review of Radical Political Economics*, 32(3).

Mehrling, Perry (1999) 'Minsky, modern finance, and the case of long term capital management', Barnard College, mimeo.

Melamed, L. (1993) *Leo Melamed on the Markets: Twenty Years of Financial History as Seen by the Man Who Revolutionized the Markets*, New York: John Wiley.

Meulendyke, A.-M. (1988) 'A review of Federal Reserve policy targets and operating guides in recent decades', *Federal Reserve Bank of New York Quarterly Review*, 13(3).

Mensbrugghe, J. (1964) 'Foreign issues in Europe', *IMF Staff Papers*, July.

Menz, W., S. Becker and T. Sablowski (1999) *Shareholder Value gegen Belegschaftsinteressen: Der Weg der Hoechst AG zum Life Science-Konzern*, Hamburg: VSA.

Mikesell, R. F. and J. H. Furth (1974) *Foreign Dollar Balances and the International Role of the Dollar*, New York: National Bureau of Economic Research.

Mishkin, F. (2000) 'From monetary targeting to inflation targeting: lessons from the industrialized world', paper prepared for Bank of Mexico Conference, 'Stabilization and Monetary Policy: the International Experience', Mexico City, 14–15 November. Available at http://www0.gsb.columbia.edu/faculty/fmishkin/PDFpapers/00BOMEX.pdf

Mishkin, F. S. (2000) *The Economics of Money, Banking and Financial Markets*, Boston: Addison Wesley.

Mollenkamp, C., D. Solomon, R. Sidel and V. Bauerein (2007a) 'Gordian knot: how London created a snarl in global markets', *Wall Street Journal*, 18 October: A1.

Mollenkamp, C. et al. (2007b) 'Rescue readied by banks is bet to spur markets', *Wall Street Journal*, 15 October.

Montgomerie, J. (2006). 'Financialization of the American credit card industry', *Competition and Change*, 10(3).

Moran, M. (1991) *The Politics of the Financial Services Revolution: the USA, UK and Japan*, New York: St. Martin's Press.

Mosley, P., J. Harrigan and J. Toye (1995) *Aid and Power: the World Bank and Policy-based Lending*, London and New York: Routledge.

Müller, M. (2004) *International Accounting Standards*, Düsseldorf: Bund-Verlag.

Munk, B. (2001) 'A new international economic policy', *Orbis*, 45(3).

Myers, M. (1931) *The New York Money Market*, New York: Columbia University Press.

Myers, M. (1951a) 'The investment market after the Civil War', in H. F. Williamson (ed.), *The Growth of the American Economy*, Englewood Cliffs: Prentice-Hall.

Myers, M. (1951b) 'The investment market after 1919', in H. F. Williamson (ed.), *The Growth of the American Economy*, Englewood Cliffs: Prentice-Hall.

Myers, M. (1970) *A Financial History of the United States*, New York: Columbia University Press.

Myers, S. C. and N. S. Majluf (1984) 'Corporate financing and investment decisions when firms have information that investors do not have', *Journal of Financial Economics*, 13.

Nazareth, A. L. (2007) *Speech by SEC Commissioner: Remarks before the Council of Institutional Investors*, Washington, D.C., 20 March, available at http://www.sec.gov/news/speech/2007/spch032007aln.htm

Nicolaisen, D. T. (2004) *Speech by SEC Staff: Remarks before the Public Hearing on the IASC Constitution Review*, Baruch College, N.Y., 3 June, available at http://www.sec.gov/news/speech/spch060304dtn.htm

Nicolaisen, D. T. (2005) 'Statement by SEC staff: a securities regulator looks at convergence', *Northwestern University Journal of International Law and Business*, April, http://www.sec.gov/news/speech/spch040605dtn.htm

Nobes, C. W. (1994) *A Study of the International Accounting Standards Committee*, London: Coopers & Lybrand.

Nölke, A. and J. Perry (2005) 'International accounting standard setting: a network approach', *Business and Politics*, 7(3).

Nudler, J. (2004) 'Que te Manyo de hace Rato', *Página 12*, Buenos Aires, 7 August, retrieved 10 December 2003, http://www.pagina12.com.ar/diario/economia/2-39308-2004-08-07.html

Nye, J. S. (1990) *Bound to Lead: the Changing Nature of American Power*, New York: Basic Books.

Odell, J. S. (1982) *U.S. International Monetary Policy: Markets, Power, and Ideas as Sources of Change*, Princeton: Princeton University Press.

Olney, M. L. (1991) *Buy Now Pay Later: Advertising, Credit, and Consumer Durables in the 1920s*, Chapel Hill and London: University of North Carolina Press.

Organization for Economic Co-operation and Development (1989) 'International and foreign bond markets', *Financial Market Trends*, 42.

Organization for Economic Co-operation and Development (1992) 'International and foreign bond markets', *Financial Market Trends*, 52.

Organization for Economic Co-operation and Development (1993) 'International financial markets', *Financial Market Trends*, 54.

Organization for Economic Co-operation and Development (1994a) 'International and foreign bond markets', *Financial Market Trends*, 57.

Organization for Economic Co-operation and Development (1994b) 'International and foreign bond offerings', *Financial Market Trends*, 57.

Organization for Economic Co-operation and Development (1996) 'Euro and foreign bond offerings', *Financial Market Trends*, 63.

Organization for Economic Co-operation and Development (1998a) 'International financial markets: overview', *Financial Market Trends*, 69.

Organization for Economic Co-operation and Development (1998b) 'Euro and foreign bond offerings: statistical annex'. *Financial Market Trends*, 69.

Ozgercin, K. (2005) 'The history of the Bank for International Settlements, 1930–1958', PhD dissertation, City University of New York Graduate Center, May 2005.

Panitch, L. (1986) *Working Class Politics in Crisis*, London: Verso.

Panitch, L. (1994) 'Globalisation and the state', in R. Miliband and L. Panitch (eds), *Socialist Register 1994: Between Globalism and Nationalism*, Halifax: Fernwood.

Panitch, L. (1996) 'Rethinking the role of the state', in J. H. Mittelman (ed.), *Globalization: Critical Reflections*, Boulder and London: Lynne Rienner.

Panitch, L. (2000) 'The new imperial state', *New Left Review*, 2(2).

Panitch, L. and S. Gindin (2002a) 'Gems and baubles in empire', *Historical Materialism*, 10(2).

Panitch, L. and S. Gindin (2002b) 'Rethinking crisis', *Monthly Review*, 54(6).

Panitch, L. and S. Gindin (2004) 'Global capitalism and American empire', in L. Panitch and C. Leys (eds), *Socialist Register 2004: the New Imperial Challenge*: 1–42.

Panitch, L. and S. Gindin (2005a) 'Finance and American empire', in L. Panitch and C. Leys (eds), *Socialist Register 2005: the Empire Reloaded*, London: Merlin Press.

Panitch, L. and S. Gindin (2005b) 'Superintending global capital', *New Left Review*, 2(35).

Panitch, L. and S. Gindin (2005c) 'Euro-capitalism and American empire', in D. Coates (ed.), *Varieties of Capitalism, Varieties of Approaches*, New York: Palgrave Macmillan.

Panitch, L. and C. Leys (2001) *The End of Parliamentary Socialism*, 2nd edn, London: Verso.

Parboni, R. (1981) *The Dollar and its Rivals: Recession, Inflation, and International Finance*, London: Verso.

Parrini, C. P. (1969) *Heir to Empire: United States Economic Diplomacy, 1916–1923*, Pittsburgh: University of Pittsburgh Press.

Paulson, H. M. (2006) *Remarks by Treasury Secretary Henry M. Paulson on the competitiveness of U.S. capital markets*, Economic Club of New York, New York, NY, 20 November, http://www.treas.gov/press/releases/hp174.htm

Paulson, H. M. (2007) *Speech delivered on current housing and mortgage market developments*, Georgetown Law Center, Washington, D.C., 16 October.

Pauly, L. (1999) 'Good governance and bad policy: the perils of international organization overextension', *Review of International Political Economy*, 6(4).

Payer, C. (1982) *The World Bank: a Critical Analysis*, New York: Monthly Review Press.

Peet, R. (2003) *Unholy Trinity: the IMF, World Bank and WTO*, London and New York: Zed Books.

Pender, J. (2001) 'From "structural adjustment" to "comprehensive development framework": conditionality transformed?', *Third World Quarterly*, 22(3).

Perry, J. and A. Nölke (2006) 'The political economy of International Accounting Standards', *Review of Radical Political Economy*, 13(4): 559–86.

Phelps, C. W. (1927) *The Foreign Expansion of American Banks: American Branch Banking Abroad*, New York: Ronald Press Company.

Phillips, C. A. (1921) *Bank Credit: a Study of the Principles and Factors Underlying Advances Made by Banks to Borrowers*, New York: Macmillan Company.

Phillips, S. M. (1996) 'The place of securitization in the financial system: implications for banking and monetary policy', in L. T. Kendall and M. J. Fishman (eds), *A Primer on Securitization*, Cambridge, MA and London: MIT Press.

Pieper, U. and L. Taylor (1998) 'The revival of the liberal creed: the IMF, the World Bank, and inequality in a globalized economy', in D. Baker, G. Epstein and R. Pollin (eds), *Globalization and Progressive Economic Policy*, Cambridge and New York: Cambridge University Press.

Pigeoon, M. (2005) 'It happened, but not again: a Minskian analysis of Japan's lost decade', Working Paper No. 303, Jerome Levy Economics Institute, 2000.

Poulantzas, N. (1973) *Political Power and Social Classes*, London: New Left Books.

Poulantzas, N. (1975) *Classes in Contemporary Capitalism*, London: New Left Books.

Priewe, J. (2001) 'Vom Lohnarbeiter zum Shareholder?', *Prokla*, 122, 31(1).

Przeworski, Adam (1985) *Capitalism and Social Democracy*, New York: Cambridge University Press.

Rafferty, M., D. Bryan and N. Ackland (2000) 'Financial derivatives and Marxist value theory', Working Papers, School of Economics and Political Science, University of Sydney.

Reinicke, W. H. (1995) *Banking, Politics and Global Finance: American Commercial Banks and Regulatory Change, 1980–1990*, Aldershot: Edward Elgar.

Rich, B. (1994) *Mortgaging the Earth: the World Bank, Environmental Impoverishment, and the Crisis of Development*, Boston: Beacon Press.

Riesenhuber, E. (2001) *The International Monetary Fund under Constraint: Legitimacy of its Crisis Management*, The Hague: Kluwer Law International.

Robinson, W. I. (2004) *A Theory of Global Capitalism*, Baltimore: Johns Hopkins University Press.

Roosa, R. V. (1967) *The Dollar and World Liquidity*, New York: Random House.

Roy, R. (2004) 'No secrets between "special friends": America's involvement in British economic policy, October 1964–April 1964', *History*, 89(295).

Roy, W. G. (1997) *Socializing Capital: the Rise of the Large Industrial Corporation in America*, Princeton: Princeton University Press.

Rubin, R. (with J. Weisberg) (2003) *In an Uncertain World: Tough Choices from Wall Street to Washington*, New York: Random House.

Rude, C. (1999) 'The 1997–1998 East Asian financial crisis: a New York market-informed view', in Barry Herman (ed.), *Global Financial Turmoil and Reform*, New York: United Nations University Press.

Rude, C. (2004) 'The Volcker monetary policy shocks: a political-economic analysis', unpublished paper, Department of Economics, New School University, January, 2004.

Ruggie, J. G. (1982) 'International regimes, transactions and change: embedded liberalism in the post-war economic order', *International Organization*, 36(2).

Ruggie, J. G. (1992) 'Multilateralism: the anatomy of an institution', *International Organization*, 46(3).

Sablowski, T. (2003a) 'Bilanz(en) des Wertpapierkapitalismus. Deregulierung, Shareholder Value, Bilanzskandale', *Prokla* 131, 33(2).

Sablowski, T. (2003b) 'Kapitalmarktorientierte Unternehmensführung und neue Branchenstrukturen: Das Beispiel der InfoCom-Industrie', in K. Dörre and B. Röttger (eds), *Das neue Marktregime. Konturen eines nachfordistischen Produktionsmodells*, Hamburg: VSA.

Sablowski, T. (2005a) 'Shareholder Value, neue Geschäftsmodelle und die Fragmentierung von Wertschöpfungsketten', in H. Wagner (ed.), *'Rentier' ich mich noch?' – Neue Steuerungskonzepte im Betrieb*, Hamburg.

Sablowski, T. (2005b) 'Handlungskonstellationen im Shareholder-Kapitalismus', in R. Detje, K. Pickshaus and H.-J. Urban (eds), *Arbeitspolitik kontrovers: Zwischen Abwehrkämpfen und Offensivestrategien*, Hamburg: VSA.

Samuels, J. M. and A.G. Piper (1985) *International Accounting: a Survey*, London: Palgrave Macmillan.

Sandleben, G. (2003) *Nationalökonomie & Staat: Zur Kritik der Theorie des Finanzkapitals*, Hamburg: VSA.

Sassen, S. (1991) *The Global City: New York, London, Tokyo*, Princeton: Princeton University Press.

Sassoon, D. (1997) *One Hundred Years of Socialism*, London: Fontana.

Scammell, W. M. (1968) *The London Discount Market*, London: Elek Books.

Scherrer, C. (2001) 'Double hegemony? State and class in American foreign economic policymaking', *Amerikastudien*, 46(4): 573–91.

Scherrer, C. (2005) 'Beyond path dependency and competitive convergence: institutional transfer from a discourse-analytical perspective', in G. Fuchs and P. Shapira (eds), *Rethinking Regional Innovation and Change*, New York: Springer.

Schinasi, G. J. and R. T. Smith (1998) 'Fixed-income markets in the United States, Europe, and Japan: some lessons for emerging markets', *IMF Working Paper*, 173.

Schinasi, G. J., C. F. Kramer and R. T. Smith (2001) 'Financial implications of the shrinking supply of U.S. Treasury securities', *IMF Working Paper*.

Schmidt, C. H. and E. J. Stockwell (1952) 'The changing importance of institutional investors in the American capital market', *Law and Contemporary Problems*, 17(1).

Scott, I. O. (1965) *Government Securities Market*, New York: McGraw-Hill.

Seabrooke, L. (2001) *U.S. Power in International Finance: the Victory of Dividends*, New York: Palgrave Macmillan.

Seabrooke, L. (2004) 'The economic taproot of US imperialism: the Bush *rentier* shift', *International Politics*, 41(3).

SEC (2006) *Accounting standards: SEC Chairman Cox and EU Commissioner McCreevy affirm commitment to elimination of the need for reconciliation requirements*, Press Release 2006-17, http://www.sec.gov/news/press/2006-17.htm

SEC (2007a) *SEC soliciting public comment on eliminating reconciliation requirement for IFRS financial statements*, Press Release 2007-128, http://www.sec.gov/news/press/2007/2007-128.htm

SEC (2007b) *SEC soliciting public comment on role of IFRS in the U.S.*, Press Release 2007-145. http://www.sec.gov/news/press/2007/2007-145.htm

SEC (2007c) *Authorities responsible for capital market regulation work to enhance the governance of the IASC Foundation*, http://www.sec.gov/news/press/2007/2007-226.htm

Seitz, K. (1990) *Die japanisch-amerikanische Herausforderung: Deutschlands Hochtechnologie-Industrien kämpfen ums Überleben*, München: Bonn aktuell.

Seitz, K. (1998) *Wettlauf ins 21. Jahrhundert: Die Zukunft Europas zwischen Amerika und Asien*, München: Siedler.

Seligman, J. (2003) *The Transformation of Wall Street: a History of the Securities and Exchange Commission and Modern Corporate Finance*, New York: Aspen Publishers.

Shaikh, Anwar (1999) 'Explaining inflation and unemployment: an alternative to neo-liberal economic theory', available at http://homepage.newschool.edu/~AShaikh/inflation2.pdf

Shook, D. N. (1987) *William G. McAdoo and the Development of National Economic Policy, 1913–1918*, New York: Garland.

Silver, B. J. and G. Arrighi (2003) 'Polanyi's "double movement": the belle époques of British and U.S. hegemony compared', *Politics & Society*, 31(2).

Simmons, B. A. (2001) 'The international politics of harmonization: the case of capital market regulation', *International Organization*, 55(3).

Skidelsky, R. (2000) *John Maynard Keynes: Fighting for Freedom, 1937–1946*, New York: Viking.

Sklar, M. J. (1988) *The Corporate Reconstruction of American Capitalism, 1890–1916*, Cambridge: Cambridge University Press.

Smaghi, L. (2004) 'A single EU seat in the IMF?', *Journal of Common Market Studies*, 42(2).

Smith, R. C. (1990) *The Global Bankers*, New York: Plume.

Smith, R. C. and I. Walter (1997) *Global Banking*, New York: Oxford University Press.

Sobel, A. C. (1994) *Domestic Choices, International Markets: Dismantling National Barriers and Liberalizing Securities Markets*, Ann Arbor: University of Michigan Press.

Sobol, D. M. (1998) 'Foreign ownership of U.S. Treasury securities: what the data show and do not show', *Economics and Finance*, 4(5).

Soederberg, S. (2001) 'Grafting stability onto globalization? Deconstructing the IMF's recent bid for transparency', *Third World Quarterly*, 22(5).

Soederberg, S. (2004) *The Politics of the New International Financial Architecture: Reimposing Neoliberal Domination in the Global South*, New York: Zed Books.

Solomon, R. (1977) *The International Monetary System, 1945–1976: an Insider's View*, New York: Harper & Row.

Solomon, R. (1999) *Money on the Move: the Revolution in International Finance since 1980*, Princeton: Princeton University Press.

Spiro, D. E. (1999) *The Hidden Hand of American Hegemony: Petrodollar Recycling and International Markets*, Ithaca, NY: Cornell University Press.

Sprinkel, B. W. (1981) 'Remarks by Under Secretary of the Treasury for Monetary Affairs at the Institute Auguste Comte', Paris.

Sprinkel, B. W. (1983) 'Statement of Under Secretary for Monetary Affairs', Senate Banking Committee (Subcommittee on International Trade, Investment and Monetary Policy and Subcommittee on Monetary Policy), 99th Congress (27 October), Washington, D.C.

Stein, Ben (2007) 'The long and the short of it at Goldman Sachs', *New York Times*, 2 December.

Steinmeier, F.-W. and M. Machnig (eds) (2004) *Made in Germany '21: Innovationen für eine gerechte Zukunft*, Hamburg: Hoffmann und Campe.

Stone, D. and C. Wright (2006) 'The currency of change: World Bank lending and learning in the Wolfensohn era', in D. Stone and C. Wright (eds), *The World Bank and Governance: a Decade of Reform and Reaction*, Oxford and New York: Routledge.

Strange, S. (1988) *States and Markets*, London: Pinter.

Strange, S. (1996) *The Retreat of the State: the Diffusion of Power in the World Economy*, Cambridge: Cambridge University Press.

Study Group sponsored by the Woodrow Wilson Foundation and the National Planning Association (1955)*The Political Economy of American Foreign Policy*, New York: Holt & Co.

Swann, C. (2007) *Chávez exploits oil to lend in Latin America*, Bloomberg, 27 February, retrieved 16 March, http://www.bloomberg.com/apps/news?pid=newsarchive&sid=atN8OPWGA4n

Sylla, R. (2002) 'United States banks and Europe: strategy and attitudes', in S. Battilossi and Y. Cassis (eds), *European Banks and the American Challenge: Competition and Cooperation in International Banking under Bretton Woods*, Oxford: Oxford University Press.

Tafara, E. (2005) *Speech by SEC Staff: Remarks before the Federation of European Accountants: International Financial Reporting Standards and the US Capital Market*, Brussels, 1 December 2005, http://www.sec.gov/news/speech/spch120105et.htm

Taylor, J. B. (1995) 'Changes in American economic policy in the 1980s: watershed or pendulum swing?', *Journal of Economic Literature*, 33 (June).

Taylor, J. B. (2007) *Global Financial Warriors: the Untold Story of International Finance in the post-9/11 World*, New York: W.W. Norton.

Taylor, L. (2004) *Reconstructing Macroeconomics: Structuralist Proposals and Critiques of the Mainstream*, Cambridge, MA: Harvard University Press.

Thacker, S. (1999) 'The high politics of IMF Lending', *World Politics*, 52(1).

Tickell, A. (1999) 'Unstable futures: controlling and creating risks in international money', in L. Panitch and C. Leys (eds), *Socialist Register 1999*, London: Merlin.

Tickell, A. (2000) 'Dangerous derivatives: controlling and creating risks in international money', *Geoforum*, 31(1).

Touron, P. (2005) 'The adoption of US GAAP by French firms before the creation of the International Accounting Standard Committee: an institutional explanation', *Critical Perspectives on Accounting*, 16.

Underhill, G., C. Stijn and Xiaoke Zhang (2004) 'Basel II capital requirements and developing countries: a political economy perspective on the costs for poor countries of rich country policies', paper presented at the annual meeting of the International Studies Association, Le Centre Sheraton Hotel, Montreal, Quebec, Canada, 17 March 2004. Available at http://www.allacademic.com/meta/p73420_index.html

US Census Bureau (1975) 'Banking finance and insurance', *Statistical Abstracts of the United States, 1975: the National Data Book*, Washington, No. 773–86.

US Census Bureau (1980) 'Public debt', *Statistical Abstracts of the United States, 1980: the National Data Book*, Washington, No. 463–68.

US Census Bureau (1989) 'Banking finance and insurance', *Statistical Abstracts of the United States, 1989: the National Data Book*, Washington, No. 781–94.

US Census Bureau (1998) 'Banking finance and insurance', *Statistical Abstracts of the United States, 1998: the National Data Book*, Washington, No. 792–854.

US Census Bureau (2004) 'Banking finance and insurance', *Statistical Abstracts of the United States, 2004: the National Data Book*, Washington, No. 1154–1223.

US Department of the Treasury (1964) *A Description and Analysis of Certain European Capital Markets*, Washington, D.C.: GPO.

US Department of the Treasury (1976) 'Foreign portfolio investment in the United States', Washington, D.C.: Department of the Treasury.

US Department of the Treasury (1996) 'Ownership of federal securities', *Treasury Bulletin Quarterly*, June.

US Department of the Treasury (2005) 'Ownership of federal securities', *Treasury Bulletin Quarterly*, June.

US Department of the Treasury (2007) 'Ownership of federal securities', *Treasury Bulletin Quarterly*, September.

van der Pijl, K. (1984) *The Making of an Atlantic Ruling Class*, London: Verso.

Vetterlein, A. (2006) 'Change in international organizations: innovation or adaptation? A comparison of the World Bank and the International Monetary Fund', in D. Stone and C. Wright (eds),*The World Bank and Governance: a Decade of Reform and Reaction*, Oxford and New York: Routledge.

Vidger, L. P. (1961) 'The Federal National Mortgage Association, 1938-57', *Journal of Finance*, 16(1).

Vitols, S. (2004) *Changes in Germany's Bank-based Financial System: a Varieties of Capitalism Perspective*, Discussion Paper SP II 2004-03, Wissenschaftszentrum Berlin.

Vittoz, S. (1987) *New Deal Labor Policy and the American Industrial Economy*, Chapel Hill: University of North Carolina Press.

Volcker, P. A. (1990) 'The triumph of central banking?' Per Jacobssen Lecture, The Per Jacobssen Foundation, Washington, D.C., 23 September.

Volcker, P. A. and T. Gyohten (1992) *Changing Fortunes: the World's Money and the Threat to American Leadership*, New York: Times Books.

von Rosen, R. (2003) 'US Corporate Governance kein Vorbild mehr', *Boersen-Zeitung*, 28 November.

Waddell, B. (2001) *The War against the New Deal: World War II and American Democracy*, DeKalb: Illinois University Press.

Wallerstein, I. (2006) 'The curve of American power', *New Left Review*, 2(40).

Walter, A. (1993) *World Power and World Money: the Role of Hegemony and International Monetary Order*, New York: Harvester Wheatsheaf.

Webber, M. J. and D. L. Rigby (1996) *The Golden Age Illusion*, New York: Guilford Press.

Weber, M. *Economy and Society: an Outline of Interpretive Sociology*, Los Angeles, California: University of California Press.

Weisman, S. R. (2007) 'At Treasury, the Secretary waits it out', *New York Times*, 17 August.

Weldin, S. J. (2000) 'A. P. Giannini, Marriner Stoddard Eccles, and the changing landscape of American banking', PhD thesis, University of North Texas.

White, E. N. (1992) *The Comptroller and the Transformation of American Banking 1960–1990*, Washington, D.C.: Comptroller of the Currency.

White, W. (1999) 'New strategies for dealing with the instability of financial markets', paper presented at the FUNDAD meeting, Budapest, 24–25 June.

White, W. (2000) 'What have we learned from recent financial crises and policy responses?', BIS Working Papers, No. 84, Basel: BIS.

Wigmore, B. A. (1997) *Securities Markets in the 1980s. Vol. 1: The New Regime, 1979–1984*, Oxford and New York: Oxford University Press.

Williams, M. (1994) *International Economic Organisations and the Third World*, New York: Harvester Wheatsheaf.

Williamson, J. (1977) *The Failure of World Monetary Reform, 1971–74*, New York: New York University Press.

Wójcik, D. (2001) *Change in the German Model of Corporate Governance: Evidence from Blockholdings, 1997–2001*, Working Paper, School of Geography and the Environment, University of Oxford, Oxford.

Wojnilower, A. M. (2000) 'Life without Treasury securities', *Business Economics*, 17(35).

Woods, N. (2000a) 'The challenge of good governance for the IMF and the World Bank themselves', *World Development*, 28(5).

Woods, N. (2000b) 'The challenges of multilateralism and governance', in C. Gilbert and D. Vines (eds), *The World Bank: Structure and Policies, Global Economic Institutions*, Cambridge and New York: Cambridge University Press.

Woods, N. (2003) 'The United States and the international financial institutions: power and influence within the World Bank and the IMF', in R. Foot, S. MacFarlane and M. Mastanduno (eds), *US Hegemony and International Organizations: the United States and Multilateral Institutions*, Oxford and New York: Oxford University Press.

Woods, N. (2006) 'The globalizers in search of a future: four reasons why the IMF and World Bank must change, and four ways they can', Washington: Center for Global Development, retrieved 11 January 2007, http://www.cgdev.org/content/publications/detail/7371

Woodward, B. (1994) *The Agenda: Inside the Clinton White House*, New York: Simon & Schuster.

Woolley, J. (1984) *Monetary Politics: the Federal Reserve and the Politics of Monetary Policy*, Cambridge: Cambridge University Press.

World Bank (1998) *The World Bank Annual Report 1998*, Washington: World Bank, retrieved 4 March 2007, http://www.worldbank.org/html/extpb/annrep98/overview.htm

Youngman, A. (1906) 'The growth of financial banking', *Journal of Political Economy*, 14(7).

Zaiat, A. (2002) 'Un Chiste Alemán de Köhler', *Página 12*, Buenos Aires, 23 January, retrieved 6 December 2003, http://www.pagina12.com.ar/diario/economia/subnotas/1125-629-2002-01-23. html

Zuege, A. (2000) 'The chimera of the Third Way', in L. Panitch and C. Leys (eds), *Socialist Register 2000*, London: Merlin.

Zweig, P. L. (1995) *Wriston: Walter Wriston, Citibank, and the Rise and Fall of American Financial Supremacy*, New York: Crown Publishers, Inc.

Zysman, J. (1983) *Governments, Markets, and Growth*, Ithaca, NY: Cornell University Press.

Index